BLIND JUSTICE

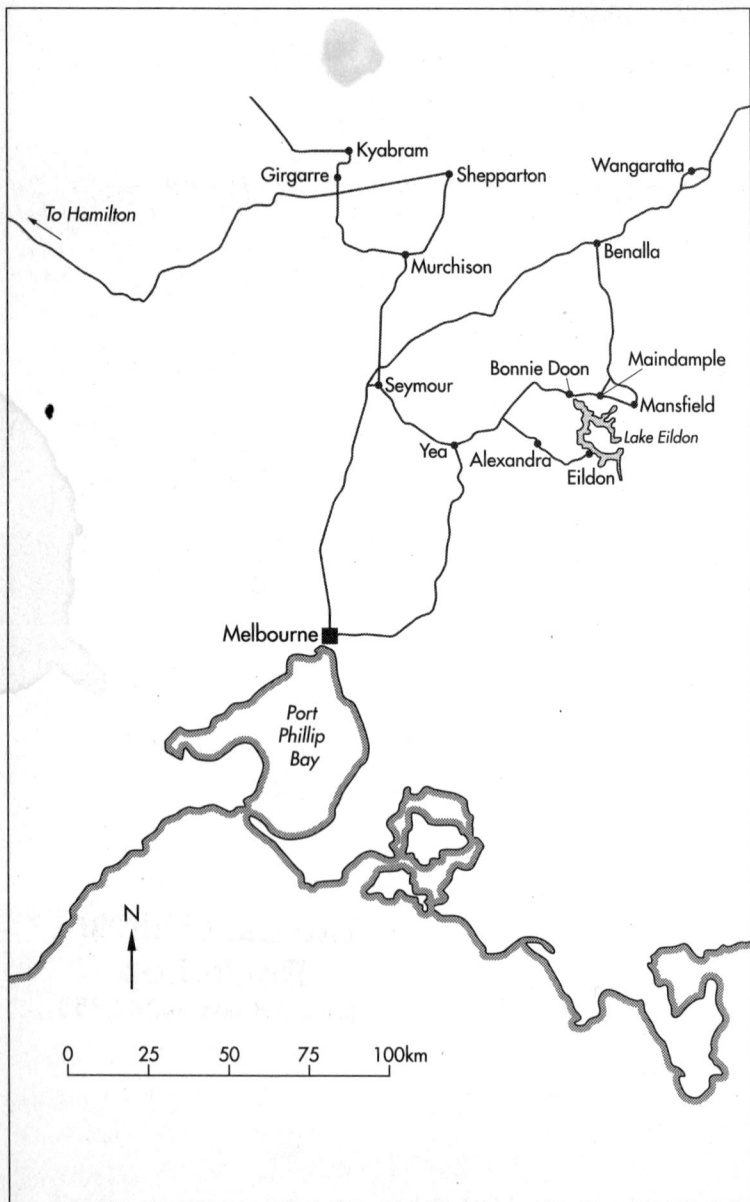

Kyabram

Girgarre

Shepparton

Wangaratta

To Hamilton

Murchison

Benalla

Maindample

Bonnie Doon

Seymour

Mansfield

Lake Eildon

Yea

Alexandra

Eildon

Melbourne

Port Phillip Bay

N

0   25   50   75   100km

BLIND JUSTICE

ROBIN BOWLES

THE TRUE STORY OF THE DEATH
OF JENNIFER TANNER

A Sue Hines Book
ALLEN & UNWIN

Copyright © Robin Bowles 1998

First published in 1998
A Sue Hines Book
Allen & Unwin Pty Ltd
9 Atchison Street
St Leonards, NSW 2065 Australia
Phone: (61 2) 8425 0100
Fax: (61 2) 9906 2218
Email: frontdesk@allen-unwin.com.au
Web: http://www.allen-unwin.com.au

National Library of Australia
Cataloguing-in-Publication entry:

Bowles, Robin.
    Blind justice: the true story of the death of Jennifer Tanner.

    ISBN 1 86448 858 1.

    1. Tanner, Jennifer — Death and burial. 2. Murder — Victoria — Bonnie
Doon. 3. Murder victims — Victoria — Bonnie Doon. 4. Homicide
investigation — Victoria — Bonnie Doon. I. Title.

364.152099455

Designed and typeset by J & M Typesetting
Printed by Australian Print Group, Maryborough, Victoria

10 9 8 7 6 5 4

For Sam

To the dead we owe nothing but the truth.

VOLTAIRE

Contents

Acknowledgements

WHERE TO begin? So many people have assisted me in the difficult, fascinating and challenging task of researching and writing this book. If I have omitted anyone I can only beg your forgiveness and extend my thanks.

So—my heartfelt thanks go to: my cherished husband, Clive, who believes in me and who gave his total support in so many ways during the two years of our lives devoted to this book; my friend, Helen Duffy, without whose glowing introduction of me to Allen & Unwin this would have been one of the hundreds of unsolicited manuscripts that make their way to publishers each week and get lost in the pile; my publisher, Sue Hines, who believed in me enough to coach, encourage, challenge and bully me and make me take out all the cute bits, clichés and exclamation marks (well most of them, anyway!); my lawyer Phil Dwyer, who read a draft for legal glitches and got so immersed in the story he spent the following weekend in Mansfield and the surrounding area absorbing the atmosphere; Jenny Tanner's parents, who trustingly agreed to permit a stranger to research a very painful and private part of their lives, with no control over the outcome; members of the Tanner family, who all spoke to me against their better judgement; all the people who have shared their memories and relived some painful times in their lives—some are named in this story and others remain unidentified, at their request or to maintain their privacy; members of the Victoria Police and other investigative experts, who have all treated me with respect and trust, again not confident of the outcome; Adele Baily's sister, for openly sharing her family's tragedy with a stranger in another country; my painstaking and pragmatic editor, J., who taught me so much and nursed me through several panic attacks—well beyond her brief; my enthusiastic agents, Jenny and Jacinta at Australian Literary Management, who signed me up 'on spec' after one phone call and a shared bottle of red wine; Keryn Robinson, who typed hundreds of pages of interview transcripts from scrawled notes and muffled tapes; David Stevens, the expert from the Coroner's Court, who explained the relevant Acts and processes; Malcolm Feiner, from the Office of Corrections Library, who minimised my isolation in Queensland by looking up or sending me almost anything I rang him about; Andrew Rule, John Silvester and the *Sunday Age*, for breaking the story in the first place; the *Mansfield Courier*, for providing photos and other material support; Kurt Weick, Alan and Phillipa Finney, Meg Butler and John Johnson, who waded through rambling early drafts and enthusiastically provided feedback, encouraging and stimulating me to prune, edit and prune again, but not give up; MDL, for some good ideas; Barkly Computers in Mackay, Queensland, who put up with my tantrums when my Mac spat the dummy and lent me another one so I could keep writing; Jodie at the Coroner's Court, who conducted a fairly gruesome tour with great aplomb; also Marco from the Coroner's Court, who provided me with reams of photocopying without complaint; Bryce Courtenay, who has encouraged me to 'Be a writer!' in a number of ways; John Thorne from Jane Franklin Hall in Tasmania, who has done likewise; friends—dozens, too many to mention—who have encouraged me with 'How's the book going?' and helped me persevere with a task very much more demanding, but correspondingly more rewarding, than I ever believed possible. Thank you all.

Any errors of fact in this story are mine alone. Reconstructions of conversations are mine; many are developed from inquest statements or first-person recollections, while others are based on my knowledge of the people involved.

Introduction

For many people, Jennifer Tanner is no more than a name attached to a series of news stories, often coupled with the phrase 'police cover-up'. For others, Jenny Tanner was 'their girl', a daughter, sister, mother, wife and much-loved friend.

My relationship with Jenny Tanner lies somewhere between the two. Although I did not know her in life, from the moment I discovered the circumstances of her death I was convinced that a terrible miscarriage of justice had taken place. The police had treated her death as a suicide. Almost no-one seemed to want to ask how a young woman who was afraid of guns could shoot herself twice in the head and through both hands with a single-shot rifle.

When I first became aware of the questions surrounding Jenny's death I was a director of a small Melbourne firm specialising in strategic communications. Although I had never written a book before, there was something about Jenny Tanner's story that simply would not leave me alone. I decided to become a writer, to tell Jenny's story. I closed my business in order to concentrate on the journey I was about to undertake. All my friends cautioned me against giving up my day job, but I took no notice.

Finding people who have been in professions or public life in some way is not very difficult in Australia, but it's not so easy to barge into their lives after they've spent twelve years trying to put an unpleasant event out of their minds. Sometimes they were relieved to have a chance to tell their side of a story, to communicate their grief at Jenny's death and their anger at the way it had been treated. Sometimes they slammed the phone down in my ear. Sometimes I was able to cajole them into sharing some memories with me, but in many cases they were close to the people concerned and felt very uncomfortable. A lot of people made me promise not to use their names. They will see this promise has been kept.

This is the strange story of Jennifer Tanner's death and its disturbing aftermath—a sequence of events that would blight the lives of an extraordinary number of people, divide a small Victorian country town, and ultimately lead to a mammoth investigation by the Victoria Police twelve years after the event. This new investigation might never have occurred but for the discovery of the skeleton of a transsexual prostitute, Adele Baily, who had been missing since 1978, six years before Jenny died. Adele's remains were discovered at the back of the property where Jenny had lived. Was there a link?

This is also the story of my own search for the truth, tracking down the key players, often one step behind the Homicide Task Force, often asking the same questions. During the two years and more than 100 interviews it has taken me to write this book, I've followed every lead, no matter how flimsy. I've conducted interviews in paddocks and mortuaries, in courtrooms and cafés; learnt about ballistics and police culture, had some fun and a few scares. And somewhere along the way I've become a writer.

At times I was in danger of allowing myself to be sucked into trying to solve the mystery, instead of recording it. At the same time, I was always aware that it was Homicide's job to solve this puzzle, not mine.

And Homicide, in the shape of a special Victorian Police Task Force, has conducted an extraordinarily thorough investigation. Despite their best efforts, they have now accepted that there is no evidence on which to charge anyone with an offence arising from Jenny's death.

All my speculations are worthless anyway; they only serve to keep me awake at night and occupy me during long car trips. Many of the questions raised by Jenny's death may never receive satisfying answers. There are some answers known only to whoever pulled the trigger in 1984 and fired the bullets that killed Jennifer Ruth Tanner.

Melbourne
May 1998

Part One

Suicide or Murder?

Sometimes when I consider what tremendous consequences come from little things, I am tempted to think there are no little things.

BRUCE BARTON

1

An End and a Beginning

BONNIE DOON, VICTORIA
WEDNESDAY 14 NOVEMBER 1984
10.15 P.M. A young woman dressed in unzipped jeans and a rumpled black T-shirt sits slumped sideways on a two-seater couch, head tilted forward, right leg fully extended and left leg bent, with her left foot under her right knee. Her feet are bare. Her right arm extends down along her body, and her hand rests on her bare stomach. Her left hand is partially wrapped around the barrel of a BRNO .22 bolt-action rifle. The butt of the rifle rests on the floor between her legs. The barrel is pointing upwards and away. A spent cartridge is on the floor near her left heel. There is a lot of blood, stark against the pale floral couch, on the cushions and around a wound in the centre of her forehead. Both her hands are injured and covered in blood.

Jennifer Ruth Tanner, aged twenty-seven, is dead.

Around her all appears normal. The lounge room in her lovingly restored 100-year-old home is full of signs of life. The television is on. The gas wall heater is on, although the night temperature is around 18 degrees. The iron and ironing-board are set up near the heater and the day's wash has been ironed. On the floor near the ironing-board are a disposable nappy and a tin of baby powder. On the other side of the heater are a half-full cup of coffee on a saucer and three biscuits on a plate. Jennifer's 21-month-old son Sam is sound asleep in his cot in the room across the hallway.

The room is neat and tidy except for the awful scene on the couch. Framed portraits of several generations of Jennifer's family look down from freshly painted white walls. An antique cedar sideboard

holds a vivid blue Mary Gregory jug. Two Moran armchairs matching the couch are upholstered in a traditional cream floral highlighted
with birds of paradise. Blue linen curtains are drawn across the window behind the couch. Three small glass-and-brass coffee tables are
spaced around the room. One holds an ashtray containing five cigarette butts. On another is a dish full of brightly wrapped chocolates,
providing the only strong colour, apart from Jennifer's blood.

Tyres crunch as a ute rolls down the drive from the highway and
stops outside the kitchen door. Jennifer's husband of just over three
years, Laurie Tanner, is home from a visit to Mansfield, 27 kilometres
away. The kitchen and lounge-room lights are on and the sound of
the TV can just be heard as he walks towards the kitchen door. Otherwise, all is quiet among the cypresses lining the long driveway. The
house nestles in its secluded garden, almost invisible from the road.

Laurie steps onto the porch and through the back door into the
big farmhouse kitchen. He puts bread, milk and a local paper on the
large wooden kitchen table, along with two Cherry Ripes as a surprise for Jennifer.

He looks through the connecting door from the kitchen to the
lounge and sees Jennifer slumped on the couch about ten metres
away. From the way she looks, he is instantly convinced she is dead.
His first thought is to make sure Sam is safe. He does not go to his
wife, but walks through the lounge room to reach the baby's room,
where Sam has apparently slept through whatever horror has taken
place this night.

Laurie walks back along the hall to the phone. He calls his parents,
then rings for an ambulance.

10.22 P.M. A phone shatters the chatter in the Duty Controller's
office at Wangaratta Ambulance Service. A male voice, very distraught,
says, 'It's Laurie Tanner from Springfield at Bonnie Doon. I've just got
home and I think my wife's dead.'

10.24 P.M. Gerard O'Donnell, duty ambulance officer, is at his
home in the centre of Mansfield. When his phone rings he glances at
the clock and wonders what awaits him at this time of night. The
Duty Controller from Wangaratta says, 'I've just had a call from a chap

at Bonnie Doon, property called Springfield on the Maroondah Highway. His name's Laurie Tanner. Thinks his wife is dead. You'd better get out there straight away—he's pretty upset.'

10.25 P.M. In a rambling, ramshackle old farmhouse across the Maroondah Highway from Springfield, Hughie and Val Almond are thinking about turning in. Val hasn't been feeling too well lately and Hughie has been up since early morning. He is waiting for his TV programme to finish before he calls it a day. The phone makes them both jump. Hughie answers.

'Hughie, Laurie here. I've got trouble. You'd better get over here, quick.'

Hughie is shocked. 'What the hell's the matter, Laurie?' But Laurie has already hung up. 'There's some kind of trouble over at the Tanners', Val. I'm going right over.'

Hughie rapidly covers the 400 metres to Springfield, not knowing what to expect. He has known Laurie since he was born, and has never had a similar call for help.

10.25 P.M. At Mansfield Police Station Senior Constable Bill Kerr and Senior Constable Don Frazer are starting to think about going home. The afternoon shift finishes at midnight. The day has been pretty uneventful—a typical Wednesday in a town with a slow pulse. Mansfield is the gateway to the snow country, but it is only home to about 2000 people. Mansfield Police Station covers a pretty large area around the district, almost 6000 people in all, but speeding tickets and the odd brawl provide most of the excitement in a police officer's life.

10.35 P.M. The phone rings, and Bill Kerr answers. The ambulance despatcher at Wangaratta tells him about the phone call he's just received from Laurie Tanner.

'Come on, Don,' Bill calls. 'There's trouble at the Tanners' at Bonnie Doon. Let's go.'

10.35 P.M. Hughie Almond arrives at Springfield. He is met by Laurie outside. 'Come in the kitchen,' Laurie says, leading the way. Inside Laurie points to the lounge-room door. 'You'd better look in there, but be prepared for a shock.'

Hughie nearly collapses. He has known Jenny for the past four years, his wife knits clothes for the baby and they are neighbours. He forces himself to walk across the room and bends over Jenny's body. He listens desperately for sounds of breathing. Nothing. He feels gently for a pulse in Jenny's right wrist. Nothing. His hand comes away covered in Jenny's blood. He walks slowly back to the kitchen, shutting the door behind him.

'The first thing we must do is call the police,' Hughie says.

Laurie replies, 'I've rung the ambulance—I'll get the police number.'

'I know the police number.'

10.37 P.M. Bill Kerr and Don Frazer are leaving the station when the phone rings again. 'It's Hugh Almond from Bonnie Doon here. There's been a shooting at the Tanners'.'

He looks sympathetically at Laurie. 'They're on their way.'

10.40 P.M. Duty Ambulance Officer Gerry O'Donnell arrives at Springfield. He is met inside the gate by Hughie Almond, who says, 'I don't think there's anything you can do, but you'd better come in and check. Nothing has been touched.'

Laurie is sitting at the kitchen table when Gerry walks in. He is obviously very distressed. 'I'm pretty sure she's dead. I just walked in from a meeting—what do I do now?' he says to Gerry. Then, turning to Hughie, 'I could do with a drink. I don't have anything in the house.' Feeling safe to leave Laurie now the ambulance officer has arrived, Hughie races home to get a bottle of whisky. He could do with a drink too.

10.44 P.M. Grim-faced, Gerry examines Jenny's body. She is about the same age as his own wife. There are no signs of life and he attempts no treatment. He notices a large wound in her forehead. He assumes she has shot herself in the mouth and this is an exit wound because of the amount of blood and what he believes to be brain tissue around it. He records detailed notes on his treatment chart, including his observations that both hands have gunshot wounds at the bases of the thumbs, but he cannot tell which are entry and which are exit wounds. He notices a large amount of blood on the back of the couch and on the cushion to the left of where Jenny is slumped.

The details of the room are imprinted on his brain.

Gerry returns to the kitchen. 'Where's the baby, Laurie?'

'The baby's fine—I've checked him. I don't want him to wake up with all this happening.'

Gerry checks him anyway, and at the stranger's touch the baby wakes.

10.45 P.M. Senior Constables Bill Kerr and Don Frazer arrive at Springfield. They enter through the kitchen door and find Laurie and Hughie sitting at the kitchen table, drinking a shot of whisky each. Hughie indicates the lounge-room door and says, 'In there.'

Gerry is checking on Sam, so Jenny is once more alone.

The police find Jenny Tanner still in the same position. They notice a heavily bloodstained white towel rolled up on the couch next to her on her left side. There are bloodstains on the back of the couch, behind Jenny's head and down the left side of her head on the back cushion. There is a large amount of blood pooled in the depression of the seat where Jenny is sitting and along her left leg, and a blood spatter on the wall behind the couch. A square cushion next to her is bloodstained as if something has been wiped across it.

Don Frazer comments to Bill Kerr, 'It looks like she could have been lying down there at some stage, don't you think?'

Bill Kerr takes in the room, then slowly says, 'I think I'd better phone the CI. You stay with the girl.' Don Frazer remains with the body. Over the cries of the baby he can barely hear Bill's muffled conversation from the kitchen as he puts through the call to the Criminal Intelligence Division in Alexandra. Never having met Jenny, Don wonders what she looked like in life. She is certainly not a pretty sight right now. He feels sad about the impact this event will have on the lives of everyone involved, although he cannot know how far the ripples will spread.

Bill Kerr returns after his call, speaking briefly to Laurie and Hughie Almond on the way. 'He doesn't want any photos if we're satisfied it's suicide. What do you think?' Without waiting for Don Frazer to answer, Kerr removes and examines the rifle. It is bloodstained from muzzle to butt. He notes it is a bolt-action .22-calibre BRNO rifle with a magazine feed. He removes the magazine and finds two live hollow-point bullets. He opens the breech and ejects a spent cartridge case, which falls to the floor, landing near one already lying between Jenny's legs.

The lower extremities of Jenny's body are showing signs of a bluish bruising as her blood pools in the tissues. The upper part is yellowish and cold. There is no doubt Jenny Tanner is dead.

Bill Kerr goes back to the kitchen to phone his Detective Sergeant in Alexandra again. He informs him about the two cartridge cases.

'But there's no need for me to come over if it's suicide,' says the Sergeant, relieved not to have to make the 70-kilometre trip at this late hour.

Bill returns to the lounge and tells Don Frazer, 'He's not coming.' Bill would like to organise photographs, but he doesn't know the whereabouts of Sergeant Neil Phipps, the official police photographer at Mansfield, so instead he does a freehand sketch of the bloody scene on the couch and puts it in his pocket. He makes a few brief notes about the scene and goes to find Laurie. He asks him some questions about the rifle, then says, 'Have you phoned your parents? What about the rest of your family? Do they know?'

Laurie tells him he phoned his parents' home at about 10.15 p.m. and spoke to his elderly father, whom he woke. His mother was at her usual Wednesday bingo night, so he left a message with his father for her to come straight out to the farm when she got home. He has not contacted any other family members.

'Do your parents know about Jenny?'

Laurie shakes his head, tears in his eyes.

'We need a doctor to certify your wife is dead, Laurie. Who's your family doctor?'

11.15 P.M. Dr Ross Gilham is at a dinner party out at Mac's Cove, about half an hour's drive from Mansfield, when he receives the call. Gerry O'Donnell tells him, 'We've got a shooting accident and some pretty distressed relatives here, Dr Gilham. Could you come and confirm the death and look after these folk as soon as you can?'

Dr Gilham owns one of the two medical practices in Mansfield.

He is family doctor to many families living in and around the district. Laurie is his patient.

Dr Gilham arrives at the house about midnight after dropping his wife in Mansfield. He has no sense of urgency, having been told Jenny is dead. By now Laurie's parents have arrived too. Don Frazer is still watching over the body. He tells Ross Gilham where the rifle was found. It is now resting against the wall.

'Probably held the barrel in her mouth with both hands and pulled the trigger with her toe,' Don surmises.

Gilham conducts a cursory examination after seeking Frazer's permission. He is asked only to pronounce her dead. Like Gerry, he assumes the bullet entered Jenny's mouth and exited through the front region of the skull. He notices the injuries to the hands, but does not examine them. He does not look in Jenny's mouth. He does not look for powder burns. He does not examine any other part of her body. He gives Gerry and the police permission to remove the body.

12.05 A.M. Jenny's body is lifted onto a stretcher by Don Frazer, Gerry O'Donnell and Ross Gilham.

Don Frazer, following the stretcher through the kitchen, notices a small poster on the kitchen wall. It is a page torn from a magazine, depicting a baby lying on its back, holding a pistol pointed into its mouth. Across the top of the poster, in letters as big as the baby, is the single word 'BEWARE!' A bit distressing for everyone tonight, Don thinks. He pulls the poster down, folds it and puts it in his pocket.

12.09 A.M. Jennifer Ruth Tanner leaves Springfield for the last time.

∽

MELBOURNE, VICTORIA
SUNDAY 9 JUNE 1996

Jenny's story began for me in the gloom of a Melbourne winter morning. I inched out of bed to retrieve the newspaper and boil the kettle. It was the Sunday of a long weekend and I'd arranged a family dinner party for that night, but there was plenty of time for one cup of tea—or even two—in bed while I read the *Sunday Age*.

As I crawled back under the covers, my eye was caught by a head-line above a single-column story on page one: 'New police probe on mystery gun death.' Above the story was a colour photo of a pretty girl, captioned 'Jennifer Tanner: Forensic experts say she may have been murdered.'

A secret police Task Force had been set up to investigate the death in 1984 of a young mother on a property near Bonnie Doon, a couple of hours' drive north of Melbourne. The new investigation was linked with the discovery of human remains in a mineshaft behind the same property almost a year ago. I vaguely remembered that story. The remains had been identified as those of Adele Evelyn Baily, a transsexual prostitute, who disappeared from St Kilda in 1978. The find had puzzled police for some months until she was identified through dental records.

A retired police officer who had led the original investigation of Jennifer Tanner's so-called suicide had come forward to tell the *Sunday Age* he believed other police had blocked his attempts to investigate suspicious circumstances concerning the shooting.

The article stated that a post mortem carried out two days after Mrs Tanner's death showed she had been shot twice in the brain and through both hands.

Sitting up straighter, I reread this section. How could this woman have shot herself twice in the brain? I'd spent some time in psy-chiatric nursing, and my experience told me women rarely use guns to suicide. They prefer poison or sleeping pills—anything less violent.

I also knew that gunshot injuries to both hands were usually classified as defence wounds. Why shoot yourself in the hands if you are trying to kill yourself? It would be agonising and not a bit fatal.

I read on. The retired police officer, Mr Bill Kerr, who apparently had the foresight to record conversations and interviews with several people involved in the case at the time, had said, 'As the investigating officer, I found it extremely hard to accept that she fired two bullets, using a bolt action rifle, when she was reported as hating firearms. There was no note and no proof of intention.'

The article went on to quote a number of experts, who all cast doubt on the suicide theory. Dr Terry Schultz, who reviewed the autopsy results for the inquest, said he believed then that Jenny Tanner was murdered, even if it was theoretically possible the second gunshot wound was self-inflicted. He felt police had been selective about their use of the findings from the post mortem provided by the original pathologist, and this had influenced the resulting investigation into Jenny's death.

Dr Schultz concluded that it was virtually impossible Jenny had shot herself and that the wounds in her hands were commonly known as 'defence wounds'.

Bingo! Now if I could work that out lying in my warm bed, why didn't the police suspect something then? Being a voracious reader of detective stories, I was already trying to identify the killer.

The investigating journalist had interviewed a number of other experts on suicide, forensics and ballistics, all of whom stated their reservations about Jennifer's ability or inclination to have pulled the trigger herself. Dr Lee, an expert in gunshot wounds, said he was automatically sceptical of any claim that a woman had shot herself if she was not familiar with using firearms, as this was so rare.

Professor John Hilton, head of the New South Wales Institute of Forensic Medicine, said that both circumstances and statistics made it 'pretty damned unlikely' that Mrs Tanner had shot herself. Other experts supported these opinions.

The scene of the death was thoroughly cleaned up early the next morning, thus destroying possible evidence before the autopsy was conducted. During this clean-up the room where Mrs Tanner died was washed, and bloodstained items were burnt. No forensic tests were done at the scene, then or later.

Jenny Tanner was buried sixty hours after her body had been discovered. Most of the mourners, including her husband and her parents, were apparently unaware she had died from the impact of two bullets to her brain, not one.

The ensuing inquest returned an open finding, although the Coroner was scathing about the police inquiry.

The Coroner formally cleared Mrs Tanner's husband, Laurence James Tanner, and his younger brother, Detective Sergeant Denis John Tanner, of any responsibility for her death. He went on to say he was 'at a loss to explain how Mrs Tanner was shot twice in the head with a manually operated rifle and why the Homicide Squad was not asked to assist from at least the day of autopsy onwards'.

But this all happened in 1984. Why was it all being reinvestigated now? It couldn't have been at the instigation of the family, as the journalist had also contacted Laurie and Denis Tanner for their comments.

Mr Laurie Tanner, 51, said he thought the original examination of his wife's death was 'very thorough'. He said he was 'shocked' to hear that experts considered it more likely she was murdered. He said he welcomed further inquiries into his wife's death. Sergeant Denis Tanner, 43, now stationed at Benalla, a country town near Mansfield, said he did not think a fresh investigation was warranted because 'as far as I'm concerned it was a very thorough investigation' in 1984.

Sergeant Tanner questioned whether pathologists who were not present at the post mortem could pass informed opinions on whether Mrs Tanner had been murdered. 'There's plenty of experts coming out of the woodwork in hindsight, like all these bloody psychologists who come out,' he said. 'They're experts about everything, but when it comes to practice they're not worth a hatful of busted arseholes.'

In spite of the police conclusion of suicide, Jenny's parents had never been convinced their daughter had pulled the trigger. Her mother, Kath Blake, told the *Sunday Age*, 'Jen hated guns. We always had a hatred of firearms, and instilled it in our children. When she was first married and Laurie used his rifle to kill a snake, instead of a shovel or something, she was so surprised she rang and told us.'

Kath also pointed out that Jenny was 'very left-handed', and would have had great difficulty operating the rifle, which had a right-handed action.

Many of the questions that had apparently troubled Bill Kerr still remained unanswered.

Two bullets were fired from a bolt-action rifle, which had to be reloaded after each shot. How could a left-handed woman who was scared of guns, with one bullet already in her brain, turn the rifle, reach over the telescopic sight to the right-handed bolt, eject the spent cartridge, reload and cock the firing pin, then turn the gun backwards towards herself and fire through both hands?

And, most importantly, how could anyone with any knowledge of what was required to perform this task believe she did so, without asking any other questions?

Once the police were aware there were two bullets in Jenny's brain, why did they still treat the case as a suicide?

The article ended with a photo of a bruised sky glooming over Mansfield Cemetery.

I went to the kitchen to pour a second cup of tea. My husband, who had been trying to sleep in with little success, buried his head far under the covers.

During the afternoon my mind wandered often to the story of Jennifer Tanner. Was that the entire story? There must be more to it. There was a strong hint of a police cover-up in parts of the article. I resolved to raise it over dinner and see what the others thought.

∞

We dissected and discussed the article throughout the evening. We had all read it. Various culprits were charged and cleared due to lack of evidence or motive or opportunity or all three. The police didn't get off lightly, and the conversation wandered through other reported cases of police conspiracies and cover-ups. It seemed everyone at the table had an opinion. I wondered what was being discussed around dinner tables in Mansfield—especially the Blakes' and the Tanners'— and how they were coping with the pain of having the story in the newspaper for everyone to discuss all over again.

For days the story popped in and out of my head, like the threads of a gripping book I hadn't finished. I'd been reading a book on forensic anthropology called *Dead Men Do Tell Tales*, which detailed

the fascinating advances in modern forensics that have made it possible to solve very old mysteries by studying the victims' bones. I
wondered if there was a pathologist like the author living in Australia.
Perhaps Jenny's parents, Kath and Les Blake, could contact him and
get Jenny's body exhumed and conduct their own investigation to
prove or disprove the suicide theory once and for all. Surely the angle
of the bullets would say something. If she was sitting on a low couch
and she was only—how tall?—could she have done it?

One day I finally got up the courage to ring Kath Blake. She
sounded a bit brusque on the phone. I stumbled through an apology
for butting into her life, and asked her if she would like to have the
forensic book I'd been reading. I told her she could probably contact
the author through the publisher and ask if there was anyone similar
in Australia. If she wanted to, that is. None of my business, really, but
I just couldn't get Jenny out of my mind.

'Neither can we,' Kath replied.

I felt very intrusive and a bit silly. 'I can't think of anything worse
than having to bury a child,' I blurted out. 'It must be awful not
knowing.'

'It is. It's been awful since it happened, but you get on with your
life.'

We talked a while and I posted the book. I received no reply.

I became a bit obsessed with Jenny. I told her story to many
people who hadn't read it in the *Sunday Age* and retold it to quite a
few who had. After a couple more weeks mulling it over I said to my
husband, 'I think Jennifer Tanner might be the subject for that book
I've always wanted to write. There must be so much more to the story
than we know from the article.'

'Well, it's not your story, it belongs to the journalist. You'd better
ask him first.'

I phoned the journalist. Yes, he thought there was a book in it and
no, he wasn't going to write it himself, as he didn't have time. 'Do
your own research, though,' he said. 'You'll find out more that way,'
and cryptically, 'Be careful. There are a lot of funny things associated
with this case. Some time after I wrote that story, my car windscreen

was smashed while my car was parked in my driveway. And you know about the fire, don't you?'

'What fire?'

He lowered his voice automatically, as if he thought someone might be listening in. 'Jenny Tanner's case wasn't reopened for a while after the transsexual's remains were found in July last year. It took that long for the police to feel justified in believing the two cases may be connected. Once it was officially reopened, like *one week* later, even though the Tanners don't still own the place, the house where Jenny Tanner was found dead burnt to the ground in the middle of the night.'

It was beginning to sound a bit melodramatic.

'Was it an accident? Was anyone hurt?'

'You draw your own conclusions. It was empty at the time.'

I phoned Kath Blake again. I told her I wanted to write a book about Jenny's death. I offered to come and meet her to see if she and her husband Les felt comfortable with me before I wrote anything. She agreed to the meeting and agreed to play it by ear from there— no obligations.

I was elated. I couldn't wait to get started. This had all the ingre-dients of a great story—a macabre find in a deserted mineshaft, an impossible suicide, allegations of a police cover-up, an investigation reopened twelve years after the event. The hunt was on for evidence and witnesses—a hunt that I would join, all being agreed.

One of my closest business associates was appalled. During lunch she echoed everyone's sentiments when she said calmly, 'It's a very intriguing story, but how on earth are you even going to begin? You've never done anything remotely like this before. This is a real murder, you know. People have actually been killed. Maybe two, maybe more. What makes you think you can uncover things the Victoria Police haven't found? What if you get too close to the truth?'

Over coffee we agreed if I was determined to be such an idiot, the best place to start would be somewhere remote like the Coroner's Court. I could still retreat with honour if the transcript didn't live up to its promise.

When I phoned the Coroner's office to make an application there was a whispered conference at the other end of the line, then I was told the transcript was not available because the investigation had been reopened.

'Is that usual? I thought this was a matter of public record,' I asked, feeling frustrated at having my first initiative thwarted.

'Well, put it this way—this is not a usual case,' came the enigmatic reply.

'But I know people who already have it—it's already in the public arena—it's been in the newspaper, for goodness sake,' I argued.

'Sorry, you'll have to ask someone who already has it, then. We can't release a copy from here and that's that.'

So much for being clever. I asked the *Sunday Age* journalist if I could borrow his copy, and he kindly agreed. I pored over the documents for days, putting different statements in piles and using the office whiteboard to develop time sequences. Gradually I pieced together a picture of what had happened on that night after Jenny's body was found. I also found plenty of testimony to support the presumption of suicide.

The inquest was told that Jenny was 'depressed' and had 'had a breakdown'. 'She seemed to have two personalities and was very moody,' said her husband Laurie. According to his brother Denis, 'She'd have arguments [with Laurie] and use a lot of bad language, which was in his opinion, out of character. She would behave in an irrational manner.'

Dr Patience, the Benalla doctor who treated Jenny during and after her pregnancy, described her as 'a taciturn and slightly depressed young woman whose emotional reaction to her pregnancy and the subsequent delivery was abnormal, more so after the birth of her son'. He also said her 'demeanour during the pregnancy was not the usual joyful expectancy of most of my young prospective mothers, but I interpreted her taciturn nature as more shyness'.

Was this the way Jenny's family and friends saw her? It was hard to reconcile this picture of her with the pretty, laughing girl in the newspaper.

The inquest record only intensified the mystery. I felt I was already getting caught up in the emotions of those involved in the case. Perhaps my best intentions to remain objective would be thwarted by my desire to solve the puzzle.

I once experienced the violent death of someone close, and I knew the aftermath leaves no-one untouched. It seems to rip through the defences we erect to cope with a more expected bereavement and leave jagged spaces and angry questions—the most common being 'Why?' And letting go of the memories isn't forgetting. It's remembering in a different way.

I did not expect Jenny's death to be any different. I was not prepared, however, for the depth of pain still remaining in so many hearts.

2

The Blakes

ON A bright day in mid-August I set off for Mansfield, treating the trip as an adventure as much as a serious exercise. If Jenny's parents don't like me there probably won't even be a book. I travel from Melbourne through the north-eastern Victorian township of Beechworth, and stay there overnight with some nursing friends who work in the area near where Jenny lived. Through them I initiate some discreet enquiries to find out if Jennifer Ruth Blake or Tanner has ever been treated in a psychiatric unit, or for a 'breakdown'.

Heading out of Beechworth, I stop to buy flowers for Jenny's mother. After protracted indecision, I finally settle on some long-stemmed white rosebuds. The patient florist is already arranging them when I stop her. 'These are for someone whose daughter has died. I hope the colour will be OK.' I'm very nervous that Kath will say no to the book, and a bit worried about how I'll go about conducting this critical interview—dredging up her old pain—without sounding too eager for her approval. But the roses are the best flowers in the shop, so the florist continues wrapping.

'The poor woman,' offers the florist along with the bunch. 'I lost my son in a car accident a few years ago. You never get over it. When did it happen?'

'Well, actually it was twelve years ago—she was Jennifer Tanner, who was supposed to have committed suicide in Bonnie Doon.'

'Oh—*that* poor girl,' says the florist. She leans over the counter so her grandsons playing on the floor can't hear. 'You know, she deserved better. They never did investigate that case properly. How is the mother, anyway?'

I haven't expected such an informed response from someone in a town 150 kilometres from Bonnie Doon, and I'm not yet in a position to reply. Nonplussed, I back out of the shop.

Kath and Les Blake live on the other side of Mansfield, about 30 kilometres from Bonnie Doon. I want to meet with Kath first to settle any doubts she might have and get the go-ahead from her before setting out on my quest in earnest.

From Mansfield I take the road leading to the looming mountain range on the horizon—the 'High Country' made famous by *The Man from Snowy River*. Several years ago I had one of the best adventures of my life in this area, bringing a mob of cattle down from the autumn-chilled High Country on a ten-day trail ride.

We rode up jagged slopes, over fallen trees, down breathtaking precipices and through twenty-one river crossings in ten days. We camped in bush huts beside rivers or overlooking purple valleys, and told tall tales around the camp-fire. We were at eye level with the surrounding mountaintops. Big, smelly, sweaty mountain cattle emerged from their hiding places and turned their shaggy heads downwards to the milder plains below, to shelter from the ravages of a High Country winter. I arrived in Merrijig with all my fingernails ruined, tired, sore, filthy and elated.

Leaving behind my memories of mountain rides, I make my way across the bridge over the Delatite River on the other side of Mansfield, to wind through a peaceful rural landscape flush with early spring.

The Blakes' compact white weatherboard is set back off the road, surrounded by a cottage garden and lawn clipped with military precision. As I pull into the driveway I think of the police car years ago, bearing the news every policeman dreads delivering. It all seems so calm and unremarkable. I think how little we know about the human dramas behind so many innocuous front doors.

Kath Blake is small and businesslike, with neat short hair sprinkled with grey. Immaculately presented in pressed jeans and starched white blouse under a navy jumper, she greets me at the back door, standing beside a profusely flowering gardenia in a tub. I'm envious—mine always die—and to break the ice, I say so.

'Oh, that old thing! I don't do anything much, it just keeps flowering. I thought I heard your car pull in. You didn't go around the front, did you? No-one uses front doors around here.'

I am glad I stuck to the white roses. She arranges them expertly in a tall glass vase and they look perfect in her blue-and-white lounge room. Les is not home. I'm not sure if this is on my account, but I try to take a positive view. Kath and I sit in the dining room, sharing tea and sizing each other up. At some point, it all seems to be fine and we just move easily into talking about Jennifer.

'Tell me about her,' I lead off. 'What was she like?'

'Well, she was just ordinary, really. She'd always have a go. She lived life to the full—did everything.

'She was born in Melbourne on 14 January 1957. We moved here when Jen was ten. Les had a job managing the Ashfield sawmill in Mansfield—it's a big timber area here—plenty of work until well into the 1970s. After the huge bushfires in the Central Highlands in 1939 there was not much timber left there and Mansfield took over. We had a little house in Ultimo Street near the state primary school. The girls went to the Catholic school near by. I had a letter from Jen's teacher, Sister Bonita, recently. She could never believe Jen had shot herself. Sister's in a retirement home now—she's very elderly, but she still took the trouble to write.'

Kath goes to get the letter, on a thrifty piece of convent-issue paper in a tight, small hand. She smooths the letter out as she has probably done many times before—it looks well read; a testament to Jenny's good character.

'See, she says Jen was a good girl—she never gave us a moment's trouble, although she could be very stubborn. We had four girls— Jenny was the oldest, then Kristine, who was eight, Miriam, five, and Clare, who was only one when we arrived in Mansfield.'

I ask if Jennifer had ever lived in this house.

'Oh yes, we moved here when Jen was in her late teens, but she wasn't living here all that long, although she had her room here, of course. She left school and took up hairdressing and moved down to

Melbourne. The hairdressing didn't last long, but then she had a job in an office for a while and came home at weekends.'

It's about a three-hour drive each way, but when I suggest it was a long trip to make every weekend, Kath waves that away. 'Oh, I often go down to Melbourne for the day, and so did Jen when she moved back here. We'd often go together—she'd ring up and say "How about a bit of shopping?" and off we'd go. My mother is still living in Melbourne, and Jen was very close to her. She stayed there when she first went to live in Melbourne.'

Sitting here in the house where she'd lived, at the table where she'd shared meals with her family, I am starting to feel more at home with this long-dead girl called Jennifer and beginning to think of her in more familiar terms.

Eventually Jenny tired of the weekend commuting and got a job in the State Bank in Mansfield, where she quickly demonstrated her ability. She was 'always smiling—into everything', Kath recalls fondly. She was very active in Young Farmers and had 'lots of friends—lots of boyfriends'.

Jenny began a fairly serious relationship with Jed Moffit, a Mansfield police officer who was separated from his terminally ill wife. He was about ten years older than Jenny and was caring for two children aged ten and eight. Kath produces some old photo albums, and happy groups leap out from the turning pages to cheer us up, as if we are having a family catch-up rather than discussing a possible murder. There are young people at barbecues, car rallies, picnics and parties. The images are eerily fresh, as if they'd just been photographed last week in the throes of the '70s revival.

In every single photo I see, one thing is constant—Jenny is always laughing. So, I wonder to myself, when did she become 'taciturn and moody'?

'Do you think Jenny was depressed?' I ask aloud.

'Of course not!' Kath huffs. 'Who *said* she was depressed? Only Denis and Laurie—and that doctor in Benalla, that's who. He only said that because he was *told* Jen was depressed. He only saw her a few times while she was pregnant anyway. No-one else who knew her agreed she was depressed. She had nothing to be depressed about.'

'Tell me about Jenny and Laurie. How did they meet each other?'

'Oh ... I'm not really sure where she met him. She was into so many things.' Kath purses her lips as if the thought of Jenny meeting Laurie anywhere displeases her a bit.

'Do you think they were happily married?'

'I think so. Never heard anything from Jen that they weren't. Oh, you know, she thought he could have done more about the place—maybe she got a bit impatient with him from time to time, but she had her own life. She was very busy, not just a housewife. She was a keen shopper and was always on the lookout for furnishings and fittings for her renovations during shopping expeditions to Melbourne. Sometimes Laurie would go with her and they'd stay at Denis's, sometimes she'd stay with my mother. She loved gardening, and was really starting to make something out of that overgrown garden out there. She did the books for a couple of bingo clubs—she was good with figures. After Sam was born she was organising the mobile toy library and had a playgroup, hosted it often. The young mums took turns, I think. In fact, it was Jenny's turn the day she died—she had the whole playgroup there that morning and not one of them noticed a single thing wrong with her. How could you change so much in one day?'

I admit I don't have any answers to that question. I ask another one instead.

'Was Jenny the kind of person who might say to Laurie, "If you don't pull your socks up, I'm off"? Do you think she could have threatened to leave him, even as a device to get him to do more with her or be around home more?'

'Jen always spoke her mind. She was very direct. She'd say what she was thinking, especially to Laurie. She probably nagged him. I suppose he could have gone home to his mother, but that wouldn't have looked good. She could have threatened to leave him, I don't know. She never said anything to me and she said to her grandmother once, "I can always tell Mum anything, but I couldn't tell Dad," so you'd think she would have told me. But she was a very private person in some ways ... I don't know ... maybe ...

'Laurie did try to confide in Les one day when Les was out there painting. He said, "We've got a problem." Les, being Les, said, "We've all got problems," and didn't ask any more about it. That was after they were married, of course. Jen and Laurie were married in March 1981—the Labour Day weekend. They'd met about eighteen months earlier, fairly soon before Jen and I went for a trip to England together. This is a photo of Laurie and Jen at the airport—he's saying goodbye—so they definitely knew each other then.'

'Oh, Laurie has a beard!' I think I was hoping to see a bit more of his face. 'Has he got a weak chin?'

Kath considers. 'Oh, I don't know if you'd say he has or he hasn't. He grew that beard because he had a bad accident with a chainsaw, which left him quite scarred. The blade snapped and flew back and cut his face. I think he's like all the Tanners, quite strong really ...' Uncharacteristically, her voice trails off a bit.

'So was it a big wedding? Did all the family come? Were they happy about Laurie marrying Jenny?'

'It was quite a big wedding. Laurie was divorced, so we had the wedding here in our garden. It was a beautiful day.'

She turns the album pages to the wedding. Jenny was a stunning young bride.

'They moved almost straight away out to the house at Bonnie Doon. It was a real dump when Jen and Laurie moved there. It almost needed a match put to it.'

Someone eventually got round to it last year, I think without speaking.

'It had been rented out a bit since Laurie's first marriage had broken up in 1978. Before that Laurie's parents had lived there for years. Laurie was born at Springfield. Anyway, Jen loved a challenge and she was determined to get that house looking good. Les went over a lot, to help out with painting the place.

'He took a lot of trouble, patching and mending before he painted. Jen wanted it all done quickly, but Les is a bit of a perfectionist. They really only had the kitchen and laundry and bathroom to go when she died. The kitchen was half done—Laurie started renovating it during his first marriage. Jen painted the cupboards white with beautiful dusty blue doors. It had a big old kitchen table, dark tiled vinyl on the floor—a bit lumpy—she was going to replace that—all white walls, a window over the sink looking out into the back yard and up into the foothills where all the goldmines were. They'd bought a new dishwasher and there was an AGA stove and a combination electric oven and stove-top as well.'

I remember AGA stoves well. Many years ago I worked as a jillaroo near Goulburn in the Southern Highlands of NSW, and we used to haul ourselves out of bed in the freezing dark to find the good old wood-fuelled AGA still warming the kitchen. I wonder if Jenny padded down the hallway in her farmhouse from the night before to the same cheery warmth.

I ask about photos of the lounge room where Jenny was found.

After a bit of rummaging through several albums we find some shots of Jenny playing with baby Sam on the lounge-room floor.

'She wouldn't like me showing you this one,' Kath speaks defensively. 'She's got her ugly old Ugg boots on.'

To be honest, I am more interested in Jenny's surroundings.

White walls, pale Berber carpet, pastel lounge suite and a matching ottoman. Kath points out that the ottoman was supporting a plate of chocolate biscuits. 'Jen had a very sweet tooth—she loved chocolates.'

Tailored blue curtains covered the window at the far end of the room, and a Victorian cedar chiffonier stood against one wall. Sam's nursing bottle was on an occasional table near Jenny. In another photo, various framed portraits looked approvingly across the room towards a pianola.

Just like home, I muse as I look around the white rooms of Kath's house, with their cheerful blue-and-white accents and powder-blue fitted carpets. In fact, I think I am looking at the same family portraits on the far wall.

'They are the same,' she agrees. 'We went to the farm for the first time weeks after Jen died—it was at least a month afterwards. Miriam [Jenny's sister] came with us to help Les pick up Sam's new bed. We got the portraits then, along with a few other things of Jenny's. Les wanted to paint the bed for Sam, as he had promised Jenny. It wasn't delivered until after … Laurie accused us of stealing all sorts of things—Jenny's cookery books, cutlery, glassware and so on. What actually happened was that Miriam went into the kitchen and saw Jenny's shopping list still next to the phone and other little reminders of her everywhere—even food still in the fridge. It broke Miriam up and she couldn't stay. Nobody took the cookery books, but we did take those portraits. Why wouldn't we? They didn't mean anything to Laurie. Later on he gave me this little jug too, for the same reason. Jen bought it at an auction a few days before she died.'

I look at the rather fine example of Mary Gregory glass, a vivid blue, matching Kath's lounge room so well—and the lounge room at the farm too. It is strategically placed on a side table between a framed studio portrait of Jenny and another of a boy in school uniform. He is about twelve years old, with blond hair and fine features. Probably Sam. Jenny's photo is the same as the one that caught my eye in June on the front page of the *Sunday Age*. I want to take a photo of this little tableau, but I don't feel confident enough to ask.

Kath picks up the jug and continues, 'When we went out to the house her lovely couch, without any cushions, was on the front veranda covered with a blanket. The cushions were burnt the day after Jen died, we found out. Much later, when Laurie decided to let the place, I discovered Sam's cot was thrown out at the tip—mice had eaten the mattress, the house had been empty so long. Before the tenants moved in, I heard that three truckloads of stuff were taken to the tip and carpet cleaners were brought in to spruce up the floors. We were never given an opportunity to recover any mementos of Jenny or Sam. Laurie only sold the place three years ago.'

For the first time a little bitterness creeps into her voice, as if she feels anger at all traces of her daughter being removed and guilt that she has to justify retrieving a few family portraits.

'How do you think Jenny got on with the rest of the Tanners?' I ask Kath, thinking a change of subject might be good for both of us. Kath embarks on a bit of family history to put me in the picture.

It seemed Jenny had her ups and downs with the Tanners, like most young married girls, especially girls with a bit of determination. Her mother-in-law, June Tanner, was large and in charge. June Tanner still treated Springfield as home, as did the whole family. Family ties to land run deep in the High Country. People would walk unannounced through the back door—a habit Jenny found especially irritating after she had Sam. She'd often sit in the warm kitchen to breastfeed him, only to have a stream of people, including the boys and her father-in-law, going through as they came in from the farm for morning tea or lunch. The Tanners thought nothing of this, and Jenny was unsure how to broach the subject without causing family friction.

Jenny was a little in awe of June and was nervous about making structural changes around the house without at least giving the appearance of consultation. She had a number of discussions with June about tiles for the kitchen, for example, before embarking on a serious overhaul. Jenny was also a little cautious about making major changes to the garden, although she actively disliked the big dark cypress trees looming over the windows, blocking the light.

After Sam was born, Laurie's brother Frank took time off from his police duties to help put another fence around the house to prevent the baby from toddling out onto the highway. But even though he lent a hand he thought Jenny was wasteful spending so much effort—and, as he saw it, money—on restoring the farmhouse.

According to Kath, Frank believed you never make any money out of a house. Being the son of a farmer, maybe Frank felt that land and livestock gave better returns on investment.

During the early part of her marriage to Laurie, Jenny seemed to get on reasonably well with Denis, the youngest but 'biggest and least popular' of the Tanner brothers, whom she had known for about twelve years. She saw him more than Frank, who was based at Hamilton police station, or Bruce, teaching in Girgarre, further up north. She still had friends in the police force after her close relationship with Jed Moffit, and was always a bit of a pushover for a uniform, especially if the person wore it with authority, which Denis certainly did. It was hard to believe Laurie and Denis were brothers, much less that Laurie was nearly nine years older. Denis always took charge. Laurie was quiet and reticent, Denis loud and bold.

Denis had an interest in the adjoining family property, Stanleys, just visible through the grove of willow trees opposite the bedroom windows at Springfield. The solid Georgian-style house was in a bad state of repair. Denis and his wife Lynne visited the area often to see Laurie and Jenny; to bring building and other materials to Stanleys; to visit his parents, June and Fred, in nearby Mansfield and assist in the day-to-day running of the three family properties. Denis was a Detective Sergeant in the CIB in Melbourne at the time, so these visits necessitated a lot of travelling to and fro.

I try to bring Jenny back to life while I listen to Kath reminisce. I sense her eagerness to share this story, but I can also see it is coming at some cost.

We need brightening up a bit. 'Do you see a lot of Sam?'

'Oh no, not at all in the last three months, since the *Sunday Age* article. It's my granddaughter's birthday today, but he won't be allowed to come to his cousin's party. He crosses the street when he sees my son-in-law, Steve. Steve's a teacher at Sam's school, but Sam's obviously been told to have nothing to do with our family any more. Sam'd work for my other son-in-law, Clare's husband, sometimes in the milk bar after school for a bit of pocket money, but he hasn't been in since the article … Sam used to be so fond of Clare—she used to baby-sit and she actually lived out at the farm for a while. They were very close, but now I don't think he's allowed to speak to us.'

I was shocked.

'But how can that be? Why do you think you can't see him?'

Kath continues calmly, 'I think they believe we're trying to cast blame on their family, but we're not. We just want the truth. The Tanner family was very unhappy about the *Sunday Age* article. Everyone in Mansfield read it and was discussing it—you couldn't buy a paper for miles around. It brought all the gossips out again.

Even back then, after the inquest, Laurie told me he never wanted Sam to have anything to do with me and Les. If Bruce hadn't intervened and spoken up for us I don't know what would have happened. Bruce was very nice then, although he's changed towards us now.'

'But why wouldn't Laurie want you to see Sam? You're his mother's parents. Don't the Tanners want Sam to know who his mother was? Maybe Laurie was just angry with Jenny for having left him alone to bring up Sam—if they really were happy, he must have been very sad at her loss and perhaps angry with you as well, just because you *were* her parents.'

'No, it goes back further than that article. The Tanners seemed to be very angry about us having legal representation at the inquest— and we only engaged a lawyer to make sure Jennifer's best interests were represented, so you wouldn't think that would upset Laurie, would you? After the inquest he was very upset. He said later we'd shamed him in the court and he didn't want Sam to have anything to do with us ever again.'

I think back to my reading of the inquest transcript and try in vain to think of a single direct question or even inferred question that could have 'shamed' Laurie. I make a mental note to reread it when I get back to the motel.

'Anyway, after a time I thought it was stupid and I just went over there to June's one day. I think Liz Thomas, Jenny's friend from Melbourne, was visiting and she wanted to see Sam anyway, so we went together. June answered the door and Liz was shocked to see how much weight she'd lost in twelve months—she guessed six to eight stone. She used to be a very big woman, but not now. Anyway, I said, "I want to see my grandson," and she called Laurie and we argued on the front veranda and he said, "Haven't you caused enough gossip?" and I answered, "What do you think us standing here arguing is doing, and I'm not leaving," so eventually he brought Sam out and we took him out for a while.

'Don't get me wrong—I didn't want to keep him, I thought his father should make an attempt to bring up his child, and all in all he seems to have done a good job. But Sam is not allowed to speak to us any more, so now we have a double loss.'

'What a waste,' I say.

I tell myself I should not make judgements or give opinions, but privately it's a bit hard to be objective about this last bit of information. We've been talking for a few hours and I feel it's time to go, even though I have many more questions. Kath is expected at her granddaughter's birthday party, and I want to see Springfield before it gets dark.

As I gather up my notes, the photo of Laurie and Jenny at the airport falls onto the polished wooden table where police sat twelve years ago, telling Les and Kath Blake their daughter was dead. 'May I borrow this?' I ask. I tell her it will help me connect better with Jenny if I can look at this snapshot from time to time. After only a moment's hesitation, Kath agrees.

'Do you think I could come back for an hour or so tomorrow? I'd like to meet your husband, and I still have lots of questions.'

In her businesslike way Kath considers then agrees. We settle on 'about 10.30' and I express a hope that Les might have half an hour.

Kath is non-committal. 'We'll see.'

Is this because she knows he doesn't want to talk to me or because she doesn't make arrangements on her husband's behalf? Maybe she knows he's already busy. Oh well, one day at a time. I'll just keep my fingers crossed.

∞

SPRINGFIELD. A battered, hand-lettered sign attached to a cyclone wire gate leaves me in no doubt this is the place. A second, smaller and newer sign hangs alongside. PRIVATE PROPERTY—KEEP OUT, surrounded by an uncompromising black border. Just in case you can't read or are a nosy writer needing further discouragement, there's a heavy chain and padlock securing the gate and a strand of barbed wire along the top of the waist-high wire fence.

I hang over the gate and peer about 100 metres down the driveway, trying to picture the scene on that night. Lights on in every room. The police car, the ambulance, the doctor's car, Hughie's truck, Laurie's ute, the Tanners' car—blue and red shafts of light swinging through the black overhanging cypresses and radios crackling sporadically. Finally, Jenny's body being carried out to make the lonely journey to the morgue. Car doors slamming, emphasising the silence, cars starting up and dispersing—Laurie, Sam, June and Fred to the Tanners'; Gerry O'Donnell and Dr Gilham home to tell their wives the sad story and the police to break the news to Les and Kath, leaving the old farmhouse to subside quietly into the blackness and silently mourn its young mistress.

Although the old house has gone, all the outbuildings and the dirt driveway are original, so it's fairly easy to imagine how it all would have been. The present house is built in a colonial style. It has a brand-new look; it's almost a year since the fire that destroyed the old Springfield. It's a bit hard to see the house properly, as it is built end-on to the road, with the front door on the side, opening to the driveway. I feel a bit sorry for the new owners—I bet they didn't realise what they were getting into when they bought Lot 1, Maroondah Highway, Bonnie Doon, before the discovery of the body in the mineshaft.

I don't see any cars, and nobody responds to 'Hi! Anyone home?' yelled spontaneously at the top of my voice before I'd even thought of a good reason for poking around. I get a bit brave and lean right over the fence to see if I can see Stanleys on the left through the clump of willows, trailing wispy branches beaded with green.

I can just make out a shape from here. I think it is the old brick or sandstone house with a bright new tin roof which I passed just before I reached Springfield. There's no use hanging around here really, but I want to feel what it's like. The evening sky is lowering over the hills behind Springfield. They seem to form a protective ring around the rear of the property. I know they're quite a distance away, but they feel very close, almost at the bottom of the garden. Up there is the mineshaft where Adele Baily lay for more than fifteen years, all alone and undiscovered. The cypresses form a forbidding barrier along the boundary on the highway side. They must be ancient—maybe they were planted when the original house was built. The enormous pair flanking the gate and arching together over my head shiver sibilantly as the evening wind picks up across Lake Eildon and gusts across the road.

I shiver too, although I'm not cold.

I back the car carefully out of the driveway entrance and drive back towards the Bonnie Doon township, which is about six kilometres down the road towards Mansfield.

Pulling level with Stanleys, I look at the old sandstone place: a renovator would say it had great potential, although the garden is a bit non-existent. The house looks deserted; all the windows and the front door are filled in with corrugated iron, matching the new roof. Either Denis has given up, or he's sold it to someone who is not the handyman type. Another sign on the fence instructs curious parties to keep out. Not a very friendly little corner of the world, I reflect.

I do have one more stop to make before I buy a takeaway chicken, go back to my motel and review the inquest notes—I want to see if Hugh Almond will talk to me.

When I asked Kath earlier if she thought I could call in and see Hughie, she couldn't really say if he'd speak to me or not. I have his phone number, but since I am right outside his front door, as it were, I decide it will be easier to drop in and surprise him, in the hope he'll share his memories with me.

At this stage I am still trying to keep an open mind about suicide. Even though I think it was most unlikely, so far there has been no proof to the contrary. Having an opportunity to talk to someone who was there on the night is an enticing prospect, especially so early in my investigations.

There is another reason why I'm interested in Hugh Almond. Kath has told me that a few weeks before, after the article in the paper, he made a special trip from Bonnie Doon to see her. 'He seemed to have come to apologise in a way,' Kath said. 'He said something like "I'm really sorry. I should have realised the rifle was in the wrong position. If I'd known what I know now I would have looked more closely, but it was all so awful ..." '

I want to ask him what he meant by this and also why a farmer, obviously experienced with firearms, could have accepted so easily that someone could kill themselves in the way Jenny was said to have done. Especially someone he knew well, who was afraid of guns.

The driveway opening off the highway to Hughie's farmhouse is exactly 400 metres from the gate of Springfield. Hughie made this trip twice on that night, once in answer to Laurie's phone call, then again to get the whisky. I pull off the road into a raised dirt access way and then into the bumpy, rutted drive.

I park next to the house, which looks pretty old, a huge brick chimney holding two weatherboard walls together. There are some black Tudor-style slats nailed onto the weatherboards, running verti-cally up towards the dark tin roof. Maybe they have a practical as well as an aesthetic purpose—like keeping the weatherboards on? Although the house is white, there's about half a metre of yellowy stain creeping from the ground up the weatherboards. It looks like rising damp. A little lean-to veranda is tacked onto the left-hand side of the house, and around to the right of the chimney I see a front veranda running the full width. There is a large front door with lead-light side panels, which looks like a good place to start.

I squelch my way across the long grass that townies like me would designate 'the front lawn', feeling rather smug that I had the foresight to wear boots. As I reach the veranda I remember Kath's words earlier today—'Nobody uses the front door around here.' I pick my way through what looks like several years' worth of garden rubbish blown onto the porch, and, just in case, go to knock on the door. I change my mind when I see that several spiders have taken up residence between the door and its jamb.

I pick my way back onto the firmer territory of the drive leading around to the back door. A white ute (do they come in any other colours?) is parked near the dusty steps and about twenty metres away Hughie's black-and-white kelpie is barking hysterically, nearly strangling itself as it twists on the chain tethering it to the 44-gallon drum called home. Several other nondescript dogs appear and bark at me from a discreet distance. I figure the one tied up is the only one to worry about, and anyway I rather fancy my dog-handling skills. So I ignore the barking and call out, trying to obtain a human response.

Not a cracker.

I feel the bonnet of the ute—still slightly warm. As I move closer to the house I hear the TV blaring out the football match of the day, and I understand why Hughie can't hear my feeble little yell over the TV and the dogs. He probably can't even hear the dogs over the TV. I step as loudly as I can onto the back porch, as I don't want to give him a fright by appearing from nowhere. He doesn't get a fright because he's not there.

Rudely peering through his kitchen window I see the TV and a table covered with a patterned plastic cloth set with the remains of a meal for two, and a couple of open cans of beer. His wife died some time ago—perhaps he has a guest.

Maybe he's out the back. I set off down the continuation of the driveway to look for him. Hughie's property rambles for perhaps a kilometre almost down to the edge of Lake Eildon, and he has more outbuildings than I have ever encountered on a farm anywhere. I try them all, disturbing various curious livestock, and by now it is nearly dark. This is a mystery I don't particularly want to solve on my own. I return quickly to my car and reverse out, trying to avoid the loose dogs, which become very brave once my car door slams.

During the drive into Mansfield I ponder his absence. Maybe he was hiding from me. I decide I'll phone him instead. This decision is a mistake.

Later that evening I make the call.

When I was preparing for my research, my husband suggested I would need an introduction to let people know who I was and encourage them to share their recollections with me. I decided on 'I'm Robin Bowles and I'm a writer. I'm writing a book about the death of Jennifer Tanner.' Hughie Almond is the first person I try it out on, and I can't say it's a roaring success. He is completely silent for a moment and then responds shakily. He seems to have tears in his voice.

'I can't talk about this any more. You don't know what it was like. I just want to be left alone. I really can't.'

I feel a wrench at his despair, but I interrupt anyway.

'I'm really sorry, Mr Almond. I just wanted to speak to someone who was there. You were one of the first people on the scene—I need to get the facts. I'm trying to interview people who knew Jenny, so I can write about her. I don't mean to upset you.'

'I *am* upset,' he shouts. 'I don't want to talk about it.' He hangs up.

I feel deflated, sitting there in my motel with the remains of a chicken and the dregs of a glass of Scotch.

∞

Les Blake is large and rugged-looking. He towers over his neat little wife, although it's not too hard to figure out who carries the most weight in family discussions. He has the damaged hands of a timber worker and thick, snowy hair, contrasting sharply with his good-looking, rather weather-beaten face. On Sunday morning he walks into the dining room while Kath and I are going through the events of the week leading up to Jenny's death and I am taking down names and contact numbers for Jenny's old friends. Les stands in the archway between the lounge and dining rooms, looking ambivalent about staying.

'I don't really know if there's anything I can add,' he says reluctantly. 'We've been over and over it so many times—I just want to see it resolved once and for all. I want it finished and out of our lives for good.'

I give him a little speech about how it is important to write down the facts of the story, so that everyone, especially Sam, knows the truth. I reassure him that I will do my best to be ethical and even-handed at all times. It sounds a bit pompous, even to me. He moves a bit closer to the empty chair at the head of the table. Kath seizes the opportunity to jump up and offer him a cuppa. Now he'll at least sit down to drink it with us. She's made a cake and it's delicious. I help myself to a second slice—breakfast. I was awake half the night thinking about the tears choking Hughie's voice and now I see more tears in Les's eyes.

On several occasions during our talk his eyes fill. He makes no attempt to hide the tears or brush them away; they just sit there glistening in this big strong man's eyes as he repeats yet again, for another curious stranger, the anguish of that dreadful night and all the days and years since then. It's almost as if the people connected with Jenny have lived their lives on two separate planes since 1984. First, not believing she killed herself and not understanding how anyone at the time could believe it and being angry or frustrated or guilty for not doing more to find out the truth. But also getting on with their lives, not 'rocking the boat' or making a lot of fuss, letting her rest in peace with whatever secrets died with her.

'We didn't want to go on a witch-hunt. We just wanted an open finding so Jen was not the only person suspected of pulling the trigger. We've got that grandson there,' he says, gesturing at Sam's portrait. 'We have to think of his feelings too in all this.'

Kath agrees. 'They said Jen was irrational. Well, if I make too much fuss they might say, "There you are—her mother's a bit nutty, so she might have been." That thought especially stopped me from making more enquiries and more fuss after she died. I really did try at first, but I kept coming against brick walls.'

Les picks up the thread as if they've had this conversation before, as indeed they must have '… and of course, you're dealing with the police here, people you want to trust. For goodness sake, we knew most of those police—they were visitors in our home, on first-name terms. Why wouldn't we believe what they had to say?' He shakes his head as if still confused by this betrayal, all these years later.

'What did you think when you found out there were two bullets in Jenny's brain?' I ask carefully.

'I remember it word for word—exactly what he said. Bill Kerr came out here on his own, it must have been a few days, maybe a week before the inquest. He said, "Les, I've got something to tell you you're not going to like. I don't think Jenny's best interests are going to be served at the inquest and I think you should talk to a lawyer.

She had two bullets in her brain, not one." I couldn't speak at first and then got really angry. Here's all this time, for the last ten months, I've been trying to come to terms with it—well, she did it and that's all there is to it—and now there's a doubt. An official doubt, we thought. But that didn't really come out very well on the day.'

Kath makes a disgusted little grunt. 'All we knew was, she didn't do it herself. We never believed it—*I* never believed it. She had too much to live for. She … only the week before she died … she asked me about the beach house at Cowes for a Christmas holiday; she went Christmas shopping in Melbourne; she was flat out preparing for the show the next weekend—it was all too much to expect we'd believe it. But if the police don't do anything, what can *we* do?'

Once again I don't have an answer, but hope I'll find one before my search ends. I feel pretty sad as I leave the Blakes. Listening to them tell their story, I had come close to tears myself.

Perhaps the local police have some information they'll share with me, and I decide to visit them next.

∞

I tuck in, nose to the kerb, between a Range Rover and a half-ton ute filled with businesslike dogs, halfway between the police station and the *Mansfield Courier* office. I want to search the newspaper archives too, so this is a perfect spot. The afternoon streetscape is quiet, with diagonal parking lines separating a few four-wheel-drive vehicles that look as if they actually use all their gears from time to time. By now I'm sure lots of people know I'm in town asking questions. Parking close to the police station might not be a bad idea.

First stop: Mansfield Police. Pretending I'm not a bit nervous and wondering if I should whistle a happy tune, I lean on the enquiries counter, open my manila folder and ask a very large policewoman if there is anyone still working here who was here in 1984—'the year Jenny Tanner died', I add, to put the date in context. She disappears. I wait. Just when I am beginning to think the entire complement of the police station has scarpered out the back door, a silver-haired police officer with sergeant's stripes on his sleeves emerges from the rear office.

'I'm Robin Bowles and I'm a writer. I'm writing a book about the death of Jennifer Tanner.'

He looks surprised and smiles. 'That should be an interesting book.' He pauses. 'Only three officers who work here now were stationed here at that time, but unfortunately two are on night shift and one is on leave. I wasn't here, so I can't help you at all,' he gets in quickly, before my next question.

My husband, the strategist, has suggested another opening gambit to help me obtain some of the information I need.

'I don't really need to discuss that particular night with you at all—I'm more interested in clarifying a few procedural matters.'

Unlike my disaster of the previous night, this works brilliantly. Mention procedure to a police officer and he lights up. This officer explains that the police force has changed a lot since 1984. I will hear that on many occasions during the next few months, always from the police.

'What was acceptable then may not be now. People in the force have more options if they want to have further investigations done, and the lines of communication are better. All violent death scenes are photographed these days. Back then, if it was a suicide you didn't have to take photos, so it's not surprising none were taken. The autopsy regulations were different too—for example, X-rays of bullet wounds were not required if the wounds were self-inflicted. Now all fatal bullet wounds are X-rayed.

'This is a small town, you know. It's pretty hard being a country copper sometimes. You know everyone in the town, and then sometimes you have to come down heavy on people—we tread a fine line. People these days are promoted on merit, not just seniority, so you get better officers who are more inclined to listen to the lower ranks. The regulations and procedures have been thoroughly overhauled and things are much better now than they used to be.'

It seems one of the problems for country police is they have to

make on-the-spot decisions, often without backup from more experienced colleagues. I ask him if that meant things were not done
properly in Jenny's case. He is unwilling to discuss Jenny at all or
apply any of the things he has just told me to her particular case.

'Do you know the Tanners?' I ask.

'Of course.'

'Do you know Laurie?'

'Yes. He's a quiet sort of a bloke.'

'I'm going round there now to see if he'll talk to me. Do you
think he will?'

'I can't see why he wouldn't. He should really, if you're going to
get the full story for your book.'

Just what I think. I feel my next stop should be the Tanners' house,
just around the corner. Now I've visited the police, it would only take
one phone call to let the Tanners know I'm asking questions, and I
want them to have exactly the same opportunity as the Blakes to tell
me what happened.

∞

I phone on my mobile as I walk towards their street. Laurie's mother
answers and is initially quite surprised, then quickly becomes very
cross after I introduce myself. She says she and her family want nothing to do with me or my book.

'This situation has ruined our lives! It's broken our family! We
have no comment.'

I am nearly at the house by now and think I will try once more
face-to-face. She might change her mind if I'm standing there,
although I do respect her position. After all, she's not obliged to talk
to anyone.

The Tanner family lives in an old white weatherboard home with
a wide veranda. Town folklore says after Jenny died Laurie 'never
spent another night' out at Springfield and has lived here ever since.
The house is set back behind a fenced front lawn interspersed with
scraggly trees. Edwardian wooden fretwork encloses the veranda,

secluding and screening the house from prying passers-by. A name plate beside the front door tells me the house is called Lorona, and I wonder who or what inspired this unusual name. Uneven floorboards have the worn look of having seen many seasons and hundreds of footsteps come and go.

In response to my knock Mrs Tanner opens the door a little way. She is elderly and much smaller than I expected, wearing felt slippers and a full apron over her dress. She looks like anyone's granny, except for the fierce expression on her face. She repeats her earlier comments and starts closing the door. I try quickly to persuade her to ask Laurie to talk to me, but she is adamant. I tell her through the crack that I will leave my card on the windowsill for her to either throw away or put in a drawer, in case she changes her mind. Then I apologise for intruding on her afternoon and walk away as the door shuts firmly. I am left in no doubt about her resolve not to have anything to do with me.

Ah, well, maybe further down the track. I have to respect people's feelings and she wasn't expecting me—I think. In one way I can understand why the Tanners don't want to drag everything up again, but if Jenny *was* murdered, surely they'd want to know who did it, at least as much as anyone else. In fact, I wonder why the Tanners and the Blakes didn't join forces to get to the truth.

∞

The *Mansfield Courier* archives are 'filed' on dusty shelves in a back storeroom. No such thing as microfiche in Mansfield. I'm really pleased about that, as I easily find 50 or so weekly newspapers in a pile labelled '1984' and I don't have to ask anyone for help. The editor kindly offers me the boardroom to leaf through the piles of dusty old papers. I'm surrounded by a hundred years of *Courier* history on walls and in cedar showcases. I bet these walls have heard a few town secrets.

My only surprise at the *Courier* is the lack of coverage of Jenny's death. I know local papers generally respect family sensitivities in cases of suicide, but this was no ordinary suicide; the case was the talk of the town when it happened. Not that there is any sign of this in the *Courier*. There are only the death notices in the classified section and a brief obituary, published on the Wednesday a week after she died, written by a former editor who was also a retired Mansfield coroner. (Later I learn that he privately told people, 'That girl did not kill herself.') In the obituary column Jenny is sandwiched between Mr G. A. (Andy) Martin, aged 73, and Mr John P. Moran, aged 81. It seems an odd obituary for a suicide:

Mrs Jennifer Ruth Tanner

A wave of sorrow swept over the Mansfield district at the news of the tragically sudden passing of Mrs Jennifer Ruth Tanner, of Bonnie Doon, at the early age of 27 years.

Mrs Tanner, whose death occurred at her home, had been a popular member of this community for most of her adult life.

She was a daughter of Kath and Les Blake of Piries, and won many friends amongst members of the general public and staff members of the State Bank, where she rendered friendly and capable service over a period of approximately eight years.

She was married to Mr Laurie Tanner, a member of a well known Bonnie Doon family and current president of the Mansfield Agricultural and Pastoral Society.

Profound sympathy is felt for Laurie, infant son Samuel and all other relatives in their very sad loss.

A service was held at St Francis Xavier's Church on Saturday morning, following which the cortege moved to the Mansfield Lawn Cemetery. Reverend Father A. Grenville conducted both services and N. J. Todd was in charge of the mortuary arrangements.

There were five death notices. One looked as if it was inserted by Laurie, though it was not signed.

TANNER Jennifer Ruth. Suddenly, November 14, loved wife of Laurie and dearly loved mother of Samuel James. In God's care.

The others were mainly from friends; Kath and Les had not lodged a notice.

TANNER Jennifer Ruth. November 14. Loved daughter in law of Fred and June. At peace.

TANNER Jennifer. Suddenly November 15 [sic]. Sincerest sympathy to Les and Kath, Laurie and families. From employees, Ashfield Sawmilling. R.I.P.

TANNER Jenny. November 14. Memories are something no-one can steal, They just leave a heartache no-one can heal, You will always be my best friend, Until we meet again. Deborah, Trevor and family.

TANNER Jenny. Passed away November 14. Much loved and loving friend. Always in our hearts. Rosslyn, Barry, Melissa and Brenton Smith, Queensland.

That was it. Hardly a ripple and she was gone.

Rummaging the storeroom piles, I look for news on other significant dates. The story about the house fire is smaller than its headline—'Bonnie Doon house destroyed by fire'—followed by four short paragraphs and a final sentence: 'The cause is unknown.'

One of the *Courier* staff tells me Mansfield is known for its unexplained or mysterious deaths. Between 1862 and 1984 there were at least 30 such incidents in the area, including unsolved murders and suicides. Jenny Tanner is included in that total. I can hardly believe there was so little made of Jenny's death at the time. When I ask why the *Courier* did not present the case in more detail, given its mystery and local flavour, the editor replies, 'The paper worries more about sensibilities than news. We can't really publish "hard" news in Mansfield—the paper is run by a family company and they don't want to upset their friends. Mansfield is a town that keeps its secrets.'

∞

The next morning I visit Jenny's sister Kris in her business in Mansfield's main street. Kris is another beautiful Blake daughter, blonde and trim, taller than her mother, but with the same aura of calm and order. She has two businesses, a fashion shop and a home-wares store. The items on display reflect the family's good taste.

Only two weeks before she died, Jenny started a part-time job in Kris's fashion shop. She was friendly and outgoing and knew every-one in town because of her time at the bank. Kris thought Jenny would be a great asset to her new business.

Kris is quite willing to have a chat to me, but doesn't hold out much hope for any positive outcome from the new investigation. She thinks, and I'm already tending to agree, that the new investigation is opening barely healed wounds and sweeping away the superficial courtesies adopted for the past few years—mostly to protect Sam and allow the Blakes to maintain their relationship with him.

'We all thought Sam was pretty special when he was born. The first grandson, a darling little boy. I don't think Jenny found it all that easy with a new baby—he was a difficult feeder and had ear problems which kept him (and her!) awake at night. But I thought everything was normal. I was younger than Jenny and a bit naive. We were all very "girly" girls at home—it was a very female house. I liked horse riding and Miriam went fishing—Jenny mowed the lawn, but gener-ally we didn't do messy and horrible things.

'We loved shopping—I still do and now I can do it professionally.' She smiles. 'I'm not sick of it yet. We'd often go to Melbourne, because that's where we spent our early lives. Local people go on shopping expeditions to Shepparton [a big regional centre about 45 minutes from Mansfield], but we thought nothing of going down to Melbourne, even for a haircut.

'We were all good savers—we knew the rules, especially from Jenny's time in the bank. Like, when we wanted to buy our first cars, we'd all chant: "Now, what are the rules? $500 in the bank for six months, then you can apply for a loan." We were all like that. If we wanted anything we'd go after it—save for it. We are a family which puts a lot of emphasis on waiting until we can afford quality. We all like antiques, because we grew up with that sort of thing.'

I ask her why the two grieving families didn't unite at the time to get to the bottom of Jenny's uncharacteristic action.

'It's so difficult to explain in a way. The phone call from Mum woke me up. You sit there in total disbelief. There was a lot of anger too—how could she do this? I felt like I could've killed her myself for doing this to me. I went round and Mum was just leaving the house. I thought she was going to the farm, but she said there was no point, they'd all left. She was going to the Tanners' to pick Sam up. I was only twenty-four and I didn't really know what I could do. You're not in the driver's seat in those situations.

'Nothing was ever done properly—not the investigation or the inquest. Laurie didn't take charge. It showed up a lot of weaknesses. He wasn't gutsy. He was a bit of a wet week generally, so we shouldn't have expected any different, I suppose, but he *was* her husband. He was nice—had good manners, but he had a lot of difficulty fitting into our family gatherings. He wouldn't sit down until you told him to—he was too timid to even ask for the sugar! If no-one passed it to him he'd go without. We were all so casual and relaxed with each other—he was probably a bit overwhelmed.

'I suppose since the *Sunday Age* article the Tanners think we're trying to blame them. But we've never personally blamed them or attacked them in any way. Frank's wife works in town and she used to pop her head in with Sam if they were passing, but that doesn't happen any more. Laurie's mother   well, no matter what the outcome from all this, I don't think we'll ever salvage that relationship.

'It's true we didn't want to go on a witch-hunt, but we didn't understand at the time that the inquest was our only chance. We thought if there's something found out it will be taken on from here—that the forces of law and order would prevail. In the end we sat through it; howled a lot; listened to the professionals; thought what they were saying must be right, even though we didn't believe she did it. You don't think people will lie in those circumstances and you don't think people go round doing those awful things to other people—so in the end, we got about all we could hope for, an open finding.'

I ask her to describe Jenny for me.

'She was the girl next door. Ordinary. A bit of an old-fashioned person rather than a young gadabout. More a girl who would settle down and get married in her life than a career girl. She had a "home" thing—Mum, Dad and the kids—quite a romantic. She always had her nose in some love story. She was just her, and killing herself was a pretty unordinary thing for her to do.'

My husband and I have speculated endlessly about possible motives for murdering Jenny. One theory we have canvassed is jealousy. I ask Kris, 'Do you think she could have been having an affair with Denis?'

'My gut feel would say no. In a country town the only new men who come here are police, teachers or bankers. She mixed in those circles, but she definitely was not a one-night-stand person. I could name every boyfriend she had until she married Laurie.'

'If she didn't kill herself, why was she killed?'

'I don't know. You can't just blame someone without knowing why. The last ten years have been difficult, but at least we enjoyed Sam, we didn't have to feel like we had to avoid the Tanners. It was an absolute blow-out when that body came to light in the mineshaft. Before that, we got on with things—it was out of our hands. We didn't think there was anything we could do—didn't think there were any avenues. Now who's to say down the track something else won't blow up? It's very unsettling—even your book. The most important thing to come out of that would be making Sam know how much Jenny loved him.'

Driving back home, I ponder on this strange case and the people I have met during the past few days. There is more than one story here. Almost as intriguing as the manner of Jenny's death is the question about why people who knew her were so ready to accept she had committed suicide—even though it seemed to be so out of character, and none of the circumstantial or physical evidence indicated she had done so.

I think back to a poignant line from the *Sunday Age* article: 'The word suicide—repeated to each new person introduced to the case—settled over the tragedy like a shroud.'

I run through the people who have repeated 'suicide' over and over in this chain of Chinese whispers. In spite of Senior Constable Bill Kerr's misgivings, the case was dealt with in indecent haste and buried quickly, just like Jenny.

If murder seems so bloody obvious now, why did everyone accept then that it was suicide? Or, if they didn't accept it, why didn't they speak up? Why didn't both her families make more fuss?

In life, Jenny was a girl her own mother described in her first few words as 'ordinary'. Jenny in death is far from ordinary. People don't just walk into the lounge room of an ordinary person and fire several bullets into them. So, if she *was* murdered, there must have been a reason. And, if she was murdered, whoever did it has been thinking all these years he or she has got away with it, that the whole town swallowed the suicide story and her death was swept under the carpet so quickly and with such authority that no-one dared ask questions, or if they did they didn't get answers.

As I drive, I think about Kath's photos of Jenny. To say I was stunned when I saw them would be an understatement. Jenny looks so like me at the same age we could be twins. I didn't say anything to Kath at the time for fear she'd think I was being melodramatic, but when I get home I delve through my old photo albums and compare my photos with the one I've borrowed. I am not mistaken.

I wonder how I'll find out about the Tanner family if they won't talk to me. While I'm waiting for inspiration on this knotty problem, I'll follow up the leads Kath has given me to uncover more about Jenny.

3

Best Friends

LIZ THOMAS is one of three almost middle-aged women I contact, all of whom refer to themselves as 'Jenny's best friend'. Jenny may have indeed been best friends to each of them. I am learning she had the capacity to be many things to many people.

I discover that Liz lives in the suburb next to me, and I arrange to visit. The Homicide Squad has already been. She married late and has a young child. Her husband has come home early to keep the toddler at bay, and I have brought a bottle of wine to help me through the interview. I should have taken beer—they don't have a corkscrew. After a bit of a rummage looking for one, which helps to break the ice, we settle for coffee and a beer later.

We move into a pale blue lounge room with a cream floral couch and chairs. I suddenly feel I've been here before. Liz seems to have been strongly influenced by her relationship with Jenny and her family. 'This room looks a little like Kath Blake's lounge room,' I comment. 'Have you been there?'

'Many times. I love that place. It's just so immaculate. Often Jenny and I would drive up to Mansfield on a Friday after work, for weekends. I remember one night we were held up and we'd told her mother we'd be there at a certain time, and Jen was really concerned Kath would be worrying. Jen was very conscientious about always letting her mother know she was OK. Kath is a worrier, even though she doesn't show it. Jen stopped at the next police station and phoned to let Kath know we were on the way. See, that just shows you, she never would have done that to her mother—killed herself, I mean. Or her father—they were very close, like friends as well as parents.'

Liz and Jenny met when Jenny moved to Melbourne to work at the State Bank. 'She was the first person I met at the bank—we got on really well from day one.' Liz was certainly Jenny's Melbourne 'best friend'. She loved Jenny and looked up to her. Liz brings out some photo albums and we slide down onto the carpet together to view pages of photos of two long-haired attractive girls engaged in all manner of activities—parties, car rallies, picnics, touring in England, and later with Sam and each other at Springfield.

'I'd go up at weekends and see them at that run-down old farmhouse. It was very dark because of the trees. Jen hated them. She would phone and say, "I've got a few trees for you to cut down," and I'd go and help when Laurie was at Apex meetings, or off shearing. We'd giggle about it afterwards—wonder if June'd notice. If the truth be known she probably wouldn't have cared, although she still treated the house as her own, even if the back door was shut. I don't think they ever locked it—but if it was locked, if you knew the house you could still get in the back way, because you could walk through a little toilet off the back porch through the bathroom and their bedroom into the kitchen. Jenny didn't like June all that much—she tends to take over, and Jenny was very much her own person.

'Jenny would keep Sam immaculate—she was so fussy about him. She'd buy only the best—she got him this really expensive Italian pusher, even though she didn't need a pusher all that often living on the farm. She bought a lovely little cot her Dad painted up—Sam always had the best of everything. June sometimes bought him things from the op-shop in town and it got right up Jenny's nose. In fact, if she had committed suicide—like *if* she had—she would have left a note for sure, because knowing Jen she would have written a detailed list of what she wanted, and one of the things on it would have been that she didn't want June to have Sam. No way!

'She wrote to me quite often. One of her letters said, "Dad's finished the lounge room—your room's last on the agenda." I had the middle room in the hall—it was called "Liz's room". Sam was at the front and Jenny and Laurie had the large bedroom at the back, straight off the kitchen. It was warm in the winter. The lounge room used to be two rooms, but they took down a wall to make it bigger and lighter.

'I've still got a few of her letters—Homicide found them quite interesting. They took them away and photocopied them,' she hints, waiting for me to pounce. I really want to see Jenny's letters, but wait for them to be offered. They are not. I store away the knowledge for another time, not wanting to risk her saying no just now. I don't want to rush her, no matter how eager I feel.

Liz continues: 'Jenny wouldn't hurt anything, not even a chook. During one of my visits we were inside chatting when she heard the chooks scratching in the vegie garden. She had incredible hearing. We went outside and cornered them by the woodpile—she gave me this big log and told me to give them a whack for her, she couldn't do it herself. The chooks ran through the trees across to Denis's place—I don't know if he was there that weekend, but she was really worried he'd shoot them. She was a bit scared of Denis. We ran after the chooks to chase them off Denis's property and then we walked over there together to look at the old house he was doing up. It was pretty close, only a few minutes' walk, but Denis wasn't around.'

Eager to itemise all of Jenny's good points, she goes on.

'Jenny was a real softie. A single mum with two little girls used to come into the bank quite often—one of the girls was retarded. The woman was getting some sort of extra allowance and she'd come in to put the money in the retarded kid's account. One day Jen asked the other little girl if she had her own account too—just in conversation—and she said her Mummy couldn't afford to put money away for her because her sister was "sick". So Jenny started up an account for that little girl—paid her own money into it until she left the bank, as far as I know. She had a full-time job at the Yea State Bank after she married Laurie. She used to send me funny little letters on the internal mail system. She found the driving in and out terrible during the first winter—the roads were so icy. She stayed for about eighteen months altogether and decided to leave before the second winter came. It was so dangerous driving early and late in the dark in both directions. She got a part-time job at the timber mill, which Laurie mostly took over when Sam was born.'

That must be the cleaning job he went to do in Mansfield the night she died, I think.

'Were they poor? Did they need money?'

'Well, Laurie was married before—he was twelve years older than Jenny. He was going to be forty in 1985, the same day I was turning thirty, and Jenny was already making plans for a big party the following October. The word around Mansfield is that his first wife ripped him off for a really big amount of money and he was heavily in debt to Denis and his parents for quite a while, because they lent him the money to help him out. I don't know if that was paid back by the time he and Jenny got married—we didn't really talk about it. She liked to work because she liked nice things for the house. She was very independent—she didn't like asking Laurie for money all the time. If she saw something she wanted which cost $200, she'd work until she got the money and buy it. She was very determined. She'd sometimes see some antique thing on a trip to Melbourne—she loved antiques—and she'd save up and go back and get it. She always seemed to get the money if she really wanted something. Laurie's brothers, some of them, thought she was wasteful, but she didn't care. And I'm not sure if Laurie felt that way.'

'How did you get along with Laurie? Did he interfere with your friendship with Jenny?'

'Oh no. I thought he was all right, I suppose—pretty easy-going. A bit of a weak prick, if you'll excuse the expression. I believe her dad thought he was a bit of a nothing person—no personality. A lot of people think that about Laurie, but I'm not so sure. Personally, I think he's still a Tanner, and Tanners are tough.'

By now Liz has settled in for a good chat. I feel like a glass of my wine, but don't suppose it'll ever be drunk in this house. We get ourselves a beer and keep going.

'Another funny thing about this so-called suicide—you know how you always have your favourite chair at home, at the dining table you always sit in the same one and usually in the lounge room, unless a guest sits there first and you're being polite?' I hope this isn't an oblique message that I'm sitting in her chair. I nod. It's true, I actually remember hearing something about it during my sociology lectures years ago—something to do with 'territory', I think.

'Jenny never sat on the couch. She always sat on one of the chairs with her legs curled under her, never on the couch. So why was she on the couch? She either had a visitor who was sitting in her chair, or she was put there after she was dead. That's what I think, anyway.

'I knew in myself she couldn't have done it. I've been carrying around baggage for years, thinking "What did I miss?" Was it my fault because she had no-one to turn to? She was seeing a clairvoyant at Werribee for a while—maybe she had some problems we didn't know anything about. I was away for three months just before Jen died, but I got back about two weeks before and went straight up to see her. Her next job was to renovate the bathroom. She didn't seem at all depressed, making plans for the Mansfield Show. I was planning to go up for that weekend too. Of course, I still went, but it was to her funeral. I keep thinking if I'd been here …' Her words finish with a little gulp, as she swallows some tears.

I am struck again by the power Jenny's death still exerts on her friends and family.

'The visit from Homicide brought it all back again as if it was last week. I thought in the beginning it might have been someone driving past, but I don't think she would have let anyone in. She wasn't all that secure in her mind out there alone at night.'

We speak a little longer about the gossip around Mansfield, where everyone has a pet theory about who pulled the trigger.

'Would you like to see her letters?' Liz asks, as if she needs a reason to stretch her legs and move away from the confinement of our intense conversation. I would.

There is a handful of letters from Jenny, in small neat handwriting. There are spelling and grammatical mistakes, and I experience a momentary twinge of disappointment.

'Jed has stopped hassling me,' she wrote, and went on to talk about her blossoming relationship with Laurie—1979.

'You wouldn't be pleased with the leaves, they're three inches thick'—autumn 1981.

In answer to a letter from Liz written when Liz was between boyfriends: 'God—oh your life sounds just utterly boring.'

'Dad finished painting the lounge room. Liz's room is last on the agenda.'

'We got rid of the black cat on the weekend. Ben's got run over and he wanted another cat. Our pig has settled in, thinks he's a bull, he sleeps on the bull's back (when the bull's lying down) goes wherever we go.'

And a little postscript on the last letter, 'Hope you're not too bored with my country married woman's letter.'

Nothing remarkable, except for the fact that these letters, written by an ordinary girl about her ordinary life, might now be evidence in a murder investigation.

Liz agrees I can see or phone her again if necessary.

'Any time. At last Jenny's death is being investigated. I knew it wasn't suicide.'

I don't comment on this for two reasons. First, I still have no official confirmation that it was definitely a murder. Secondly, I keep thinking if all these people were so sure she didn't shoot herself, why didn't they say something then?

∞

Still very puzzled about why Jenny's death was so easily accepted as suicide, I decide to conduct a test of my own, to see whether Jenny could have shot herself. I need to understand why people who were so familiar with guns accepted the suicide hypothesis so readily. A gun shop listed in the Yellow Pages is ten minutes' drive from my house. I tell the salesman I want to buy a BRNO .22 rifle as a gift for my son. The gun he produces is a surprise. It's so long! More than a metre—three and a half feet in the old measurements. The barrel alone is over sixty centimetres long. I ask him if I can test something. He asks if I have a licence—gun-shop owners are wary of nutters.

I confess my ulterior motive. 'I need to conduct a little experiment,' I cajole. 'Please make sure it's not loaded.' He removes the magazine and hands this slick instrument of death across the counter. It's much lighter than I expect. Taking off my shoes, I sit on a wooden chair and arrange myself in a similar position to the one in which Jenny was found. From reports of her height by family and friends, at 170 cm (five feet seven inches) I am a little taller than Jenny, and I am sitting on a straight wooden chair, not a soft low sofa. I hold the muzzle against my forehead. It sits uncomfortably at my hairline. Then I awkwardly manoeuvre my toe into the trigger mount area and depress the trigger, asking the salesman how hard I have to press to make it work. By now his hand is hovering over the phone. He tells me I've just done it—the pressure needed is very slight. Another surprise—this bit is easy.

So it is possible for me to activate the trigger of a BRNO .22 rifle with my big toe. But it would be almost impossible for any resulting bullets to travel a horizontal pathway through my brain. The path of the bullets would be upwards (perhaps at forty-five degrees or more) and possibly out through the top of my skull. If I'd been on a lower chair or been shorter, the barrel would have been too long to put against my forehead. If Jenny did shoot herself, she must have stood up and bent her head over the top of the rifle, twice. This would have been difficult while keeping balance on one leg, especially with one bullet already in her brain. And if this is what she did, how did she manage to sit down again so neatly before dying, in the middle of the couch? And why was there no blood reported on the floor? I cast my memory back to the photos of Jenny's lounge room. Was there a floor rug? I can't remember.

The salesman grabs the gun roughly as I hand it back. Perhaps he's cross because I've spun him a story and he's wasted time on a 'no sale'. I thank him anyway and leave, convinced there was no physical way Jenny could have executed this deed. Why did everyone accept she did? Anyone could have done exactly the same test I've just done. Not scientific, but pretty common sense.

∞

I hear back from my nursing friends at Beechworth. No Health Department history anywhere in the district of Jenny having had a breakdown. Of course, if it had been in Melbourne, the information would be more difficult to track down, but it had supposedly happened after Sam was born, when Jenny was living at Springfield. My contact also makes a suggestion, heavy with meaning but scant on detail.

'You'd do well to try to contact the Whistleblowers' Association. I'm told there are certain people involved with them who might be able to give you some information.' This little gem sets me off on a real-life cloak-and-dagger exercise, trying to find the Association and then being vetted before anyone will even meet me, much less talk to me.

There is no listing in the phone book (well, that may sound naive, but I had to start somewhere), so I ring a few media contacts to obtain a lead. I finally get through to a recorded message, and the former president phones me back. We agree to meet in a very public coffee lounge in inner-city Carlton, and go through the 'I'll be wearing so-and-so and carrying such-and-such' routine.

He is small, grey-suited and ordinary-looking. He is probably equally disappointed with my appearance—tall, casually dressed and ordinary-looking. Neither of us looks very 'undercover'. Once he is satisfied I really am writing a book about a case involving a possible 'police cover-up', he relaxes and tells me some incredible tales about the fate of whistleblowers in today's community. He is certain his phones are tapped, and warns me to be careful about what I say on the phone. He also says, 'Watch out for your car and your dog if you have one. That's how people are warned off.'

I am stunned by his serious approach to life, and laugh at the possibility of having my phone tapped—or worse.

'It's illegal. Even the police are not allowed to do it,' I scoff.

'Let me tell you something for once and for all. You may still think there is such a thing as truth and justice. I'm telling you—there's no truth and justice. Go on, write that down.' He jabs at my note-pad with a fierce forefinger. 'There's no truth and justice—there's only power.'

A bitter man, but I obey him and write in big capitals on the front page of Jenny's inquest transcript: NO TRUTH AND JUSTICE.

Later, as I get further into my investigations, I will begin to agree with him.

My new-found mentor says I should protect myself by ensuring that as many people as possible in influential positions know about my involvement with Jenny's story. He says I should meet an investigative reporter from the ABC's *7.30 Report*, who is particularly interested in alleged police cover-ups. I'm still inclined to be sceptical, but I agree to go along out of curiosity.

When we subsequently meet the reporter, I have no intention of saying much—experience has taught me that, contrary to general belief, nothing is 'off the record' for a journalist. We have a whispered and furtive chat in the staff canteen, but I don't give much away. I leave after half an hour wondering what the real agenda is. Maybe my whistleblower owes the journo a favour and sees me as a good story? The whole conundrum becomes irrelevant a few weeks later, when the reporter is excised in an ABC TV 'downsizing'.

Soon after my clandestine meetings and late-night phone calls with the whistleblowers, one of whom has achieved great notoriety for his information about a police scam, two strange events occur.

I have a new boxer puppy, ten weeks old, which becomes morbidly anaemic from rat-bait poisoning. Luckily, with my nursing training, I notice her pale gums in time to save her—at great expense. There is no way she can have eaten rat bait on our property, as I won't even put snail pellets around the garden in case I poison wild birds. As she hasn't had her injections, she has barely put a foot outside the gate since we bought her.

Then one night, when I finish work around 7.30 p.m. at our Carlton office, I try to phone my husband to tell him I am leaving. I get a recording, 'This number is temporarily unavailable,' so I try again. After three attempts I get through, but there are a couple of loud clicks on the line before my husband answers. I tell him about the clicks, and he advises me to report the difficulty immediately in case someone is messing around with the phone. He reasons that perhaps if someone is interfering, they would feel fairly safe with a business phone at that hour. So, with paranoia ascending, in spite of my scepticism, I report the difficulty straight away.

Next morning I have a call from a man who says he's a supervisor with the phone company. He has checked my line and it is fine. I ask how he knew about the problem and he tells me he was advised that morning. I ask for his name and extension number, which he supplies without hesitation. I write them down very carefully. I'm now feeling very paranoid, and decide to think up an excuse and call him back, to check he is real.

The phone rings all right, but it is an air-conditioning company whose receptionist has never heard of my telephone 'supervisor'. I get a few goosebumps. I don't tell my husband. I don't want to frighten him. There's bound to be a simple explanation.

When I first started working on Jenny's story, my husband and I decided to move away from Melbourne for the writing stage. That way I'd have no excuses about being interrupted by clients, attending meetings or having to do lunch. If I failed it wouldn't be for lack of application, only lack of talent.

This decision, once made, was implemented with amazing thoroughness, maybe because my husband couldn't wait to slam the door of his consulting office shut. So, while I've been researching, he's been putting his considerable planning talents into our relocation strategy. He's given me a copy, complete with deadline dates and action responsibilities.

Now, after the incident with the phoney supervisor, I'm starting to look forward to getting out of town.

∞

Still trying to discover the real Jenny, I telephone another of her 'best friends', Roz Smith, who has lived for some time in Queensland.

Roz and Jenny had known each other at school in Mansfield, but didn't become close friends until Jenny was involved in hairdressing. They also knew each other from a church group, and shared an interest in netball and swimming. Roz said Jenny was 'full of life', a real party girl—into everything.

Roz liked Laurie and thought he was 'very nice, a lot quieter than Jenny—more reserved. He was really devoted to Jenny and she to him. They were happy together, got on well. They both visited us in our last house at Sorrento Waters, came to stay a couple of times, and I visited them too at Bonnie Doon. If they weren't happy, she never told me. Jenny was a happy wife and mother and a good cook—she was very homey and very motherly to Sam.

'She sewed lots of things for Sam and the house. When she visited a few months before she died I gave her my old sewing machine, as she didn't have her own and I had a new one.'

I sit at the other end of the phone taking notes and wondering if anyone else is listening in to this tale of domestic bliss.

'Did you know Denis Tanner?'

'I only ever met Denis once. He didn't come to the house often, as far as I knew. He's big, with short hair and he's very broad—looks very strong. I was a bit ambivalent towards him then. I didn't warm to him. Later on I hated him. I never believed Jenny killed herself. She wasn't a person to cop out, and a lot of strange things happened a short time before she died. Laurie's valuable pedigree dog was shot when they were both out one night two weeks before she died, and a strange car came up the drive one night when Laurie would have normally been out at one of his meetings, but he wasn't well so he didn't go. Jenny looked out of their bedroom window and saw this car reversing down the drive and thought they must have seen Laurie's car in the shed. She rang Kath the next morning and told her about it, but didn't report it to the police. They did report the dog's death, and an officer came over from Alexandra CIB to investigate. I've always been really angry that they'd send someone over to investigate a dog's death, but they couldn't be bothered to come over for Jenny.'

In a statement to the police after Jenny's death, and in her evidence at the inquest, Roz had detailed another phone call she'd had from Jenny shortly before she died. This evidence had been crucial in casting some early suspicion on Denis Tanner, and as a result he had been asked to provide the police with a statement of his whereabouts on the night of Jenny's death.

According to Roz's inquest evidence, Jenny had phoned to tell her about a strange visit she'd received from Denis on a Monday evening when Laurie was at Apex. Roz could pinpoint the date, as Jenny said daylight saving had just started in Victoria and she was having difficulty getting Sam to bed. Jenny said Denis had told her he had come to borrow Laurie's rifle for some shooting. He hadn't told his wife he was coming from Melbourne to Bonnie Doon, and didn't want Jenny to tell Laurie of his visit. He then sat on the lounge-room floor, loading the rifle as they spoke. Suddenly he asked Jenny if she was planning to leave Laurie. Jenny told Roz she'd indignantly denied this and wanted to know where he had got the idea. 'A friend,' he said, and refused to elaborate. Denis Tanner, in his evidence at the first inquest, has denied that he told Jenny he had come to Springfield to shoot, that he asked her not to tell Laurie about the visit, that he handled any of Laurie's guns during that visit, or that he asked Jenny about her personal life.

According to Smith, Jenny had told Laurie as soon as he returned, but she felt disturbed enough about the incident to phone Roz next morning and tell her about it too.

'I've thought and thought about Jenny's death and weighed things up,' Roz tells me. 'I really don't know, but I have my suspicions. It has really affected my life since then.' She excuses herself and blows her nose.

'I'll always remember Jen. There's days even now when I sit and think about her—birthdays, Christmas, things for a reason, things for no reason. Homicide came to see me a couple of months ago and reopened some pretty buried stuff. Now I feel like I'm going through it all over again.'

And I phone out of the blue, making you even worse. I feel guilty about barging into her life without notice, but I want to find out what really happened. It seems to justify almost anything.

She finishes hopefully, 'Maybe the truth will come out this time.'

I nod as I put the phone down. 'What do *you* think?' I ask the silent phone and the possible listener-in.

∞

Memories are something no-one can steal,
They just leave a heartache no-one can heal,
You will always be my best friend,
Until we meet again.
Deborah, Trevor and family

The Deborah who inserted this notice in the *Mansfield Courier* is an angry woman. Her response to 'My name is Robin Bowles and I'm writing a book about the death of Jennifer Tanner' is 'Good! It's about time someone got all that out into the open. I've always been angry about it—in fact, I rang Kath up after the *Sunday Age* article and gave her a real serve. How could they let it go like that, knowing Jenny was murdered? Her own daughter!'

I speak up on Kath's behalf. 'I don't think they knew about the two bullets until just before the inquest.'

'Rubbish! I knew about two bullets at the funeral, or soon after. The whole of Mansfield knew, for goodness sake. That's why there was so much gossip. I knew she didn't do it—all her friends knew! It was totally at odds with the Jennifer we knew. There was no way anybody could do what she was supposed to have done. I couldn't understand why the police dropped it—why was it stopped? Over the years I've wondered what I could do to get the case reopened.

'Jen and I were arm-in-arm friends from Year Seven. The boys at school used to tease us about being lesbians, we were so close. We always stayed in touch after we left school and I spent about as much time at the Blakes' as I did at my own parents'. I knew the Tanners very well too. Denis partnered my sister at her deb ball. I've known for years about Laurie's first wife—he wanted kids and she didn't— not with Laurie, anyway. That's what I think broke up the marriage. It almost bankrupted Laurie, and if Jenny was thinking of leaving him

he would have been frightened that Jenny would get more money—
and Sam. I don't think he could've emotionally gone through it again.

'They say people who are close to you sometimes come back in
dreams and speak to their best friends—I'm waiting for Jenny to
come and tell me who killed her.'

'Could Jenny have been having an affair with anyone? Perhaps Jed
Moffit, or someone down in Melbourne—maybe Denis?'

'Not Denis! He might have tried to put the hard word on her but,
as I said, she couldn't stand him. And Jed—well, she was very upset
when they split up, but no, I don't know if she was having an affair. I
have no idea if she was having family problems. She wouldn't blurt
out personal problems anyway—she'd try to work them out herself.
When I came down on visits from Echuca, she'd drive into town to
meet me at the Witches Brew for coffee, or I'd go out there to see her
and we talked every so often on the phone, but just family and personal news—nothing about any problems.

'She used to call Sam "the little shit", because he was naughty at
times. One time I was on the phone to her and he took a bowl of
sugar and up-ended it all over her new carpet. She was furious—she
was very house-proud—but I already had kids of my own and I told
her she'd be lucky if that was the naughtiest thing he ever did. She
never smacked him, though—she was so sensitive she couldn't even
bear to see a fly squashed. My sister and I were planning to spend a
weekend down there a couple of weeks after she died. I was going to
stay with Jen and my sister with her best friend. I ended up going to
her funeral instead.'

No tears from Debbie—her anger is still sustaining her. At the end
of our conversation, she wishes me good luck.

∞

And I'm beginning to feel I'll need a bit of luck to get to the bottom
of the Jennifer Tanner enigma. She seems to have had the knack of
presenting different faces to different friends, and so far nothing that's
been said casts any light on why someone would want to murder her.

My husband says, 'Find out the why and you'll find the who.' True, but unearthing more than warm memories isn't so simple.

Even though Jenny's female friends and family are all convinced she was murdered, none of them can offer a credible guess about why and by whom. And I'm only getting one side of the story so far, as her former husband and his family are not talking to me. There are other people who knew her—her doctors, for instance—but I want more personal information.

I decide to look for Jed Moffit. Maybe he and Jenny had started up their affair again, and perhaps he knew something.

Someone tells me he's moved to South Australia. I go through the phone enquiries for every area code in the State. I'm already familiar with this routine, as I've been searching for Gerry O'Donnell, the ambulance officer, the same way. I've had no luck with Gerry, but Moffit is a more unusual name, and I track Jed down in a country area without much trouble. In Australia, unless people deliberately try to hide themselves, they aren't hard to find.

Jed's wife Shirley answers the phone, and we have a friendly talk. At the time of Jenny's death, she says, they were living in Gippsland, in eastern Victoria. Jed heard through the police network that Jenny had shot herself, and it really 'rocked him'. Jed has now left the police force and is away doing a refresher course, preparing for a return to his former career as a prison officer. She gives me his motel number.

I catch him by surprise a few evenings later, in a motel room he is sharing with a colleague. His early responses are cagey, as you'd expect from an ex-cop. He tells me he wants to check me out with Homicide, which I say doesn't bother me. I think that reply reassures him, as he doesn't hang up.

He says he and Jenny 'just grew apart—there was no animosity'. I tell him I've seen a letter from Jenny saying he was 'hassling her and making her name mud around town'. Jed strongly denies this, but he does say he did his best to try to get her back. 'She was a spunk. Tall, about 5 foot 6, beautiful hair—she was so full of life.' At this point Jed Moffit, 51 years old, ex-cop and prison officer, starts to weep. I hear his embarrassed room-mate excuse himself. Jed reassures him, 'It's OK, mate, I'll be fine.' Again I feel as if I have barged clumsily into someone's life as I sit listening to him sobbing hundreds of kilometres away, not knowing what to say, wondering if he'll feel like going on. He recovers and continues.

'My first wife and I transferred to Mansfield in July 1977 after an operation she had for a breast lump removal. We'd only been in Mansfield about three months when my wife suddenly became ill with lymph cancer. Doctors told her she had three months to live. She went back to her parents to spend time with her mother and the family, leaving me to care for my boy aged ten and a girl aged eight. Some time after that I met Jenny. She was tops.

'My wife was ill for much longer than three months and died in December 1978. Jenny and I had become quite serious by then. During that period she'd put in for a more senior job with the bank—it was either that or get "shanghaied", as she put it, to somewhere she didn't want to be. She was bright enough to get the Melbourne job and so she lived in Melbourne and came home at weekends. We often discussed where we'd eventually live—should we build or buy, in Melbourne or Echuca? She had a good friend at Echuca, others in Melbourne. She didn't want to be stuck in Mansfield for ever.

'We still had the relationship, but I found myself sharing her more and more with other friends and family. She was enjoying Melbourne and the night life and I was isolated in Mansfield, looking after two kids. When she did come back at weekends there was also a tribe of people that were part and parcel of the Mansfield scene—Young Farmers, for instance, people like Curly McCormack and Laurie Tanner. In the seventies they were a bit like Jaycees. I was eleven years older than Jenny and didn't have a lot in common with a lot of her friends. I think her parents liked me, though.

'I remember her twenty-first birthday—I went out the day before and helped to put up the marquee and lay the dance floor. That would have been January 1978. All her aunties and uncles came as well as the friends. It was a great success, lots of people and presents.

Good weather, tons of food. There was a band. Her family treated me A-OK.

'After we split up, Jenny was still with the bank. We'd see each other in town and say "G'day Jed," "G'day Jenny"—quite friendly. She left the bank and got a job at the timber mill, but I think that was a while later.'

I ask him if he knows Laurie and Denis.

'Oh yes. Laurie's not a bad bloke. Denis is the authority on everything. He's an 18 number—his police number starts with 18—and I'm a 17, which means I was senior to him. I met him a couple of times in Mansfield. He wasn't working there—I met him with Jenny. I can tell you, I wasn't overly impressed.'

Another Denis fan! I move away from this contentious subject. 'Tell me about Jenny's death. What did you think when you heard the news?'

'Bullshit! We'd moved to Gippsland in 1982. Jenny had been married to Laurie for a while by then—I think she was pregnant with Sam when I left. Shirley and I were married and very happy together. We had a young son of our own. My ex-Senior Sergeant, Neil Walker, rang me from Mansfield and said, "One of your old girlfriends shot herself." I couldn't even think who it could have been, but I certainly didn't think it was Jenny. No way! I knew the girl—she never would have done it. Three or four weeks later, Kath rang me as well, in case I hadn't heard.

'I couldn't work it out. I thought I knew Jenny better than that, especially in view of her attitude to firearms. I had to leave mine in the boot when I went to see her. Her dad hated guns too, so I was always conscious of remembering to take mine off. In those days, early 1977, the police force had just changed over from pissy little Browning .32s and Colt .32s to big automatic .38 Smith and Wesson pistols. We weren't obliged to wear them at that time—they weren't part of the uniform, as they are now. Up until the mid-eighties it was at the member's discretion to wear firearms or not. She didn't know how to shoot, so I knew she couldn't have done it.'

Another one, I think to myself.

'Were you ever a suspect, do you think?'

'Oh yes. I've had Homicide at home—two of them came over from Melbourne. They questioned me and my family. Some relative of Laurie's told the police that in August 1984 I was at a pre-recording of *The New Price is Right* for Channel 7 on the same day as Jenny, at Festival Hall. They suggested it might have been a liaison. It would have been a bit difficult—I was with my wife and her family, and Jenny was with two female relatives—I think one was her mother-in-law. We were several rows apart and didn't even speak, we weren't close enough. We were shown directly to our seats and left after the show.

'My wife and I joked about it with Homicide. Can you believe, they'd gone to the trouble of getting copies of those tapes from the Channel 7 archives? I think someone put the wind up the police there may have still been something going on between me and Jenny. We sat down at home and watched the tapes together. I was also asked about my movements on 14 November 1984, which of course I couldn't remember. Fortunately my wife is fastidious about dating all our family photos, and it turned out I was right here at home at some family function—luckily, with photos to prove it.'

'So if you don't think Jenny shot herself and you are innocent—you're an ex-cop and you knew her—who do *you* think did it?'

'I've drawn conclusions and they are the same as Homicide's theories. I think Bill Kerr was badly treated in a way. I've worked with Bill at Mansfield, and he was treated within the system as a bit of a joke. The police department even treated him as if he was somewhat lacking. I've treated him that way myself, although he was a 16 number and had four years' more experience than me.

'I also knew [Detective Sergeant] Ian Welch and his offsider [Detective Senior Constable] Jimmy Sullivan, and they had the reputation of being good country detectives they'd always turn out I don't know why they didn't go over that night. Told by Bill it was suicide, I suppose. It was late at night; Jenny was dead; the ambulance and doctor had been notified; next of kin were on the way to take care of Laurie and the baby—probably saw no need.'

'I hear they call Ian Welch "Columbo". Did you know that?'

'Oh, yes. He wore the raincoat, shambled and mumbled a bit and smoked a lot. He couldn't handle a tinnie—for some reason he needed a straw. He likes a drink, though. Sullivan moved to Warrnambool. He retired early. What you should ask yourself is: why did a certain Detective Sergeant make a statement about where he was that night which later proved to be incorrect?'

'Why didn't the police ask more questions at the time, especially after they knew there were two bullets? Bill Kerr always had suspicions—surely his superiors should have followed them up? Or Don Frazer, even. He was there on the night.'

'I think they initially treated the case as a simple suicide, and then when they realised they'd stuffed it up there was no going back. Fortunately for them, Bill Kerr wasn't taken seriously about a lot of things, so maybe that made it easier. I'm not sure why Donnie Frazer didn't say more. He was a pretty good operator, quite well respected. I don't know if anyone was actively exerting pressure to cover it up. It did go down to Homicide in Melbourne for investigation, but was returned with "Further Investigation Not Warranted" on it, I believe. I heard after Jenny died Bill wanted to move. He was on the lookout for a one-manner somewhere in Victoria. He checked out Penshurst in February '86, and the same year he moved out to Macarthur in the far west of the State. I ran into him in another country town one day and had a conversation with him. He told me he wasn't happy about what happened with Jenny, but what could he do—one constable against all the establishment? I also ran into Don Frazer in Horsham. He wasn't very forthcoming, but he had his reservations. He wouldn't say much other than it was a "stuff-up". Seemed to me that he and Bill had both moved about as far away from Mansfield as you could get and still be in Victoria.'

I have visions of Bill Kerr finally getting out from under in Mansfield and moving miles away to his 'one-manner', where he's the boss, taken seriously by folks in Macarthur as their town police officer. I feel sorry for him and cross with him at the same time. Why didn't he try harder? Why was it so difficult to get his superiors to keep the investigation going? I plan to ask him those questions soon.

∞

I am beginning to sense a hint of a PR campaign being done on me about Jenny. Apparently she was almost too good to be true. Laurie reportedly holds other views—but he hasn't agreed to speak to me. In his statement to the police the day after Jenny's funeral and in all subsequent interviews, he has stuck to the same tune: 'After the birth of Sam she became very depressed and seemed to have two personalities. She would become very moody but would hide her bad moods when we had company. I tried to get her to go to a doctor in relation to this, but she would not go. She insisted there was nothing wrong with her.' When asked if Jenny had ever given him any indication that she might commit suicide he responded, 'No, she didn't say it in those words. When she got depressed and—she seemed to think I had the best end of the stick because I went out a lot to working bees and work—she might say, "Life wasn't worth living like this" several times over a period of time … You know, my wife had plenty of opportunity to go out and join things and enjoy herself, but she just wasn't that way inclined.'

Laurie told the inquest that his wife's moods changed after the birth of their son. She became short-tempered. He often had to bath Sam if he was home. 'She got cranky, specially at night when she had to get up to the baby. She didn't like getting up through the night.' Three months before she died he had unsuccessfully tried to persuade her to visit her doctor in Benalla, to seek assistance for her depression. 'She said she'd get over it in time and in the meantime she was good at putting on a happy face for visitors.'

This evidence doesn't sit well with what I have been told so far. Where is the party girl, the loving young mum who 'kept that baby immaculate', the enthusiastic shopper, the girl who kept the bingo books, planted a garden, renovated a gloomy old farmhouse and 'lived life to the full'? What had happened to laughing Jenny? Do people really change that much after they are married? And does post-natal depression last almost two years without anyone except your husband noticing? Or does the fact that only Laurie had seen these depressed and 'cranky' moods mean they were rare?

Dr Patience, Jenny's doctor, had confirmed in his evidence that Jenny had lacked the joy one usually associates with having a first baby. But he had also told the court that in late July, around the same time Laurie spoke to him about Jenny's moods, Jenny had consulted him without Laurie's knowledge about the possibility of having another child. She wanted to know whether she would have to have another Caesarean, and underwent tests to see if she would. Not exactly the actions of someone planning to leave her husband.

∞

I review my notes and try to get inside Jenny's head. I can understand if she was a bit cranky from lack of sleep—after all, sleep deprivation has been used as a form of torture. Was she depressed? Perhaps a bit bored or fed up with her husband being away a lot? I remember years ago, as a young mother, I was tired, depressed and cranky at times, often simultaneously. I resented my husband's freedom as he departed for work each day, leaving me with monosyllabic toddlers and never-ending piles of washing, vegies to cook and mash and arguments to resolve. Any woman who's had children could identify with these circumstances.

Do I know Jenny yet? Not really, although a picture is emerging of a young, attractive, apparently uncomplicated person whose favourite reading material was Mills & Boon romances. She was settled in relative isolation on a farm with an older, very quiet husband who was absent most of the day—a rather awkward man who was perhaps intimidated by the Blakes' casual familiarity and boisterousness, who may have found it difficult to express feelings and emotions. I think Jenny was very strong-willed and highly emotional. I can also identify with her daily activities—renovating, gardening and

participating in her local community. These are the things you throw
yourself into when you're cut off from the familiar routine of working in a job. With the renovations on her house nearing completion,
she had begun looking for other interests to keep her active and
occupied. Somehow I can't imagine Jenny knitting by the fire.

When Jenny started work in Kris's new fashion shop, she selected
a dress and some accessories in lieu of her first pay-packet. She said
she planned to continue this form of payment for a while to 'build up
a new wardrobe'. Maybe she was ready to emerge into society again
on her own terms and wanted to spruce herself up, as Sam was almost
two. Which young mother couldn't identify with those feelings?

∞

It's time to return to Mansfield, to attempt an interview with Laurie.

A call at the council chambers provides some local historical
information. Then I walk to the Tanners' home near by. The house
looks deserted and unwelcoming, but I have decided to attempt contact each time I am in town.

My knock echoes loudly. Someone toils slowly up the hall. An old
man, still tall in spite of leaning heavily on two walking sticks, opens
the door. Fred Tanner. I introduce myself and ask if Mrs Tanner is
home. He says she is at golf, but will be back soon.

I'm very keen to engage Mr Tanner in some sort of discussion, and
ask if I can wait for his wife.

'I don't know,' he says. 'I'm not allowed to talk to you. We're not
talking to reporters. I've been told to shut my gob and say nothing.'

'I'm not a reporter, Mr Tanner, I'm a writer. I'm writing a book,
not a newspaper story. I want it to be fair and I'm talking to a lot of
people about your family, so I'd appreciate the chance to talk to you
too. We don't have to talk about anything to do with that night if you
don't want to. Perhaps I can just wait out here on the veranda until
Mrs Tanner gets back?'

He wobbles through the doorway and sits down crookedly on the
porch chair. He invites me to sit down too, so I grab the opportunity

and sit on a bench directly opposite him. He describes in detail a fall he's had recently, necessitating the two sticks. While he itemises all his bruises, my brain busily explores my dilemma.

Fred is an old and frail man who has been firmly told not to talk to strangers. He is a bit vague, but not at all stupid. I have him all to myself, and I know from nursing elderly people that I could get him to talk to me, but I don't want to get him into trouble with anyone. Self-interest debates with concern for him. I wonder who he'd get trouble from—his wife or his sons? Or all of them? I decide to stay on the safe side and ask him instead about his early life in Bonnie Doon.

Mr Tanner is not only expecting his wife, but Sam as well, home from school. This information sharpens my dilemma—if Sam arrives home, I don't really want to meet him. I feel he's had enough to deal with already, but he'll have to walk straight past me to go inside. If that happens, I decide I'll just give him my name and tell him I'm waiting to see his grandmother. Most 13-year-old kids would make a stab at politely mumbling something and disappear anyway, I reason. Mr Tanner and I chat for a while until Mrs Tanner arrives home with Sam in the car.

Sam goes around the back and Mrs Tanner shoos her husband inside. She is quite polite to me, but does not want to talk. She is concerned for Sam. 'We want to protect that poor boy from all this.'

'But don't you think he would want to know if his mother didn't kill herself and abandon him?' I ask.

'Well, she did. And I just wish they'd let the girl rest in peace.'

'But Mrs Tanner, if she was murdered, how can she rest in peace?' My question is left hanging as the front door shuts firmly behind her.

4

The Tanners

BONNIE DOON began as a hamlet known as Devil's River. Before the flooding of Lake Eildon, the town nestled in a verdant valley among the foothills of the Strathbogie Ranges. Behind it the mountains loom high and mysterious, often swathed for days in grey-black, swirling clouds.

The local legend is that in 1839 a party of explorers camping beside the junction of the Delatite River and Brankeet Creek, below the twin peaks now known as The Paps, overheard the sound of a nearby corroboree and were so alarmed by the unholy noise that they named the river by their campsite Devil's River.

If gold had not been discovered in the Strathbogies in 1851, and bigger deposits in 1858, the valley would simply have remained a fine farming district. But the discovery of gold changes many communities, and Devil's River was no exception. Miners of several nationalities flocked to the area to search for gold. From 1858 Chinese gold seekers and traders arrived in large numbers, contributing to the growth of the settlement. The *Mansfield Independent* reported a sports meeting at Christmas 1869 attended by 300 to 400 people, and as late as 1877 the *Mansfield Guardian* estimated the population around the Strathbogie goldfields at upwards of 500 people.

Villages and towns grew around the Devil's River County. The largest was originally called The Battery, but its name was changed to Mansfield, after a town near Sherwood Forest in England, by a local squatter, no doubt nostalgic for green fields and forests far away. Much of the mining was alluvial along the river banks and gullies, but on the slopes of the Strathbogies deep shafts were sunk. Profitable sheep and cattle farms also sprang up. Men who worked the farms on the steep slopes of the High Country became skilled horsemen, earning a reputation for their daredevil riding.

In the valley on a property called Wappan Run lived a devout Presbyterian lady, Anne Bon, who became a matriarch and benefactor for the entire area during her long life. She abhorred the name 'Devil's River', referring to it as 'that river with the unmentionable name'. She had come to Wappan (called after the Aboriginal name for the Delatite River) as a young bride from Perthshire in Scotland. Her sensitivities influenced the decision to rename Devil's River 'Bonnie Doon'.

Bonnie Doon today is a town with a pioneer past and not much future. Its main attractions are the Strathbogies in the distance and man-made Lake Eildon, which wraps itself around the foothills and completely covers a good part of the old township. Newcomers from the city have discovered cheap houses and subdivided farmlets fronting the lake. They keep the town active in the winter with skiing parties, and in summer with boating and fishing.

There's a strong sense of community in Bonnie Doon, and some people who have lived in the area for forty years still don't consider themselves 'locals'. 'It takes more than just living here to make you into a local,' pronounced a resident of more than twenty-five years' standing.

Bonnie Doon people have their own yardsticks for measuring time. They talk in terms of generations, or before and after 'the water came up'. It's things like this that make you a local.

The water came up with incredible rapidity in 1956, a year after Lake Eildon was enlarged to a volume about seven times as big as Sydney Harbour. Bonnie Doon had been relocated, and city experts had told the displaced townspeople they would have up to six years to shift buildings and other items before they were submerged, but unusually heavy rains in 1956 saw everything disappear within the year. Only the cemetery, three churches and the football field survived.

'It was terrible, really,' recalls a member of the Historical Society. 'It filled in five months! A lot of people didn't have time to clear out sheds, much less remove them. The pub couldn't be saved and the publican couldn't retrieve his licence, either. Had to build a new pub. And a new community hall—for bingo and so on.'

The Tanners are definitely considered local. Three generations of Tanners have farmed the area and contributed to the community's development. A fourth generation is now growing up in and around the district. Like the Blakes, the family is very highly regarded in Mansfield and Bonnie Doon, and many people express strong feelings of sympathy for the Tanners' experiences since Jenny Tanner died.

Laurie's grandfather, Frank, was a teacher. He was moved around a bit by the Education Department and ended up in Greensborough, down in the city. But Frank didn't like city life and returned to Bonnie Doon to teach. He was headmaster at the old (now flooded) school from 1930 to 1936. He was tough but fair, and local people remember him as 'a very good teacher'. He married a Davon from Maindample, whose family were original selectors of the property known as Springfield. Frank and his wife lived there in a house built around 1900 of locally milled cypress pine.

Laurie's father, Fred, was born at Springfield in 1910 and grew up there, farming the property with his brother Sandy. Fred may be stooped and gaunt these days, but he must have been a strong man in his prime. He was very reserved, and was never seen at local dances. He told me he 'spent most of the time working with his brother, didn't hang around with girls—too busy on the farm'. He met June Palmer when she was up from Melbourne visiting her sister, whose husband, a young blacksmith, had come to Bonnie Doon to work and eventually settled in the town. Later June would walk from her sister's house to visit Fred. 'I don't think he did much courting, he was so shy,' a local recalled. 'June most likely made all the running. Once she sets her mind on something, she usually gets it.'

When Fred and June were married, June was small and alert, with a clipped way of speaking. Where Fred was quiet and easy-going, she was always a lady who spoke her mind. She is about ten years younger than Fred, and seems to have been the driving force in the family. She and Fred lived with old Frank and his wife until Frank ran his car off the road and killed himself after a long night at the pub celebrating his retirement that day. Local gossip has it that Frank's widow ran off to live in New South Wales with 'a younger fella'; true or not, she eventually sold the farm to June and Fred to support their own growing family.

Laurie was born in 1945, when Fred was thirty-five. Over the next ten years four more children came along—Bruce, Frank, Denis and a daughter, Carol. June Tanner became involved in community affairs and actively supported the group raising money to build the new community hall after the water came up.

'She was a very strong and compassionate person,' a neighbour related. 'If anyone needed help, June'd be the first to make a cake or lend a hand. You'd see them all together often—they were a pretty close-knit family. Kept themselves to themselves, though.'

'We had a grand time in those days,' another told me. 'Everyone pitched in and the new people contributed too. June took everything in her stride. She was always in control. They were a nice family—it's terrible all this has happened to them. They didn't deserve it. Laurie's a lovely bloke—very quiet, like his dad. He's always polite, always waves, always chats.'

A woman who went to school with Fred and was taught by Frank Tanner tells me she hasn't spoken much to June since the tragedy was so extensively aired in the *Sunday Age*. 'I wouldn't know what to say. I feel terrible sorry for June. I don't think she knew anything, like, but it's her sons under the microscope now, isn't it? It must be terrible for her and that little boy.'

The Tanner children grew up in the open-air freedom of the property, which stretched almost as far as the forbidden old goldmine shafts in the foothills of the Strathbogies. They knew every pathway and hiding place in the district. As a young policeman at his first posting in South Melbourne, Denis worked with young men who knew the city well. In response, he often spoke of knowing the hills and countryside around home like the back of his hand.

The younger boys were fit and strong, but Laurie suffered from poor health in his childhood, probably glandular fever, which left him quite debilitated and unable to participate in many sports. The Tanners went to Bonnie Doon primary school and were 'just the usual boys—very sporty'. Football was popular and everyone would turn out to watch the Tanner boys play. They were very good tennis players too. Frank was the best at football, with Bruce and Denis giving a fair showing. Laurie hung back at most of the school events, content to cheer his brothers on.

Frank continued to play football for Bonnie Doon Football Club well into his thirties. He was still playing competitively when his eldest son started playing for the same club.

Denis was the leader. He was a big, strong boy, which earned him the name 'Mudguts' at Mansfield Higher Elementary—a name that followed him into the police force. As he got bigger, and some say meaner, his nickname changed to 'Lard'.

'Denis always wanted to "be a buddy chopper", right from when he was a little fella,' his father recalled. 'Almost at the end of his apprenticeship at O'Brien's motor mechanics he left and joined the police. It was what he always wanted.' Denis was posted to Melbourne and during the mid to late '70s was working at St Kilda, where he was to work with Brian Ritchie, who would later cross his path at a crucial time.

Denis was married to another 'member', Lynne, who was a Senior Constable at St Kilda at the time Adele Baily disappeared. Lynne was a well-liked, compassionate person who spent most of her professional life in Community Policing. She acted as a mentor to some younger policewomen, who still remember her with affection, even though she has been gone from Melbourne for about ten years. Lynne and Denis had renovated 'a beautiful home in Williamstown', an old dockside suburb that was gradually being gentrified. 'It was a lovely house, very tasteful, antique furniture, exceptional attention to detail—she had excellent taste in everything,' one of her colleagues told me. At the time of Jenny's death Denis was attached to the Traffic and Patrol Group in the city and Lynne was on maternity leave from her Community Policing position in Flemington. They had a four-month-old baby boy—the first of their four children.

After Jenny's death Denis and Lynne moved to Benalla, about 70 kilometres from Mansfield. Denis's father said the move was to enable Denis to be 'closer to his family after the tragedy, so he could look after us'. One of Lynne's friends said, 'I'm sure it was a huge wrench, but country postings are hard to get, especially near your family, so she packed up and followed Denis.'

Denis had already applied for a forthcoming vacancy at Mansfield before Jenny died, but two days after Jenny's death, on Friday 16 November, he sent an official typed request to police in charge of manpower allocations, asking for the vacancy in Mansfield to be given to him on compassionate grounds, to enable him to care for his brother and family. The inquest was later told that this request was forwarded from Denis's Traffic and Patrol Group office in Flinders Lane, in spite of the fact that he was in Mansfield making arrangements for Jenny's funeral and looking after Laurie and his family.

∞

In early November 1996 I ring Denis at Benalla Police Station to ask him about a newspaper report that said the Jenny Tanner Task Force had asked him to come in and answer a few questions. He has no obligation to take my call, or to co-operate with his police colleagues either, but he agrees to both. When he answers me I open with 'I'm a writer and I'm writing a book about the death of Jenny Tanner. I suppose your mother may have mentioned me?'

'She did say someone has been pestering her, yes.'

'Oh, that wouldn't have been me. I've only been there twice and she's been very polite to me. I read in the paper you've been talking to the Task Force investigating Jenny's death and wondered if you had anything you'd like to say to me about that?'

'I don't really know—I hadn't thought about it much.'

'How did you feel about it?'

Apparently the interview with the Task Force lasted an hour or so and was videotaped. For much of the interview Denis says he responded, 'No comment.'

'My only comment is no comment. At this point in time I have no comment to make to anyone. The *Sunday Age* story was not balanced and there's another inquest coming along—I want a fair assessment next time.'

I refrain from saying that the coroner absolved him of any involvement in Jenny's death at the last inquest, so why didn't he think it was fair? I ask instead, 'Does it worry you, being questioned by your colleagues?'

'Not at all—the outcome of the next inquest will show they're wrong.'

'Denis, you probably know I'm talking to a lot of people around Mansfield and elsewhere. Many of them are saying you might have had something to do with Jenny's death.'

'So what—they're only making their assessment based on a biased newspaper article. I'm not worried at all.'

He excuses himself to take another call and I hang up, thinking what a nice voice he has. Doesn't fit his reputation at all.

Bruce Tanner followed in his grandfather's steps. He left his childhood sweetheart behind in Mansfield and went away to teachers' college. He married someone else, had a son and a daughter and eventually left teaching to establish a very successful business. After his first marriage failed he re-established contact with his Mansfield sweetheart and they finally married each other. At least this family saga has one happy ending.

I reach Bruce Tanner on his mobile phone. He sounds sad and angry about the events that have so damaged his family and the treatment dealt out by the media, even though his direct involvement seems to have been slight. Like all strong families, the Tanners present a united front, no matter what is said in private. During my chat with old Fred, he told me the family 'had a lot of secret meetings'. I asked him what they were about and he said he didn't know, because he and the boy were left outside. He immediately looked as if he was sorry he'd told me this. 'Probably about what they were going to do with the bulls,' he suggested.

Bruce is cross that I've called him on his mobile phone and wants to know how I obtained the number. We speak briefly. 'There's no way I'm going to discuss this. We'll sit it out—I believe it will blow over. I've had lots of things sprung on me over the past twelve months. There's been so much stuff said about our family. We haven't done anything wrong.'

I tell him everyone I have interviewed has told me of his family's generous involvement in local activities.

He sounds eager to agree with me. 'That's quite right. We have lived a wholesome life and contributed to the community.'

I ask if he still thinks Jenny committed suicide. 'Yes, I still believe it was. I think the police are a bunch of wankers. I have a business to run—I'm trying to run it the best I can. This has affected things. I don't want to talk about this now—I'd rather wait until the results of the next inquest—if there is one. I'm confident the outcome of the next inquest will show things up as they are.'

I ask him why he thinks Laurie won't talk to me to offer a balanced view of present and past events.

'We're not going to contribute to public debate at this time. There's a lot of gossip in the town—fifty per cent don't even care, but how can you have a fair inquest when you've been reading biased newspaper articles? I am confident there will be no shred of evidence to show anything different.'

That comment prompts me to ask him who cleaned up the farm the day after Jenny died. I emphasise that there could have been a quite innocent motive for doing this—if the family thought it was suicide they would not want Laurie to have to return to such an awful scene.

Bruce says, 'I know what the truth is. Everyone wants to know who cleaned up the place and why. I'll see if you write an unbiased story and I may open my heart to you once this is over.'

He says he has to go, and I can't think of anything else to say. I sit at my desk miles away from Bruce, in his car out in the country somewhere, upset and rattled that I have phoned him on his business mobile. His role seems to have been that of supportive brother and concerned uncle. I remember how Kath told me he stuck up for her when Laurie didn't want Sam to see his grandparents any more. I feel sad for Bruce and his new family, as well as his old one.

∞

Frank, named for his grandfather, joined the Victoria Police around the same time as Denis and remained a police officer for five years before resigning and returning to farming. Old Fred told me softly, 'Frank's a gentle young bloke, like Laurie. He pulled two little kids out of a dam when he was working in the police force, drowned. It really affected him. Some time later he left the police and moved out to a farm at Howquadale. Frank has two boys and a girl. The oldest boy is going to be the coach at Doon Football Club this year.'

When Jenny died Frank was still in the force, based at Hamilton in the Western District. He was told of Jenny's death by phone, but tells me he can't remember what time or who called. He says he and his wife and three small children made the six-hour drive to Mansfield the next morning.

I speak at some length to Frank, who is a very private person, made even more wary by the renewed spotlight being focused on his family. He does not want to be included in this book and quite reasonably asks me to allow him and his family to get on with their lives in private. I tell him this is a true story and he exists, so he's in it, but I agree not to quote him on any part of our long conversation, which concludes with him informing me that he is still convinced Jenny killed herself. We agree that a more thorough police investigation at the time could have spared the Tanners and the Blakes much heartache.

According to his father, 'Laurie was the quiet one. A good worker. He helped me run the farm and did a bit of contract fencing and shearing to help out with the finances. We farmed stud Hereford cattle and sheep.' He recalled the day they were out cutting fence posts together on the old farm property. The chain on the saw snapped and lashed back around Laurie's neck. It cut through the jugular vein and right through his ear and cheek. His strength driven by fear, Fred lifted a trailer-load of fence posts off the truck and drove Laurie about 30 kilometres to hospital. 'Doctor Vine told us Laurie was lucky to be alive. He was bleeding like a stuck pig when we got there.'

Unlike his brother Denis, Laurie is universally liked. All of Jenny's girlfriends liked him. He cared for Jenny and 'was devoted to her'. He is a good, steady worker, reliable and affable, although he is not known for initiative. A close friend of the Tanner family who has known and worked with Laurie for many years describes him as 'a champion bloke' and thinks Jenny was 'a great person, I thought they were very happy out at the farm', but when pressed for more details says nervously, 'No, I can't say any more—I gotta be careful.'

Even Kath and Les Blake express little bitterness towards Laurie. He has been 'a good father' and they have no complaints about the way he was a husband to their daughter, at least up until when she died. Les, though, was always a bit confused about what his beloved Jenny saw in Laurie. 'Why him?' he quietly asked one of her friends on her wedding day.

I have often asked myself why Jenny married Laurie. The most obvious and popular answer is that she loved him. I've made a few other guesses. She was nearing twenty-five and still not married, with a few casual liaisons and at least one serious relationship already behind her. She may have worried about becoming an 'old maid'—an important consideration in the late '70s. There were not many eligible bachelors in the district. Jenny enjoyed the good life and maybe thought marrying an easy-going farmer with his own property would provide her with lots of freedom without having to work to save up and pay off a mortgage. Laurie was good to her and she seemed to prefer older men, maybe because she was so close to her father. Although a farmer, Laurie had a bit of 'clout' in the town and was prominent in local community groups, including the Agricultural and Pastoral Society, which was responsible for the annual Mansfield Show. He was easy-going and fairly malleable, where she was pretty assertive and tough. Perhaps she thought Laurie would be a pushover and she could have the security of marriage while still doing almost as she pleased.

Another of Laurie's friends told me, 'Laurie's mother used to push him to do all those things you have to do to get anywhere in the country, like go to Apex and so on.' He started courting his first wife, Sally, when he was twenty-four. She was a teacher, and her brother had been close friends with Laurie at school. Their 'dates' often consisted of riding around the Tanner properties doing stock work, or digging out and blocking rabbit burrows at weekends, or occasionally attending old-fashioned country balls held in woolsheds and local halls around the district. It was nothing to drive a hundred kilometres to one of these balls, camp overnight and return the next day.

By '70s standards, June and Fred had a very progressive attitude towards the relationship between Laurie and his then girlfriend. This was not shared by other members of Laurie's family. The senior Tanners bought Laurie a double bed and dealt with opposition from younger family members by telling the lovers to keep their window blinds closed.

During the early days of his first marriage, Laurie and Sally lived near the Mansfield Racecourse in a primitive cottage without any hot-water service. Tired of trying to wash clothes greasy from hours of shearing, Sally borrowed a hot-water urn from a male friend. Laurie was horrified. He made her return it in case 'one thing led to another'. Sally also claims that Laurie was unwilling to allow her to go out without him. Visits to art galleries, skiing trips, shopping in Melbourne were all seen as threats to his hold on their relationship.

Laurie and Sally later bought the house in Mansfield now occupied by the Tanner family. Then, early in 1977, they moved to Springfield to enable Laurie to work the farm more efficiently, doing a virtual financial swap with Laurie's parents. Sally had contributed to the purchase of the Mansfield house, and cashed in her superannuation to pay for a stud Hereford bull. Laurie started breeding pedigreed kelpies and Herefords, as well as running his own sheep and doing contract shearing.

Life on the farm did not appeal to Sally, and in mid-1978, less than eighteen months after this move, she left the relationship, feeling stifled by a life that had never consisted of anything more than school, house and farm. They had no children, though Laurie had been keen to start a family. Sally moved to Melbourne, where she found a house she wanted. She asked Laurie to buy out her share of Springfield and give her the sum of $20 000 towards the purchase. She calculated this amount to be her foregone savings, as she stopped teaching during the ten years of their marriage.

Accounts of the separation differ. Sally says it was fairly amicable, and claims Laurie was left with a 'fair share' of household goods. Town gossip, however, has it that Laurie was 'suicidal'. It's said one of his parents found him sitting with his rifle at the kitchen table at Springfield and persuaded him to move back to town with them. Laurie immediately closed the joint account, consulted a solicitor and asked for a divorce. While locals often claim that Sally ripped Laurie off when they separated, she is adamant that she only received $20 000 and an agreed share of the household contents.

According to Laurie, when Jenny moved to Springfield she tried to rid the place of any vestige of his first wife. Among the possessions Sally had left behind was an antique blackwood table and matching chairs, which she'd bought for Laurie as a wedding present. Laurie tells of coming home to Springfield one day to find all the glassware smashed and the furniture burnt. The only surviving item was an old pewter mug given to Laurie by Sally's grandfather. Kath Blake strenuously denies this story and says there was nothing of any value in the farmhouse when Jenny moved there.

Laurie's friends and people who knew him from school describe him as a clean-living, quiet sort of bloke—a taciturn fellow who just gets up every day and goes out to tend the land and stock. How could such a terrible tragedy have befallen him?

'He's had an awful lot of bad luck, really,' an old school friend tells me. 'The chainsaw, and another accident driving the truck with Fred on the Melbourne road—they were both pretty smashed up. I never believed he had anything to do with Jenny's death himself. I ruled him out because of his nature and the difficulty he would have had doing it.'

Another professional person who knows Laurie a little says, 'He's a very up-and-down-the-wicket, simple sort of guy. He was very traumatised by the event and to a certain degree has been since, although it seems to have made him a lot tougher.'

Laurie's emotional health was a bit fragile at times, and some people say he was experiencing problems with Jenny, an impression that is reinforced by his statements at the first inquest. Someone in whom Laurie occasionally confided tells me, 'People are wrong saying the relationship was happy. She was unhappy and difficult, and Laurie didn't find it easy at all. She wasn't the type of person who'd pull herself together—a pretty narky sort of person at times. The only people who wouldn't have found her unhappy were her farming girlfriends. It was not a close relationship. I'm not sure what the problem was, but there was a problem. Laurie was set in his ways, a bit complacent, not very bright. He was older, more of a country boy. It was his property and she'd married into the family. I don't think she was very happy.'

Still only twenty-seven, and having led a very active social life before she married, perhaps Jenny sometimes felt she'd made a mistake marrying Laurie, twelve years older and so settled in his ways. At one stage Laurie told a couple of close friends that Jenny was threatening to leave unless he sold the farm and found himself a 'nine-to-five job up north'. Jenny had always been fond of Echuca, but maybe she meant further north—Queensland perhaps? Laurie didn't say. His friends' advice was 'Don't do it. You'll hate it.'

Yet Roz Smith had told the first inquest that Jenny had said she liked living at the farm. In any case, even if she did feel she was being left to her own resources, she didn't sit around and mope. As well as caring for Sam and doing all the extra washing and ironing created by a new baby, Jenny had her own busy life, involving herself with community groups and home activities.

Jenny threw herself into most things she did. She was not a near-enough-is-good-enough type; things had to be exactly as she planned. Laurie's laid-back and let-it-be attitudes could easily have created friction and tension between them. Small irritations, like Laurie not being very communicative, his habit of firing his rifle out the back door to quieten the dogs, his close involvement with his family and his long absences from parenting, could only have intensified her dissatisfaction.

When I interview Dr Ross Gilham, he recalls that Jenny was often abrupt when she brought Sam to see him. 'She was never my patient, Laurie was. Jenny brought Sam in to see me a few times about ear and throat infections—you know the sort of things babies get. She was very ungracious, she didn't open up, never filled any silences. It was like pulling teeth to get information out of her—she never volunteered anything. I don't remember her being forthcoming with happiness and joy at social occasions either, but I hardly saw them socially. I'm not aware of any reason why she wouldn't like me. Perhaps she just didn't like doctors. But I felt the relationship between her and Laurie was not very close.'

People who knew Jenny well agree that she was very private about parts of her life, and it's possible she wouldn't have told anyone—even Laurie—that she had decided to leave him until she had definitely made up her mind. Perhaps she didn't want to be seen as a failure in her marriage, or maybe she thought she could work things out herself. If she couldn't get Laurie to move, maybe she contemplated moving herself.

On the other hand, Roz Smith recalls that Jenny stopped taking the Pill after a visit to her clairvoyant, Mrs Bond, in 1984, as she wanted to have another baby that summer. Dr Geoffrey Patience, Jenny's doctor, confirmed that Jenny visited him about three months before she died and discussed the possibility of having another baby. Perhaps, like many young mothers, she thought a second child would shore up a failing relationship.

The notion that Jenny's marriage to Laurie could have been at risk is partly supported by Roz's version of Denis's behaviour during a visit to Springfield, which she claims happened on 22 October.

In her evidence at the first inquest Roz recalled that on the morning of Tuesday, 23 October Jenny phoned her at her home near Brisbane and said, 'A funny thing happened last night. I took Laurie into Mansfield to Apex and came back to put Sam down. I'm having a lot of trouble settling him down at the moment because of that darn daylight saving. He thinks I'm having him on, trying to put him to bed while the sun's still up. It was after 7 o'clock, but he thought it was more like 6 o'clock and we were battling. Anyway, as he wouldn't settle, I decided I'd better stoke up the Aga before it went out altogether. I opened the back door and found Denis standing on the porch. He had not knocked or come in, he was just standing there.'

Jenny got a bit of a fright, as she had not heard Denis's car. 'He must have walked across from Stanleys. I was surprised because Denis knows Laurie's at Apex on Mondays,' Jenny continued. 'I said, "Good heavens, what are you doing just standing there? Come in, why don't you? Laurie's at Apex, you know. What are you doing in Doon at this hour anyway?" '

According to Roz, Jenny went on, 'Denis came into the kitchen and told me he had come up from Melbourne to go shooting. He told me he'd had a fight with his wife and had told her he was going to the races. He was quite sober, definitely hadn't been drinking. Then he asked if he could borrow Laurie's gun. I went to the bedroom and got the gun and then to get the bullets from the top of a kitchen cupboard. He just hung around, so I offered him a coffee. He said he didn't want one. I told him I had to get Sam into bed and he followed me in and watched while I got Sam down. Then we went to sit in the lounge, since he didn't seem to want to leave. He sat down on the floor and started loading the rifle. Then he asked me if I was planning on leaving Laurie. I said, "No, and who told you I was?" He just said, "A friend," and wouldn't tell me any more. He still had the loaded rifle on his lap, just lying there.'

Roz asked Jenny if Denis had threatened her with the rifle. 'Were you frightened?' she asked.

'No,' Jenny said. 'He never pointed it at me, just sat there with it on his lap. He told me not to tell Laurie about this conversation and left soon afterwards.'

Roz asked, 'Did you tell Laurie?'

'Of course I did. As soon as he came home. If I'd thought of it at the time I would have told Denis to mind his own damn business. He's trying to interfere too much in my relationship with Laurie.'

If Denis had arrived at the time Jenny has stated—that is, when she was trying to get Sam to bed around 7 p.m.—and Laurie did not get home until after 10 p.m. from Apex most nights, at least a couple of hours could have elapsed during Denis's visit. What else could have been discussed while Jenny says Denis sat on the floor with the rifle across his lap?

In his statement to the police, given after Jenny's death, and again in his sworn evidence at the inquest, Denis Tanner agreed he visited Jenny at the farm that night, but disputed Roz's version of her conversation with Jenny. He denied borrowing the rifle or discussing the possibility that Jenny was planning to leave Laurie.

Denis Tanner also told police he 'was aware of private matters between him [Laurie] and the deceased which he had told me and I considered it was not directly relevant to what had happened, because it was an intimate matter, solely confined to a husband/wife relationship'.

All these hints were tantalisingly vague. Several people claimed there was a problem, but no-one was willing to say what it was.

5

That Night

THERE WAS an atmosphere of expectancy in Bonnie Doon and Mansfield during the weeks leading up to Jenny's death. Jenny herself was caught up in the endless preparations for the Mansfield Show, planned for Saturday 17 November.

Country shows represent much more to a district than sideshows and an opportunity to display produce and livestock. For many small towns scattered around Australia, 'the show' is the highlight of the year. It is like a huge family gathering, with all the town and country folk in their best Akubra hats and Blundstone boots coming to see and be seen, to strut their stuff, show off their prize hens or strawberry jam and have a good time. A stud farm's future brightens when a bull wins a blue ribbon, and many a country romance has been kindled behind the Agricultural Displays shed.

The Mansfield Show has been such an occasion since 1868, when it was first put on by the Agricultural, Pastoral and Horticultural Society. It was held on the Recreation Grounds, which also played host to cricket and football matches and annual picnics organised by the surrounding hamlets of Tolmie, Boorolite and Barwite. These were great social occasions, with everyone getting gussied up in their Sunday best to go to 'town'. The picnics featured foot racing and other games—mostly for the men and children, as the women's best outfits were too cumbersome for them to become starters in most events. The women had their place, however. Under the shady trees they set up tables laden with food and drink to revive the competitors skills and show off their baking. A contemporary photo taken in

1909 shows a grand picnic of more than 50 people, all dressed up and enjoying a traditional country day out.

The first Mansfield Show attracted many eager entrants in all fields of agriculture and horticulture. It is recorded that a Mr Loudin was awarded a special prize for his basket of flowers carved in butter—quite an achievement on a warm spring day with only primitive refrigeration.

The 'new' Mansfield Agricultural and Pastoral Society was formed in 1887, and the show was moved to a twelve-acre block of land known as the Police Paddock, where it has been held ever since.

In 1984 Laurie Tanner was president of the Agricultural and Pastoral Society and his friend Curly McCormack was vice-president. Because of the demands of this responsible honorary position, Laurie was even busier than usual in the weeks leading up to the show. As well as doing maintenance work around his own property, managing his own flock and the dogs, Herefords and fat lambs, Laurie was a member of Roy Friday's team of contract shearers, working the properties around the district from August through to Christmas—the busiest time of the year for shearing. He was also overseeing a myriad of tasks to ensure the smooth running of the show—checking fences around the stock pens, cleaning up around the grounds, testing electrical supplies for sideshow alley and organising a number of working bees with the society committee—so he was often home late and gone early. If Jenny was disgruntled about his long absences, the weeks leading up to the show could only have made matters worse.

Liz Thomas, recently back from an extended overseas holiday, visited Springfield two weekends before Jenny died, arriving late on Friday. Jenny could always identify different friends from the sound of their cars in the driveway, a trick country people often develop. Since Jenny had lived at Springfield Liz had driven up often to visit after work, arriving late at a darkened farmhouse. By the time she'd parked in the drive and walked to the farmhouse Jenny would always be out of bed with a cup of tea ready on the kitchen table—'Heard your car,' she'd say. During the weekend Liz showed Jenny photos and told her stories about her great holiday. Jenny was a bit envious of Liz's freedom to travel and have fun, but said she wouldn't swap Sam for anything. They toasted the demise of yet another cypress tree and wondered if June would notice the gap in the windbreak. Laurie was home at teatime on Saturday, but he soon left again for the show-ground. Liz arranged to return for the show and left on Sunday in high spirits.

Jenny stood in the afternoon sun in the driveway, with Sam sitting on her hip. 'Wave bye-bye to Auntie Liz,' she said. 'Bye-bye! Bye-bye! Sucker! Having to go back to work. Drive safely.' These were the last words Liz heard from Jenny Tanner.

On the weekend before Jenny died, she was occupied with the usual family and work activities. On Saturday Laurie had a full day at the Alexandra Show to check out their organisation and presentation and pick up any tips for the following weekend. He also had farm business to conduct there.

Jenny drove with Sam to her mother's place and they all went to a clearing sale at a property in nearby Kilmore. A number of items caught Jenny's eye, in particular the beautiful blue Mary Gregory jug, which she set her heart on buying. After spirited bidding between Jenny and a friend, it was finally knocked down to Jenny for about $100. Her friend said ruefully, 'He looked at you last—you only got it because you are beautiful.' Jenny laughed, holding the jug up to admire the pattern as the light streamed through. 'So's this,' she chuckled. She loved to win.

She also fancied a pair of crystal glasses or vases, but having paid $100 for the jug, agreed to bid and share them with her mother, who liked them too. Towards the end of the day Jenny bought two little activity tables for Sam's bedroom, exhausting her budget. It was a very hot day and Jenny changed Sam often to prevent nappy rash. Before leaving she begged a disposable nappy from a friend, having exhausted her own cloth nappy supply.

Triumphant with their bargains, they returned to Kath's house and called Laurie to come over for tea and bring a change of clothes for Sam and Jenny. Jenny bathed Sam and had a shower herself, as they were often short of water at Springfield. Les arrived home from golf

BLIND JUSTICE

and they decided on takeaway Chinese—a firm favourite with everyone, even young Sam. Laurie drove Jenny and Sam home, leaving
Jenny's car at her mother's house to be collected the following day.

On the Sunday afternoon, Laurie brought Jenny and Sam to
Kath's house and dropped Sam off, so that Jenny could do her twice-
weekly cleaning job in the shop at the front of Yenken Dyason's timber mill. Jenny cleaned the shop and put polish on the floor. While it
was drying she walked a couple of blocks to visit her mother-in-law.
Laurie picked Jenny up back at work when the polishing was done
and they drove back to Kath's house to have tea.

The next day Jenny, Kath and Jenny's youngest sister Clare
embarked on a Christmas shopping trip to Melbourne. Kath was a
little reluctant to go as she had a pile of ironing staring at her accus-
ingly, but Jenny encouraged her: 'Oh, come on, Mum! I'll do your
ironing for you this week—just chuck it in the car and I'll take it
home and do it while I watch TV.'

On the way they discussed Christmas gifts. Jenny wanted to get
Laurie a portable fridge to plug into his car cigarette lighter so his
lunch wouldn't spoil when he was out all day shearing. As well as the
Christmas presents, Jenny bought a generous portion of wrapped
chocolates for herself and a new whitewood trundle bed with a
matching wardrobe for Sam. 'He's nearly two—he'll need a bed soon.
It's getting too hot for him in his little cot, and I'm scared he'll try to
climb out and fall. And he'll need a bed for his friends when they
come to stay later on. Might as well get everything together, so it
looks nice for him.' Her father would paint them as well as any fac-
tory—if not better—and she saved $100 on the unfinished versions.
They arranged for the earliest delivery to Bonnie Doon, the following Thursday. 'I should be there, but if I'm out just leave them on the
front veranda—they'll be safe,' she instructed. Her final purchase was
a cute pair of sandals for Sam. On their way home Jenny and her
mother and sister called into her grandmother's to change Sam and
have a coffee before driving home.

'I've spent all my money today, Nan, but I was pretty smooth with
the furniture people,' she reported. 'I'm going to put the $100 I saved

towards a Christmas holiday at Cowes, if the house is available this year, Mum? I can't wait until I get my Christmas Club money.' Ever since she worked at the bank Jenny had operated an annual Christmas Club account. 'Then I'll be back down to finish my list. How about coming to Springfield this year, Nan, for Christmas lunch, Jenny-style?'

In previous years Jenny and Laurie had gone to other relatives for Christmas dinner, but this year, with her house newly decorated and Sam old enough to be aware of Santa and presents under the tree for the first time, she wanted to cook at her own home for her precious Nan.

After Jenny's death, her family analysed and agonised over this happy day and Jenny's plans for Christmas. How could Kath have known this would be the last time she would see her Jen alive? What changed so drastically that 48 hours later she took her own life?

On the Tuesday Jenny's friend Debbie phoned from Echuca to discuss when and where they'd meet at the show the following Saturday. It was an unremarkable chat between two friends who phoned to keep in touch every few weeks. Apart from Kath phoning Jenny briefly to confirm delivery arrangements for Sam's furniture, nothing else is known of Jenny's movements that day. The Blakes usually spoke or visited every day, but on the day of Jenny's death, Wednesday 14 November, Kath was preoccupied with one of Jenny's sisters, who had been in a minor car accident. To her lasting sorrow, she had no contact with Jenny.

Wednesday was a crisp spring day. Laurie left after breakfast to go shearing with Roy Friday. Jenny did an early wash—loads of Sam's clothes and Laurie's work gear—and hung it out. She intended to do the ironing that night, as Laurie had agreed to do her cleaning job in town, which he could fit in before a few maintenance checks requiring his attention at the showground. It was her turn to host playgroup that morning, so she prepared Sam for his young visitors and made some morning tea. About six or eight young mothers attended playgroup that sunny day. None of them noticed anything wrong with Jenny; she was 'just her usual happy self'. Laurie came home for lunch, then went to Mansfield at about 1.30 p.m.

After Laurie left, Jenny rang Roz, who was out picking up her daughter from kindergarten. Roz returned Jenny's call around 3.30 p.m. Jenny related her glee at her purchase of the Mary Gregory jug and how beautiful it looked in her lounge room. Roz later recalled that they talked about their children, and Jenny promised to record a tape for Roz for Christmas. She was in high spirits and there was no discussion of their previous phone call or the peculiar evening of 22 October.

Laurie's later evidence to the police partly fills in the next few hours. He returned home from Mansfield around 4 p.m. He intended to check on his own sheep and cattle in the paddocks, as he had been away most of the day.

'I'll take Sam along for the ride,' he told Jenny.

'Oh, Laurie, I haven't seen you all day and it's a great evening. I think I'll come too.' They all piled into the ute and drove around checking on the stock. Laurie had new lambs and ewes about to drop lambs, and he wanted to check none were in difficulty. In 1984 fat lambs were averaging about $18 each, so they were a valuable source of income, along with his stud Herefords. He had started the herd during the early days of his first marriage, and many years of selective breeding were beginning to pay off.

The little group returned home soon after 5 o'clock and Laurie volunteered to bath Sam while Jenny brought in the washing before the evening mist came up from nearby Lake Eildon. The wash was fresh and sweet-smelling after drying in the country air. She carried it to the lounge room and added it to the pile of ironing she had brought home from her mother's on Monday night.

While she was sorting the washing, Denis rang. Jenny answered and spoke to him for a few minutes before passing him on to Laurie and going to complete Sam's bath. The bathroom was beyond the kitchen and the main bedroom, so it is unlikely she heard what was said. Denis told police later he had called about breaking in a horse.

They ate early and watched *Sale of the Century*, one of Jenny's favourite TV shows. At 7.30 Laurie got up to go and vacuum Yenken and Dyason's shop and attend to his responsibilities at the showground. Jenny picked Sam up to put him to bed. 'Give your daddy a kiss,' she told Sam, who obligingly presented his little pink cheek.

Laurie was almost out the back door when Jenny called after him, 'We need some milk and bread, love, I haven't been out today. And a paper if they've still got one. And what about a little surprise for Jenny?'

Laurie made a mental note to add a Cherry Ripe to his list of purchases, and headed towards the car. This inconsequential little exchange between husband and wife would be their last. Laurie drove off in the early twilight towards Mansfield, leaving Jenny to her fate.

Not knowing what time he'd be coming back through Bonnie Doon, but certain it would be after closing time, Laurie stopped on the way at Clancy's General Store to pick up Jenny's requests.

We know a few facts about Jenny's activities after Laurie left. She did the ironing and stacked it up neatly, ready to put away, but she didn't put away the iron or the board and the iron was left on. Did she do the ironing talking to a visitor, or simply watching TV?

At some stage Sam could have woken, as it appears she may have changed him on the floor in front of the gas fire and left his wet nappy there with the talcum powder to put away later—but this was unlike Jenny. She was very neat. The nappy, according to later evidence, was disposable. Strange, when she had dried a line full of washing that day.

Jenny, or someone, smoked five cigarettes, although all her friends say she was only a 'social smoker' and unlikely to be smoking while she was ironing or watching TV at home alone. She made a cup of coffee, put some biscuits on a plate and brought them into the lounge room. She, or someone, drank half the cup of coffee and maybe ate some biscuits, leaving three on the plate. If there was a visitor, it was someone she knew. It's unlikely she'd offer a stranger coffee and biscuits on her own in a secluded farmhouse—she would be unlikely to invite a stranger in.

After calling at Clancy's, Laurie arrived in Mansfield around 8 o'clock and completed his cleaning by about 8.30. Then he went to the showgrounds and drove around the perimeter of the arena to see how the fencing work was progressing. Someone told him there was a plumbing job that needed urgent attention. It was still not too late, just getting dark, so he called in to see his plumbing mate, Marty Briscoe.

At around nine o'clock Curly McCormack, not knowing Laurie was in town, decided to give him a quick call before he had tea. He wanted to let Laurie know about the plumbing job at the show-ground. Jenny answered the phone. 'Laurie's in town,' she told Curly. 'He might drop by, he didn't say.'

'Hey, Ange, you want to talk to Jenny?' Curly called out to his wife Angie. She picked up the extension and they all talked about the show for a few minutes—the preparations for Miss Showgirl, the fine weather and if it would hold and so on. Curly excused himself to go and wash before tea. Angie, who was pregnant with her first child, stayed on to talk to Jenny.

Angie recalled later that Jenny had seemed reluctant to get off the phone, even though she must have heard Curly bawling out in the background for his tea. Eventually, around 9.30 p.m., Angie cut her off and moved in an ungainly shuffle down the hall to put out Curly's tea.

Only minutes later, Laurie arrived. Angie greeted him with surprise. 'We've just been looking for you. Rang home and I've been talking to your missus for ages. Couldn't get her off the phone.'

'Oh,' replied Laurie. 'How is she?'

'She's good. Just doing a pile of ironing.'

'What did you talk about?'

'Babies,' Angie chuckled and patted her large tummy. 'She's been telling tales about how much work they are—*and* husbands!'

Laurie sat at the table while Curly got stuck into his long-awaited dinner. 'There's some plumbing needs doing urgently at the sideshows, Curly, and I'm not sure Marty can get it done in time. Who do you think I could get?'

While Curly ate, they talked about this and other outstanding jobs that needed doing before Saturday. Laurie was organising a big working bee for very early the next morning and asked Curly if he could join in. Curly said he might not get there at the beginning as he had to move a mob of sheep, but would get there as soon as he could.

'Well, I'd better be off,' Laurie said, looking at the wall clock. 'Early start tomorrow.' It was about 10 p.m. when he left to drive home.

We don't know what happened at Springfield after Angie and Jenny completed their conversation.

What everyone was *told* was something like this:

Apparently Jenny drank half a cup of coffee. She might have had a biscuit. She left the TV, the iron and the heater on. At some point she decided to kill herself. She did not write a note to anyone, and gave no reason for this sudden decision. She took Laurie's rifle, which had presumably been returned at some time during the past two weeks (if Denis did borrow it), from the bedroom wardrobe into the kitchen, where she inserted a ten-bullet magazine.

She went to the couch and sat in the middle of the two-seater's cushions to kill herself. She tried to reach the trigger with her hand while the rifle was pointed at her forehead, found her arms were too short, took off her shoes, unzipped her jeans and repositioned the rifle against her forehead. She leant forward and reached over the barrel of the rifle with her left hand, cocked the rifle and used her toe to pull the trigger and fire into her brain.

She was not successful. Although the bullet entered her brain, it did not kill her. We are dealing with a very determined young lady here, though. Jenny was not going to let the fact she apparently missed first time beat her. So, despite having a bullet in her brain and bleeding profusely all over the couch, she sat herself up, reloaded and recocked the rifle, wrapped her big toe around the trigger, put both hands over the end of the barrel to hold it in position again and fired the fatal shot, which passed in a straight line through both hands into her skull.

She timed her demise neatly between 9.30 p.m. and 10.15 p.m., although she didn't know if Laurie would walk in before, during or after her dramatic gesture.

If it wasn't so serious, it would be funny. But the real tragedy is that people took it seriously at all.

Laurie arrived home at around 10.15 p.m. He called for help from his parents, the ambulance and Hughie Almond, in that order.

When the police arrived, Laurie couldn't be much help with details about which other members, if any, of the family had been notified.

I asked his father if June had called back to find out what had happened before leaving Mansfield.

'No. We just went. When you're told to come out to the farm, you just go.'

When June and Fred arrived at Springfield, June asked Bill Kerr if she could see Jennifer, to see 'if there was anything she could do'. The police and ambulance officers dissuaded her, thinking the scene was not one she'd want to remember. June went to Sam's room to pack up some clothes, while Fred remembers sitting drinking a cup of tea at the table in the kitchen, feeling a bit useless with so much activity and anguish going on around him. He couldn't help thinking about how many lunches he and Jenny had shared around that table—almost daily in busy seasons. He was going to miss that girl.

Dr Ross Gilham arrived around midnight to find everyone waiting, unable to do anything until he certified Jenny was officially dead. He told me he had no real cause to doubt that Jenny's death was suicide. He was told it was suicide by Laurie, the ambulance officer and the police, who had all been there long before his arrival. He remembered being 'a trifle annoyed that I was given this information so dogmatically', but he never considered the possibility of murder, and so did not mentally canvass any possibly suspicious surroundings. Jenny was not his patient, so he didn't know her very well, and he'd had a female patient who shot herself couple of months before—'These things happen,' he said. Don Frazer told him where the gun had been found and outlined the theory that Jenny had shot herself with her toe, and this influenced Ross Gilham's behaviour during his examination of Jenny. He told me he 'would have undertaken a completely different set of examinations if there had been any question it wasn't suicide'.

The police, Senior Constables Bill Kerr and Don Frazer, seemed to accept on the night that Jenny had shot herself. Bill Kerr says he always had private doubts, but that night did not seem to be the time to express them. He did, however, make note of all the little things that jarred, and made a freehand sketch of Jenny in place of photos. He noted the bluish tinge already developing in Jenny's legs below her knees.

Bill told me he searched the house for a note, and in his sketch he highlighted the blood-soaked towel on the couch. It had two blackened holes through it, which he marked as 'powder burns'. When he asked Laurie about the extra cartridge found in the magazine, Laurie told him he sometimes left a spent cartridge in the rifle 'for safety reasons'.

Don Frazer thought about making a sketch plan of all the rooms and marking the position of the couch where Jenny's body was found, but he did not want to leave Jenny's body unattended, so he decided to return to the house in the near future to fulfil this requirement. As the house would be empty overnight, Bill figured he could come back in the morning and have another look around if necessary. The CI had said something on the phone about coming over, anyway. He still had to tell the parents and do the paperwork—he felt that would be plenty for that night. Bill Kerr filled in the form on which Hughie Almond formally identified Jenny's body. There was some quiet discussion among the professionals at the scene, Kerr, Frazer and O'Donnell, about whether Jenny could have been killed by a 'passing stranger', but that was quickly ruled out because nothing had been disturbed or stolen.

Gerry O'Donnell, the young ambulance officer, fulfilled his role in textbook fashion. He took professional observations and recorded them on his charts. He stayed with Jenny's body until he was able to hand over to a doctor. Based on the information before him, the only conclusion he could draw was that all was as it appeared—that is, the suicide of a young woman, a little boy who had lost his mother and a bereaved and grieving husband.

The players in this drama left Springfield for their various destinations. Laurie and Sam went with June and Fred to their house in Mansfield. Gerry O'Donnell took Jenny's body to the Mansfield Hospital morgue. He drove without flashing lights or siren—there was no need to hurry any more. Ross Gilham followed to make sure

Jenny was accepted by the hospital, then went on to the Tanners' house to sit with June and Fred and Laurie. Laurie was sedated and put to bed, while Dr Gilham stayed on with the parents—'June was always a bit of a tough nut, the matriarch—she took everything in her stride—she was never anything but in control at the Tanner house.' But the events of that night were quite outside June Tanner's control.

For Bill Kerr and Don Frazer, the night was far from over. No-one had phoned Jenny's parents, so the police still had to perform a task every policeman dreads. They reluctantly climbed back into their car to visit the Blakes. Bill activated his two-way. Laurie's brother, Denis Tanner, was a police officer—'a member'—in Melbourne, and Bill thought it would be better for Denis to receive the news from his colleagues in person rather than over the phone.

'Mansfield 204 to VKC—do you copy?'

'VKC to Mansfield 204—reading you, over.'

'There's been a death at a member's family place in Bonnie Doon. The member works in Melbourne and lives in the Altona area, Sergeant Denis Tanner. Could you please get someone over there to let him know? Over.'

'Copy—will send it down straight away. You OK? Over.'

'You could say that—we're on the way to the deceased's parents.'

'Oh—good luck. Over and out.'

As they pulled into the Blakes' driveway, a little after 1 a.m., the radio crackled noisily back to life, making them both jump. It was Benalla Base patching through a call from D24 in Melbourne.

'VKC Benalla to Mansfield 204.'

'Mansfield 204 receiving, go ahead.'

'Re that call to attend Tanner house in Altona. Two members have been round, but unable to raise anyone. Will keep trying. Over.'

'Copy, VKC. Thanks. Please keep trying, it's a bit messy here. Tanner will probably want to know as soon as possible. Over.'

'Roger, 204, and out.'

Inside the house, Kath Blake woke up. She saw the headlights on her curtains, heard the tyres on the driveway and the indistinct static of a two-way radio and buried herself under the blankets with dread in her heart. 'Which one?' drummed repeatedly in her brain. She knew it wasn't Clare, safely asleep in the next bedroom, but she had three other girls out there in the dangerous world—'Which one?' Who had been out driving this late at night?

Les Blake got out of bed in his pyjama pants and singlet and opened the door to Bill Kerr and Don Frazer. 'They always send two for a death,' ran through his mind. Where had he heard that?

'Les, we've got some bad news. It's about Jennifer.'

Kath was straining her ears from the bedroom—wanting to hear, but not wanting to know. She got up and joined her husband, who was sitting with two awkward-looking policemen at the polished blackwood dining table. So many family dinners had been held around that table. Whose chair would be empty? She looked small and vulnerable with her tousled hair and dressing gown, not the businesslike Kath, but a stricken mum.

'It appears Jennifer may have shot herself.' Bill Kerr, as the senior officer, got the words out. 'I'm afraid she's dead. It looks like suicide.'

A small voice spoke one word: 'NO!' Then, 'She wouldn't know how. She couldn't have shot herself!' Kath was adamant. The officers described the scene as much as they thought was wise.

'She's really dead?' Les wanted to be sure.

'I'm very sorry, Les, yes, she is.'

'What's happened to Sam?' Kath's thoughts raced to her grandson.

'He's fine. He's at the Tanners' in Mansfield just now, but he's OK. He appeared to sleep through the whole thing. He didn't see anything.'

'Les, we must go and get him. June'll have her hands full with Laurie. How is Laurie, how's he taking it?'

'He's pretty devastated, Mrs Blake. I think the doctor was going over to see him.'

Recognising they both needed something positive to do, Les agreed. 'We must let the girls know, Kath. Will you ring or will I?'

'I'll do it.' Kath needed action to keep her from falling to pieces. First, Clare, asleep down the hall, was roused and told. Then Miriam, in her flat in Melbourne, was woken by a shrilling phone soon after

1 a.m. 'Bad news' was her first thought, but until the call was answered by her housemate, she couldn't imagine how bad. She heard the news from him in stunned disbelief.

The last call was to Kristine, living near by in Mansfield. 'Oh, Mum, I can't believe it! Not Jenny! Not with a gun! She was only here a week ago at my birthday party. Oh, I can't believe it! How could she do such a thing? I'll come over.'

Miriam phoned back. 'It's really true, isn't it? He didn't just imagine what you said? I wish I was there. I want to be at home,' she sobbed as her friend stood helplessly by.

Kath and Les drove to the Tanners' house, its windows beacons in the dark street. Lights were on next door too, although it was now about 2 a.m.; Gerry O'Donnell was a neighbour of the Tanners. Dr Gilham was with June and Fred. There was no sign of Laurie. Little Sam, oblivious to all the anguish and happy to see both grandmothers in one night, was handed over to Kath and Les and they drove home again, their hearts aching for their Jen.

Meanwhile, Bill Kerr and Don Frazer examined Jennifer in the morgue. They stripped her body and bagged her jeans, T-shirt and underwear. She was wearing a pair of gold ear-studs but no rings. She was left alone in the cold dark, naked and bloodstained, her once pretty face almost unrecognisable.

The final job of that long night for the two country coppers was to return to the station and for Bill Kerr to fill out a Form 83—the form required for every non-natural death attended by the police. This form had to be forwarded to the Coroner's office first thing next morning. The last line read, 'No suspicious circumstances' with a little space to tick. Bill's pen hovered over the space for a few seconds and moved away.

Some time after 5 a.m. the Altona police succeeded in rousing Denis Tanner and his wife at home. He seemed surprised by the news. It seemed no-one from home had rung him before his colleagues came round to the house. He phoned headquarters at Russell Street and spoke to a friend on the night shift. 'Listen, mate, I can't come in today, I've got to nick off to Bonnie Doon. Jenny Tanner, my brother's wife, has shot herself.' Lynne Tanner also phoned a friend and police colleague to tell her she would be unable to attend the funeral of her friend's grandmother that day, as her sister-in-law had shot herself. That colleague, Sergeant Helen Golding, would later tell the Coroner that Lynne seemed very upset. Denis's mate got off work at 6 a.m. and drove around to Denis's house to see if he could help in some way. He arrived around 6.30 a.m. to find Denis in the car with Lynne and their infant son, backing down the drive to set out for Bonnie Doon.

∞

Early Thursday morning, Mansfield was already buzzing with the news. At around 6 a.m. June Tanner phoned Curly McCormack. He had already left to move his mob of sheep, and Angie answered the phone.

'Is Curly there, Angie?'

'No, Mrs Tanner, he's moving a mob over at Scully's Lane for his brother.'

'Laurie asked me to call—he's not able to run the working bee today for the show. I wondered if Curly could take over for him. He's quite worried about it going ahead. Jenny shot herself last night. She's dead.'

Forgetting respect for a minute, Angie responded, 'Don't be stupid! I was talking to her last night.'

'Well, be that as it may, she shot herself anyway.'

'Oh, I can't believe it! It can't be true! I'm so sorry. I'll see if I can get Curly.'

Angie got her brother-in-law on the two-way. 'Can you get Curly? There's been trouble. Jenny Tanner shot herself. He'd better get into town.'

'Jenny Tanner's shot herself! Curly's a fair way up the road with the mob. I'll see if I can get him.'

When Curly got the message, he left the mob to his brother and went to find out what he could do. June met him and told him the boys were on their way to clean up the house, but Laurie needed

Curly's help to make sure the show went ahead as planned. Curly saw a heavily sedated Laurie for a few minutes and went to break the news to the members of the working bee.

Some time later that morning Kath returned to the Tanners' to get some more clothes for Sam. She did not see Laurie. While collecting the clothes, Kath mentioned to June that the police had not yet been to see her to take a statement from her. 'Aren't they kind?' June responded, as if Kath's opinion about her daughter's recent state of mind was not really worth the fifteen-minute trip out to interview her. June Tanner also told her the boys had gone over early to clean up the farmhouse. For a long time I was confused about which boys, but Frank and Denis were police officers, experienced with crime and accident scenes, so no-one would have thought it strange that either of them could have been involved in the clean-up, as they would be 'used to that sort of thing'. The clean-up may have been simply intended to remove all traces of the dreadful scene at the farmhouse as quickly as possible and prevent Laurie from ever seeing it again.

I later found out that it is not considered unusual for relatives to clean up the scene of a suicide to protect the next of kin. Often family members 'go to ground' afterwards—they just don't want to face anyone, so they disappear for a few days interstate, or to relatives in the country. They go incommunicado, and in any case they don't have to talk to the police immediately if everyone is satisfied the death is suicide. Other factors can intervene—police might have four days off after attending the scene and then get busy on another case. After a suicide, it can sometimes be up to two weeks before an interview takes place.

Denis said in his evidence to the first inquest, 'My wife, baby and self went to Bonnie Doon and later to Mansfield Police Station.' In the course of my research for this story, Denis has never denied to me he went to Springfield on the way to Mansfield that morning, but the versions of events have varied a little. I phoned him again when I reread his statement and asked him about this detail. He agreed he'd met his brother Bruce at the farmhouse and cleaned up while Lynne and the baby drove on to his parents' home. Later during the same conversation, he said he had a broken fan belt near Springfield, hitch-hiked to the property to get some tools, fixed the car and then went to clean the house while Lynne drove on to town. He said, 'There was a lot of blood and it was hot. The place could have been left for a week if we hadn't done something about it. We never would have got rid of the mess if it was left that long.'

Whatever Denis's motives for allocating top priority to this clean-up on the morning after Jenny's death, the couch cushions and the bloodstained towel and the nappy were burnt; the coffee cup, ashtray and plate washed up; cigarette butts and other evidence thrown out; bloodstains and fingerprints wiped away. The house was then locked up.

Just as there is a 'golden hour' of elapsed time to get the best results from treating people suffering from severe trauma to prevent shock, Homicide investigators believe they have a 'golden twenty-four hours' to obtain the clearest picture of what happened at a crime scene. As time passes, things and people change or disappear. Immediate witnesses can discuss the event with each other and change their stories. Their recollections can be enhanced by each other's perceptions. Evidence can be destroyed or moved so that its context is lost. The chances of accurately assessing the situation and making an arrest diminish.

In the 24 hours following Jenny's death, no attempt was made by any police to examine the scene of her death, cleaned up or not. None of the immediate witnesses were asked for statements. Jenny's relatives went through the motions of everyday life while they tried to absorb the enormity of the previous night's events.

On Thursday morning, after leaving June Tanner, Kath went on to Dr Gilham's surgery and told him she wanted to see Jenny, who was still in the Mansfield Hospital morgue.

'Mrs Blake,' said Dr Gilham kindly, 'I have to tell you, Jenny shot herself in the mouth. You wouldn't want to see her right now.' He refused to make the necessary arrangements, probably feeling it would be better for Kath to remember her daughter as she looked in life. Kath had no idea how she could go about getting through the red tape herself and no strength to try.

The same afternoon in Melbourne, Liz Thomas picked up the bank phone at about 4.30 p.m. A voice she didn't recognise said, 'It's Lynne Tanner here, I'm Jenny's sister-in-law. You're a friend of Jenny Tanner, aren't you?'

Liz gripped the phone tightly and said, 'Yes, I am. Why?'

'I rang to tell you Jenny is dead—she shot herself.'

'Bullshit! I don't believe you! I'm ringing Kath right now to find out what's going on.'

'Don't ring Kath today, she's very upset.'

'How's Sam? Is he OK?'

'Yes, he's fine. He's at Kath's place. Look I'm sorry, I have other people to call. I have to go.'

Liz couldn't believe it. The thought of Jenny shooting herself would not penetrate her brain. She sat mesmerised by the phone, peering at it, waiting for it to ring any second and it would be Lynne Tanner again telling her she'd just been practising her April Fool's pranks in November and they could have a stupid laugh and she could tell Lynne off for being a sick bitch and Jenny wouldn't be dead … but in spite of her wishing and willing, the phone sat there quietly. Liz leaned over the phone. She hugged it to her and rocked and sobbed. 'I can't believe it. I can't believe it. Oh, God! I can't *believe* it!'

Debbie thinks it was Lynne Tanner who phoned her too. A woman introduced herself and said, 'I've got some bad news. Jenny's been killed.'

'Oh, my God! How?'

'She shot herself.'

'Oh no she didn't,' was Debbie's instant reaction.

From the first minute she heard the news until today, Debbie has had a strong sense of anger mixed with her sadness. 'Everyone let it go, knowing even then it was murder. I'm angry with myself for not trying to get it reopened, but I had my reasons.'

At the Bonnie Doon pub people spoke of nothing else. All the menfolk were endlessly speculating on how it could have happened. How could a girl that size shoot herself in the mouth with a rifle that long and why and so on and so on. The women who'd been out to Jenny's for playgroup the morning before huddled together in a little shocked group, protecting each other as if suicide might be contagious. 'My God!' echoed through both townships as the news was spread from person to person. 'Poor Laurie! Poor Sam! The poor Tanners! The poor Blakes!' Sympathy for the survivors of this disaster flowed awkwardly. What is left to say when someone deliberately kills themselves? Suicide is the ultimate angry act, the final 'So there—cop that!' nose-thumbing gesture towards loved ones. How do you find words to counteract that in a small community where everyone knows everyone else?

During the day on Thursday, Bruce Tanner contacted the Mansfield agent of Mr N. J. Todd, Benalla Funeral Directors, to commence arrangements for Jenny's funeral. Laurie was so sedated and shocked that he was content to leave all the arrangements to Bruce and Denis, the 'fixer'. Other than a brief discussion with Denis, who told them the service would be held in the Catholic church because 'Laurie thinks that's the best thing to do', Kath and Les Blake were not consulted about any of the funeral arrangements. On the Friday morning they were simply told that the funeral would be 'tomorrow'.

Late on Thursday afternoon Don Frazer accompanied the police photographer, Sergeant Neil Phipps, while he took five photos of Jenny's wounds. Two photos of her face, showing a single large hole surrounded by blood just below her hairline; one of her right hand, showing a wound in the fleshy part of her hand between her finger and thumb; and two of her left hand, displaying an injury at the base of her thumb. Following this photo session, her body was moved by ambulance to Goulburn Valley Hospital in Shepparton for the autopsy next day.

In Queensland the phone rang at Roz Smith's house early on Friday morning and Roz's husband answered. His voice deepened as he took the call and Roz, still in bed, wondered who it could be. She heard, 'Thanks for letting us know. Yes, I'll tell her. I'm so sorry,' and then he was next to her.

'I've got some bad news, girl,' he said quietly. 'That was Kath Blake on the phone. Jenny Tanner is dead. I'm really sorry, love.'

Roz, small and a bit frail-looking, seemed to shrivel and collapse as the words sank in. Jenny. Dead. Jenny. Dead. Jenny. Dead. How could it be? She was so numb, she couldn't make her mouth work to ask any questions. She rolled over and sobbed and sobbed into her pillow, while her husband stood near her, unsure of what to do next.

'They are saying she shot herself.'

'No! No! No! I only spoke to her on Wednesday. On Wednesday! What is it today—Friday? Yes, Friday. When did it happen?'

'Wednesday night, when Laurie was in town.'

'Wednesday night! I don't believe it!'

Back in Melbourne, Liz Thomas didn't go home from the bank on Thursday night. While her colleagues left one by one, going home as if nothing in the world had changed, she put herself on automatic. 'Night, see you tomorrow'—'Bye, no I won't work too late.' She worked right through, locked in with the cleaners, the paperwork and other people's money. Might as well keep the old brain busy on something else, to block some of the pain. She waited until a decent hour—'What is a decent hour to ring someone whose daughter and my best friend has shot herself?'—and when she could see daylight outside and bear the silence in the bank no longer, she dialled Kath's number—one she knew by heart.

'Yes, Liz. It's true. The funeral's tomorrow.'

'Tomorrow! But she only ...'

'It's all being organised by the Tanners. We're inviting people back here afterwards, but so is June—I'm not sure what's happening.' Kath's voice trailed off. Liz had never known Kath not to be in command of her feelings, but today she sounded so unsure.

'We hope you can come,' just like a polite invitation to a cocktail party.

'Of course I will come. I'll drive up later today. I was coming up anyway—for the show ... you know ...' she explained lamely, trying to fill the silence. 'Well, I'll see you later, then.'

'Right-o,' Kath said.

∞

The morgue at the Goulburn Valley Hospital is next door to the staff canteen. This location is the source of black jokes among the staff, who often speculate about whether deliveries are being made to the correct entrances. Across the staff car-park, a short stroll from the morgue itself, is the department known to hospital staff as 'Path.'—a little soft-sounding word to cover a multitude of activities most people would rather leave to the trained professionals who work there. The Pathology Department is responsible for the morgue and the autopsy theatre—a fitting setting for the dramas of death.

This was the domain of Dr Peter Dyte, a respected pathologist, who was paid to perform coronial autopsies, as they were known at the time, as a part-time service to the police and the Coroner. Most of his day-to-day work was structured to meet the service needs of the hospital; until the Institute of Forensic Science was established after the new Coroner's Act of 1986 came into effect, autopsies on suicides or suspicious deaths were conducted almost as an 'extra' by obliging pathologists in hospitals with the necessary facilities. The Institute now provides police with specialised forensic services, but when Jenny died it was just a dollar figure in some minister's forward planning budget, and calling on the skilled services of Peter Dyte was the natural course of events.

Most pathologists take their relationships with their patients very seriously, and death does not diminish the doctor's wish to treat the patient with care and respect. Doctors work gloved, masked and gowned, in a surreal environment—silent apart from murmured comments by the pathologist and his assistant, or the sound of instruments being picked up and put down. Overhead halogen lights bounce white light off gleaming stainless steel, and the surroundings are suffused with a sweetish cloying smell of disinfectant, formaldehyde and putrefied organs. Some pathologists, like some surgeons, prefer to work to the distracting noise of Triple J or a tape of Beethoven's Fifth. Some measure the number of operations they have done by which Mozart composition they are up to in his life works and later tell their colleagues, 'Right in the middle of the second *adagio* I pinpointed the precise cause of death ...' Now and then the theatre is filled with the scream of the buzz saws when they are switched on to expose cranial or thoracic cavities.

It was into such an environment that the body of Jenny Tanner was wheeled at 10 a.m. on Friday 16 November 1984. Dr Dyte planned to conduct the autopsy alone, scheduling it early in his day before he became caught up with the constant stream of requests coming down from the operating theatres and the wards. He viewed his task as routine, and didn't expect any surprises. The body was naked under green drapes, which fell to the trolley wheels. He placed various buckets around the stainless-steel autopsy table to receive organs and other detritus. The table was like a large flat colander with drainage holes in regular rows along its length to allow fluids to fall into a collection area below. Scales with fine gradations in grams were set up to weigh organs lifted from the body. Dr Dyte was a neat and orderly man. He checked his array of instruments, laid out in symmetrical rows in sequential order, awaiting their grisly task. Then he lifted the green sheet to meet his patient. He was saddened by the sight of the hole in her forehead and the amount of dried blood and tissue surrounding it. Dropping the sheet and shaking his head at the same time, he called for assistance to move Jenny onto the autopsy table. While not large in life, in death she was too heavy for him to move alone.

'Why do they do these things?' he asked himself. A family man with a son and daughter, he pondered the parents' sorrow at having to bury their child. 'Not the proper order of things at all,' he mused.

A routine autopsy follows a specified sequence, and Dr Dyte followed this practice automatically. First, the external examination. When Jenny's body was washed clean Peter Dyte received his first surprise. He discovered four wounds, not three. There were two wounds to Jenny's head. Her hair was matted with blood, and underneath it was a second wound, which had been missed by every professional to examine her so far. The word 'suicide' had stemmed any curiosity to look further than the obvious. At this point Dr Dyte made his first call to the Mansfield police, informing them of his discovery.

He spoke to Sergeant Neil Phipps. The conversation was recorded, and the transcript indicates his concern.

Dyte:	Uh, I was ringing up to confirm you had no suspicions about this death.
Phipps:	No, we haven't at this stage. Um, what seems to be the …
Dyte:	Oh well, no, I thought I would talk to you before I proceeded with the PM. Just to check really … There are two definite wounds in the forehead of this lady and apparently she wasn't cleaned up before she was looked at … They're close together, but they're only a few centimetres apart, but they're two quite distinct wounds, which look like entrance wounds.

Phipps did not appear to be alarmed and he went on to detail the theory of Jenny firing two shots with her toe.

Dyte conceded that the wounds were 'still consistent with her holding the rifle up to her forehead and firing twice … she could still be alive after the first one, particularly in that area'.

Reassured by Neil Phipps, Dyte continued the autopsy, detailing the head wounds in his report. He states 'both being round to ovoid, the lower wound measured 0.5 centimetres in diameter with an area of blackening of the skin a further 0.5 centimetres in diameter. This wound had a clean edge and was situated 1 centimetre above the upper border of the eyebrows. 1 centimetre above this wound was a second wound of similar appearance, but more stellate [star-shaped] outline. It measured 1 centimetre in diameter and showed a less well defined 5 millimetre area of blackening of the surrounding skin.' He then described her hand wounds in minute detail, noting that the wounds to the back of the hands were round, while those in the palm were more stellate, but he drew no conclusions as to whether the bullet (or bullets) had travelled from the back of her hands to the palm or the palm to the back. The wounds to the back of the hands were five millimetres in diameter, as was the wound in Jenny's right palm, but the wound in the left palm was significantly larger, being eight millimetres in diameter. It's possible that these wounds were caused by two different bullets.

In his report Dr Dyte made no mention of any blackening around either hand injury. This is significant, as 'powder burns', or blackening around a wound, usually occur if the end of the weapon is less than 30 centimetres from the point of impact on the skin. The two wounds on Jenny's forehead showed powder burns. One was larger than the other, with the smaller and therefore possibly closer shot showing a greater area of powder burn than the larger, possibly more distant shot. If the accepted scenario of her death was that she had fired both shots herself, and one of them had gone through her hands before entering her head, there should have been powder burns on her hands and no powder burns around at least one of the shots to her forehead.

Bill Kerr labelled two 'powder burns' on his drawing of the bloodied towel next to Jenny on the couch. Could a bullet (or bullets) have been fired through a towel folded to muffle the noise, and could Jenny have instinctively thrown her hands up to protect herself? If more than two bullets were fired, but only two were found, what happened to the other spent bullets and cases?

Conjecture plays no part in an autopsy. Dr Dyte recorded what he found without suppositions. Moving from Jenny's wounds he used his scalpel to cut a large Y-shaped incision from each of her shoulders to her chest bone, under her breasts and straight down to her pubic bone. Using a big metal power saw, he sliced through Jenny's sternum and ribs to expose her organs. Her heart and lungs were normal for her age. Her heart, which lay flaccid and almost empty of blood, weighed a mere 260 grams. Blood samples were drawn from the cardiac chamber for drug screening and alcohol estimation, which later came back zero.

Her lungs showed moderate vascular congestion, consistent with a sudden trapping of venous blood, cut off from its return to the heart when the heart stops beating suddenly. He recorded no stomach contents at all, which would have been consistent with Jenny having last eaten at around 6.30 p.m., but not if she had consumed coffee and biscuits soon before she died. It takes about 45 to 60 minutes for the stomach to empty after eating a snack, depending on its size and composition.

In spite of her interest in becoming pregnant again and possibly not being on the Pill, Jenny's uterus 'showed no evidence of pregnancy'.

Completing the examination of her organs, Dr Dyte turned to examine Jenny's central nervous system, which is regulated by our most complex organ—the brain.

In 1984, if bullet wounds were thought to be self-inflicted, there was no regulation requiring X-rays to be taken before disturbing with invasive surgery the path and location of the bullets, although teaching texts recommended X-rays. The 1986 Coroner's Act makes X-rays mandatory for all bullet wounds, self-inflicted or otherwise.

Although Dr Dyte was told this was suicide, he arranged for some X-rays of Jenny's skull. These have never been produced, and are presumed lost. They might have provided a clearer picture of the path of the injuries, thus showing whether or not their angles indicated self-inflicted shots. X-rays are not conclusive, but they help to clarify the total picture.

A scalpel slit her skin from ear to ear and the scalp was peeled back to expose her skull. The hand-held buzz-saw screamed as the top of Jenny's skull was removed and lifted off neatly. The whole front area of Jenny's brain, measuring 10 × 8 × 5 centimetres, showed bruising caused by bleeding into the tissue. There was a smaller area of bruising and haemorrhage, 3 × 2 × 2 centimetres in size, at the back right-hand side of the brain, and another smaller area on the right side of the midbrain. Two bullets and a bullet fragment, presumed to have broken off one of the bullets as it spread, were removed from the brain.

At this point Dr Dyte began to feel uncomfortable with what he saw. In all his years of experience and study of pathology, he couldn't recall a suicide being effected with two bullets in the brain. One, certainly, but two was very unusual. A pathologist who encountered such a situation today could phone the Forensic Science Institute for guidance, or perhaps consult the Internet. But at that time, in that situation, Peter Dyte decided to take his cue from those responsible for the body—the police. He took off his gloves, went out to the phone in his office, called the switchboard and asked to be connected once more to the Mansfield police. It was nearly lunch-time, but he hoped they would be there, because he didn't want to leave Jenny like this any longer than necessary. Bill Kerr answered the phone, passed the receiver to Sergeant Phipps and pressed the 'Record' button on his tape recorder again as he did so:

Dyte asked Neil Phipps to explain how he thought the two injuries might have occurred.

Phipps replied: 'Um, what we deduced that happened or tried to work out was sometimes hubby went outside and fired a shot in the air and he'd leave an empty shell in the case. Next time he wanted to use it he'd eject it and put another live round in, um, and we sort of tried to fit that into the pattern with where the shell was in the first place in that she may have tried to discharge the firearm and it didn't operate. She ejected the empty shell and then fired a shot that subsequently killed her. Now, the two holes in the head, um, and you're satisfied she would have lived after the first one?'

'Well, I'm saying it's possible.'

'It's possible, yeah. Then that would fit in with what the two shells were, one empty, one in the gun and one on the floor.'

After reassuring Dr Dyte again with an elegant explanation of how they believed Jenny accomplished her own death, Sergeant Phipps concluded that it was important for Dyte to finish off as soon as possible, as the funeral was scheduled for the following day and the family wanted the body back. Dr Dyte concurred, saying he had already been phoned by the undertaker and the autopsy would be completed about lunch-time.

After this call, still uneasy, Peter Dyte disrobed, washed his hands and walked across the car-park to his deputy's office. His deputy, Dr Norm Sonenberg, was an eager young pathologist in his first post-graduate position. He was enthusiastic, but did not have Peter Dyte's years of experience.

'Norm, can you spare a few minutes? I want to show you something.'

They returned to the autopsy theatre. Peter Dyte explained his findings and his misgivings about whether it would be possible for someone to survive a first shot to the brain and still have all the fine motor skills to fire a second shot.

They discussed the various possibilities at length. Peter Dyte had studied under the highly respected pathologist Dr Plueckhahn, who had written a number of textbooks in which gunshot wounds were analysed and discussed. They consulted the relevant Plueckhahn text together. Norm Sonenberg looked at Jenny's injuries and reviewed his superior's findings. He agreed it was possible one of the bullets fired had not been fatal and that Jenny could have been conscious and fired a second bullet herself.

Aware of the family's wish to go ahead with the funeral, Dr Dyte repaired Jenny for the undertakers and sent her body back to Mansfield.

The final line of his report reads, 'CAUSE OF DEATH: In my opinion due to GUN-SHOT WOUNDS TO HEAD WITH GROSS CEREBRAL CONTUSION.' [His capitals.]

∞

Saturday 17 November was the day of the long-awaited Mansfield Show and another unscheduled event—Jenny Tanner's funeral, which was set for 11 a.m. The weather was perfect for the show, hot and cloudless. The families had finally been able to have some quiet time alone with Jenny late the day before at the funeral directors', and now the time had come to face the friends and relatives in public. Kath had kept herself busy since dawn, preparing refreshments for people coming back from the cemetery.

Jenny's funeral was memorable. Inside the old Catholic church, St Francis Xavier, it was cool and sombre—'very morbid and depressing' for those gathered to bid Jenny farewell.

Many people were angry with Jenny for taking her own life so violently and abruptly without confiding in anyone or leaving a note explaining why. In the hot noonday sun at the grave-side Kate McCormack, who had introduced Laurie and Jenny, was seen kicking the dust and muttering, 'Bugger Jenny, why did she go and do this?' through her tears.

Debbie, who had driven down from Echuca, felt it was unfair that more of Jenny's friends were not there to give her a proper send-off. She thought they were probably embarrassed about what to say to the families. Most of the people attending were friends of the families, not Jenny's personal friends—unusual for a popular girl. Debbie looked fiercely over and glared at Laurie, hidden behind dark glasses and surrounded by his family. He didn't seem to notice. 'He was so spaced out he didn't give a shit about what was going on.'

Laurie's first wife wanted to come, but Denis told her to stay away. The rest of the Tanner family were there. Kath had left Sam at her home in the care of a friend he knew, but all of Jenny's family attended.

Liz Thomas remembers a solemn priest. 'It was awful. I'd never been to a funeral before. There was no eulogy, no-one said anything nice about her and she'd been so lovely. There was "Jenny's side" and "Laurie's side"—all the Tanners huddled around Laurie, we couldn't get near him to express our sympathy and talk to him about Jenny—we loved her too. We were just shut out. He looked stoned out of his tree, as if he'd been drugged.' As she stood by Jenny's grave she remembered the sunny picture of Jenny waving her goodbye two weeks earlier—a snapshot in her mind. 'Typical of Jen to be concerned for *my* safety,' she pondered miserably.

The mourners returned to Kath and Les's house for a subdued lunch.

Debbie stopped by her baby-sitter's to give her new baby a quick feed and then went out to the Blakes'. Feeling alone in the crowd, she went into the garden and sat looking back at the home she had 'practically lived in' during her teenage years. She remembered giggling and sharing secrets during Saturday night sleep-overs and having to reluctantly go home on Sunday mornings while the Catholic Blake family attended church; dancing at Jenny's twenty-first; throwing confetti at her wedding; birthdays, barbecues and Christmases. Tears prickled and her chest hurt.

'Oh Jen, what *happened*?'

Kristine, Jenny's sister, came and sat with her.

'Let's try to remember some happy times,' she whispered, and gradually they did, ending up laughing together at their recollections of Jenny sparkling with life.

Laurie didn't stay long and everybody understood. Other people gradually moved off, and finally Clare, Kath and Les were left to clean up after the last event they would host at their home for their eldest daughter. While they were washing up Clare said, 'I don't think you're meant to have Sam, Mum. I think they want him back.'

'Well, of course Laurie should have him back. He's Sam's father. He should be the one to bring him up.'

The same afternoon, two cars pulled into the driveway. Kath says June and Laurie were in one car, with Denis 'riding shotgun' in the other.

'We've come to pick up Sam.'

Kath handed her motherless grandson over to his father and felt an enormous sense of loss. Of course it was the right thing, but now she would have to make arrangements to see Sam; there wouldn't be the spontaneous visits she'd enjoyed with Jenny. She wouldn't share so closely in watching him grow up. Nothing would ever be the same again.

Part Two

'No Truth and Justice'

When you have excluded the impossible, whatever remains,
however improbable, must be the truth.

ARTHUR CONAN DOYLE

6

Memories and Alibis

I'VE NOW heard a lot about how the Tanner family closed ranks and began to exclude the Blakes from the day of Jenny's funeral, but I feel the Tanners' perspective is still missing. On my next visit to Mansfield I arrange to visit Curly and Angie McCormack. Angie was the last known person to talk to Jenny before she died and Curly was probably Laurie's best remaining friend from primary-school days. At the time of Jenny's death they lived in the centre of Mansfield in Curia Street, just around the corner from Laurie's parents, but they have since moved to Scully's Lane on the far side of Mansfield. They can't see me till 'after work', meaning it will be dark when I drive out there alone on deserted back roads. I'm not too thrilled at the prospect. Many people are telling me to be careful, without indicating exactly what I should be careful of. I have no other appointments and some daylight to spare, so I drive out and find the place, to avoid getting lost in the dark. I soon locate it—a hilly property dotted with sheep and horses, kept in order by miles of white fences.

During my second trip I feel a little more relaxed, but still not completely at ease. I tread in a deep puddle as I open the main gate, and swear into the darkness. Should've worn the bloody boots again. Various dogs bark to signal my arrival at the small gate leading to the garden surrounding the house. At the back door I'm surprised by a couple of cranky chihuahuas, prancing around a collection of outdoor shoes and rubber boots discarded beside the doorstep. I thought country people viewed pet dogs, especially toy ones, as a waste of space.

Curly and Angie are quite different from my expectations. I have a vision of Jenny at twenty-seven and subconsciously expect her friends and contemporaries to be young too. I visualised Curly as tall with lots of curly dark hair, and Angie as small and countrified. Not so. Curly is a little nuggety bloke of about fifty in working overalls, with tough country hands and a beard growing up into the remains of his curly red hair. Angie is rather formally dressed for a country housewife. At first I assume she's put on good clothes in case I want to take photos, but it turns out she has to leave for work shortly. They have a cleaning business in addition to the farm and stud. She's a big no-nonsense woman, a country girl from up north, and looks a lot younger than Curly, although maybe he's aged tougher than she has, working outside all day. The kitchen is warm and friendly. Completing the family picture, a couple of young teenagers are watching a very loud TV in the next room while they wait for their tea.

After I go through my usual introduction we settle around the kitchen table to talk. Angie has lately earned a few critics in this close community because she agreed to be interviewed on a national television show after the reopening of Jenny's case. Some people were quite angry about this break in the ranks, especially coming from a 'newcomer', but Angie looks as if she'll cope.

'Why do you think the media approached you, Angie?' I ask.

Curly cuts in with a quick answer. 'Well, we were Laurie's alibi, weren't we? We were the last people to talk to Jenny, and Laurie was with us only a few minutes later. He walked in and I told him we'd just tried to ring him and Angie had a talk to his missus instead. He called in to see us in town. He'd been to the showground and there was a plumbing problem he wanted to talk about. The show was only a couple of days off and he had a lot to do. Angie had just finished talking to Jenny on the phone. I told her to get off the phone because I wanted my tea.'

'Yes, she didn't seem to want to hang up' says Angie. 'She didn't usually talk a long time on the phone, just enough to say why she was calling or what she wanted. I've often wondered if someone was there and she couldn't say anything—too scared maybe and didn't want me to hang up.'

'How come you were having tea so late?' I ask. This late meal of Curly's had bothered me since I read about it in Angie's statement to the police. Country people generally eat much earlier than 9.30 at night.

Curly shrugs and Angie laughs. 'Just was,' he says. 'We eat any time around here, when the food's ready and when we finish work. Depends when we get in. That was spring, daylight saving means longer hours outside and I was vice-president for Laurie, so I was pretty busy myself that week, with the show and all.'

'Could you have been mistaken about the time? Could it have been earlier?'

'No. We've been over and over it. A few minutes each side, maybe, but he definitely arrived about 9.30 and it was around ten o'clock when he left.'

In order to determine the latest time Laurie could have left the McCormack's; earlier in the day I'd timed the trip from the old Curia Street house to the front gate at Springfield. I risked a speeding ticket on the way out, reasoning that Laurie would have felt pretty safe going over the limit at ten o'clock on a Wednesday night.

It took me thirteen minutes.

On the way back, obeying limits, it took twenty, in a fast car on a good road. No idea what the road was like then. Laurie's first call to the ambulance was logged at 10.22 p.m.

'Does he still visit you? You were best friends for so long.'

'He went right back into his shell after Jenny died. I'm a bit surprised he didn't do something else with his life. I saw him at an Agricultural Show meeting the Tuesday after the *Sunday Age* article and we sat next to each other and I shared his reading glasses because I'd left mine at home. He seemed fine then.'

'He hasn't visited for years. Never comes out here. After Jenny died Laurie looked after Sam and worked and we just grew apart.'

Angie has to leave, so she finishes her part of the story. 'Jenny was very busy that week preparing for the show. She was expecting friends from Melbourne to come up and stay. When we were on the phone that night she didn't mention a thing about it. It was just about babies and stuff. I gave it all to the police in my statement. When Curly called out for his tea she said, "It's a bit like that around here sometimes. The only time I know Laurie lives here is when I do his washing. You'll know it when you get a baby—they make as much washing as two adults." She was really hard to get off the phone.'

I think perhaps she just didn't want to return alone to her pile of ironing—or was someone already there, warning her not to say anything that might give them away?

I ask if they know how Jenny and Laurie met.

Curly takes up the story. His family knew the Blakes from primary school. Curly's younger sister Kate carted everyone around to the local dances, and Jenny and Kate were friends. In September 1979, Laurie and Curly were at the Melbourne Show. Laurie had unofficially commissioned Curly, the extrovert, to find him a new girlfriend after his first marriage had ended. So far, Curly was not earning his stripes.

Jenny was living in Melbourne at the time and gradually distancing herself from Jed Moffit. On Show Saturday the girls had been invited to a party in Broadmeadows, a working-class outer Melbourne suburb. Kate told Curly to bring himself and Laurie to the party after they left the show, as Jenny wanted to meet Laurie. Curly used a biro to write the party address on his hand, forgetting it was going to be a long, warm day. The street number inevitably became a bit blurred and at their first attempt they bowled into the wrong party. They were beaten up for gate-crashing, but eventually arrived at the right address, where Jenny and Laurie were introduced. In spite of Laurie's rather dishevelled appearance, Curly says, Jenny was impressed that he had persevered. She began a friendship with him almost immediately. About eighteen months later, Laurie and Jenny were married in Jenny's parents' garden.

Angie and Curly impress me as 'salt of the earth people'—no bullshit and no subterfuge.

Back at the motel I plan my visit to former Detective Sergeant Ian

Welch the next day. He is retired and still living in Alexandra. I can call in on my way home if I go the long way. It's a pretty drive down to Melbourne through Healesville and Lilydale, and the opportunity to eyeball him is too good to miss. I prepare a list of questions I want to ask, based on my reading of the inquest notes and some of my interviews. I reread his evidence a couple of times, so I have the words and sequence almost by heart. Just because he's retired doesn't mean he's a doddery old fool.

Ian Welch is another linchpin in Jenny's unexplained death. He was the person who instructed Bill Kerr not to bother with photos of the scene. As the CIB officer for the area, he would have had to authorise further investigation into queries raised by Bill Kerr and others at the time. I want to ask him about a few things he did after Jenny's death, and some he didn't do. I particularly want to ask him why the CIB came 70 kilometres from Alexandra to investigate the shooting of Laurie's dog, but not the shooting of his wife. I hope he will talk to me.

∞

Uncertain how houses are numbered on country highways, I drive straight past Ian Welch's front gate and into the little township of Alexandra. I think about asking at the police station, but change my mind. One phone call from them and he might not answer the door. On my way to the post office to ask the posties, I pass an excellent op shop I discovered on my last visit here. The volunteer ladies in the shop will be sure to know the Welch family. I'm in luck. One of them lives close to Welch, and she gives me very detailed directions. Hugging my little bag of goodies, I return to my car and go back along the highway.

The house is well hidden from the road. I wind slowly along a rutted dirt drive towards a roof peeping through the trees. As I approach I hear a strange drumming sound—or a thumping, I can't work it out. It gets louder and more mystifying. The house suddenly appears as I round a bend. My tyres reverberate on a grid over a little creek. On my right I see at least a dozen big emus craning their long necks over an electrified wire fence, staring at me with their goggle eyes and vibrating their throats to make that weird drumming noise.

Just as I'm thinking the Welch family wouldn't need a watchdog, a big friendly black-and-white kelpie comes bouncing over to check me out. His tail is wagging, so I walk past him through a blossoming cottage garden to the front door. A lady peers around the flyscreen.

I give her my name and ask for Ian Welch.

'He's up the back. Just follow the sound of the whipper-snipper.' She inclines her head to the rear of the house and then disappears inside.

The noise is about 500 metres away. I follow it to an enclosed run about two metres wide and ten metres long, full of dozens of baby emus, running up to one end, then back, up and back, as if they are training for a race. The biggest is only about 35 centimetres high. Black stripes split their yellowy baby fluff into neat longitudinal sections, and their strong legs are going like pistons. I have never seen anything like it.

On the other side of the run, a smallish middle-aged man in gardening gear and enormous rubber boots is facing away from me, leaning over the whipper-snipper. Its noise drowns out my call, and I can't get any nearer because of the emu race. He only sees me when he changes position and we both get a fright—me because I think he is going to cut his foot off when he jumps.

He turns the whipper-snipper down and I call across the two fences separating us to ask if he can spare a few minutes. He turns the engine right off and leans on the top wire on the far side of the emu run. I move closer and lean on my side. Welch has a very 'lived in' face, one that I guess has experienced a lot of cigarette smoke and a fair share of social drinking. He lights a cigarette. This is a good sign; he'll probably talk at least until it's finished. The baby emus keep up their perpetual motion between us, making it hard to remember my lines. My notebook is still in the car, although I have my tape. I hope I've done enough preparation, although nothing could have predicted the location of this interview.

Welch's police training proves too smart for me, and he doesn't give much away. For the first five minutes he repeats his inquest evidence verbatim, as if he'd somehow known I'd be dropping in and he too learnt it off by heart the night before. I am so familiar with it I know exactly which phrase he'll use next, but I listen politely, as if it is all brand new.

I am struck that he uses exactly the same phrase as Laurie did at the inquest: 'She felt Laurie was enjoying himself and got the best end of the stick.' I wonder if it's a common phrase around this district. When he's finished outlining his exemplary role in the whole series of events, I ask him if he still thinks it's suicide.

'I've always thought it was suicide. It was entirely possible, even with two bullets in the brain. The first one only nicked her.'

Nicked her! A hollow-nosed bullet, designed for maximum impact on the target, lodged in your midbrain is just a nick? That's what I think. But I don't say it. Instead, I ask him about something else.

Six months after Jenny's death Ian Welch made a special trip over to Shepparton to see Peter Dyte, and it seems that as a result the pathologist altered his report to say the death was suicide. This was most unusual; normally pathologists only state the physical cause of death, and don't make judgements about the circumstances.

'Why did you find it necessary to go and see Dr Dyte to get him to verify suicide?'

'I wanted to satisfy myself, once and for all, that's all—just doing my job. I made a tape of my visit to Dr Dyte and I've given it to Homicide, along with my own personal file of the case, which I kept when I retired.'

I wonder if this is regular police procedure, taking home official files and tapes. It seems a few people kept their material for a long time, just in case this investigation—or lack of it—ever came back and stung them on the tail.

'Were you hassled by Bill Kerr to keep the inquiry going?' I want to find out where the blockage occurred and if Bill Kerr really did push as hard as he is now saying he did.

'Look, you don't want to take anything Bill Kerr says too seriously.

I prepared a report for Homicide in Melbourne with a request for them to interview Denis Tanner due to the evidence Kerr got from that woman in Queensland [Roz Smith]. Tanner had to be interviewed, but I wasn't going to do it. The file was sent back to me with Homicide recommending no further action.'

'Do you still have the file?'

'No, the file and the report from Homicide was lost before the inquest, and the rest of the file disappeared after the inquest.'

I barely resist saying 'How convenient' and opt for 'Is that common? Maybe the file is down in Melbourne somewhere with the Coroner's Court. How could you follow up the open finding if you didn't have the file?'

'Of course we never closed the case. I was keeping an open mind. It wasn't my fault, all this, I was only one person and it was all just before Christmas and I was the only one available to investigate. Look how many people they have on it now! I wish I'd had the same amount of time and people.'

'So you think it could have been murder?'

'If it was, it was a very vicious crime—I still think it was suicide.'

He stubs out his second cigarette and I sense my time is up.

'Do you know Denis Tanner—did you work together?'

'No, never. Tanner moved up from Melbourne as my counterpart in Benalla, around 1989 I think. We were the same rank, but I had very little to do with him. I mostly dealt with Seymour if I needed backup.'

To wind up our interview easily, I ask him about the chicks. He offers to show me 'the babies', and I follow along the wire until it converges into a big shed, where an open incubator like a small rain tank—about two metres across with walls about fifty centimetres high—is sitting on the floor. The chicks are miniature versions of the ones outside, all very active except for one little fluffy doing the splits, its long legs splayed out in a rubbery pose.

He leans in and picks it up. 'I'm going to have to wring this little fella's neck,' he says sadly. 'He hatched two days ago and I thought he might get up on his feet, thought I'd give him a chance, but he won't make it.'

I suggest it needs to be separated out and given some intensive therapy. 'I'll take him home and work on him,' I joke.

'No. He's going. Can't let them linger on when they're like this.'

So Welch is kind enough to give a little emu a chance to come good, but tough enough to wring its neck if it doesn't. I wish he'd been a bit tougher on Jenny's behalf.

He walks me to my car and the emus start drumming again. 'It's their warning to each other in the bush,' he tells me. 'I told you Bill Kerr was invalided out of the force, didn't I? He was supposed to be injured from lifting a traffic camera, but he has a long history of stress.'

'Could his stress be related to the Jenny Tanner case, do you think?'

'Not at all. He's always been stressed. He's mad. Bill Kerr should carry most of the responsibility for all this. He didn't secure the crime scene and allowed it to be cleaned up.'

Crime scene, huh?

'Thanks so much for your time, mate,' I say in farewell. 'I love your emus. They must be worth a packet.'

'Not really. You've got to create a market first, but we're getting there.'

The emus drum and his dog barks as he lights another cigarette and heads towards the house. So that was Ian Welch—a pretty cool customer, protecting his arse.

∞

There were so many twists and turns in this story and so many people trying to be wise with hindsight—including myself. I puzzled over the lost file and wondered if Denis *did* borrow Laurie's rifle, and whether he returned it on the night of 14 November. I was still no wiser about who had benefited from Jenny's death—or who would have had the guts to pull off her staged suicide and live with it all these years.

Was there any link between the deaths of Adele Baily in or around 1978 and Jenny Tanner in 1984?

Time to see if Homicide have any answers yet, or at least any they'll share with me. I'm pretty sure they know I'm out there somewhere, and I'm not sure if they can take any action to stop me doing my own research, so I ring to introduce myself and make an appointment with the Inspector leading the Task Force.

My first impression of Police Headquarters is a bit intimidating because of all the private security staff protecting the front desk. I wonder why they don't use police—must be a safety precaution. A big plain-clothes police officer, Detective Senior Sergeant Jeff Calderbank, comes to collect me and escort me upstairs to meet the Inspector. The Sergeant seems pretty friendly, with a broad smile and a crushing handshake. I glance sideways at him in the lift and see he has a jaw-line like Chesty Bond. A good man to stay friends with.

We walk through narrow corridors and security doors into a big open-plan space painted in public service cream. A dominating whiteboard on an easel is covered in lists and dates of different colours, arrows leading from one list to another and question marks all over the place. Across the top of all this information 'Jennifer Ruth Tanner' is printed in red.

Sergeant Calderbank hurries me on, joking, 'I probably should have put a blindfold on you.' I don't have time to read anything any-way. We enter a tiny office, where he introduces me to the leader of the Task Force, Inspector Newman. A large desk, like a partner's desk in an old law firm, almost fills the space. One end is rammed hard against the window, with an outlook over treetops to the city. The Inspector is sitting at one side of the desk, papers strewn in front of him. There is just enough room for the big Sergeant to manoeuvre around to his seat on the other side, while my chair is pulled up to the protruding end. I sit half-in and half-out of the office, blocking the doorway. On the wall behind the Inspector is a cork noticeboard, almost covered with the *Sunday Age* article, 'Jennifer Tanner—how did she really die?' This question hangs over both these officers every day.

The Inspector looks a bit like his namesake—Paul Newman. To loosen myself up, I joke about whether his mother knew he was going to grow up good-looking or whether she just hoped he'd grow into the name. He smiles politely. Probably heard it at least a hundred times before.

They want to know why I'm writing the book and I want to know how much they can help me. We tic tac around the answers. We all recognise we could be useful to each other; it's really only a matter of degree and a question of trust. In addition, police regulations prevent them from divulging too much before it becomes public knowledge at the inquest.

'You'll get a book out of the inquest on its own,' Inspector Newman assures me. I can hardly wait, but I guess it will come too soon for some people.

'I'm not trying to solve this mystery,' I reassure them. 'I see that as definitely your job. I want to tell the story, which obviously includes the role of the police—then and now.'

I tell them there's been talk of a police cover-up at the time. 'Are you just going through the motions, or are you serious?'

Paul Newman is stung. 'We are very, very serious. We had to start out with a premise of suicide, but that is ruled out now ...'

This is my first official confirmation it's a murder inquiry.

'... then you investigate a wide pool and rule people out one by one and end up with a few, or maybe only one suspect.' He and Jeff Calderbank look at each other.

'Let's just say we're working with a very short list at the moment,' Jeff says.

Although the Inspector is senior, he often looks to Jeff Calderbank before answering questions. I'm a bit confused by this apparent tendency to defer to his Sergeant. Jeff Calderbank was in charge of the investigation into the body in the mineshaft, and then moved into the new investigation of Jenny's death, so maybe that's the reason.

'So what *is* the link between Jenny and Adele?' I ask.

They tell me they can't tell me much. A brief for a case to hold a second inquest into Jenny's death is being prepared and the investigation is active and therefore, confidential. There will be an inquest into Adele Baily's death, but it's not certain there will be another inquest into Jenny's death. The Coroner's Act changed in 1986, but old cases still have to be heard under the old Act, so if they do get permission to hold a new inquest it will set a legal precedent.

'All we can say at the moment is that Jenny Tanner and Adele Baily died almost on the same property—the mineshaft is on Crown land directly behind the Tanner property. Denis Tanner knew the area like the back of his hand and was working in St Kilda at the time Adele Baily disappeared. He had some links with Adele Baily that we can't divulge at the moment. When we started asking questions around Mansfield about Adele Baily, there was a strong groundswell of local opinion that Jenny Tanner's death was never properly investigated and a lot of people believed she couldn't have pulled the trigger herself. In 1978, when Adele Baily disappeared, Denis Tanner was a part-owner of Springfield and could come and go as he pleased. He was also Jenny Tanner's brother-in-law, so who do you think could be the link?'

'Is he your prime suspect?'

They look at each other and laugh. 'We don't have "prime suspects". Let's say he's *a* suspect.'

'Have you questioned him?'

'No, not yet. We're conducting a very open investigation, talking to his friends and neighbours, trying to talk to his family, but his family won't talk to us. They don't have to if they don't want to. We're hoping he might come forward and see us.'

'Why would he do that if he thinks you think he could be involved?'

Newman continued. 'Well, if he's not involved he could demonstrate that, couldn't he? A funny thing about Sergeant Tanner. Since he's been in Benalla, for about eight years on and off he's been trying to get the Mansfield CIB area changed from Alexandra, to come under his jurisdiction from Benalla. He's tried a few times, unsuccessfully. Every time the slightest little incident has occurred involving the Alexandra CIB, like a theft, car accident, bashing—anything, big or small—Tanner is on the phone, getting all the details from his mates at Alexandra and Mansfield. He says that as he's often in Mansfield and people know he's a cop, but don't always realise he has no jurisdiction over Mansfield, they say, "What happened about that …

whatever it was?" and he doesn't want to look like an idiot, not knowing. That's his reason and people would believe it, because he's an arrogant prick.'

'How likely is it you'll get a new inquest? Surely since the last finding was left open and you have new evidence, there shouldn't be a problem?'

'Well, it's not really that simple. Firstly, we might get some smart barrister arguing for Tanner—or any other suspect for that matter— that there's not really enough new evidence to warrant a new inquest. We're essentially using the same witnesses, but we've asked them a lot of different questions. So we have to be prepared with all our new evidence and convince the Supreme Court there is sufficient cause to reopen the case.'

He goes on to explain the technicalities and some major differences between the old Act and the new Act. The old Coroner's Act provided for the Coroner to compel people to be committed to trial for murder, manslaughter and infanticide, plus culpable driving or arson, where these caused a death. The current legislation specifically stipulates the Coroner may *not* commit a person for trial on matters connected with culpability or otherwise. If the Coroner believes an individual has committed an indictable offence, he refers it to the Director of Public Prosecutions, who then asks the police if they have enough evidence to present to a trial. If they have, they make an arrest. If not, they don't proceed—it goes on the shelf till someone comes forward or something happens. A murder case is never closed—it can be instantly reactivated if something comes up.

Under the old Act the Coroner had to have an inquest into every non-natural death, which is why there was an inquest on Jenny at all. These days, if the Coroner believes it's a suicide he can dispense with the inquest, but still carry out his own investigation to exclude other causes of death and deliver a finding.

Inspector Newman concludes, 'Under these new rules the Coroner could have been told it was suicide, like everyone else was at the time, and if he believed it, like everyone else seemed to, he may not have held an inquest at all.'

As I listen I realise the various levels on which the investigation rests. It's not only the endless hours of following up threadbare leads and doing boring interviews that produce little of any value, but also being properly prepared to comply with all the legal processes, in case the huge amount of leg-work founders on a technicality.

'Why do you think Bill Kerr's questions didn't go further? How come he was blocked—or at least he says he was.'

'Probably because he was a uniformed cop—not CI [Criminal Investigation] trained. The culture of the day was that uniforms knew nothing.'

I know from my research that there is still a strong distinction between uniformed and plain-clothes police.

Paul Newman continues, 'The Homicide Squad today are different, structured differently and not so cliquey, there's not as much cronyism as there used to be. The whole police force is structured differently nowadays. You're looking at fifteen years ago. Promotion was only on seniority then, now it's on merit and exams et cetera, as well as experience. Allegedly there was a call to Homicide in Melbourne at that time and Homicide said, "If local CI are happy then let's let it go." '

And that seemed to be the way it was, all down the line. The local CI, of course, was my emu-breeding mate, Ian Welch, who was so anxious to assure me that it was definitely suicide, but if, by some wild outside chance, it wasn't, then the lack of investigation was all Bill Kerr's fault, as he hadn't 'secured the crime scene'.

'Bill Kerr seems to have made several claims to the media that he tried very hard to keep the inquiry going. Can he demonstrate that? Is the file really lost?'

'Yes, it's lost all right. Another one of the many coincidences associated with this case. It's basically Kerr's word against his senior officers', few of whom are still in the force now. The inquest brief is pretty pathetic, only fifteen statements, and we have over 100—around 1800 pages, six inches thick. We've had a bit of a word to the officers from that time, but there's not much point at this distance.'

I asked him how a file could disappear.

'I'm blowed if I know. But I do know there is not one sheet of paper relating to that file in any drawer or records room we've searched. It's done a complete disappearing act.'

'Is that common?'

'Not very!' He and the Sergeant exchange another look.

We agree politely to keep in touch, but on first impressions I don't think they'll be much help after all, as they have so many constraints on what they can say and they're pretty cagey. It is early days, though. Maybe I can earn their trust further on. Jeff Calderbank takes me back to the ground floor.

I mention in the lift, 'A lot of people have warned me to be careful. Do you think I am at risk from anyone in any way?'

'Look, *we've* been told to be careful! I don't think anyone could risk doing you any harm—you're too much out in the open about what you're doing. We'd be instantly suspicious. Keep an eye on your car and your dogs, though—if you have any.'

I relate the story of my poisoned puppy. He says there's not much they can do about it, but he enquires about the date it happened and says he'll make a note on the file.

'Sometimes a bit of damage can be used as a warning—nothing too obvious, but you'll get the message. Do you plan to include any information about our operation in your book?'

'Of course, as much as you'll tell me—now and later.'

'We might have to get permission from higher up to allow us to co-operate with you officially. We'll look into that after the inquest. If you're using my name, could you make sure you spell it properly? The last time someone wrote about me they got *both* names wrong!'

'Of course I will,' I say sweetly as I move past security, out of his reach. 'That's R-O-B-E-R-T R-E-D-F-O-R-D isn't it?'

Jeff Calderbank has a nice laugh, which follows me out the door.

∽

My own feelings fluctuate as I become more addicted to trying to uncover the 'real' story. New leads come from all directions. One of my clients says, 'You should talk to this staff member of ours, she grew up in Mansfield and shared a flat with one of the Blake family.' I accumulate a long list of names, which are all tantalising enough to follow up. Sometimes they are essential to the story; others yield only one line of local colour. The web around Jenny's death has incredible dimensions.

The more I dig, the more I realise that this is no simple suicide. There are frustrations as well. A lot of people around Mansfield don't want to say much, or make me promise not to use their names. Even a family member says, 'I've been told not to say anything because people misconstrue things.'

On the other hand, I am amazed about how open most people are with me. Even professionals who ethically could not (and did not) share detailed information with me are quite willing to have general discussions about procedures and their own thoughts and feelings. I am often just a disembodied voice on the phone, and they trust me with all sorts of information. While interviewing some people I learn to keep silent about things others have said, to obtain a full picture from many perspectives. I am often forced to bite my tongue and not rush in to fill up silences, as people think their way through what they'll tell me.

A key police witness has received sympathy cards and other threatening material through the mail. Through a circuitous method, I unwittingly phone her, but as soon as I realise who she is and how distressed she is that I've 'tracked her down', I say I'll interview her after the second inquest.

There are missed opportunities too. I take a plane trip to Brisbane, looking for a bolt-hole to write in. Sitting next to me is a fiftyish, well-dressed man. The flight is delayed out of Sydney (as usual) and we both have to catch connecting flights. As we approach Brisbane the flight attendant leans across me and says, 'Dr Gilham, what time is your flight to Bundaberg departing, so we can radio ahead for them to wait for you?' He pulls out his boarding pass and I crane my neck—R. Gilham. I feel weak. After the flight attendant leaves, I lean towards him and whisper, 'Is your first name Ross, by any chance?' It is. I feel overcome. I've given him my bread roll and orange juice and

Jenny Tanner.
Courtesy Blake family.

Laurie Tanner farewells
Jenny at the airport, 1980.
Courtesy Blake family.

Les and Kath Blake at the table where they first heard the news of Jenny's death.
Photo by Penny Stephens, the *Age*. Reproduced by permission.

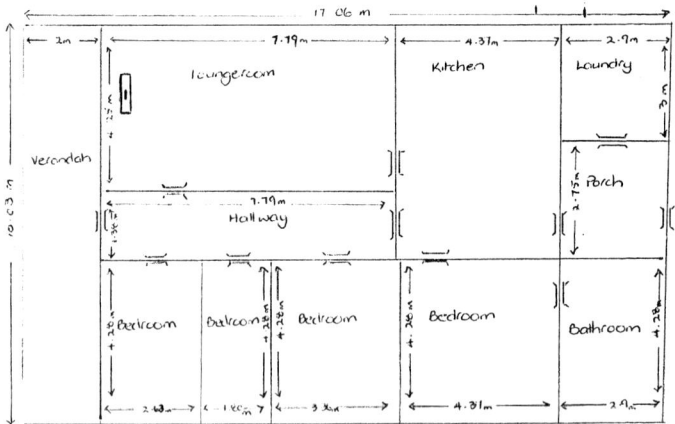

Don Frazer's freehand sketch of Jenny's house, 1984, an exhibit in the first inquest.

The BRNO bolt-action rifle,
an exhibit in the second inquest.

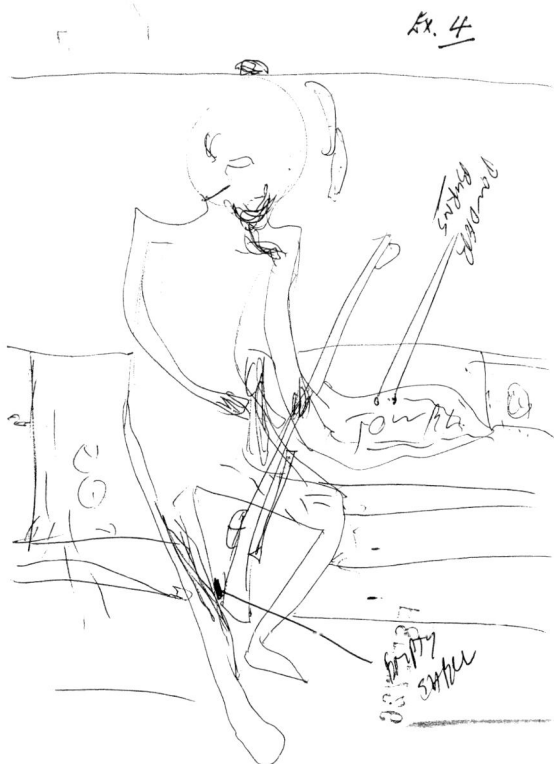

Bill Kerr's freehand sketch, done in his notebook at Springfield the night Jenny
died. This is the only official record on which further conclusions of suicide
were partly based.

Baby Beware!—a poster taken from the fridge in Jenny's kitchen, an exhibit in the first inquest.

we've swapped magazines, but we haven't exchanged another word during the flight, although I've already interviewed Dr Gilham on the phone. I'm beginning to feel Jenny is following me around.

∞

I decide it's time to track down Bill Kerr. He was there on the night, and I need to 'be there' through his eyes.

I find Bill in retirement in Macarthur, where he ended his career in the police force. Our first interview lasts for about an hour on the phone. In 1992, at the age of forty-four, he was retired from the force on medical grounds. He says he had a back injury while lifting a speed camera. I tell him Ian Welch said he'd 'always been stressed', and Bill agrees that stress, rather than his bad back, was the main factor leading to his early departure from police work. While he will not say so directly, he indicates in an obscure way that pressures applied to him after Jenny's demise could have contributed to his own demise from the force.

Bill might have seen a lot, but he doesn't say much. He's fairly heavy going on the phone, with silences lasting longer than his sentences. He was born and raised in Stawell, another country town, and was brought up in the small-town tradition of respect for the local police, but he soon discovered that inside the police station respect gives way to a powerful pecking order and a sense of 'us against them'. The brotherhood doesn't take kindly to members who rock the team dinghy. This is one of the reasons Bill gives me for not 'sticking his neck out' further than he did after Jenny's death. He just couldn't, all things considered.

Bill's two daughters are married and he now lives with his wife in a little farmhouse, which they will renovate when they get around to it. It's a small beef cattle property in the farthest corner of western Victoria, a world away from Mansfield. Bill watches every strange car that drives by in case one day one of them slows down. We go over his old evidence in great detail on the phone and he is fairly open with me, but I can't help feeling there's a lot of 'wink, wink, nod, nod' going on at his end. I wish I could see his face—he seems to be leaving a lot of things to my imagination. He also seems to be enjoying the renewed interest shown in his opinion; perhaps he feels it's about time after all these years. I decide I'll have to make the eight-hour return journey to go and see him.

Fortunately, he is still active in Neighbourhood Watch and this involvement affords us an opportunity to have a face-to-face chat when he comes to a district meeting in Melbourne. Against my better judgement, and to the chef's dismay, I buy him a 'very well done fillet steak' at Jimmy Watson's, a Carlton wine bar.

Although not yet fifty, Bill looks like a man who's had a tough life. Sitting opposite him I try to imagine him at the lonely farmhouse confronted with that bloody scene, projecting a description for his Detective Sergeant at the other end of a phone line—a description that would tip the scales on whether the investigation took one path or another, and affect dozens of lives for years to come. Bill is a man of few words, preferring understatement to exaggeration. Although he now says he described the scene faithfully, it's possible some degree of understatement influenced Welch's decision that 'it sounds like a simple suicide to me'. We go over and over Bill's story, although he has to take his time as he needs to chew each mouthful of steak thoroughly.

'But if someone killed her, what was the motive?'

'Family money. Jenny was extremely close to Old Man Tanner, and she was known to have known more about the Tanners than anyone else. Laurie's first wife got a big chunk of family money. Big legal bills, heavily fought. Denis bought an interest in the property to help Laurie. Springfield has been in their family for a long time—another legal battle could've sent Laurie to the wall. And Jenny had a kid—she probably would've got more.

'You see, if I'd known on the night there were two bullets, there's no way known I'd have accepted suicide.'

I wonder why he wasn't alerted by the two empty cartridge cases, but I don't interrupt.

'I'd been in the force fourteen years by then, been to a number of suicides and a couple of murders. But you never know what to expect. People do funny things, especially if they're in the frame of mind to kill themselves, if you know what I mean. Within a week I thought the Tanner family was involved, but as soon as I knew there were two bullets—by Friday afternoon—I thought it should be investigated further. You see, it looked like suicide, with the exception of a note. That's how it was *meant* to look, so we wouldn't secure the scene and start looking for a killer.

'Within four days I got new information about Denis Tanner— why would a certain Detective Sergeant lie about where he was on the night? Where was he? He told me on the Sunday after Jenny died he was at the trots on the Wednesday night and, unluckily for some, I got that on tape. Then he changed that to bingo in his statement to the inquest, and now that alibi can't be verified because the bloke who gave it to him is dead. But his statement's not worth a pinch of moist goat shit. He can't even remember the date and he was a bookie, probably owed Denis one. Denis used to moonlight as a bouncer, even though it was against police regs—he didn't give a bugger. He thinks he's above everybody—God's gift to women. Maybe he was putting the hard word on Jenny and she told him to bugger off— I don't know. He wouldn't have liked that. But I think the motive was plain family money—just to protect the family from being shamed.'

I'm thinking the farm couldn't have been worth that much in 1984, which was well before it became fashionable for townies to buy up parcels of land around the lake, although it was rich grazing land.

'Do you think Jenny knew about the body in the mineshaft? Perhaps she threatened to tell and someone shut her up.'

'No. I knew that girl. She was as straight as they come. If she'd known about Adele Baily she'd have been the first to the cop shop— no matter who was involved. It really shits me, excuse me but it does, that all that time when I was suspicious I was pushing my head against a brick wall and no-one would listen and then they discover that body and suddenly everyone's saying, "What about Jenny Tanner— no-one ever investigated her death properly," and they reopen the case, just like that, all these years later. But I tried! I'd like a dollar for every phone call they ignored then—but at last someone's finally picked up the phone down there. They'll get the killer this time.' He nods slowly and smiles conspiratorially. 'You have to understand the way things were then. It wasn't easy, the position I was in. I went over my superior's head to talk to Roz Smith—nearly got a disciplinary board for that—and I got the file sent to Melbourne to get Tanner interviewed. It came back "No further investigation." And there was the gun. They didn't even look at it. I put in a report to Inspector MacLennan—suppose you've heard *his* nickname?' He grins.

I shake my head. Does everyone have a nickname in the brotherhood? I wonder about Bill's.

He leans across and waves a ruined bit of steak on the end of his fork. 'I got the file back marked "simple suicide" in red texta, "not warranted" two or three times. If someone hadn't wanted it pushed aside as suicide and if I'd been asked, I would have pursued it.'

'One of the people I've interviewed said you were lazy. Would you agree?'

'No! I wasn't lazy at all. As soon as I found out about the two bullets I wanted Homicide right away. I was very competent and methodical, but to call in Homicide I needed Welch or Jimmy Sullivan [Welch's deputy] to authorise it.'

'It's a pity for your sake in a way about the file going missing,' I say, putting a bit of scepticism there for his benefit.

He agrees ingenuously, like an eager kid. 'Yes, that would clearly show everyone I did try. There's a lot of unfinished business about this case.'

Unfinished for lots of players, I register

'A lot of coincidences too. I don't believe in coincidences—show me a copper who does. Like that house burning down a week after the investigation reopened, the dog getting shot a week before Jenny gets shot. What does a dog do? He barks if someone's trying to sneak up on a place. Denis offering two alibis and only the Tanners saying Jenny was depressed. How come no-one else noticed? She can't have been *that* good an actress—I've got girls of my own. They can't keep a secret to save themselves! It's always possible someone tried to set it up to look like suicide.'

'Someone—who?' I lean right across the small table so he won't have to say the name too loudly.

Bill looks at his watch. 'Time to go to my meeting. You ask your mates at Police headquarters.'

7

The Aftermath

IN THE early hours of Thursday 15 November 1984, Senior Constable Bill Kerr was an unhappy man. He was just a fairly basic seat-of-the pants country copper, but there were a number of things that just didn't add up, and he didn't quite know how to go about making them tally. He made a mental list as he drove home around 3 a.m.

Scene:	No note
	½ cup of coffee
	½ eaten biscuit and others on a plate (entertaining?)
	TV going (lousy program, thought she'd kill herself?)
	Iron on and ironing not put away (out of character)
	Heater on high (room very warm)
	Bloodstained towel, cushions, pools of blood on couch, etc
	5 cigarette butts in ashtray (brand? did Jenny smoke?)
	nappy on the floor (did something wake the baby?)
Victim:	Left baby alone in house (out of character)
	Seemed pretty happy last time I saw her
	Women rarely use guns
	Holes in her hands (unusual way to do it)

Post mortem melidium* (wonder how long that
takes to show)

Suspicious circumstances?

No sign of violence
Nothing missing
Two cartridge cases
No sign of break-in
Husband distraught
Doctor didn't argue with suicide
No problem with CIB (arse covered, made two
calls, obeyed instructions, wish I'd been able to get
hold of Phippsy though.)

'Yeah. If the CI thought there was any need he would've come over.
Poor bloody Laurie. What a mess! That poor little kid. And Kath and
Les. Sometimes this job is a bit of a shit.'

His wife didn't even feel him get into bed. When a country copper gets home after the afternoon shift, that's when he gets home. No
point waiting up for him—you'd never get any sleep.

Over breakfast next morning, he told his wife the story. 'Funny
she'd choose that way to do it. Doesn't fit, somehow,' was the only
comment he made over tea and toast.

While Kath Blake was numbly trying to keep her life in some sort
of perspective and seeking permission from Dr Gilham to see her
daughter, Detective Sergeant Ian Welch was on his way to Mansfield.
During our little chat across the baby emus, he told me he did not
make a special trip, 'probably had some other reason to go'.
Nevertheless, according to his evidence later, he went directly to the
police station when he arrived in Mansfield at about 10 a.m.

---

* In fact, this phenomenon is called post mortem lividity. The venous blood pools in the
lower parts of the body, causing bruise-like mottling of the skin. The opposite effect is
found above the heart, where the oxygenated blood gradually drains downwards, causing
a greyish or yellowish pallor. The lividity can begin developing almost immediately, but
is not usually obvious until a couple of hours after death.

Bill Kerr had arrived at work feeling decidedly gritty. Sergeant Neil Phipps had only just discovered the drama he had missed the previous night. Station Sergeant Neil Walker was furious that Phipps had not been available. Don Frazer was still not in. The station was in confusion.

Welch and Sergeant Phipps 'viewed the deceased at the Mansfield Hospital'… and made a note of 'a wound in the centre of her forehead and one to each of her hands'. At around 11 a.m. they left for Springfield. On the way, they received a radio message not to bother, as the house had already been cleaned and locked and the key was back at Mansfield.

Bill Kerr learnt about the clean-up before Welch's return to Mansfield Police Station. 'It's been fuckin' *what*?' Bill yelled in dismay and anger. 'Fuckin' who bloody gave permission for that? Which one of you fuckin' dickheads would let them do something like that?' He kicked himself for not making the house more secure the previous night, or insisting on photos.

The Station Commander took him to one side. 'There's no need to speak like that to other members, Bill. It's done now.' Bill was still furious, but reminded himself that the family would have had a key anyway; short of mounting a guard on the house, it would have been hard to keep them out. At the same time he was conscious an opportunity had been irretrievably lost. In the past, pictures, diagrams, measurements and notes had cemented dozens of other scenes in Bill's mind. This time, his only records of the scene were his hand-drawn sketch and a memory vividly engraved on his mind. But his memory might differ from that of others who had seen exactly the same awful scene. To ensure he didn't overlook anything else he made a suggestion to Welch on his arrival back at the station.

'Sir, I'd like to get the rifle examined. There's a partial bloodied palm print we could get tested and we could check for fingerprints, you know … Just to rule out any …'

'Look, Constable,' barked Welch, using Kerr's rank to make it official, 'it's a simple suicide. Got it? Don't make waves. Let me have a look at this rifle. Where is it?'

'I have placed it under safe-keeping, sir.' Bill matched his formality. 'I'll get it.'

He collected the rifle and the two cartridge cases from his clothes locker at the back of the station, where he'd locked them the night before. He called Don Frazer, who had just come in, to join them. They showed Welch the rifle, smeared with dried blood, the two cartridge cases and the magazine with two bullets remaining.

'How many bullets does it hold altogether?' asked Welch.

'Ten, sir. I asked Laurie, the husband of the deceased, if he usually unloads after using it and he said he puts away the shells, but he's not sure if he put away the magazine after the last time he used it.'

'So eight shells have been fired from this magazine?'

'If it was full to start with, yes sir.'

Don Frazer unfolded the poster of the baby and the gun that he'd pulled from the fridge in Jenny's kitchen.

'This may or may not be relevant, sir. I took it down mainly to save people's feelings last night.'

Not much attention was paid to this poster, and Don placed it in the new slim manila file entitled 'TANNER Jennifer Ruth'.

Bill Kerr says he drew 'a number of irregularities' to Welch's attention at this time, but was abruptly dismissed with 'simple suicide—don't interfere with things'. Bill couldn't approach Homicide without clearance from the local CI.

A ripple went round the station as Denis Tanner made an entrance. He was not attached to Mansfield, but needed no introduction to the local police and walked in with a certain familiarity. He was introduced to Ian Welch, who had not come across him before. They had a conversation (not a formal interview) about Jenny's state of mind, and Bill caught some snatches as he rewrapped the rifle in plastic. 'After Sam's birth she'd had a breakdown … rifle kept in bedroom wardrobe … Laurie owned a shotgun and a rifle … normal family quarrels …' Bill walked out the back and secured the bloodstained rifle in his locker. He was a bit peeved his superior had not even wanted to measure it or examine it in any way. For the time being, he wasn't going to let anyone else near it.

At about 12.30 p.m. Ian Welch and Don Frazer, accompanied by Denis Tanner, walked around to the Tanners' to see Laurie. Laurie did not make a formal statement, but Welch took notes of the conversation. He asked Laurie about the rifle. Where was it kept?—'In the bedroom wardrobe and the ammo on top of the cupboard in the kitchen.' When did he last use it?—'Two days before, to shut the dogs up.' Was it kept loaded?—'I usually pull the shells out, I'm not sure if the magazine was out.' Did Jenny know how to use it?—'When the escapees* were out I taught her how to use the .22.' What were his movements on Jenny's last day, and finally, 'Have you any reason to suspect foul play?'

Laurie answered, 'No', the interview was terminated and Ian Welch headed for home. It was now early afternoon.

After Welch's departure, Bill Kerr was again left to his own thoughts. It was a bit of a puzzle, but he wasn't going to be able to solve it on his own. What a bugger he hadn't stuck around last night—if he'd got on to Neil Phipps, the police photographer, this morning he could've gone out and taken a few shots. Then Bill wouldn't have to rely on his memory. It was such a sad scene. The futility of it all and the pain of the relatives interfere with objectivity sometimes.

As far as everyone at the station was concerned, the case was pretty much over and done with. On to the next. By noon on Friday, however, Bill was very edgy. Dr Dyte had made two calls, which his senior officer, Sergeant Neil Phipps, took over from him. Bill taped the calls as a precaution. Phipps seemed quite convinced it was suicide, but when Bill heard 'two bullets' he was not sure at all. He decided to try to get the gun tested ballistically and suggested this to both Welch and Jimmy Sullivan in separate phone calls, but kept getting the same answer: 'It's a simple suicide—don't rock the boat. There's no evidence now anyway, since you didn't secure the scene.'

---

* The 'Jika Jika escapees', four of the most dangerous criminals in Victoria, hid out in Bonnie Doon after escaping on 30 July 1984 from Jika Jika, the maximum security ('escape proof') section of Pentridge Prison in Melbourne.

All during Friday, Bill and Don Frazer were occupied obtaining routine statements. Bill questioned Dr Gilham and Don went over to Angie McCormack's to go through the details of Jenny's last phone conversation and Laurie's visit.

On Sunday, the day after Jenny's funeral, Bill went to see if Laurie was sufficiently recovered to make a formal statement. Laurie seemed to have already come to terms with Jenny's death, and Bill took a long statement from him. Denis Tanner was present during this interview, watching over Laurie. After Bill Kerr had switched on his tape, but before they started with the statement, Denis cautioned Laurie: 'Don't say anything about your personal life.'

Laurie said Jenny put Sam to bed as he was leaving at 7.30 p.m., though the nappy found on the floor suggested a baby was changed in the lounge room later. He also recollected arriving at the McCormacks' at 'about 9 o'clock' and leaving at '10 or quarter past'— a much longer visit and at different times from Angie's recollection. He must have left by 10 p.m. or he wouldn't have been able to call the ambulance at 10.22.

When the police arrived Laurie said the magazine for the rifle 'is not normally left in the rifle, but it would normally have been fully loaded and left in the kitchen'. This differs from what he later told Ian Welch, that he normally removed the shells, but left the empty magazine in the rifle. So which was it? Bill pondered: two bullets left in the magazine, two in Jenny, and where are the other six?

Before switching off the tape, Bill turned to Denis and said lightly, 'And where were *you* on the night of the fourteenth, Denis?' Denis replied, 'I was at the trots until about 10 p.m. and then went home and went to bed.'

Later on, Bill drove out to see Hughie Almond to obtain a statement from him. Hughie didn't add anything new to the puzzle and clearly had not yet come to terms with this terrible event. Before heading back to town Bill drove the extra half kilometre past Springfield, deserted and nestling quietly under the trees in the sun. There were no outward signs of the drama it had hosted only days before.

No-one asked Gerry O'Donnell or the Blakes or the Tanner parents for a formal statement.

Bill was faced with some difficult and uncomfortable choices, but he didn't want to back off the case. Something jarred. He was confused about the conflicting information he'd received about Denis. At 1 a.m. D24 had said they couldn't contact Denis at home, but according to Denis's statement he would have been back from the trots hours before. Either Denis and Lynne had very bad hearing or neither of them was home until 5 a.m., as the police said they'd gone to the house several times. It's possible that the police said they'd gone around when they hadn't, but this would be pretty unusual in a 'death call', especially for a member's family. Bill didn't know if Laurie or the senior Tanners had tried to phone Denis before 5 a.m., but it seemed a bit out of character if they hadn't. There was a good chance Denis hadn't heard anything about the previous night-time visits from the police because he'd departed in a rush on the Thursday morning and hadn't gone home since.

Early in the week after Jenny's death, a call came in to Mansfield from Queensland. It was a woman wanting to speak to 'whoever was investigating Jenny Tanner's death', and Bill took the call. It was from Roz Smith, who identified herself as 'Jenny Tanner's best friend'. Roz told Bill her cousin was married to Constable Jeff Adams and she had discussed the information she was about to give Bill with her cousin and Jeff Adams. She then told Bill about the phone call she had received from Jenny, informing her of Denis's strange visit. She also told him she had received a call from Denis himself on the Sunday night, the night after the funeral.

'I couldn't believe it when my husband came in and told me Denis Tanner was on the phone. I'd been stewing about this phone call I've just told you about and then he rang. If he'd been in front of me I'd have smashed him!'

Bill was not in a position to see the irony in that comment, but Roz is about a quarter Denis's size.

'So I took the call, out of curiosity really, I wanted to see what he had to say for himself. He was calling, *the day after Jenny's funeral*, to see if I knew if she had a will and where she kept it! I found out later he also rang Kath that night, asking about her address book and whether they knew if she had any insurance. Can you believe it? I told him I didn't know anything about a will, but I've been thinking and thinking about the two calls and since I don't believe Jenny killed herself, I thought you should know.'

'Was she depressed at all that you could notice, or did she say anything?'

'Nothing! She was just the normal happy Jenny and had a good relationship with Laurie as far as I could see.' Pausing in his note-taking, Bill asked Roz if she would be prepared, if necessary, to make a formal statement to the police.

'Of course I would. If Jenny was killed, I'll do anything to help.'

'I'll see if I can get someone to come and get a statement from you. In the meantime, keep this to yourself will you, Mrs Smith? And thanks for taking the trouble to call.'

Bill hung up and stared at his desk. 'I wonder which trots Denis Tanner went to last Wednesday?' He dialled 013 and asked for the number of the Victoria Racing Club.

A week after Jenny's death, on the day her obituary was published, one of Laurie's old school friends, a man called Bob, advertised a saddle for sale and Hughie Almond went to check it out. They sat together examining the saddle in Bob's shed, and Bob asked Hughie about what had happened on the night. Hughie described the scene and told him what a tremendous shock it had been. Hughie left Bob in no doubt he thought Jenny had shot herself. By this time, only a week later, the gossip about the incident had almost died out. People refrained from further conjecture out of sympathy for the Blakes and the Tanners. For most people in Bonnie Doon and Mansfield, life returned to normal.

Bill Kerr knew full well the file was about to be shelved. That was the way of it—the steady progression from the investigation to the official wrap-up to oblivion. But Bill simply could not forget it and let go. He looked at his own working file and made up his mind. He put the manila folder, statements and his own tape recordings into his desk drawer, so he could pull them out whenever he wanted. He was not satisfied that the whole truth had yet come to light.

Don Frazer felt much the same. He had felt from the beginning something was 'not right', but he would soon be leaving the case behind, as he was up for a transfer. The call from Roz Smith only reinforced both constables' dissatisfaction. Bill kept his head down and got on with his job, using his meagre unofficial networks to begin a few quiet inquiries in his own time.

He approached Mrs Blake for a list of Jenny's friends. No matter how many times he approached the question of Jenny's emotional stability, Bill got essentially the same answer. All who knew her said she was a completely normal young woman.

He phoned Liz Thomas and asked her to come in to make a statement next time she was in Mansfield. They set a date for 10 December, when she had plans to see some friends before Christmas.

He contacted a Constable Niland at Southport police station in Queensland and asked him to 'do him a favour' and go out and get a statement from Roz Smith. 'Keep it unofficial at this stage, will you?' said Bill. 'I'm just conducting a few background inquiries.'

He found out from the VRC there were no trots anywhere in Melbourne on that Wednesday night—the only meeting in the State was at Bendigo, a long way from the city.

He did not tell the Blakes there were two bullets in Jenny's brain. No-one else who knew seemed to think it was important enough to tell them either.

Liz Thomas came to the police station accompanied by a cousin for moral support. She had no idea why Bill Kerr wanted to see her. Bill Kerr told her there had been two bullets in Jenny's brain, which was why he was making 'further inquiries'. Liz wasn't very surprised—she'd known all along Jenny couldn't have killed herself. He asked her not to say anything to the Blakes about the second bullet 'at this stage'.

Bill showed her the poster Don Frazer had pulled off the wall of the kitchen. 'Yes, I can remember that. I can't remember when I first saw it. It's been there as long as I can remember. Jenny had it there to remind

Laurie to put away the guns, because of Sam.' The statement Liz made that day says: 'Jenny did not like guns and would have nothing to do with them. Her husband Laurie owned a gun and on the times I was at the property, Jenny would always tell Laurie to put the gun away.'

During that visit to Mansfield Liz saw Kath Blake coming towards her in the street. Not knowing if Kath knew about the second bullet and at a loss about what to say to her either way, Liz hid in a doorway. She did not see the Blakes that Christmas, for the first time in many years. She could hardly wish them a merry Christmas, and didn't know what else she could say.

∞

Meanwhile, the Blakes and the Tanners were trying to settle back into some form of normal life.

June made room for Laurie and Sam in the family home in town. Sam may have missed his mother, but was too young to fully understand her absence. Old Fred Tanner told me during our chat on the veranda, 'He acts like he never had a mother', which, in effect, he didn't. I wonder how the person who deprived him of his mother feels about that? June began a new career as a mothering grandmother, and earned everyone's respect for taking on the job and doing it so selflessly and so well. Laurie continued to work the family farms and kept up with his presidency of the Agricultural Society. Curly told me that in 1985, at the end of Laurie's two-year term, he was re-elected for a further two years to give him something to occupy him and get him out and about.

June went away for a short break a month or so after the funeral and left Sam with her daughter Carol in Albury. She didn't ask Kath if she'd like to look after Sam. This was Kath's first inkling that she might be shut out of Sam's future life.

In the days and weeks following the funeral, Gerry O'Donnell's wife saw a lot of June and baby Sam next door. She recalled in a statement made to police in 1996 that June was convinced Jenny was having an affair with someone and was planning to leave Laurie. Gerry

O'Donnell also recalls that June told him 'the boys had cleaned the mess' at the farmhouse and burnt the couch.

Kath Blake still had great difficulty coming to terms with the fact that her daughter was gone from her life for ever. Hundreds of incidents, large and small, became constant reminders that Jenny was dead. She told me she passed Mrs O'Donnell in the street one day wheeling her new baby in exactly the same style of Italian pusher Jenny had bought for Sam. She felt a surge of anger and longing, thinking. 'I wish my girl was still here to push her baby around like that.'

In Mansfield and Bonnie Doon, Jenny's death was a taboo subject when the Blakes and Tanners were around. The townsfolk acted as if nothing had happened. There was a collective embarrassment, not knowing what to say to the survivors. A neighbour at the time felt 'Jenny's parents were so shocked they didn't make waves. It was like a movie—not really real. It needed a stronger person to say, "This can't be right." '

Jenny's sister, Miriam, was such a strong person. She was very angry with the police for their apparent lack of interest and even with her parents for their seeming acceptance of the way Jenny died. She contacted Dr Dyte directly. He was seriously ill, having recently been diagnosed with a virulent form of cancer, but Miriam told someone he said she could have a strong case against her sister having committed suicide. Miriam didn't want her sister's death to slip into history without a fight.

With the information they had at the time, though, the Blakes seemed to have no alternative. While Kath couldn't believe Jenny had killed herself, she did not have a shred of evidence to the contrary, and the whole police force seemed to agree it was suicide. Jenny's father did not want to discuss it any longer; it was too painful. Discussion about Jenny's death had already created deep family divisions.

The Blakes were annoyed that they were not asked to make a formal statement. Bill Kerr came out to the house and asked if they knew if Jenny had had a breakdown and they emphatically denied it—'What rubbish!'

They were kept away from Laurie before the funeral and had hardly seen him since. Most contacts with Sam were made through June. It was not until the inquest that Kath and Les heard Laurie tell the full story. Until then they only had the official police version of what happened on the night, in spite of their natural wish to find out as much as possible about the way their daughter had died. Kath made several trips to the police station, but was not given any additional information. She was treated kindly, but firmly. The official line had the case virtually closed.

In one of the few conversations they had during this period, Kath told Laurie of her doubts about Jenny killing herself. He told her to leave it be. He was certain she'd committed suicide, and he had incurred a huge amount of extra expense since she died. He reminded Kath his life was never going to be the same again either.

But the loss of a child is the hardest experience of all. Over the weeks that followed, the Blakes concealed their loss in the routines of a life that had to go on. Christmas was a terrible ordeal. Jenny's twenty-eighth birthday would have been on 14 January 1985. The Blakes formed themselves into a tight defensive unit and supported each other through another milestone and through the next eight months. Jenny's death was still unfinished business.

∞

In mid-February Constable Niland in Queensland finally went to see Roz Smith. Forgetting Bill Kerr's request that he conduct the interview unofficially, he sent her statement down through the normal channels. When the hierarchy saw it, they were not impressed. Bill had unilaterally involved an interstate CIB without going through his chain of command in Victoria, earning the wrath of the CIB, his station commander Neil Walker and other colleagues. At the same time it was hard to ignore the content of Roz Smith's statement, which appeared to have the potential to implicate Denis Tanner as a suspect. He had allegedly made a veiled threat to the victim and had allegedly told Bill Kerr he was somewhere he couldn't have been on the night of her death. Denis seemed to be still unaware that Altona police had repeatedly failed to raise anyone at his house between midnight and 5 a.m. that night. Bill had kept this bit of information to himself but did eventually share it with Welch, as further leverage to get Melbourne police to interview Denis.

Welch had little choice but to ask Homicide in Melbourne to interview Denis about his whereabouts on the night of 14 November 1984. He sent the file to Melbourne with this request late in April 1985.

On 30 April 1985 Welch made his visit to Shepparton to see Dr Peter Dyte in person. He took a tape recorder and recorded the interview. Welch was not aware at this time that Dr Dyte was terminally ill. Welch says that, because of the subtle and not-so-subtle pressures being exerted about the finding of two bullets in Jenny's brain, he wanted to clear up once and for all whether she could have actually fired both bullets herself. The information Welch obtained from Dr Dyte differed in some ways from that in Dyte's earlier report. Whereas his first report contained details about the wounds on her hands, this time Welch reported that Dyte had added: 'With the injuries to the hands the entrance wound appeared to be on the rear of each hand, as powder burns were evident on both.' He went on, 'Dr Dyte could not define the effect of the first bullet [to the brain] except that the minimum effect may be only to make the subject groggy.' He did, however, say 'it could be possible for the deceased to fire a second shot'.

According to a later transcript made from Welch's tape recording of this meeting, during a discussion about whether Jenny could have committed suicide or not, Welch said, 'Those wounds on the hands look like ...' [Pause]

Dr Dyte filled the gap: 'It's possible she could have put her hands up in defence and been shot by someone.'

Welch did not pursue this possibility, and neither of them seemed to want to think about how you could get powder burns around four wounds if they were self-inflicted. If, as the police reconstruction at the time alleged, Jenny held the rifle to her head to fire the second and fatal shot, and absorbed the powder burns on her hands, the severe head wound would not have had powder burns. And why would Jenny shoot herself with the backs of both hands resting on top of the barrel?

In spite of these apparent discrepancies, Welch persuaded Dr Dyte to take the unusual step of taping an alteration to his original report stating that the cause of death was 'self-inflicted gunshot wounds'. Dyte did not provide this addition to his early report in writing.

Clutching the vindication of his earlier conviction that Jenny's death had been suicide, and certain Denis's interview would demonstrate no cause for alarm in that regard, Welch headed back to Alexandra with a relieved conscience, ready to tell Bill Kerr he'd better be very sure of himself from now on before he dared to raise one more question—about anything.

∞

The Homicide Squad interview of Denis Tanner at the Russell Street CIB Headquarters was not conducted by an officer, as is usual in cases where a member of the force is being interviewed about a serious situation, but was conducted by Detective Senior Sergeant Jim Fry on 20 May 1985. Denis stated that on 14 November he telephoned Springfield at about 5.30 p.m. and spoke briefly to the deceased. I spoke to my brother in relation to a young mare that I was to have broken in. Later on that evening, at about 7.45 or 8 p.m., I went to a bingo game at the Carmelite Hall ... in Middle Park ... Jack O'Hanlon MC'd the proceedings ... I arrived home at about 10 p.m. to 10.15 p.m., checked our newborn baby and went to bed. At about 5.30 a.m. I answered the door and police told me about the deceased.'

This version of Denis's whereabouts on the night differed from the one he unofficially gave Bill Kerr, but when I interviewed Jim Fry he said he was quite satisfied with it. The alibi was not checked. The file was sent back to Mansfield with the official notation from Fry and his superior officer, Inspector Brian Ritchie, 'further investigation not warranted' and the unofficial comment that if the local CI was happy it should be left be. The brotherhood did not want to be seen to be checking up on its own members.

Bill Kerr was not satisfied, but what could he do now?

∞

No-one seemed to be in a hurry to hold an inquest into Jenny's death, even though the law required one. The date was eventually set for 18 October 1985 at Mansfield, in front of Mr Hugh Adams, Senior Magistrate and Assistant State Coroner from Melbourne. As the date approached it became obvious to a few intended participants that the lack of any proper investigations had resulted in numerous gaps in the brief.

In particular, no-one had yet told Kath and Les Blake about that extra bullet. Roz Smith's cousin had several conversations with her husband, Constable Jeff Adams, who had known for months there were two bullets, but had not told the Blakes. Roz told her cousin it was time the police told Jenny's parents. 'We can't let this be consigned to the filing drawer without trying to get justice for Jenny.' Eventually Jeff went to Bill Kerr and said, 'Don't you think you should tell the parents before the inquest?' and Bill agreed.

The Blakes were dumbfounded. There was only about a week to go before the inquest. How were they going to make sure Jenny's interests were represented? It had never occurred to them that they might need a lawyer. In the past, their only need for lawyers had been buying a house and making their wills. The oldest legal firm in Mansfield was Mal. Ryan, Jackson & Glen. The Blakes rang for an appointment. When they arrived, they were shown into Mr Rodney Ryan's office. Mr Ryan told them across his desk, 'We were initially concerned your visit might have put us in a difficult position. You see, we have represented the Tanner family on various matters for a number of years, and, while they have not yet issued us with any instructions on this matter, they might have still wanted to. Mr Glen phoned them after you called to sort this out.' Kath and Les looked at each other. Why would the Tanners need a lawyer?

Mr Ryan told them June Tanner had said 'the boys' already had a Melbourne lawyer—a Mr Joe Gullaci, who was well known for his support for police needing legal representation. He had been appointed some time before to represent Laurie and Denis Tanner at the anticipated inquest.

'So you can represent us, then?' asked Kath, a bit confused. She was beginning to agree with Miriam, though; perhaps this ought to be pursued with a bit more vigour.

Les, however, was mindful of Sam and the effect of dredging up the whole situation all over again. 'We don't want a witch-hunt. We're not interested in placing blame on anyone—we just want it known Jenny couldn't have done it.'

'An open finding,' said Mr Ryan. 'Is that what you're after?' He explained what this meant.

'Yes, an open finding,' Kath agreed. 'Once I get up there and tell them about my daughter ...'

Mr Ryan interrupted. 'Mrs Blake, you may not be able to attend the inquest—it might not be a bad idea if you stayed away, really.'

'Stayed away! Whatever for? This is my daughter we're talking about, Mr Ryan! The police haven't even been to see us about Jenny. I heard Denis Tanner's made some sort of statement and he'll probably give evidence and we haven't. Of course we shall go. We'll be there for Jenny.'

'Mrs Blake, an inquest is not a very nice place for the next of kin. There'll be very graphic descriptions, the autopsy report—there may be distressing photos—people like Hughie Almond will have to describe in detail what they saw ... what happened ... on the night. It could be very upsetting for you.'

Kath's mouth set in the line Les knew well. He knew they'd be there at the inquest, even if Mr Ryan had doubts.

'Well, now,' Mr Ryan said in a placating voice, 'we'll see what happens. I will represent you in court, so I'd better take some notes.' He asked them a lot of questions and made a pile of notes. Kath and

Les went home and told the family about their visit.

Some of the family were unimpressed with Mal. Ryan, Jackson & Glen.

But the Blakes' minds were made up and objections were over-ruled. They were locals and they'd have a local lawyer and all they wanted was the truth—Jenny didn't kill herself. The truth should come out in a court of law.

They spent the next few days dreading the inquest.

∞

A few weeks earlier in Melbourne, Senior Sergeant Peter Fleming, the police officer assigned to assist the Coroner, was looking at the rather slim brief he had to present to Mr Adams on 18 October. He did not feel warmly disposed to the colleagues who had prepared the material in front of him. On 16 September 1985 he met with Mr Stocks, the Coroner's Clerk, to discuss the unsatisfactory standard of the investigation and inquest brief. He subsequently drew the poorly prepared brief to the attention of his superior, Acting Chief Super-intendent Werner, who advised him to inform Internal Investigations because a police member was under some degree of scrutiny. Fleming asked to handle the investigations personally. This request was denied. He was told to see Homicide and discuss his concerns with their investigating officers.

Just one week before the inquest, Fleming met three Homicide detectives—Senior Sergeant Jim Fry, Inspector Merrigan and Inspector Ritchie—to detail his misgivings about the inadequacy of the investigation and gaps in the brief. Sergeant Fry was adamant that Jenny Tanner had committed suicide, but did admit he hadn't checked the alibi he had taken from Denis Tanner in May that year.

At a meeting lasting nearly two hours Fleming was told categori-cally that Homicide were not prepared to investigate the case further. On 14 October he met with Mr Adams to advise him of this and other facts. There had already been an unacceptable delay in the scheduling of the inquest, so it was agreed he would make as many inquiries as possible beforehand and the Coroner would then consider adjourning the inquest part-heard for further inquiries to be made if necessary.

Fleming found Dr Norm Sonenberg at Southern Memorial Hospital in Melbourne and asked him to come to the South Caulfield police station. Sonenberg gave a half-page handwritten statement saying he was present at part of the autopsy performed on Jenny and that he supported Dr Dyte's findings that she could have fired both bullets herself.

On the same day Fleming set up a temporary office at Middle Park police station to take a statement from John Francis O'Hanlon, the bookmaker Denis had named as MC at the bingo game. Sergeant Fleming was uneasy about O'Hanlon's statement for two reasons. First, when asked for a statement, Mr O'Hanlon mentioned how unfortunate Jenny's suicide had been, which showed he had discussed the matter with someone and had already been told Jenny had committed suicide. Secondly, it was quite apparent he was not sure about the dates and times, and he had no written records to back up his recollections. He did think the night in question may have been a farewell for Joy and Keith Brown, who were moving to Queensland. During the interview O'Hanlon placed a call to the secretary of the bingo, Mrs Shirley Pike, who recalls him saying, 'I need to know *now* when Joy and Keith actually left.' When Shirley told him she'd have to get out all her records and check, he said 'Never mind' and hung up.

In his statement O'Hanlon said, 'I have been asked to recall the bingo evening that I said farewell to Mr and Mrs Keith Brown, I can't remember the date exactly, but it was after the Melbourne Cup Race and the calcuttas* had been held. I can't remember whether it was a Wednesday or a Friday night but I can vaguely remember Dennis [sic] Tanner standing at the back of the Browns ... We had been held up by gunmen previously and Dennis was there to assist the committee.

---

* The Melbourne Cup was held on 6 November 1984. A 'calcutta' is a form of sweep on a horse race. Each horse known to be in the race is 'auctioned' off to the highest bidder, and all the money paid goes into a pot. The 'owners' of the winning three horses earn a percentage of the pot and the balance goes to the house —usually a charity

I can't recall any conversation I had with Dennis that night. [I can't remember making-—crossed out] I can remember making a presentation of a bottle of whisky to the Browns which was wrapped up and brought to me by Dennis. After thinking about it I am pretty sure that it would have been a Wednesday night and it would have been the Wednesday after the Melbourne Cup. The Browns left for Queensland in December some time because I can remember us saying they were leaving us early. Jack and Sheila Hill and Shirley and John Pike could possibly verify this … On the night of the Brown presentation I can't say what time Dennis Tanner left, but it would be approximately 10 p.m. I think he lives in Altona. I have a feeling he has to go over the bridge. Prior to November last year I have known Dennis Tanner for some three or four years.'

I feel a bit uneasy myself when I finish reading this.

This statement formed part of the evidence produced at the first inquest, but Mr O'Hanlon was not asked to appear and so was not cross-examined about its vague contents. It did, however corroborate Denis Tanner's official statement to Sergeant Jim Fry.

Sergeant Fleming contacted another pathologist, Dr Terry Schultz, at Wangaratta Hospital to ask him to review Dr Dyte's report and to appear as an expert witness. Schultz was known to the police and Coroner in Shepparton, and had performed many autopsies for them in the past. Dyte's report was sent to him a few days before the inquest.

Before appearing at the inquest, Dr Schultz felt it important to visit Dr Dyte, even though Dyte was very ill, to tell him he had been called to give evidence. He wanted to discuss his review of Dr Dyte's report, as his opinion differed from Dr Dyte's in some areas. Dr Dyte, however, stood by his original report and the supplementary one given to Detective Sergeant Welch.

In a letter to me, Terry Schultz says, 'I mentioned only that I had been called to give evidence. I do not recall his exact words, but I gained the impression that he had no change of mind, and the subject was dropped. He was very ill at the time.'

Sergeant Fleming also tracked down Gerry O'Donnell, the ambulance officer, in his new job in Melbourne and took a statement from him on 17 October, the day before the inquest. He asked him to attend the inquest in Mansfield the next day.

That night Fleming drove up to Mansfield with a small folder containing fifteen statements and some incomplete evidence to be presented to the Coroner in relation to the alleged suicide of Jennifer Ruth Tanner.

8

The First Inquest: Mansfield

THERE WAS a small audience at the first inquest into Jennifer's death. It was now eleven months since she was buried, and few people were interested apart from immediate family, a couple of friends and those who had to appear and give evidence. In any event, it isn't usual practice for spectators to attend an inquest unless they have 'an interest', that is, an actual reason to be there.

The inquest was convened before Mr Hugh Adams SM on 18 October 1985 at a Mansfield church hall, which was used because the old red-brick courthouse was being renovated.

Although Jenny's inquest had taken an unusually long time to prepare, the process more or less followed the usual guidelines for developing a brief for the Coroner. Witnesses were interviewed and their statements taken down in a laborious longhand, then typed up for inclusion in the brief that eventually found its way into Senior Sergeant Peter Fleming's hands.

At an inquest, either a barrister or a fairly senior police officer is appointed from the Coroner's office to assist the Coroner and ask questions in court on behalf of the Crown. At Jenny's inquest this role was fulfilled by Sergeant Fleming. When witnesses are giving evidence, the clerk or the officer assisting the Coroner reads their earlier statements to them for confirmation. They are then questioned about their statements and any other relevant issues. If the Coroner has questions of his own to ask, he can direct them to anyone in the court, not just the witness giving evidence at the time.

At Jenny's inquest there were fourteen witnesses, two lawyers— Mr Joe Gullaci for Laurie and Denis Tanner and Mr Rodney Ryan for the Blake family—and a few spectators. Most of the witnesses sat in the court while others gave evidence. Roz Smith had been brought down from Queensland, Denis Tanner and Gerry O'Donnell came from Melbourne and Dr Terry Schultz from Wangaratta. Sworn depositions from a number of minor witnesses formed part of the evidence submitted in the Coroner's brief. Kath Blake insisted on attending.

The court commenced at 10.10 a.m. The first person to give evidence was Senior Sergeant Ian Welch. Like all the witnesses who followed him, he was sworn in and his statement was read to him. He told the court about the events on the night, his investigations in Mansfield the following day and the visit to Dr Dyte in April 1985.

When Welch outlined his conversation with Dr Dyte, there was a loud disturbance at the back of the court. Hughie Almond, who had been leaning forward and straining to hear the last few words of evidence, turned to Curly McCormack and cried out in an anguished voice, 'Two bullets! Oh, my God, did he say *two* bullets?' Curly nodded, pale and serious. 'Two bullets! Two bullets!' The words buzzed around the court like small missiles. Many people were stunned.

Mr Adams banged his gavel, making everyone jump. 'Silence in this court! If there is any more disturbance at the back I will ask you to remove yourselves from this chamber. Please continue, Sergeant Welch.'

Ian Welch told the court he was satisfied Sergeant Tanner's alibi for his whereabouts on the night had been substantiated. There followed some questions about his visit to Dr Dyte, in particular discussions with Dr Dyte about one bullet maybe 'nicking' the brain and the other causing a greater injury. Welch agreed that Dr Dyte was unable to say which bullet entered first and which bullet entered second. Welch told the court he had been in charge of the investigation and 'had overall supervision—until he was satisfied'. He was satisfied Laurie Tanner was not involved in his wife's death.

Welch was not questioned about why he had not ordered photos be taken on the night or why he didn't go to Mansfield until the following day, or whether any subsequent investigations had been initiated on the rifle. Nor was he questioned about his assertion that

Dr Dyte had said in his amended statement 'there were powder burns on both hands'.

The second witness was Laurie Tanner, who had little to add to the two interviews he had already given the police.

His statement said that when he arrived home, 'I noticed through the lounge room, which was open, Jenny on the couch, covered in blood and the rifle between her legs. I didn't think there was anything I could do for her. I believed, from the way she looked, she was dead. I'm not sure what exactly I did but I'm pretty sure I checked the baby and found that he was asleep in bed. I had not gone into the lounge room apart from when I went through the lounge to check the baby's room, to check that he was OK. I came out along the passage. I think I'd left the door between the kitchen and lounge open.'

There was a quick indrawn breath from Kath Blake as she turned angrily to her husband. Mr Adams made no move to stop their whispering.

Laurie told the court he could not think of any reason why Jenny would take her own life except that she was depressed after the birth of Sam.

Senior Sergeant Fleming asked Laurie whether he attached any significance to the poster on the fridge, and whether Jenny had been reading articles about suicide in the *Police Journal*, which was still delivered to Denis Tanner's old address at Springfield. Laurie did not feel either was very important. Fleming then asked, 'Did your wife ever mention the visit of your brother Denis on the 22 October to you?

'22 October—that'd be the night that I was at Apex, is that the night you're referring to? Yes, she did.'

'Did she say anything about Denis's movements whilst he was there that night?'

'She said he'd delivered some stuff to his house, which is next door, the old house he's renovating and he—which was a common thing for him to do, he walked across and—to say 'hello' and I was at Apex that night. He played with the baby, which he—he hadn't been settling down too well because of the daylight saving and had a cup of coffee or something with Jenny and general discussion, I think, and waited around for me—I'm not sure what time he waited till, but I got home fairly late that night from Apex and he'd gone.'

Laurie was questioned by Mr Ryan about his wife's height, the height of the couch seat and the length of the BRNO rifle. He did not know any of the measurements.

Mr Gullaci spent some time eliciting information about Jenny's bad moods, her unwillingness to care for Sam and Laurie's desire for her to consult a doctor. Then he asked, 'Did you notice any change in her attitude towards you—say, if somebody arrived at the house, what was her reaction to some third party coming to the house?'

'Well, her moods could change like that,' Laurie replied. 'She might be in a bad mood, a depressed mood or a bad mood and if someone came in, my parents or her parents, or one of her sisters or my family, she could just change like that and act like a normal person.'

'Would she try to put a happy face on for people who came into the house?'

'She did.'

The Coroner completed the cross-examination with a question about Jenny's visit to Dr Patience.

'You say your wife did not like to care for the baby and she was not keen to get up at night to attend to him. Would it come as a surprise to you that she had consulted Dr Patience in Benalla in respect of seeing whether she could become pregnant again?'

'I've since learned about that,' Laurie replied. 'She did that without my knowledge.'

'There was no discussion between her and yourself?'

'I'd tried—well, I was keen to have another child and she wasn't. She was worried about having another Caesarean birth.'

'So that consultation with Dr Patience was unbeknown to you.'

Laurie was also obviously unaware that Jenny had told Roz Smith she was hoping for another baby in the summer of 1985. It seems strange that she discussed this with her friend and not her husband.

Laurie's account of the times he arrived at and left the McCormacks' house differed from the other evidence, but counsel didn't follow up these discrepancies. Mr Ryan didn't pursue Jenny's reputed fear of guns or her knowledge of how to use them. He didn't ask the question that had struck me when I first read Laurie's evidence: how could he be so sure that Jenny was dead from approximately ten metres away? Why didn't he check her pulse or her breathing—or even look closely at her?

∞

Hugh Almond was the next witness. He was obviously still distressed about the entire episode, and had no new information to give the court, other than some specifics about the position in which he found the rifle and the location of the white towel on the couch.

∞

Gerry O'Donnell, the ambulance driver, was the first professional on the scene and 'took notes on an ambulance case sheet because of the circumstances of the death'. In his observations he said he had 'noted at 22.44 hours that she had no pulse, no blood pressure and was not breathing. Her right pupil was dilated, fixed and glazed. I couldn't make an observation of her left eye. I didn't attempt any treatment.'

As there was no blood elsewhere in the room he was satisfied the body had not been moved and assumed she had shot herself in the mouth. The body was not moved until Dr Ross Gilham arrived and certified death.

The Coroner had a question for Gerry O'Donnell: 'Just one matter, Mr O'Donnell. You say the rifle was between her knees and her knees were apart?'

'Yes. Apart and she was slumped down in the couch with her head to the left.'

'Where was her left hand?'

'I don't recall whether it was actually holding the barrel or was over the barrel,' Gerry said, 'but I observed on the case sheet that it was holding the firearm. It may have been over it. She may have been holding it. I don't recall.'

'Yes, that was leading to my next question as to whether the fingers were tightly around the barrel or not. You do not know?'

'I don't know.'

Constable Don Frazer was sworn in next. He said that he thought the body could have been moved at some stage.

'I also observed the cushion resting on the seat and armrest of the couch to the left of the deceased. There was congealed blood on the left thigh of Tanner, which, along with the bloodstains I have already outlined, indicated to me that Tanner, at one stage, had actually laid on the couch with her head on the cushion. There were smeared blood-stains on this cushion.'

Much was made of the poster Don Frazer removed and the fact that Jenny read copies of the *Police Journal*. The main source of inter-est was because the issue from which the poster was torn had featured an article on suicides. Copies of these articles were submitted to the court as supporting material. The inference was that Jenny might have been contemplating suicide for some time, and possibly considering taking Sam with her.

♋

Every participant in the inquest was tensely waiting for Senior Constable Bill Kerr's turn in the witness box. Bill had been through a rough eleven months. By now, he was out of favour at Mansfield Police Station and with Denis Tanner, although Denis probably regarded him more as an irritation than a serious threat. Some of the witnesses present—in particular, Denis Tanner and Roz Smith—were there because of his persistent nudging.

Bill's statement summarising all the events at Springfield was read to the court. Jenny's family sat transfixed, hearing the full details for the first time. Bill's sketch of Jenny was produced as Exhibit 4. He was questioned about why tests were not conducted on the deceased at the time or on the rifle later on.

After Bill explained the absence of any testing, Fleming continued, 'Now, did you see any powder burns on either side of the hand? Or hands?'

'I'm not dead sure what a powder burn looks like,' Bill replied. 'I can't say that I did.'

'Did you discuss with anyone the possibility of getting paraffin wax tests done in relation to the feet and the hands?'

'No, I haven't discussed paraffin wax. I—it's the first time I've heard about it,' Bill confessed.

'Had you mentioned to the detective, Sergeant Welch, anything in relation to your opinion of how the trigger was pulled or pushed?'

'One theory that was mentioned was that it may have been operated by the toe of the foot or alternately [sic] by reaching down with the hand. I don't think the deceased had a sufficient reach to operate the trigger mechanism by hand.'

'Well, in the position you found the body, did you consider it possible that the firearm trigger mechanism could have been pulled or pushed by a toe of the deceased?'

'Yes, it is possible.'

Fleming then asked, 'How many wounds did you see on the body, firearm wounds? Or appeared to be firearm wounds?'

'One on each hand and one in the forehead,' Bill replied.

'What observations did you make of the deceased's mouth area?'

'The mouth area of the deceased—there was a fair bit of congealed blood with some type of whitish content, which I took to be possible brain tissue which had flowed down through the nose and then out the mouth. I've seen other bodies where similar things have occurred and that has been what it was. That's what I took it to be—possibly brain tissue that had flowed down, either through the back of the mouth or more than likely down through the nasal passages.'

'That tissue you observed, could that possibly be part of the hand tissue?'

'That I couldn't say.'

Mr Ryan then asked a series of questions about the condition of the BRNO rifle on the night and whether any tests had been conducted on it since.

'Have you measured the length of the rifle since this incident, Senior Constable?'

'Yes, I have,' Bill replied, 'but the exact measurement I can't recall.'

'In the vicinity of 104 centimetres?'

'That figure rings a bell, yes.'

'Do you agree with the estimate of height of the front edge of the couch given by Mr Laurie Tanner of approximately fifteen inches?'

'That would be approximately right, yes.'

'And would you agree,' Mr Ryan asked, 'that the deceased's height would have been—I think Mr Tanner said slightly in excess of five feet three inches?'

'I would say five feet four, five feet five.'

'You were the one that ejected the bullet from the breech of the rifle?'

'That's correct.'

'At the time you ejected the spent cartridge, do you recall how much force, strength you had to use to actually open the bolt action and cause the ejection motion?'

'The exact amount of force, no,' Bill replied, 'but it was just a normal bolt-action rifle operation.'

'It would be fair to say, would it not, that a degree of strength was necessary to open the breech?'

'Yes,' Bill said. 'It takes a certain amount of pressure to release the—open the breech. You've first got to move the bolt up and then slide the bolt backward.'

'Yes, so there is also a—if I may put it this way—a thinking component necessary to actually open that breech, and eject a bullet and thus cause another bullet to come into the breech?' Mr Ryan asked.

'Yes, there's a certain amount of knack to it.'

Mr Ryan then quizzed Bill about the injuries to Jenny's hands. Bill agreed that Dr Dyte's report was consistent with her having been shot in the back of the hands. He added, 'There was a fair bit of blood around the hand when I observed the wounds and I didn't remove any of the blood to have a close examination.'

'You have indicated that you felt that the deceased was not tall enough to lean down and activate the trigger by hand from the position where you found the body?'

'That's correct.'

Bill seemed ill at ease when Mr Gullaci cross-examined him about his original belief that Jenny had suicided.

'Now, Mr Kerr, you, as an experienced police officer, concluded on the night that you attended the scene, that this was an unfortunate suicide?'

'The initial picture that we had, when I rang the Detective Sergeant, I described the picture to him. It appeared on the face of it to be what appeared to be a suicide, yes.'

'… The police view was that no tests were done on the rifle because experienced police were all of the opinion that Jenny had shot herself … That is so, is it not?'

'Um'mm.'

'Yes. So the police department, acting on your observations and Mr Frazer's observations, took the view apparently that there was no need to have any further tests carried out. That is the situation?'

'I wouldn't quite put it that way,' Bill said, apparently coming back to life. 'I asked for the tests to be done on the rifle but they said that there was no necessity for it to be done.'

Mr Gullaci immediately dropped this line of questioning and turned his interest to powder burns. This series of questions was crucial; Gullaci was attempting to discredit Bill Kerr as an expert witness and deflect any inference that someone other than Jenny could have been involved in her death.

'Now,' Gullaci began, 'you indicated that you did not know what a powder burn was like. On this diagram you drew there appears to be powder burns. What do they refer to?'

'A couple of black marks that are on the towel,' Bill replied. 'I took it that they may be powder burns because I expected that black marks would be the result of a powder burn, particularly on a white cloth.'

'So because there were a couple of black marks there you decided they were powder burns?'

'It's only an assumption on my part,' Bill admitted.

'You have never seen powder burns before, I think you indicated?'

'That's correct.'

'You did not—would not know what they looked like?'

'No.'

'And for all you know, they could leave different types of marks?'

'That's right.'

'That is the situation, is it not?'

'Yes,' Bill confirmed.

'So again that is just simply an assumption on your behalf that they were powder burns. It was just simply a guess, was it not?'

'That's true. Yes.'

After confronting Bill Kerr with seven separate questions about the powder burns on his drawing and getting the same answer each time, Mr Gullaci turned away. This is a common and very powerful tactic used by lawyers to ram home an answer that is favourable to their position.

For all his lack of expertise on the matter of powder burns, I couldn't help noticing that Bill Kerr was very careful in his responses to the previous series of questions from Mr Gullaci. He mentioned several times, directly and indirectly, that he had in fact asked Ian Welch to have tests carried out on the rifle. He also was careful to say, 'It appeared on the face of it to be what appeared to be a suicide'—a fairly ungrammatical but very significant way of expressing his doubts, then and at the time of the inquest. Neither lawyer followed this up.

The Coroner asked Bill what he thought of Don Frazer's suggestion that Jenny might have been lying down on the couch at some stage.

'It is possible,' Bill said. 'The amount of blood that was over the couch—there were blood spatters down to the right-hand side of the couch and dripping—what appeared to be blood drips down the side of the couch over the end of it—possibly where one of the arms or hands of the deceased had been thrown by the impact of the—of one of the shots. It is possible that, because there's been two shots fired, the first shot would've undoubtedly thrown the body around to some extent. That could be the reason why the smears are on the cushion and the drips down one side of the couch.'

'From your observations and investigations, is there any evidence to suggest the deceased may have left the couch at any stage?'

'No.'

The Coroner then followed up his earlier question to Gerry O'Donnell about the position of Jenny's left hand: 'And you say from your observations the thumb and the forefinger of the left hand were round the barrel near the top of the stock?'

'That's correct.'

'Were those two fingers gripped tightly around, or were they loose?'

'No. Slightly apart and just resting on the webbing between the forefinger, and the thumb was actually resting on the wooden stock.'

'The fingers were not gripped?' the Coroner asked again.

'They were not gripped, no.'

'Was there no sign of any struggle or forced entry to the premises?'

'No, there wasn't.'

∞

Dr Ross Gilham arrived at the court just before he was due to give his evidence. He took the stand and was sworn in.

His statement described Jenny's injuries with clinical composure. He was then questioned by Sergeant Fleming.

'Doctor, at the time that you examined the deceased at the home, how many wounds to the forehead did you observe?'

'Well, I didn't examine the body closely and I couldn't be certain how many wounds there were to the head.'

'Did you observe any powder burns to any part of the deceased's body?'

'No, but I didn't examine the body with that in mind,' Gilham said. 'I felt that my role was to confirm the death of the deceased. And I didn't undertake any full examination.'

Mr Ryan then asked, 'Doctor, you did not actually examine the inside of the mouth of the deceased?'

'No, not in any detail,' Gilham replied. 'I did look inside. I didn't have a torch. It was difficult to see. And I really didn't want to interfere with things at all. I didn't feel that was my role and I thought that I might only obscure the facts and so I didn't pursue any detailed examination.'

Mr Ryan changed the subject. 'Only one other thing, I think, Doctor—you say that you noticed the injuries to the hands. Did you observe those or did you look at those in the lights of bullet wounds?'

'No, I just repeat what I said before, that I didn't undertake any full examination and I just noticed that there were injuries to the hands but, again, I didn't interfere in any way.'

'You are not in a position to indicate which—if there was entry wounds or exit wounds or which side of the hands they were on?'

'No, I'm sorry.'

Later, when I interview Dr Gilham, he tells me that he gave all his evidence to this inquest without knowing there had been two bullets in Jenny's brain. He says he first discovered this crucial piece of information eleven years later in the *Sunday Age*. When I express incredulity that this could be so, he says he has given evidence at many inquests during his career and has rarely waited around to hear others' evidence—it would have kept him away from his practice too long.

Perhaps he would have known about the second bullet on the night if he'd examined her more thoroughly, or if he'd found out soon afterwards he might have been able to recall more details about the room and Jenny's presentation. As it was, he examined Jenny after spending the evening at a dinner party. He did not have a torch. He did not examine her in any detail, and merely pronounced her dead, because that is what he'd been asked to do.

By the time of the inquest Dr Peter Dyte was near death. In

accordance with Peter Fleming's request, Dr Terry Schultz had reviewed the autopsy results for the court.

Dr Schultz's evidence is mainly significant because he was the first expert who publicly said what others may have been thinking—it was unlikely Jenny could have pulled the BRNO trigger herself after receiving one bullet wound to her brain.

He told the court, 'The possibility of the wounds being self-inflicted cannot be excluded and there are many cases in the literature of suicide with multiple gunshot wounds. However, in my opinion, I think it unlikely that the deceased would not have lost consciousness after the first wound to the head, whichever of the two it may have been. In addition, it is noted that the rifle was a bolt-action type requiring manual operation.'

In deference to his more experienced colleague, however, and also bearing in mind Dr Dyte's reference to the well-regarded texts by Dr Plueckhahn and the fact that Dr Schultz had not examined Jenny himself, he did concede that self-inflicted injury could not be altogether ruled out.

Dr Geoffrey Patience was next.

Senior Sergeant Fleming read out a letter Dr Patience had sent to the police in response to a request for his opinion about Jenny's state of mind. This was the letter in which Dr Patience said Jenny's 'demeanour during the pregnancy was not the usual joyful expectancy of most of my young prospective mothers'.

Dr Patience's letter went on: 'Her labour was long and she eventually required a Caesarean section because she was obstructed. She was delivered of a live and healthy boy on 14 February 1983. Immediately post-operatively she did well and I reviewed her some five weeks later when this state continued and her young son was thriving. I saw her twice with her son Sam subsequently for minor problems regarding him. He was a healthy and normal boy. However, her demeanour remained unchanged. She was having no joy in raising her infant son.'

Dr Patience had last seen Jenny on 30 July 1984, when she asked him to arrange an X-ray test to determine whether she would require a Caesarean section if she had a second child. He wrote that she 'seemed to be reasonably happy to embark upon a further pregnancy in the future'. She later phoned to get the results of her tests, which showed she would need to have another Caesarean.

The doctor concluded, 'It could be argued, in retrospect, that her pre-morbid personality was further depressed by her pregnancy, but I at no time either suspected or had intimated by Jennifer that she ever intended to take her own life.'

Mr Ryan said to Dr Patience, 'I suggest to you the fact that you had been told that she committed suicide no doubt coloured, be it subconsciously, your view when you were asked for a report?'

'Perhaps to a small degree, yes,' Dr Patience admitted.

'And in fact were you asked specifically by the police in relation to such matters as ante-natal [Mr Ryan probably meant post-natal] depression? Did they raise those with you?'

'M'mm.'

Then Mr Gullaci began his examination. He asked, 'Doctor, you know of course the husband of the deceased, Laurie Tanner?'

'I do.'

'And did he express to you some concern about her behaviour or her depression prior to her death? Did he express to you a desire that she come and see you and seek some assistance?'

'He did.'

'And it was apparent, was it not, that she did not want to do that? And I suppose it follows that if she did not want to come to you for assistance, it was very difficult for you to offer that assistance?'

'That is correct,' Patience replied.

Mr Gullaci asked several more questions in this vein, then the Coroner himself stepped in.

'Doctor, when you last saw Mrs Tanner on the 30th of July of last year, in relation to her depression, what was her condition then?'

'I would say it had slightly improved due to the fact that she had come to consult me regarding these tests. Initially, after I saw her immediately post-natally, she indicated she wasn't keen to embark upon another pregnancy fairly soon, and several times when she came over with her son. Yet on the last occasion, on the 30th of July, she came over with that view in mind and her mood did seem to be slightly less depressed then.'

Dr Patience's evidence was significant because he verified Laurie's description of Jenny's 'depressed' demeanour—although the picture he presented was hardly that of a woman on the verge of suicide.

∞

The next witness called was Sergeant Denis Tanner, who was mainly present to clear up any suspicion cast upon him by Roz Smith's statement to the police. The statement he made to Sergeant Jim Fry of Homicide on 20 May 1985 was read to the inquest.

Denis said he had known Jenny for somewhere between twelve and fifteen years, since before she married Laurie. Denis was best man at their wedding. He outlined the family's property arrangements: 'Shortly after the marriage the deceased and my brother moved into Springfield. It was about this time I relinquished any ownership rights in so far as Springfield was concerned and with the capital I gained from this settlement, I commenced the partnership with my parents in relation to Stanleys, leaving Laurie the sole owner of Springfield with finance commitments.'

Denis's statement went on to discuss Jenny's relationship with him and his wife Lynne: 'Also during the period of the last five years or so, both the deceased and Laurie visited my wife and myself in Melbourne at my home address. Because of the work commitment of Laurie and the deceased's shopping needs, it was not uncommon for her to attend without Laurie. Before she had baby Samuel, she often used to visit us and after the birth she often stayed several days at a time. We all got on very well. It became apparent to both my wife and myself that something was bothering the deceased, because there was a definite change in her following the birth of the child. Before the birth she was a normal open person with an easy-going nature. After the birth she progressively changed. My wife more particularly was concerned about her.

'I have been asked to recall if I visited Bonnie Doon on the 22nd of October, 1984. By looking at my diary, I believe this to be the night I drove to Bonnie Doon to deliver some plaster bags and cement to Stanleys. I unloaded this and finished just before dark and walked across to Springfield and saw the deceased as she came out the back door. We spoke and I went inside and told her what I was doing there. She told me she was having a lot of trouble putting Samuel, the boy, down of an evening because of the recent change over to daylight saving. The deceased also told me that Laurie was at an Apex meeting.

'I waited at Springfield until 10.00 p.m. as I thought Laurie may get home by then. Whilst waiting the deceased and I had general conversation and I had coffee. I also played with Samuel for some time. Nothing appeared to be out of the ordinary. I did not mention to the deceased that I had gone there to go shooting. I told her why I was there and that if Laurie came home in time I'd say hello to him. I did not look at any of Laurie's guns. I'd no reason.

'My movements on that night were consistent with my usual pattern, as it was on many occasions that I would go to Bonnie Doon, and still do, unannounced.

'I didn't inquire into the deceased's private life and she did not volunteer anything that I can recall that was out of the ordinary.'

On the night of Jenny's death, Denis had phoned Springfield at about 5.30 p.m. After exchanging a few words with Jenny, he spoke to Laurie about a young mare that he wanted to have broken in.

'Later on that evening', his statement continued, 'at about 7.45 p.m. or 8.00 p.m., I went to a bingo game at the Carmelite Hall at Richardson Street, Middle Park. The hall is generally full and was so on this night. I am a regular visitor. Jack O'Hanlon MC'd the proceedings.

'I arrived home at about 10.00 p.m. to 10.15 p.m., checked our newborn baby and went to bed.

'At about 5.30 a.m. I answered the door and police told me about the deceased.

'As soon as possible and after making family telephone calls, my wife, baby and self went to Bonnie Doon and later to Mansfield Police Station.

'Since this unhappy occasion I have assisted my brother in any matter that he required, both in his personal grief and the general running of the property.

'I have absolutely no knowledge as to whether the deceased was going to part from Laurie, she had never mentioned anything remotely similar and likewise my brother had never mentioned anything along these lines.

'I have been asked to comment if during the course of my brother making a statement to police, I said to him words similar to "Don't go into your private life." As to whether they were the exact words, I'm not sure, but I know my brother, he is a sincere type, rather shy, and I explained to him that what he says in his statement would be read out in court and I was aware of private matters between him and the deceased which he had told me, and I considered it was not directly relevant to what had happened, because it was an intimate matter, solely confined to a husband/wife relationship. It was on that basis that I said words similar to "Don't go into your private life." I also added that what he said would be public, and not necessarily just for whoever was actually in court.

'I share the thoughts of my brother Laurie, that we are at a loss, as is all the family, to why this unfortunate and unforeseen event occurred.'

Senior Sergeant Fleming probed Denis on his alleged visit to Springfield in October: 'You mentioned that by checking your diary you can recall having visited Bonnie Doon on 22nd of October?'

'Yes.'

'Was that your official police department diary, or was it a personal diary?'

'No, it was a personal diary.'

'Yes, and what entry did you have in your personal diary?'

The question seemed to catch Denis off-balance. 'There's no entry, it was just the—whilst I was making the statement there was no calendar available, so I just counted the weeks back and worked out that it would've been on that night. That was the night that I did go.'

'On that particular night when you were at your brother and sister-in-law's place, you mention that there was some discussion in relation to the child finding it difficult to be put down because of daylight saving?'

'Yes.'

'What did your sister-in-law actually say to you in relation to daylight saving?'

'She said that she was having troubles with Sam going down for the extra hour, or the hour earlier, because his routine had been broken, from the normal time that he was due to go down.'

'Now, that discussion took place on the 22nd of October, from your recollection is that right?' Fleming was pushing this quite hard; I wondered what he was driving at.

'That's right.'

'Are you aware of when daylight saving started in 1984?'

'No, I'm not,' Denis said. 'It's only from recollection and—'

'Well, if I put to you that the daylight saving period was between 28 October 1984 until 3 March 1985, do you have any comment to make in relation to the discussion about daylight saving problems?'

'No. Probably if that was the date, it may have been the following Monday. As I said, I had no entry in the diary, it's just that I went back over the Mondays. I knew it was a Monday night because of the fact that Laurie had been to Apex, and that occurs on Monday nights*.'

'So it was a reconstruction more than anything, is that right?'

'That's correct.'

'Yes.' Fleming now changed tack: 'Did you speak to your brother about the death?'

'Yes, I have.'

'And is there anything in the discussions you have had with your brother that has not been said here today, that you think is important for the Coroner to know?'

'I probably can't enlighten the matter any further, except that just from conversations I've had with my brother over a period of time since the birth, but there was a distinct change in the nature of the deceased.'

---

* Apex meets in Mansfield every second Monday, not weekly.

'Had your brother discussed any marital problems that he was having?'

'I hadn't finished, I was just—'

'Sorry.'

'In as much as at various times, for various reasons, she would break out into—have arguments, it'd be—she'd use a lot of bad language, which was, in his opinion, out of character. She would behave in an irrational manner. This had all been discussed between Laurie and myself because there was something wrong and he was looking for some way he could seek treatment for it. Jennifer wouldn't go to a doctor for treatment because she believed nothing could be done to assist her. It'd be a thing that'd just fade away. That's all.'

Fleming asked again, 'Had your brother discussed any marital problems that he and his wife were having with you?'

'No, he had not. I considered his relationship to be a reasonably normal relationship, but the fact that she was experiencing some problems with regard to the birth was no marital problem, it was just a thing that was there.'

'Right. You were at Bonnie Doon on 22 October or thereabout?'

'The Monday night?'

'The night that your brother was at the Apex meeting, what did you do when you were at your brother's place?'

'I had a cup of coffee,' Denis said. 'We spoke about the baby and the difficulties she was having with putting him down—she had to at that stage put him down at the older time, which was the time he was used to, and played with him for a while and we just generally talked. I had quite a good relationship with Jennifer and Laurie, as did my wife.'

'Did you see any firearms at the premises that particular evening?'

'No, I didn't.'

'Was there any mention of firearms?'

'No. I knew where the firearms were.'

'Did you leave a message with your sister-in-law to give your brother?'

'Just to say hello, which was the normal thing.'

Mr Ryan began his examination. He challenged Denis's version of

Jenny's emotional state. 'You expressed the view that your brother had been concerned at what you called his wife acting in an irrational manner?'

'That's right.'

'You heard your brother asked about those things this morning; he did not put it as high as that, did he?'

'I heard him. It depends how you—'

'Well, you heard him, did you not? And he did not use that term this morning did he?'

'I heard him. It depends—as I was about to say—Not that I recall, no.'

'Do you think it may be somewhat of an overstatement on your part?' Mr Ryan pressed.

'No,' Denis said. 'I was only relying on what I'd been told. But as I said—or as I should've possibly said, it never occurred in my presence, ever.'

This was a remarkable admission, but Mr Ryan didn't pursue it. Instead, he returned to his earlier question. 'Well, could you be mistaken then in the fact that your brother used that particular word "irrational"?'

'It was probably a word that I'd used to describe what he'd told me, I would say.'

'I am putting to you, are you swearing that he used that word to you?'

'No, I didn't say that he used it.'

Mr Gullaci's first question took the heat off Denis: 'Mr Tanner, as I understood your evidence you did not purport to give evidence that your brother had said that her behaviour was irrational, is that the situation?'

'That's right.'

'That was your assessment of what he had told you?'

'That's correct.'

'And you made that assessment having known the deceased for a number of years?'

'Yes.'

'Having enjoyed a close relationship?'

'That's right.'

'Over that period of time,' Gullaci emphasised. 'And she had been a—prior to this—to the child being born, she had been a frequent visitor to your place, had she not?'

'On numerous occasions, yes.'

'She would often go to Melbourne to go shopping?'

'That's right.'

'And stay at your place?'

'For sometimes a week or two weeks at a time.'

'And subsequent to the birth did those visits continue or did they stop or did they slow down or what was the situation?' Gullaci asked.

'She came down—she still kept coming down, but towards probably—getting this in the right perspective, she did come down on a number of occasions after the birth and she stayed with the baby, and she also stayed with Laurie and the baby. They're two occasions that spring to mind.* She—I think one or two occasions she did come to Melbourne and stayed at her grandmother's place because geographically it was more convenient for her on that side of the city.'

'Yes, thank you, I have no further questions.'

Again, Mr Gullaci used his 'broken record' technique to ensure those listening were left in no doubt of the good relationship between the Tanner brothers' families.

There were several things about Denis Tanner's evidence that made me uneasy. None of them were challenged by Sergeant Fleming, Mr Ryan or the Coroner.

In his discussions with Ian Welch the morning after Jenny's death, Denis said Jenny and Laurie had 'only the normal family quarrels', but in his inquest evidence he cited different reasons to explain why he advised Laurie not to be completely open with police in his statement.

From the conflicting versions of his whereabouts on the night of

---

* Sam was 21 months old when Jenny died, yet Denis could recall only two visits since he was born.

Jenny's death (of which Fleming, at least, was aware) it seems Denis may have done some checking about the trots after he gave his statement to Bill Kerr. Bookmaker John O'Hanlon's vague recollection was the only supporting evidence for Denis's sworn statement regarding his whereabouts on the night Jenny died. The police have said no-one answered the door at Denis's home between around midnight and 5.30 a.m.

Denis also mentioned that Jenny made frequent overnight trips to Melbourne without Laurie before Sam was born and sometimes stayed for one or two weeks. What was she doing all that time in Melbourne?

And what were Denis and Jenny discussing for a couple of hours at Springfield during his visit in October?

It is interesting that Mr Ryan did not challenge Denis Tanner about Roz Smith's statement or follow up his comment that Jenny's alleged 'irrational' behaviour 'never occurred in my presence, ever'. Again, we only seem to have Laurie's word, supported by Dr Patience, that Jenny was depressed and moody—no-one else had ever observed it at first hand.

∞

Angie McCormack was the next to give evidence. After telling the court she had known Jenny for about five years, she recalled the phone conversation she'd had with Jenny.

'I suppose we spoke for about twenty minutes or so. I can remember that I had said that I had not read any books or got around to doing anything much in relation to preparing for the birth of my child. Jenny said that I should go to classes that are held at the Benalla Hospital and Curly, my husband, should go to the films that are held in Benalla. She sounded quite cheerful and said that she would drop some stuff in to me.

'I noticed that she seemed hard to get off the phone. I had to say things like "I've got to go and get Curly's tea." It's usually Jenny that cuts the conversation short. One thing that I noticed odd was the fact that she never mentioned the Mansfield Show, which was only a couple of days away. We had put a lot of work into it and she never mentioned it. Jenny often went to Melbourne shopping, yet she often said that she never went out anywhere.'

Angie told the court 'Laurie left soon after 10 p.m. to go home', which she estimated by the fact that Curly had finished eating when Laurie left. She estimated the driving time between her home and Springfield at about twenty minutes.

Jenny's friend from Queensland, Roz Smith, was the final witness for the day. Feeling too upset to sit through all the details of her friend's death, she had waited outside the court since the morning.

Roz described Jenny as 'a person of good temperament and very confident in most matters she was involved with. She was very strong-willed and self-assured. As far as I knew, the deceased and her husband enjoyed a healthy relationship. Jennifer enjoyed living on the farm and had stated on previous occasions to me that she would not like to live in the same situation as I do, i.e. a close neighbourhood.'

She gave details of the peculiar phone call she'd received from Jenny about Denis's evening visit, repeating the information she'd given in her statement earlier in the year. Then she spoke of her conversation with Jenny on the afternoon before her death.

'At approximately 3.30 p.m. on 14 November 1984, I had a further telephone conversation with Jennifer. She did not in any way sound distressed or depressed. She had rung to tell me of an antique jug she had purchased at a clearing sale. We had a discussion about our children and how she was going to tape a record for me at Christmas… she was in high spirits and did not make any mention of the peculiar evening of 22 October 1984. She was just the normal Jenny that I knew. Happy, just talked for ten minutes about our children and just anything in general.'

Mr Ryan did not ask any questions about Jenny's apparent high spirits and plans for the immediate future. Although Roz Smith's evidence seemed to offer Mr Ryan a good opportunity to highlight the different versions of Denis's earlier visit to Springfield, he asked no questions at all.

So Mr Gullaci commenced examination.

'Dr Patience gave evidence this morning that he saw Jennifer on some ten occasions prior to the birth and subsequent to the birth, and that it was his opinion that she was having difficulties with the rearing of the child and that she was suffering from depression, and had done so for some time?'

'Well, she'd never mentioned depression to me,' Roz said.

'No. So she was able to present a side to you which never displayed anything like that?'

'I never heard her sound depressed and the times I'd seen her since Samuel had been born she was normal.'

'And does it come as a surprise to you that it was his professional opinion that she had been suffering from depression, post-natal depression, and things of that sort?'

'Yes—she loved that baby very much.'

Mr Gullaci employed his repeat-question tactics again here, asking Roz five times if she was 'shocked or surprised' about the doctor's evidence, before moving on. He questioned Roz about any knowledge she might have of an article entitled 'Case History of Crimes'* published in the *Police Journal*. Roz knew nothing about any interest Jenny might have displayed in this article. He turned back again to the phone discussion Roz alleged had taken place on 23 October.

'And in respect of this conversation that you say you had with her on the 23rd, how do you know it was the 23rd?'

'We've worked it out with daylight savings with the police in Queensland.'

'What, the police helped you out with the date?'

'No, with a calendar, my husband and I worked it out.'

'But apart from your husband and you working it out, you really do not have any memory about that date, do you?'

---

* 'The Case History of Crimes' article, which was part of the brief prepared for the inquest, consisted of case histories of crimes studied by the police. Exhibit 7 was a series of photocopied pages from this book discussing a case of 'Suicide or murder?' where a woman appeared to have committed suicide by shooting herself twice—but not twice in the head.

'No.'

'And there has never been any other support for that conversation. In other words you did not raise it with her husband?'

'No, I didn't.'

'Her family?'

'No.'

'Or anybody else?'

'No.'

'And of course you are simply recounting what she told you?'

'Yes.'

To work out the date of Denis's visit to Jenny, both Roz Smith and Denis independently worked backwards through their respective diaries and calendars to arrive at a date that seemed right. In both cases they arrived at an impossible conclusion, as daylight saving in Victoria started on 28 October. Regardless of this confusion, the visit took place within three weeks of Jenny's death. If Denis arrived just before dark and left about 10 p.m., as he claimed, he could have stayed at the farmhouse for at least two hours—longer if it was before daylight saving began. Sunset was at around 6.45 p.m. in Mansfield on 22 October and 7.45 p.m. on 29 October. As Jenny usually put Sam to bed between 7 and 7.30 p.m., this would explain her difficulty in getting him to sleep when it was still light. And, depending on the actual date, there might or might not have been an Apex meeting that night. If it wasn't Apex week, where was Laurie until after 10 p.m.?

Why would Jenny make up a story to tell Roz on the phone? There could be no reason for her to invent the details of Denis's visit on either 22 or 29 October. Did Jenny tell Laurie about Denis's visit, and did Laurie take Denis to task over it?

∞

After Roz Smith gave her evidence, the Coroner told the court his office had found Dr Norman Sonenberg, who was in attendance at part of Jenny's autopsy. The Coroner thought it would be a good idea to hear what Dr Sonenberg had to say. He also thought it would be more than timely to conduct some ballistics tests on the BRNO rifle. Bill Kerr's face creased into a quiet little smile. The court was adjourned to a date to be fixed, before the end of the year.

Sergeant Peter Fleming accompanied Bill Kerr to the police station, where they met Detective Chief Inspector Tom O'Keefe to collect the BRNO rifle for examination at last.

9

The First Inquest: Melbourne

PART TWO of Jenny's inquest was held in Melbourne at the imposing buildings in Flinders Street. Most of the key players reassembled in case they were called again to provide further information. Court commenced at 11.07 a.m. on Wednesday 11 December 1985.

The first witness was Dr Norm Sonenberg, Dr Dyte's former assistant, who now occupied a more senior position in another hospital.

His statement was brief.

'I was present during part of the post mortem and discussed the case with Dr Dyte.

'It is my opinion that the deceased suffered two wounds to the head, one of which was fatal affecting the mid-brain, the other appeared to be non-fatal with a path across the base of the brain and not hitting a vital structure.

'During the discussion of the case I was of the opinion that the deceased would probably have been able to inflict both wounds to herself.

'The hand wounds would support the opinion of the muzzle of the weapon being held in the hands of the deceased near the entry sites.'

Sergeant Fleming asked Dr Sonenberg a series of technical questions about Jenny's injuries and their likely effect on her brain functions. Sonenberg explained that Jenny received injuries to three parts of her brain, the frontal lobe, the occipital (back) lobe and the mid-brain. Any minor injury to the mid-brain could be very significant, and the injury sustained in this case would have been sufficient to cause death.

'So death occurred presumably by the second bullet?'

'I would assume so, yes.'

On the question of the hand wounds, Dr Sonenberg said, 'I think the entry wounds were on the palmar surface.'

Fleming obviously felt that this was the wrong answer—after all, the clean-edged wounds had been on the back of Jenny's hands and the 'stellate' (ragged) wounds in the palm. In his interview with Ian Welch, Dr Dyte had interpreted this as indicating that the entry wounds were at the back. Fleming, however, was determined to be polite. He invited Sonenberg to refer to Dr Dyte's report, and they discussed each wound in turn. A few moments of confusion ensued. Commenting on the ragged wound in the palm of the right hand, Dr Sonenberg said, 'I think that is—similar sort of appearance of—except that it's caught a bit of bone as it's gone through.' Was this a flicker of doubt about his earlier assertion that the bullets travelled from front to back? If so, it wasn't followed up. Sergeant Fleming asked Sonenberg if he still believed that the wounds were consistent with Jenny's hand holding the muzzle of the firearm. When Sonenberg stuck by his earlier statement, Fleming moved on to discuss the head wounds again.

The coroner and Mr Ryan both quizzed Dr Sonenberg further on the hand wounds, and both received the answer that an entry wound from a .22 bullet could either be round or stellate, depending on how close the muzzle was at the time. Sometimes the wound was very clean at both entry and exit sites, if the bullet passed only through soft tissue. Eventually, following a series of questions on this issue from Mr Ryan, Dr Sonenberg agreed that he really didn't have any firm policy about whether entry wounds or exit wounds are clean or stellate.

Mr Ryan went on to ask a series of questions intended to throw doubt on whether Jenny would have been able to fire a second shot after the first bullet had entered her brain. He asked whether her sight would have been affected, whether she would have lost consciousness or become confused. Dr Sonenberg's answers were equivocal. At one point he simply said, 'I don't think I have the expertise to tell you exactly what happened to that person.'

Finally, Mr Ryan tried to ask Dr Sonenberg if he thought that a left-handed person could have reloaded a bolt-action rifle with a bullet in her head. This line of questioning was stopped by the Coroner, who suggested that the matter was 'beyond [Dr Sonenberg's] field of expertise'.

Mr Ryan went on to establish that Dr Sonenberg had read, discussed and agreed with everything in Dr Dyte's report. He then obliquely broached the question of the supplementary statement Dr Dyte had made during Ian Welch's visit.

'If, at that stage, you had been approached by the investigating authorities or anybody, would you have added anything to that report?'

'It is not our practice to provide any other comments apart from the pathology findings, unless—'

'No, but I mean—you accepted it totally and would not have added anything to it, is that so?'

'Well, I may have—if I was involved in the case, may have made comments regarding the wounds and the lack or absence of powder burns around the various sites,' Sonenberg conceded.

This was the key question. If there were no powder burns around Jenny's hand wounds, the police theory that she shot herself through her hands the second time was untenable. On the other hand, if there were powder burns on her hands, as Dyte had told Ian Welch, then there shouldn't have been any around the fatal head wound. It is difficult to understand why experienced pathologists did not ask themselves these questions—or, if they did, how they arrived at the answers they gave.

Mr Ryan, however, did not probe Dr Sonenberg about his reply. He was still intent on establishing why the first report hadn't referred to the wounds as being self-inflicted. 'See, there is no reference in that report, Doctor, to self-inflicted gun wounds. Now if that was your view, did you suggest to Dr Dyte that he should have made some reference to self-inflicted gun wounds?'

'It is not our practice, it wasn't our practice up there to indicate on our pathology report that they were self-inflicted. That is not a practice that we—as a pathologist you do.' Sonenberg seemed quite emphatic on this point.

'I see. Well, can you explain then why Dr Dyte made a supplementary report purely and simply to say just that?'

'Probably because he was asked to.'

It seemed a pretty limp answer. In fact, I wasn't impressed with Sonenberg's evidence in general. He agreed with Dyte even though, as he said elsewhere in his evidence, he knew of no photos or X-rays being taken, nor had he examined the whole body. He had merely viewed the head and hand wounds after Dr Dyte had conducted his autopsy.

Mr Gullaci may have felt the same as I did. To recover ground for his expert witness—the only expert witness who had been involved at any stage of the autopsy—he gave Sonenberg the opportunity to emphasise Dr Dyte's professional expertise and outline his own experience in assessing gunshot wounds. Sonenberg had only examined one body that was the subject of a homicide inquiry, but he felt confident enough to say that the fact there were no other signs of violence to Jenny's body suggested that homicide was unlikely.

Although the Coroner probed a bit further about the damage the bullets could have inflicted on Jenny's brain tissue, Mr Fleming and Mr Ryan did not ask any further questions of this witness. I came away from reading the transcript with a sense of opportunity lost.

⚮

Senior Sergeant Adrian John Barry of the Firearms and Toolmarks Branch of Victoria Police had been given the BRNO rifle by Sergeant Fleming and asked for his professional opinion. He was sworn and examined. This was his report.

On 24 October 1985 I received from the liaison officer a sealed bag labelled 1146/856 22/10/85 2.25 p.m., signed P. L. Fleming, Senior Sergeant, 16469, containing the following items:

Item 1 was a .22 calibre BRNO rifle fitted with a telescopic sight.

Item 2 was two .22 calibre fired cartridge cases.

Item 3 a .22 calibre magazine.

I have examined these items.

Tests conducted showed that the barrel of the firearm was at a maximum angle of fifteen degrees from vertical at the last time of discharge.

In cross-examination, Sergeant Fleming asked whether the test results were 'consistent with a firearm being placed with the head tilted down and the firearm being placed against the forehead of a person?'

'Well, it's consistent with an area of damage or wound having been placed against the muzzle when the firearm was in a vertical position.'

'Yes. You state that tests conducted show that the barrel of the firearm was at a maximum angle of 15 degrees from vertical at the last time of discharge?'

'That's correct.'

'How do you ascertain that?'

At this point Senior Sergeant Barry launched into a lengthy and very precise explanation of the peculiarities of .22 calibre bolt-action rifles, which retain a powdered residue in the barrel after being fired. The tests done on the rifle and the deposit of unburnt grains of powder left in the bore indicated conclusively the position of the rifle when last discharged.

'You mentioned you have been called to crime scenes in relation to firearm wounds,' Fleming said. 'Have you been to any crime scenes and examined firearms, where it has been established that they have been suicides, where more than one wound has been self-inflicted?'

'Yes, I have.'

'And have you had any situations where you would have two wounds from a shotgun to the head area of a person?'

'Not to the head area,' Barry conceded. 'But I have seen some diagrams drawn by Mr Dyte in his resumé. I've seen no other photographs whatsoever of the area, but with his description and with the calibre and type of weapon involved, it's been my experience that without outside contamination … for there to be a residue of unburnt grains of powder around the wound, the muzzle would've been within a distance of ten to twelve inches at the time last discharged. For it to be a clean wound, I believe there would have to be interference from some other body or there must have been an obstruction between the muzzle and the wound.'

'In any known suicide matters that you have investigated, is it common to see injuries to a deceased's hands in relation to self-infliction of gunshot wounds?'

'No, I wouldn't say it is common to see injuries in relation to their hands.'

'Well, could we go to the other end of the spectrum and say it is a rarity?'

Barry's reply was cautiously worded: 'That is, in my experience and as per every other section—there's six members in the laboratory related to firearms examination and we do confer, time permitting, on a lot of jobs, and it's something I haven't heard of being a familiar-type process or procedure that's been adopted. It's uncommon to me.'

Mr Ryan asked Sergeant Barry if he thought it would have been difficult for an inexperienced left-handed person to re-load a bolt action rifle.

'It depends solely on the person's familiarity. I'm left-handed—with handling them daily, I have no problems.'

Mr Ryan asked the witness to provide opinions regarding palm and fingerprints and bloodstains on the rifle. Barry refused to be drawn. With a scientist's precision, he felt unable to offer opinions.

Mr Gullaci took over the detailed examination of Sergeant Barry, emphasising his certainty regarding the rifle's last position.

'All the indications that you have been able to ascertain from examining the weapon is that certainly on the last occasion that the weapon was fired it was essentially in a vertical position?'

'That's correct, yes,' Sergeant Barry confirmed.

'There is no indication at all which would suggest that it was in a horizontal position at the time it was being fired?'

'I can only comment on the last time discharged. Without doubt I say that it was in a position of fifteen degrees in either direction of vertical.'

'And it would be, in your experience, it would be consistent with a person having the stock of the weapon on the floor and firing it in an upward direction?'

'That's correct, yes.'

In January 1997, when I reread this evidence for the third time, Sergeant Barry's comments on the rifle leapt off the page at me. I hastened to phone the Firearms and Toolmarks Laboratory to check if my sudden flash of inspiration was possible. Could 'fifteen degrees in either direction of vertical' mean the rifle was pointing downwards rather than upwards? If so, Jenny could have been lying down and been shot from above. Why wasn't this interpretation canvassed at the time? It seems that everyone wanted to believe the nice neat solution of Jenny inflicting the gunshot wounds herself, so some key pieces of the jigsaw were overlooked—or interpreted in a way to make the facts fit the story.

Sergeant Barry gave his evidence very carefully and only answered what he was asked. I believe he didn't want to be the only expert at the inquest to cast doubt on the police theory. I also noticed that the bullets were not on the list of items Sergeant Barry received for examination. How could he match the bullets that killed Jenny with the gun found with her body if he didn't have both items?

After these two witnesses had given evidence it was time for the lawyers and the Coroner to sum up and for the Coroner to deliver his finding.

∞

Mr Ryan opened his address by directly asking the Coroner to make an open finding.

'At the outset, Sir, I make the position of my clients and myself perfectly clear. We are not before this inquiry on any witch-hunt, but purely and simply to ask Your Worship to take into account all those areas of uncertainty and confusion and return an open finding.'

He then summarised the medical, physical and emotional evidence, and pointed out the lack of consultation with Jenny's family regarding her state of mind and her relationship to her infant son. He severely criticised the absence of forensic evidence and the inadequacy of the police investigation. 'The police assumed from the word go that the death was a suicide and acted accordingly,' he said. He drew the Coroner's attention to Dr Terry Schultz's 'grave doubts that the deceased could have fired the second bullet'.

'Unfortunately, probably nobody will ever know exactly what happened on this particular night at this particular place, and we respectfully submit Your Worship should certainly go no further than finding that she died as a result of gunshot wounds to the head, but that the origin of those gunshot wounds should be a matter which should be left open.'

Ryan never suggested the Coroner consider murder. Or even 'person or persons unknown'. True to his brief, he sought an open finding, no more, no less.

When Mr Gullaci rose to his feet he immediately repudiated Mr Ryan's claim that Jenny's parents did not want to blame anyone for the death of their daughter. Gullaci cast Jenny's parents in the role of the bad guys persecuting his clients, and claimed that Mr Ryan had 'asked Your Worship to join the witch-hunt and to leave this unhappy situation in a further unhappy state by ignoring the evidence that Your Worship has heard'.

Mr Gullaci hung his case for suicide mainly on the evidence of Dyte and Sonenberg, 'two eminent pathologists who actually examined the deceased' and he made little of Dr Schultz, 'eminent or otherwise as he may be', because he had not viewed the body.

Mr Gullaci didn't mention Denio, but suggested that his other client, Laurie Tanner, 'bears the greatest burden, in my respectful submission. He is the one who has been subjected to some innuendo, who has been subjected to some questions, he has been subjected to enormous pressures. For you, in my respectful submission, to come to a decision of an open finding would be to fly in the face of the evidence. Credible, cogent, relevant evidence.'

Mr Gullaci then spent some time itemising the scientific expertise of Sergeant Barry and his significant findings. 'Now, if there is some suspicious circumstances which would leave an open finding open to Your Worship, how on earth can that stand with the evidence of Mr Barry, whose opinion has not been challenged?'

After sitting through this performance (which at times reminded me of the trial in *Alice in Wonderland*), the Coroner delivered his finding. He was critical of the development of the brief and the time taken, the police investigation, the autopsy and the lack of involvement of the Homicide Squad. He then went on to say, 'The initial investigating officer should have been alerted to the situation of possible non-self-inflicted injuries because of some unusual features which were evident at the scene … two expended cartridge cases … one entry wound … a manually loading rifle … the absence of any apparent reason at that stage for the deceased to take her life. Other evidence was noted at the scene but the scene was allowed to be cleared and no autopsy performed until the 16th.

'A lot of unanswered questions could have been resolved and suspicion removed from certain persons if proper initial investigations and tests had been instituted by the police officers concerned and the pathologists.'

He expanded on those unanswered questions, saying the medical evidence was inconclusive on the question of whether the wounds were self-inflicted; there was no checking done to corroborate Denis's alibi, and he was at a loss to know why Homicide had not been called in as soon as two bullets were discovered.

He concluded, 'The question then arises, who other than the deceased may have been responsible? The evidence indicates that Mr Laurie Tanner could not have been responsible for his wife's death. And likewise the same situation in respect to Mr Denis Tanner. His movements on the night of the 14th have been investigated. His answers substantiated. I am satisfied that he was in no way responsible.

'There is another possibility: that an unknown person inflicted the wounds. This person would have had to have known the location of the weapon and the magazine. The evidence shows that they were kept in different areas.

'Before a Coroner can return a finding that a person has the intention to die by their own hand and in fact did so, there must be clear and conclusive evidence to that fact. And here in my opinion that is not so.

'And in light of that, I formally find that Jennifer Ruth Tanner died on 14 November 1984 at a property known as Springfield situated on the Maroondah Highway at Bonnie Doon, from the effects of gunshot wounds to the head. And on the evidence adduced I am unable to determine if the wounds were self-inflicted or otherwise.'

After reading this finding, I felt uncomfortable. The Coroner said the killer (if there had been a killer) would have needed to know the exact location of the rifle and the bullets, as they were kept separately. Yet there was no hard evidence to link the rifle with the bullets, as the bullets hadn't been submitted for ballistics tests. It seemed they had been lost or thrown away.

There was so much left unsaid in the evidence at the inquest that I couldn't understand how the Coroner could decisively draw a conclusion that *anyone* could be exonerated from suspicion in this matter. His finding, I was convinced, was flawed.

∞

As people left the courtroom Curly made his way over to Laurie. 'Well, that's not much of a help, is it—an open finding? I don't think much of that meself, eh, Laurie?'

Laurie brusquely pushed him aside. 'It's better that way, Curly. Just leave it be.'

Kath Blake also moved to Laurie's side. 'Laurie, it's good, isn't it? That's all we wanted—an open finding.'

'Well, you got what you wanted, didn't you?' he snapped. 'Now, just leave me and Sam alone!' and turned away before Kath could reply.

June Tanner brushed against Kath as she made her way out.

'I'm so pleased with the open finding, June. What do you think? At least it shows that my girl didn't shoot herself.'

'Well, my two boys didn't do it either! I think we should let her rest in peace and get on with our lives,' said June grimly as she followed Laurie from the court.

Recounting this moment to me so many years later, Kath could still recall how she felt, left standing, wondering what this open finding meant to her life. Nothing was properly over, so how could she ever put it behind her and start again? All she could do was wait and hope something would come up to show once and for all that her girl did not kill herself.

And ten years later, something did.

Part Three

The Hunt

Your mind is like a parachute—it has to be open to function.

DENIS TANNER

10

The Body in the Mineshaft

Mick Bladen had spent his holidays in Bonnie Doon for as long as he could remember. He stayed with a friend of his mother's in McIntyre's Lane, opposite the Bonnie Doon pub, and spent many adventurous hours roaming the foothills of the Strathbogies. When he and his mates were little, they played bushrangers and goldminers; then, as they got older, they'd go bushwalking and shooting rabbits. Mick and his mate Dave Worsley often came up from Melbourne together for a few days to test their mountain-climbing skills and their endurance on treks through the High Country. Sometimes they took their dogs and camping gear and stayed out overnight.

Tuesday 19 July 1995 was one of those nights. Even though it was very cold, they were used to roughing it. Dave was at a loose end, as he'd had to postpone a planned trip to England the following day, so he persuaded Mick to spend a few days up at Doon.

Leaving McIntyre's Lane, they whistled up their dogs, Bundy and Tyson, and headed for the hills. They camped for the night and spent the next day hunting and exploring along the mountain ridges, then headed back towards Bonnie Doon along Prowd's Gully. The hilltops started turning charcoal as the watery sun slid behind the jagged horizon. On a windy ridge top at the head of the gully they came across the remains of the famous Jack o' Clubs mine.

The mine was famous for a number of reasons. Its first owner was an unnamed miner and farmer, and it was called the Jack o' Clubs because of his reputed skill at blackjack games around the campfires.

The mine yielded superfine quality gold, which fetched a premium price of £4 3s 5d per ounce at the Melbourne Mint.

After he died, the ownership of the mine passed to a woman called Sarah Brown, who in 1896 contracted with Albert Jewell to keep working the mine on her behalf for 5 per cent of the takings. He must have had great faith in the mine's potential. As miners are a superstitious lot, and the previous owner had met an unhappy end, the mine's name was changed to the Queen of Hearts. Maybe Albert was a bit taken with his lady boss, Sarah Brown? Locals, however, still knew it as the Jack o' Clubs.

In its early years the mine yielded very rich concentrations of gold in the veins between the soft sandstone and iron-hard quartz that are features of the Strathbogie Ranges. It was quite a big mine, employing several local miners, but eventually they ran into a fault in the rock, which cut the rich vein off. Albert Jewell found a new employer and the mine fell into disrepair. The mine was later taken over by another miner and farmer, James Ryan, who was killed in 1933 by lightning strike while working in a nearby district known as Glen Creek.

Now the only remnant of the mine was a huge native cherry tree growing at its entrance, kept watered by one of the waterlogged shafts near by, and a few shafts going straight down to the old reef workings.

Mick and Dave came across one of these shafts on their descent through Prowd's Gully.

'Have you ever been down one of these?' Dave asked.

'Nah. Too dangerous on yer own. We could go down this one, though, if you want to. We've got a long enough rope and a torch.'

'How far down does it go?'

'I don't know, you dickhead,' Mick replied. 'I just told you, I haven't been down one.'

'Well, how do you know the rope's long enough then, you dork?'

'Let's try it and see, will we?'

Dave hesitated. 'It's nearly four o'clock. It'll be dark soon. What do you think?'

'I think it's going to be bloody dark down there anyway, so who gives a shit? Let's try it.'

Mick wrapped the rope tightly around a solid-looking tree and swung over the lip of the shaft. Using the sides to brace his feet, he slithered down to the first level, approximately ten metres below the surface. He was joined in a rush by Dave, who landed on a pile of rubble a bit to Mick's left. The tunnel inclined downwards to follow the used-up vein of gold. A couple of metres ahead of them was another shaft leading to a second level about five metres further down. They peered through the deep dark, with only the thin line of their torch outlining the depths and the thinner line of their rope connecting them back to the outside world.

'Not much to see, huh?' said Mick with a swagger in his voice he didn't really feel. 'We don't need to go any further down, eh?'

Dave agreed. This was quite dark enough for him. 'What's that over there?' he asked, waving the torch he was carrying. He shone it back into the tunnel they were in, lighting up the area behind where Mick was standing. 'Look. It's red. Is it a jumper? It looks a bit funny, like a bundle of something.'

'Probably some sheep fallen down the shaft. I don't know.'

'Sheep don't wear red jumpers, you dickhead. Here. Have a look.' He couldn't get past Mick in the narrow space, so he handed him the torch. 'Go on. Have a look. I reckon I can see some green underpants.'

'Fair dinkum? Green jocks? Shit, I can see them too—they look lacy!'

'Oooah! Well, that's for sure it's not a sheep. Not with lacy green jocks. Give us your knife for a minute.'

Dave took Mick's knife and squeezed past him in the tunnel.

'Here. Over here. Shine the bloody thing here.'

'Cut the jumper open, Dave. See what's in it.'

'Ooh shit! I can't. I can't. You do it.'

'Oh, go on, you wuss. What are you, a girl? Go on, just cut it.'

'OK. I'll cut, but you've got the torch—you can look.'

With this division of labour sorted out, Dave shut his eyes and sliced through the red fabric on the ground at his feet. He felt 'something like gristle' as the fabric parted and then, unable to contain his curiosity, he opened his eyes and saw—nothing but blackness.

'There's no bones in it,' he reported to Mick, who was still holding the torch, but otherwise hadn't moved.

Mick raked the beam of light over the mound of rocks and red clothing.

'Look, that looks like a rib-cage. Well it *could* be a sheep. They look the same, you know. Ribs—look the same on everyone.'

'Bullshit! Look there's one sticking up at the end. I'm grabbing that and I reckon we should get out of here. What if it's a real skeleton? Oh shit! Let's get out of here right now!'

Clutching their trophy piece of bone they slid and slithered all the way down to Bonnie Doon—the dogs cavorting and jumping around them, thinking this was a new game. It was around 8.30 p.m. when they arrived back at McIntyre's Lane and decided to phone a police mate in Melbourne to ask him what to do next.

Still holding the rib bone, Dave jabbed it through the air as he described the scene ten metres below the ground at the Jack o' Clubs.

'What'll we do?'

'Ring the local coppers,' his friend replied.

'What if it's only a sheep?' Now he was standing in the well-lit lounge room, Dave was being cautious. He didn't want to look like an idiot.

'What if it isn't? Ya gotta phone them. Just tell them what you've told me.'

So Mick called the Mansfield police station. At first they treated the story as a bit of a yawn. Mick got frustrated and yelled, 'Look, you lazy bloody wankers, I'll bet you a slab it's a body.'

That's when the police took him seriously. 'We'll come over then, soon as we can get hold of the CIB.'

'Yeah, well I should bloody think so. Got nothing better on, have you? We'll be over the road in the pub. It's nearly nine o'bloody clock and we're starving.'

It was almost 10 p.m. when three police officers walked into the pub. The eyes of everyone in the room fixed upon them as they called out, 'Mick Bladen?'

'Yeah, mate. Over here.'

Over a last beer before closing the young men took the police through the details again from the beginning. The CIB officer took them seriously this time. 'Could you take us up and show us where you found this mineshaft?'

'What, now?' they asked in unison.

'We could go now, but it would be better if we went first thing,' replied the CIB officer.

'Yeah, much better idea. And there's no way I'm walking back up with you blokes,' Mick replied, eyeing their thickening waistlines. 'Chopper or four-wheel-drive'd be the go, mate.'

'I'll organise that now,' the officer agreed, pulling out his mobile phone. 'I'd better take that bone with me, David. It may be needed as evidence.'

Rather reluctantly, Dave handed over the only visible reminder of their find. Could it really belong to a dead body? The whole thing was starting to feel like a dream. These things only happened in the movies—or to other people.

The CIB officer finalised his phone call and told them, 'We'll assemble at 7 a.m. at the service station—the chopper will pick us up there. Thanks fellas. See you tomorrow.'

The dawning of the following day brought the slow realisation they had become local celebrities overnight. Gathered on the bitumen outside the service station were about six Search and Rescue officers; three Homicide officers from Melbourne, led by Jeff Calderbank; a constable from Mansfield; Detective Sergeant Ian Coutts from Wangaratta; two forensic specialists, Dr Matthew Lynch and Dr Chris Briggs from Melbourne and other police—about twenty people in all.

The chopper hovered over the service station in the grey light and radioed down to the waiting crowd telling them the space was too tight to set down. The blades whipped up gravel and intensified the wind cutting across the parking lot from Lake Eildon. Dave's heart beat fast. What if it *was* a sheep?

The little group, by now the subject of intense scrutiny from almost everyone in Bonnie Doon woken by the noise, moved along the street to the back of the pub, where the chopper set down.

'OK, Mick. We're first up,' Jeff Calderbank said. 'You'll have to direct the pilot.'

With a cheeky grin, Mick disappeared into the cabin for his first chopper ride. Even if it was a sheep, this bit would be fun. Once he'd identified the spot, the helicopter made half a dozen trips, ferrying men and equipment up to a flat ridge area near the Jack o' Clubs mineshaft. Harnesses, lifting equipment, trolleys and boxes of tools were all assembled to be used in the task of getting the mineshaft to part with its gruesome secret.

The Search and Rescue team went down first, to secure the area and to assess the situation. The message came through on the two-way: there was something down there, probably dressed in a red jumper, but almost completely covered with fallen rubble. 'Looks like it's been here five or six years,' came over the air. The two boys relaxed a bit. Apparently they'd done the right thing after all. After a short time, two silicon breast implants were found and sent to the surface.

'Bet she didn't know when she got these done they'd last longer than she would,' someone said. No-one laughed. Everyone was cold and nothing much was happening on the surface. The uncovering of the body had to be done meticulously, and it took hours. Evidence that might have been with the body had to be preserved. Everyone involved went about their tasks with grim humour. The remains were reduced to calculations of time frames, geometric measurements and photo opportunities.

The winter wind whipped up through Prowd's Gully and cut through jumpers and sweatshirts. The adventure of the mineshaft only the day before had evaporated into irritation and boredom. Mick and Dave sat huddled up together, watching people emerging from or disappearing into the black hole in the ground. Some of the police searched the area around the shaft, probably as much to keep warm as with the hope of finding anything.

Eventually, Mick got brave and asked if they could get the chopper to take them back down the hill. 'Why not?' Jeff Calderbank agreed. 'But we'll need to come and see you for a statement when we come down. Will you stick around?'

'Yeah. We're here for a week—when are you guys going back?'

'Don't know yet. We'll need to ask a few questions around here.'

'Why don't you stay at my place, then?' asked Mick. 'It's better than the pub and we can talk by the fire—if I can ever get my mouth to move again properly.'

'Done,' said Jeff. 'We'll come over when we get off this hill. We'll meet you at the hotel.'

Mick and Dave got a lift down and thawed out in the pub, telling all who'd listen about the activity going on at the Jack o' Clubs. Late in the day they heard the chopper returning, bringing down the living and dead. Talk flowed freely with the beer, as local people called in for a drink on the way home.

'One thing's for sure,' said a farmer, 'you'd have to be a local to find that mineshaft.'

'Yeah. But how would a body be got up there? You'd need a four-wheel-drive—anyone'd notice a stranger going up. You'd have to go in daylight—too bloody dangerous in the dark. Be a bit embarrassing if you did an axle with a dead sheila sitting next to you!'

Laughs rang out as people imagined the scene. 'Be a bit difficult to call the RACV, eh?'

'Could've had something to do with drugs, maybe. All these townies coming up the highway—God knows what they get up to.'

'Not just townies, mate. A few locals have been involved with drugs in their time, mark my words.'

'Ah, she could've easily fallen in. A stranger rambling around up there wouldn't know about those holes.'

'But how would she get up there? You'd have to pass quite a few houses and you'd need a pretty solid truck—it's four Ks off the road.'

'Nah—you could go round to the caravan park on the other side of the lake and use the SEC track. That goes up from there somewhere.'

'But who knows about that? Hardly anyone, except people who live here.'

'Aw, yeah, you could've had an old mine map and followed that— if you were an outsider, I mean.'

'Naah! You wouldn't want it to be your first time up there trying to find that shaft. It'd have to be someone who already knew where it was to be able to take a body to it. Pity for them she didn't bounce down to the next level—she never would've been found, eh, lads?'

Dave agreed. 'It was at least another five metres down and really dark. We never would've seen her if she'd rolled into the next level.'

'Assuming she was dead when she hit the deck,' someone else chipped in. 'What if she was chucked in alive and left to rot?'

This cast a silence over the group.

'Nah, you wouldn't do that to a dog, mate. You'd finish it off first.'

'Any mongrel who'd do that—drag someone up there and chuck 'em down the hole—would be capable of anything, I reckon.'

Speculation continued until Jeff Calderbank arrived.

'Did you get her out?'

'Yep. Dr Lynch is already escorting the remains back to Melbourne. Now, where's that fire you mentioned?'

∞

The following morning, Friday, Jeff Calderbank visited the offices of the *Mansfield Courier*. Photographers from the paper had been out the day before, but the police had not released any information the previous night.

'We'll need your help on this,' said Jeff. 'We don't know how long the body has been down there, could be quite a few years. Following an examination by Dr Lynch at the scene, this is what we do know.

'A complete skeleton was removed. The body was probably Caucasian and 25 to 35 years old. The person was between 164 cm (64.5 inches) and 172 cm (67.5 inches) tall. The remains had natural teeth, with dental work done to upper and lower teeth. A pair of silicone breast implants were removed with the body.

'The cause of death has not yet been determined, but several bones were broken. Missing person files are being searched nationally, but this person could be local, or related to a local resident, due to the location where the body was found. We need any information at all to assist us with our inquiries. All information will be treated confidentially.

'Items recovered with the body were: a red woollen jumper, green/blue lace panties, cream coloured woollen socks, a Timex brand wristwatch with a brown leather strap, a silver coloured ring, a silver bracelet, a cream coloured plastic bangle and brown/burgundy high-heeled ankle boots.

'The significance of the boots is that it is very unlikely anyone would be bushwalking in those boots. Because of the remote location and inaccessibility of the mine, we believe someone with local knowledge may be involved.'

The *Courier* ran the story on its front page on Wednesday 26 July, a week after the remains were discovered. I remember glancing at a story in the Melbourne press as well, thinking you'd hardly go bushwalking in high-heeled boots, jewellery and underwear. It was reported as an oddity. The bones were those of a man, but the clothing was definitely a woman's, and the silicone breast implants suggested the body could be that of a transsexual. In August the police released a detailed description and photos of the clothing to *Outrage*, a gay and lesbian magazine.

Early in September, Jeff Calderbank took a call from a woman in New Zealand.

'I think you've found my sister, Adele Baily,' she said.

∽∾

The discovery of the body in the mineshaft was a catalyst for the reopening of investigations into Jenny Tanner's death. The Jack o' Clubs mine was at the back of Springfield, and when the police began asking questions, there were a lot of hints—'While you're looking into this one, you should check out that poor girl who was supposed to have shot herself twice in the head.' Not only did the location link the two deaths, but it also emerged that Adele Baily was known to Denis Tanner. Jeff Calderbank had a Homicide detective's hunch that genuine coincidences are pretty rare.

When I first start tracing other possible links between the two deaths, I visualise the connection in very simple terms. Maybe Adele and Jenny were shot with the same gun, or something similarly nice and neat.

I begin by tracking down Adele's sister, Karen, in the usual circuitous way. I get her name from Kath Blake, who spoke to Karen soon after the investigation into Jenny's death was reopened. Karen phoned Kath when she heard the news, and they had a friendly conversation about long-buried feelings and hopes, sharing their despair of then and now. Kath doesn't have Karen's phone number or address, but she thinks New Zealand *Sixty Minutes* is planning a story.

Armed with this piece of information, I ring 0103 and luckily get a helpful operator, who agrees to try the New Zealand operator. 'They'll know which channel it's on over there, won't they?'

First up we connect with a bloke who never watches TV, but he asks around the other operators, and soon we're having a trans-Tasman conference about *Suxty Mununtes* and why I need the number. (My operator in Australia has by now elevated me to the status of a 'famous author' and Jenny to a 'celebrated case', and all in New Zealand are duly impressed and correspondingly helpful.)

As soon as I obtain the number, I make the call. The phone rings for ages, then a male voice answers. '*Sixty Minutes*, please,' I ask.

'No-one there at the moment, love. I'm the cleaner, just passing the phone.'

'Where is everybody?'

'Home in bed if they've got any sense! It's 12.30 in the morning.'

For the first time in hours I look at the clock. 'Oh, of course, I'm sorry, I'm calling from Australia—it's only 9.30 p.m. here. I'll try again tomorrow.'

As bad luck would have it, it takes three days and seven phone calls to track down the right producer, who then wants to include me in the *Sixty Minutes* story. We negotiate a raincheck on this and she gives me Karen's phone number—at last!

When I first call I'm told Karen is 'out with her granddaughter'. Granddaughter! I keep forgetting that so much time has elapsed.

Adele disappeared in 1978 and was not found until 1995, seventeen years later. She was about twenty-three when she was killed, so she'd be around forty now if she had lived.

I call back repeatedly and leave three or four messages on an answering machine, with no response. I decide she is avoiding me. But one weekend afternoon, almost three weeks after my original calls, Karen rings.

We have a long talk about her sister Adele and her incredible family. Adele looks distinctly exotic in her photo, and I ask if they are Maoris.

'No way! We're from New Orleans Negro stock, mixed with Portuguese, Irish and Tahitian—direct descendants of Fletcher Christian from the mutiny on the *Bounty*.' An image of Marlon Brando in tight trousers springs to my mind.

Karen continues, 'My great-grandfather was a slave from New Orleans, working on a whaling ship. He jumped ship near Norfolk Island and swam ashore, where he was sheltered by Evelyn Christian, one of Fletcher Christian's daughters—her mother was the daughter of the chief of Pitcairn Island.'

The whalers put ashore to search for the escaped slave and came perilously close to finding the couple. The young lovers were smuggled by relatives across to Pitcairn, where eventually they married. They had fourteen children. 'One of them was my granddad, Harry, who came to New Zealand. He married an Irish woman here and they had eleven children including my mum, Evelyn, called after her grandmother. That's why Adele called herself Adele Evelyn, see, to keep the link going. My dad is Portuguese and we had ten kids in our family. Adele was number four. She was Paul then, but always wanted to be a girl, played with us girls and used to dress in our clothes.

'In 1972, when she was seventeen, she moved to Sydney and had her boobs done the next year—she went to the best surgeon at the time. She always had nothing but the best. She came back to New Zealand for a while and then went off to Cairo in 1976 to have the sex-change operation.'

'Cairo? In Egypt? Why Cairo?'

'Well, that's where they did them then. In Australia you had to live as a woman for two years and go through all sorts of psychological tests and stuff, and she just knew what she wanted and did it.'

'So it was obviously a success, then?' I ask. 'She went ahead and lived as a woman—whereabouts, in New Zealand or here?'

'No, Melbourne, St Kilda. She was probably working as a prossie even then, she liked the good life. She had a beautiful little furnished flat in Grey Street, St Kilda and a car—used to write and send photos to my mum or phoned'

'Have you still got the letters?

I hold my breath.

'No—you don't keep things for that long.'

I breathe out.

'So when did you know she was missing?'

'In September 1977 my eldest sister died and my eldest son was born. It was like a new life kind of starting in exchange for the old. Adele came home for a visit then, stayed a little while and went back to Oz.

She was meant to go and see friends in Adelaide later on that month—that's why she went back—but we found out later she never went. No-one has seen her since. She didn't write or ring at Christmas and didn't send cards on birthdays either, and Mum started to worry. Adele was always good at keeping in touch. Mum knew even then something was wrong. Around April, our letters to her started coming back "Return to Sender".

'Mum went to the New Zealand police and filled out all these Missing Person forms. They were not very interested—I'm sure they never contacted the Melbourne police or put it out on Interpol or whatever they do—just stuffed it in a cubby hole somewhere. Mum even rang the Melbourne police at St Kilda. They told her to fuck off, they were not interested in a transsexual hooker, or something like that. A lot of transsexuals went missing in them days—it was the time of Mr Asia and all that, and people didn't accept people like Adele like they more or less do now. It was pretty much "Good riddance".

'Mum knew a priest in Melbourne and she rang him to ask his help. We didn't hear anything for a few months, and then he rang back and told her he'd been through all the dingiest places looking for her or information about her, but she'd just disappeared. Her unit was rented to someone, her car and her furniture had disappeared and she had vanished—like she'd never existed.'

'What did you do then?' I ask, wondering how someone can just 'vanish' without help of some kind.

'We waited for news and talked about her. Prayed. No-one went over—no point really, if the priest couldn't find her and the police wouldn't help.

'I went to a clairvoyant who told me Adele was dead in a dark place. Fair dinkum—I've still got the tape of that session, almost twenty years ago! Bit weird, eh?'

It certainly is. So is the disappearance of Adele's belongings. Karen says Adele had a car, a unit in Grey Street, and at least one bank account. She told her family they were beneficiaries of her life insurance policy and explained how to claim the benefit if she died. After she disappeared physically, she seemed to vanish altogether into the ether. There was no record of her belongings or a lease at Grey Street. Her car disappeared and the Motor Registry had no record of her having owned one. There was no record of a driving licence in Paul or Adele Baily's name. Her family knew her bank account details, as she sometimes sent them cheques, but apparently the St Kilda branch had no record of her ever having an account with them. The insurance policy no longer seemed to exist.

Later, when I ask the police about this, they say Adele lived in a crappy little flat with no belongings to speak of. If she had a car it was probably hauled off as abandoned. They haven't heard about any of the other 'disappearances' but seriously doubt their validity—relatives' fables, they say.

Adele's family was distraught. 'One of my mother's best friends was with us through this time and she said to my mum, "I will never forget Adele. If ever I hear anything, no matter where I am, I will remember your pain at not knowing where she is." She didn't forget, either. It was through her we found Adele again, really.'

This friend of Adele's mother had moved a long way away, but she saw the article in *Outrage* and sent it with a note: 'I thought this article may be significant to you ...' Karen and her mother looked long at the clothing. The boots, especially, were just the kind of footwear Adele had favoured all her life, cute and fashionable, cut off at the ankle to show her pretty legs. The two women were certain Adele had been wearing them on her last visit home.

They showed the article to another sister, who agreed it was certainly worth following up. Karen took it to the local police and was asked dispassionately to fill in yet another form. Frustrated by the apparent lack of interest from the New Zealand police, in early September Karen phoned the 1800 number at the end of the *Outrage* article and connected directly with Jeff Calderbank.

After taking her through a number of questions, Jeff indicated he thought it could be Adele, but they needed proof. 'Do you know where she got her dental work done?' he asked.

'Yeah. Same place we all got it done.'

'Is the dentist still practising? Could we get access to her dental records?'

'We sure can. I'll fax them to you tomorrow.'

The family dentist who had actually done the work had retired and the practice had moved premises, but fortunately all the records from years before were stored in the attic of the new surgery. Once he knew what Karen wanted, the new dentist was very helpful. Together they searched through piles and boxes of patient records until—bingo!—there it was—Paul David Baily. Karen took the cards to the retired dentist, who copied all the information onto a fax format to send to Jeff Calderbank. Jeff showed this fax to a group of senior dentists in Sydney, who all agreed there was a perfect match.

This news was brought to the people of Mansfield in the 6 September issue of the *Courier*: 'Police identify Doon Mineshaft Skeleton'. It was a front-page story, with a pocket version of Adele's life history and an appeal from the police for assistance.

At the end of September, forensic examinations completed, Adele Baily's remains were accompanied to New Zealand by Jeff Calderbank and another member of the Homicide team. They were handed over to her mother in Wellington for her funeral.

The family asked the local undertaker to lay out Adele's bones for viewing at the funeral parlour. He was able to do this almost exactly; although many bones were broken, the skeleton was intact. 'You could see Adele there,' said Karen. 'You could see her shape all around where the bones were. We covered her with a lovely crocheted blanket and wrapped rosary beads around her head. We wanted her friends to be able to say goodbye to her properly and show she was a really loved member of our family. After the public viewing we had her put in a closed casket and we had her in our house for three days for friends and family to come and pay their respects.

'The funeral was beautiful. We had a full choir and a Requiem Mass and then the funeral procession took her to all the old places on the way to the cemetery—first to our home where we all grew up together, then the primary school, college, her first job, our old church and finally past the airport where at last she came home.'

Jeff Calderbank went to the funeral as a guest of the family. Adele's mother wrote to David Worsley thanking him for finding her daughter. 'Now I know again where all my children are.'

Forensic investigators could not conclusively establish the cause of Adele Bailey's death and her inquest has not yet been held. Privately, police officers have told me she may have either been kicked to death or 'copped the chicken'—a police slang term for almost wringing someone's neck and then letting them drop—perhaps this time down a ten-metre mineshaft.

We will not find out much more about Adele Baily. Her trail is cold and her inquest will be held separately to Jenny's. Her inquest, like Jenny's, may never answer all the outstanding questions about how she died. But her story deserves to be told. She lay alone—maybe for days before dying—at the bottom of a mineshaft for seventeen years while her family waited and prayed for her return. With all the intrigue and publicity associated with Jenny's death and subsequent investigations, it is easy to forget another family in New Zealand which also lost a loved daughter and sister.

∞

In early September, the Jenny Tanner case was officially reopened as a possible homicide.

On the night of Monday, 11 September at around eleven o'clock, Bryan Shannon, Volunteer Fire Captain for Bonnie Doon Brigade, received a Fire Reporting Service alert from Dennis Clancy, the general storekeeper in Bonnie Doon.

'There's a fire at a property in Bonnie Doon, mate—on the highway. Someone driving by has just called it in, said the name on the gate was Springfield—that's Tanners' old place, isn't it?'

And it was—ablaze and beyond rescue by the time Bryan and his crew arrived. The old house was made of tinder-dry cypress pine and parts of it were clad with fibro-cement sheeting, causing a concentration of heat inside. It was closed up because the new owners had gone away while the house was restumped. This was common knowledge locally, so no-one had made any attempt to effect a rescue. The heat was too intense for a lone garden hose to have any impact anyway.

The interior of the house was completely gutted. Bryan was confused about how the fire could have started. He told me the electricity switchboard was not connected to the house. The outbuildings were only scarred from the heat of the fire, but the entire innards of the house were destroyed. What remained of the frame showed no obvious sign of forced entry, but because of the unusual nature of the fire, Bryan decided to call in the professionals from Wangaratta to ascertain the cause. Bryan explained to me the reasons for his concern:

'The Lockhart brothers were first on the scene. Mrs van Winden saw the house on fire as she drove out of Bonnie Doon and called into Lockharts', which was almost next door. They raced across in their truck and cut the gate open—although Jeff [Lockhart] had a key to the gate, Archie got there first. Archie's a fencing contractor, so he had the right gear in his truck. There were no people or cars at the site when the Lockharts arrived. We arrived a couple of minutes later. The fire was all through the house, across all the floors and up the ceiling in all six rooms. This was very unusual. House fires are usually confined to one room for a start, or contained in the roof. Once the oxygen gets to it, though, it'll take off. If you don't get to the base of the fire within fifteen minutes you've usually had it.

'During that year we had sixty or seventy fires in our volunteer district. I attended about twenty myself, but only saw one other anything like the Springfield fire. That was when a kero heater was thought to have exploded and spread the fire across the floor really quickly. So, because Springfield had been empty and the fire so widespread and I couldn't see any obvious reason for it starting, I called in the Wangaratta professionals.'

The Wangaratta fire officers sifted through the debris and searched for any 'hot spots' indicating an accelerant or a place the fire had been more intense, but they found nothing. Still not satisfied the fire could have started spontaneously, Wangaratta called in Melbourne Arson Squad investigators. This initiative was supported by Jeff Calderbank from Homicide, who was very suspicious about such a huge coincidence, the total destruction of the scene of the possible crime occurring within a week of the reopening of the investigation into Jenny's death.

The police investigation revealed that the first person to see Springfield on fire was Brian Maher, a truck driver heading east to Bonnie Doon to make a delivery to the general store, at about 10.30 p.m. As he drove past he noticed a car in the driveway and thought he saw a figure running towards the back of the house. The flames did not look as if they had really taken hold. He was worried by this shadowy figure and no-one came running down the driveway to seek assistance, so he decided to drive to Bonnie Doon and call the fire brigade.

At the same time, two young women were pulling out of the petrol station, heading west towards their farm. Driving past Springfield they apparently noticed the gate open and a car in the driveway. They did not see anyone. The house was well alight and they decided to drive on and get help. They returned with reinforcements about ten minutes later, arriving just before the fire brigade. When they arrived the gate was shut and padlocked. There was no car and no sign of anyone. The house was a roaring inferno.

Paul Newman asked the owners of Springfield about who had a key to the padlock. The police say they were told only three people had a key—the owners, Jeff Lockhart, who was minding their house while they were away, and Laurie Tanner, who needs access to his paddocks and shearing shed. Apparently it was not Laurie Tanner's car in the driveway that night—so whose was it?

Fascinated by this additional evidence, I phone the new owners of Springfield. They know who I am and think they know all about me. They think I'm writing this story because I'm 'a friend of that crazy Mrs Smith'. It takes me a while to realise they mean Roz Smith. I'm not sure why they have this idea—perhaps because I've phoned from Queensland.

The new owners have had property around Bonnie Doon for years. They're good friends with the Tanner family—they spoke to Laurie this very afternoon—and are unwilling to discuss the case in detail. They say it's 'too dangerous'. Eventually they tell me a couple of interesting things. They say in the country who knows who has a key to a gate? They dispute the police version that only three people had keys. The padlock was put on to keep out nosy reporters ('and writers', I add silently), not locals. They tell me that after the fire, one of the commercial television stations kept coming onto their property filming the burnt ruins and outbuildings, and tourist buses often stopped outside to show passengers the ruins. They say the truck driver's 'evidence has been discredited', because he told the police the car he saw was on the left-hand side of the property, not the right-hand side, where the driveway actually is.

But if the plan was arson it would be very easy for anyone without a key to drive into Tanners Road—the track running down the left-hand side of the property—and climb over the side fence. The arsonist wouldn't need a key. There's no lock on Tanners Road.

The insurance company paid up without any qualms, and that's quite an important bit of information, as they are usually pretty difficult to satisfy. The owners say the electricity was definitely connected to the house as well as the outbuildings. This would have been an important factor in the insurance investigations. There was a time-lapse light in the kitchen, which came on at 7 p.m. and went out at 11 p.m. This wouldn't have fooled any of the locals, who knew the house was empty at the time, but it would have kept passing opportunists away.

The house was purchased in 1991 and had been tenanted since the purchase, until there was a dispute about the tenants' dogs chasing sheep—a cardinal sin in the country. In the true spirit of the High Country, where dogs have a value only if they work for their living, the owners issued an ultimatum: 'Move out or your dogs will be shot.' The tenants obviously liked their dogs better than their surroundings and went. This enabled the new owners to use the farm kitchen for comfort during the shearing season and to begin a few renovations. They say Springfield was a lovely old farmhouse with 'no aura' of past sad events, and they see themselves as just people who bought a house where something bad happened a long time ago.

The restumping was to have started on the Monday, and when the owners heard of the fire they initially thought the builders had left something burning. But the restumpers were delayed and had not started at all when the house went up on Tuesday night. Maybe whoever set the fire (if someone did) knew about the proposed start date and hoped the builders would be blamed? The fire's intensity was so great that only powder ash remained, leaving no clues for arson investigators to deduce the cause of the fire.

When I hear about the possible surfeit of keys and the truck driver's confusion, I begin to doubt the information given to me by Paul Newman. I feel quite upset, as if I have been betrayed in a relationship of trust. Paul Newman has made no secret of the fact he is using me at times as 'a tool of his investigation'. As long as he doesn't expect me to be working for Homicide I don't care, but now I wonder if the Task Force has been feeding me selected information to keep me from straying off along my own pathways. I spend the whole evening pacing up and down and taking my peevishness out on my husband, who, having a more cynical and paranoid nature, is not nearly as disillusioned as I am.

The fire is an example of how one story can change with the telling. The fireman told me no electricity was connected to the house, the owners say it was. The police say there were only three keys and a car in the driveway; the owners say many keys and a car in the roadway on the outside of the property. A small puzzle, but indicative of the difficulties involved in reaching the truth.

The final conclusion from the Melbourne Arson Squad was 'cause unknown'. Just one of those things?

The fire received a couple of small paragraphs in the *Courier* on 13 September. The only implied link to the new investigation was the phrase: 'The house, originally owned by the Tanner family, was unoccupied …'

The word around Mansfield was that it was a last-gasp attempt to cover up anything that might have been missed.

∞

Still searching for the links between the country housewife and the transsexual St Kilda prostitute, I contact a previous manager of the Maindample pub and a neighbour of the Tanners at Springfield for ten years. Ray is now elderly, semi-retired and living near a beach, a long way from the High Country.

His main contribution to my research is his local knowledge of both the area and the farmers themselves. He also recalls a number of gatherings of prostitutes and transsexuals and their friends in local pubs in the late '70s and early '80s. Could one of these girls have been Adele Baily, visiting someone she knew in the area?

He tells me, 'It'd be hard to get a body up to that mineshaft without people seeing it. You'd have to pass several houses and you'd have to know the area pretty well, but a lot of people did know about that mineshaft. It wasn't a secret or anything. I was down that shaft meself about ten years ago and I saw a heap of debris in one corner, bit of red rag sticking out under the leaves and sticks and stuff. Didn't look closer though—never thought it'd be a body or anything.'

Imagine if Adele had been found ten years earlier, I think, just after Jenny died. What a difference that could have made to the now cold trail of evidence and recollections!

'How about the way Jenny Tanner died? Was there much gossip at the time?'

'There's always gossip in country towns,' he replies. 'Word was she'd shot herself twice—wounded herself and then shot again. Suicide was put out, even though she'd been shot twice. I didn't know Laurie's first wife. The Tanners have been there a long time, you know. You don't become a local in ten years. Anyway, the way it sounds is that a farmer or someone used to killing animals done for the Tanner girl. Didn't get her with the first shot and just walked up and executed her with another shot through the head. That's the way you put down injured animals, as you know.'

For once I have nothing to say.

∞

Much investigative police work is tedious in the extreme. Every lead, piece of gossip, name dropped or hint given must be followed up—sometimes along a tortuous trail—until it is confirmed and added to the body of evidence, discarded as irrelevant, or simply hits a stone wall. Investigations begun twelve years after an event have almost no chance of a major breakthrough. Straight plodding and determined follow-up produce the small layers of information that gradually build up to an outcome—maybe. Vital information can be lost through fuzzy memories, removal, time or distance.

Many of the locals questioned by the Task Force after the reopening of the Tanner investigation added only minute pieces to the long-buried jigsaw puzzle. Many clammed up altogether—or told the police what they thought they wanted to hear. There was gossip, suspicion and innuendo, but no hard evidence.

The taskforce had some bad moments in the early stages—not least the unfolding knowledge that some of their own members, at all levels, had not adequately performed their duty following Jenny's death. The initial investigation had been short-circuited; relevant evidence was not checked or thoroughly investigated; at the inquest, conflicting versions of events were not pursued. The Coroner could only deliver his finding based on the evidence he was given, but even at the time there were some raised eyebrows around the Coroner's Court and a feeling that 'this looks a bit funny'. An undercurrent eddied, as staff and magistrates discussed the case socially and professionally.

The reason for the paucity of investigation at the time might simply have been that the police realised an almighty stuff-up had occurred and felt they needed to save face after not securing and photographing the crime scene. Or it might have been something more—a realisation that one of their own might be incriminated in some way. Without the actual file it was difficult even to make assumptions, much less come to definite conclusions.

In May 1996 Inspector Paul Newman from the newly created Police Ethical Standards Division (formerly known as Internal Investigations) was seconded to Homicide, where he had previously worked for six years, to head up the investigation into both deaths. It was considered necessary to transfer Inspector Newman because a serving police officer had become a possible suspect for one or both killings. There is also a school of thought that suggests Paul Newman was moved in because the hierarchy realised they had a potential public-relations fiasco on their hands.

The Victoria Police were already under pressure. Their colleagues in both New South Wales and Queensland were reeling under the impact of damaging public disclosures at official inquiries and Royal Commissions. Top echelons of both interstate forces were being shaken and split. There were signs of division in the ranks in Victoria as well. Long-term senior officers had been passed over for promotion when the Chief Commissioner's position became available in 1993 and a perceived outsider, Mr Neil Comrie, was appointed. At least three senior members of the force resigned amid a flurry of media coverage to take up improved prospects elsewhere.

The daily media were peppered with allegations from whistle-blowers and 'unnamed sources' about police incompetence and corruption. Shootings of civilians by police in the line of duty reached double figures in one year, severely embarrassing Force Command and enraging the public—stimulated to new levels of anger by regular front-page media coverage, editorials and interviews with weeping relatives. The bad news just kept on coming: a window-shutter kick-back scam; failure to inform the Ombudsman of suspected paedophilia in the force; a senior police officer allowed to retire on full benefits while being investigated for alleged improper relationships with a female witness; the deputy head of the internal investigations department admitting on tape that a 'brotherhood' within the Victoria Police was protecting and encouraging corruption; allegations that officers in a country town had sexual relations with women at a local refuge, which was closed down while an internal investigation was proceeding; and the saga of reprisals against Karl Conrad, who blew the whistle on the window-shutter scam in the first place. It was in this climate that the police found out the *Sunday Age* was launching its own investigation of the Jenny Tanner case.

∽

In about January 1996 a reporter from the *Sunday Age* was allegedly approached by a well-placed police contact, who expressed a concern that the investigation into Jenny Tanner's death was stalling and certain members of the police hierarchy appeared to be taking 'very short steps towards a possible solution'. This intriguing piece of intelligence spurred the reporter to start his own three-month investigation, which led to the publication of the story I eventually read in June that year. He followed Homicide detectives around asking many of the same questions. He also visited most of the key locations, including the Jack o' Clubs mine, and contacted quite a few people who had not been spoken to by Homicide. The reporter formed his own opinions about what had happened, and finally published some of them on 9 June 1996.

The *Sunday Age* investigation led to friction between the newspaper and the police, who feared that information could be inadvertently passed from one witness to the next. The police were also concerned that the publication of the story might alert suspects to certain aspects of the investigation, and that some potential witnesses might be influenced by reading the article before they were questioned.

Two members of the Task Force met the reporter in early May to discuss keeping the story on ice until they had progressed further with their own inquiries, which seemed to have been noticeably stepped up after the *Sunday Age* demonstrated such an interest in their outcome. The reporter was willing to give them a little leeway, but had concerns of his own that his competitors from a rival newspaper might pick up the story—either from someone he had interviewed, or through a leak from the police themselves. He threatened 'dire consequences' for the police if they leaked anything to the opposition.

Several days after this meeting the police sought a Supreme Court injunction to have the story kept on hold for at least two weeks. The *Sunday Age* was quite angry about this, but in early May Justice Barry Beach granted the injunction and the story was temporarily suppressed. The only consolation from the *Sunday Age*'s viewpoint was that the injunction applied to the opposition as well.

This was a fairly unusual step to take in a police investigation. In the previous few years of police operations in Victoria, only stories perceived to be jeopardising life or against the true public interest had been suppressed—usually not by injunction, but through a 'gentlemen's agreement' with news editors. So the desire to keep the *Sunday Age* version of events away from the general public by injunction could have been partly driven by a desire to ensure that when the story did hit the papers the police would appear to be on top of the investigation.

The stated reason the police wanted the injunction, however, was in case the *Sunday Age* article stimulated a spate of phone calls between major suspects. The injunction gave the Task Force time to apply for a Supreme Court warrant to install listening devices on the relevant telephones. Under the Listening Devices Act of 1969 police can obtain permission to install listening devices on suspects' phones if they are able to satisfy a Supreme Court Judge on two criteria: that there are reasonable grounds to suspect that an offence is being, is likely to be, or has been committed; and that the use of a listening device is reasonable and necessary for the purpose of investigation and obtaining of evidence. The police were able to obtain their warrants, and on Friday 6 June the injunction on the media was lifted. The story appeared the following Sunday. It was billed as a special investigation, and ran for three broadsheet pages.

There is a school of thought that says the whole police investigation could have been abandoned on the grounds that it was 'too little, too late' if the *Sunday Age* had not broken the story. Paul Newman disagrees. He says the investigation never slowed down and was certainly never going to be shelved. His appointment to the Task Force took place in May 1996, only weeks before the first article was published, but after the police found out it was being written—a decision by the police hierarchy that could be interpreted either way.

Paul Newman is known to everyone in the police force as one of the straightest officers in town. He is not large or overbearing, but is of medium height with piercing eyes, iron-grey hair and usually a suit to match. Although the two murders he had been assigned to investigate were old and ragged trails, he decided to seek some answers from the one person *known* to be present on the night Jenny was killed— Jenny herself.

He decided to try to determine forensically whether or not Jenny Tanner could have pulled the trigger of the BRNO rifle. If the answer was a definite no, then they had a definite murder investigation on their hands. He began to prepare a brief for the Coroner requesting her exhumation.

∞

Almost twelve months later, my own investigation into this period of the official process leads me into a search for information about the complicated and rarely implemented process of exhumation.

I am casting around for leads when a computer serviceman in our office overhears me talking to someone about Jenny on the phone. After I hang up, he says hesitantly, 'I wasn't eavesdropping, but I heard what you were saying. If you want to know something about how the police treat these forensic cases. I have a mate in Wangaratta who works in forensics. A beaut bloke—he might be able to help you with some general background stuff if you want to ring him. Tell him I gave you his name. If he knows what you want to know, I'm sure he'll help.'

I ring his friend, Detective Sergeant Ian Coutts, and we both get a shock. He was involved in the recovery of the bones from the mine-shaft *and* at Jenny's exhumation! This fount of potential information immediately runs dry, as he feels he cannot share very much detail with me, being directly involved in both cases and not knowing me from a tabloid reporter. We speak about a few generalities. Eventually, I suggest he checks me out with Homicide and say I'll call again.

It takes several phone calls around the halls of justice to track down Mr Hugh Adams, now semi-retired and working part-time at the Guardianship Board. I want to ask him if he felt at the time more could have been done to keep the case going, to ensure his open finding was not ignored. He is kind and friendly, but says he can't tell me anything because the case is being reinvestigated. He refers me to David Stevens, who worked at the Coroner's Court for almost twenty years and is familiar with Jenny's story, as he was working at the Coroner's Court at the time of the first inquest and for Jenny's exhumation.

David leads me through the legal complexities surrounding the exhumation, some of which are a result of the change in the Coroner's Act. 'Section 5 of the new Act says that any death which occurred under the old Act should be investigated under the old Act,' he says. 'Strictly speaking, this meant that we had to have grounds under the old Act to exhume Jenny's body, but she was actually exhumed under a number of different rules.'

Paul Newman asked Laurie Tanner for permission to exhume

Jenny's body. At this meeting Laurie agreed he'd 'like to get to the bottom of it'. Does this mean that Laurie could have stopped the exhumation if he'd refused permission? David explains: 'The exhumation licence was originally obtained under the Cemeteries Department auspices, which can order that a body be exhumed with permission of the next of kin. This was obtained from Laurie Tanner. Before approaching Laurie Tanner, Paul Newman obtained a licence to effect the exhumation with or without Laurie's permission. His visit to Laurie was largely only courtesy.'

There were complications, however, as David explains: 'To conduct a new post mortem on the remains, we couldn't really continue under the old Act, which placed some constraints upon us because of the way the body was exhumed. For example, the old legislation says the Attorney General can order exhumation of a body and investigation of a case. Jenny's exhumation was at first being conducted under civil, not criminal rules, so was not ordered by the Attorney General. However, Section 30 of the new Coroner's Act allowed examination of Jenny's remains as evidence in the process of investigating Adele Baily's death, so a warrant was obtained to cover this, in case there were procedural queries at a possible later trial.'

I am scribbling furiously. This is like a mini-tutorial in coronial law. David goes on to say that the problems encountered in this case have been such that the Attorney General has been asked to amend the Act. It was also necessary to ask the Supreme Court to quash the findings of the first inquest so that Jenny's case could be reopened and a new inquest held.

'There are a lot of things in this case we have never come across before,' David says. 'The next interesting thing is that the Coroner might have to conduct Jenny's inquest under the old legislation, which means he will be asked to do a committal. Under the old Act, in cases of homicide there has to be a committal unless the finding is "insufficient evidence"—then there will be another open finding.'

'So they could go to all this trouble and still not get an arrest?'

'Of course—how are they going to prove anything after all this time? Even if the Coroner ordered that anyone stood trial, the

Director of Public Prosecutions would be responsible for bringing a case against them, not the Coroner's Court.'

'What happens if the Coroner believes someone should stand trial and the DPP doesn't think there's enough evidence to arrest and prosecute him or her?'

'The DPP can issue a *nullae prosequae* and it can be filed away in a bottom drawer. The old Act is the only one with the provision for the Coroner to direct that a person should stand trial. To my knowledge a Coroner has never directed that a person be tried before the police have arrested them. It may be another one of the unusual aspects of this case if that does happen. Usually a person has either already been arrested, or the Coroner adjourns the case part way through and suggests that the suspect obtains legal advice before being arrested.'

The Coroner's decision is complicated by the rules of evidence, David says. 'In an inquest the rules of evidence are different. Under the old Act there are no rules of evidence—hearsay and speculation can be introduced. Under the new Act there *are* rules of evidence, but not as tight as trial evidence. However, if the Coroner is going to commit someone for trial, it has to be based on admissible evidence only, that is, evidence that could be produced at a trial. He has to disregard all the hearsay or other speculation which might have been put forward at the inquest. He has to separate these before making a decision.'

'What can be released to the public from an inquest?'

'In Victoria, the way the Act is set up, unless the Coroner orders suppression under provisions of 'Public Record Power' the whole proceedings can be released nationally as a matter of public record. Suppression would be a bit self-defeating in this case really, but the Coroner's powers are broad, sweeping and general.'

I feel dispirited that more questions were not asked at Jenny's first inquest, and fervently hope the police are successful in getting a second chance—for everyone's sake.

11

Jenny Tells

JENNY'S BODY was exhumed on 9 July 1996 by Curly McCormack's brother Mick, who is now the local undertaker. It was a chill, murky day, quite the opposite of the day Jenny was buried. A huge dank cypress overhanging her grave dripped moisture onto long grass. Its branches were home to a thousand parrots, whose droppings had encrusted the gnarled, exposed roots with polka dots. A handful of tired cornflowers drooped over Jenny's simple gravestone. Jenny's grave was at the end of a row, so the group attending the exhumation felt no discomfort about disturbing others' silent rest as they moved around the grave site. All the city people had worn ordinary shoes, and their trouser legs, socks and feet were soaked by the time they had walked from the gate to the grave. The locals wore gumboots. In Mansfield it has been known to snow in the middle of summer.

The Mansfield cemetery was established in 1870 at the far end of Highett Street, then on the outskirts of town. The cypress beside Jenny's grave is one of many planted at that time. Jenny has some famous neighbours in repose. Among them are Mounted Troopers Scanlon and Lonigan and Mounted Sergeant Kennedy, who all died in the line of duty apprehending Australia's most famous bushrangers, Ned Kelly and his fearsome gang. The troopers' three graves have tall, ornate headstones, donated by a grateful Victorian government. In spite of some latter-day vandalism, since repaired, they are an imposing reminder that the High Country has always had more than its share of violence and death.

Jenny's exhumation was a melancholy affair, attended only by those required to be there. Media from Mansfield and Melbourne were roped off at a distance, recording the action through telephoto lenses. The police had phoned Mick McCormack that morning and asked him to bring out the small bobcat. They gave him little warning, probably to divert the media, although that plan failed. Talk around town was that the exhumation would be any day. Mick had planned a four-day trip to Melbourne, but his instincts told him not to go until it was over.

Jeff Calderbank and Paul Newman had already visited the Blakes to warn them of the approaching event. Kath, for one, was very happy about it. 'At last my Jen might get to say something on her own behalf about how she died.' By this time Kath had read the book I'd sent her, and had some idea of what was possible with the advances made in forensic science since Jenny's death. Laurie and the Tanner family were already aware of the date. No representative of either family was there.

Squares of grass were removed and placed in a pile under the cypress to be replanted when Jenny was reinterred. The ground was wet and sticky, red clay reluctant to surrender its booty. Carefully manoeuvring the bobcat, Mick dug to within about a foot of the coffin, then police specialists took over the painstaking work of hand digging to expose the lid. They dug carefully with hand trowels to ensure the Forensic Science Institute eventually received Jenny's remains in the most pristine condition possible. The coffin lid was quite rotten, and extreme care was needed to ensure it was not broken through. Hand trowels were exchanged for spatulas.

The coffin was lifted out gently and Sergeant Ian Coutts removed the lid. The plastic lining inside the coffin was used to lift Jenny's remains and gently transfer them to a new coffin intact. The same afternoon, Mick drove the hearse containing this vital forensic evidence to Melbourne, escorted by Senior Constable Charles Fleming from Mansfield police. Naturally they discussed the case on the way. Fleming was convinced Jenny had committed suicide. He didn't believe any of the Tanners were involved in the way she met her death. 'Even if Laurie wanted stock put down he'd get someone else to do it,' he told Mick with conviction.

Forensic examinations lasted some weeks. Jenny was then returned for her second funeral, which took place on 16 August 1996.

This was a low-key affair on another bleak, damp day. Moisture-laden clouds swirled around the cemetery perimeters, seeming to insulate the sad little tableau from the curious eyes of the neighbourhood. White parrots supervised noisily from nearby branches, then jibbed away. A perky Jack Russell terrier sniffed around the tombstones until a shrill call caught his attention and he obediently trotted home. Only Laurie, Jenny's parents and a handful of relatives and family friends could summon the emotional energy to revisit the scene of eleven years before. Jeff Calderbank and Marty Allison represented the police. The service was completed with an almost embarrassing haste.

Big clods of clay were shovelled back into the grave, forming a lumpy red scar in the surrounding grass. Single roses and simple bunches of flowers still wrapped in cellophane were laid on top. There was no get-together afterwards, as the Tanner family was now openly hostile to the Blakes and none of the friends of both wanted to be seen to be 'taking sides'. The living victims of Jenny's murder dispersed quietly, with silent hopes all this would finally be resolved.

∞

One of the whistleblowers I met during my early investigations has a close understanding of the workings of the police department, having been part of it for a number of years. When I discuss the progress of the police investigation with him, he expresses doubt about the investigation going much further.

'The problem is the evidence was so covered up at the time,' he says. 'All the forensic evidence was destroyed. Because of the way the brotherhood is now, and was then, if you start digging about anyone, you start pointing guilt in that person's direction. The only way to keep the investigation going will be for the parents to keep jumping up and down. It's a very important case and it should be kept going, because it proves this whole point about the brotherhood covering up. There's no benefit to any of the police involved to get it solved now. Anyway, even if all the evidence they find points in one direction, getting the proof together is another matter. If you arrest a copper then the coppers hate you, unless it's very special circumstances. If you don't, the public hates you. Either way, the media loves you, but there are no winners.'

'What about Jenny?' I ask, outraged at the thought that the case would be shoved back in the archives again. 'I've met the detectives involved and I think they're genuinely serious about following up every suspect and if one of them happens to be a police officer, well, too bad!'

'Look, get real. Even if Homicide do have the investigation's best interests at heart, there's such a thing as Force Command. They have the final say. They tell Newman "Charge someone" or "Don't charge someone". He's only got those two choices. The parents should go to their local MP and say the investigation has slowed down—they need politicians involved.'

I don't think Kath and Les actually believe the investigation has slowed down and I know the Task Force is keeping them informed of any new developments, but I conclude that a trip to Mansfield is overdue.

I head straight for the Tanners' house and as always, try my luck there, but no-one is home. I leave my card, feeling a bit like the Wormald Security man, and cross the road to look for a public toilet and walk my little dog, whom I've brought along for company. We run around on the wet oval for a while. I notice a big sign on the door of the Football Club rooms—'BINGO—Mansfield Football Club, Highett Street Mansfield, every Wednesday night. Eyes down at 8 p.m.' Things go on forever in the country—this is probably the very bingo game June was attending when Laurie rang from Springfield in 1984. My next stop is Bonnie Doon and Springfield again.

∞

Today is a very different day from my last visit. Then, I was full of curiosity and excitement about my own adventure. Although it was winter then and late in the day, the sun had been shining. Now, even though it's spring, the warm weather still seems far away. I am much more aware of Jenny's death being a real murder and feel a bit spooked by being back at the scene. The hills behind the house are instilled with a new significance now I know Adele Baily lay up there so long. They are green as Ireland and just as soft-looking. Above them no blue is visible, simply a dark grey swirl of rain-laden clouds. The farmhouse and the drive alongside it seem sinister. The front gate is open and a white car is parked in a rusty tin shed where the dirt drive ends. Some landscaping has been done along the edges of the drive—two little rows of something green surrounded by white windbreaks, dwarfed by all the large old trees.

The gate is wide open, so I take a chance and walk up to the front door, calling out as I go. There's no sign saying 'Trespassers Shot', but you never know in the High Country. No-one answers, so I walk around the back and look at the outbuildings, blackened by fire—a little white weatherboard shed, which could have been the toilet or laundry, and a larger weathered timber shed for ... maybe some of Laurie's pedigree dogs? There's rubble on the ground around these sheds—all that is left of the kitchen chimney, probably. Feeling like a thief, I quickly take a few photos and remove myself from the danger of being nabbed for trespassing. Writing a book about real people *is* a bit like trespassing—you keep treading on forbidden or sensitive territory.

I decide to try following the dirt road next to the house to take some more photos. The entrance is the only gate within cooee that doesn't wear a 'KEEP OUT' sign—maybe it's a public road. Venturing onto this track is a big mistake. This is definitely four-wheel-drive country—haven't I been listening to *anyone* who's told me how diffi-cult it is to get up into those hills? My low-slung car keeps grazing the hump in the ground between the tyre tracks. It's muddy and slip-pery and there's nowhere to turn around. Long sodden grass on either side of the car could hide a sea of soggy clay for all I know. The parallel red tracks, which look quite negotiable from the highway, actually consist of hell-holes of water and mud, and they're getting narrower and rockier by the metre. Right now I'm as scared as I've ever been. I don't want to damage the car (hell to pay with the husband) or get caught out here (hell to pay with the owners if it's private property) and I have this irrational panic that I might get stuck and no-one will pull me out because it serves me right for being such a nosy parker.

Then the skies open. The dark grey clouds become dark black and roll down the slopes like gigantic dirty snowballs. They enshroud my steel-grey car and we merge in one enormous downpour. I seriously doubt if I'll get out tonight at all. Not even a chocolate bar for emergencies. Thank heavens I brought the dog—at least I'll have someone to unburden myself to. I feel like crying with anger at myself.

The rain drums itself out to a steady downpour as its fury passes on to replenish Lake Eildon across the highway. I crawl along a bit further and find a slightly flatter, wider, rockier piece of track with shallower holes and decide this is it. I execute a three-point turn in triplicate, gaining about thirty centimetres each time. At last I'm facing the right direction and now only have the slightly lesser peril of renegotiating my return to the highway.

Oh, blessed bitumen! How happy I am to reach you with my car and my ego more or less intact. I get out in the pouring rain to take photos of this driving hazard as evidence of my stupidity. I vow to put one on my fridge to remind myself I'm not invincible.

I sneak the dog into the motel room to watch TV with me and share my takeaway chicken until I put him in the car to sleep. The motel owner finds out and is not amused. Not my best day so far.

The following morning I have arranged to meet Kath at the cemetery to visit Jenny's grave. I could have gone on my own, but I now feel closer to Jenny, and I think an introduction by a family member will be more meaningful. The dog and I arrive early, as I want to walk him after he's been cooped up in the car all night. (Didn't want to risk the motel car-park and the owner's rekindled wrath.) He runs joyfully around the tombstones and encounters a Jack Russell, who is like a cemetery ghost, will o' the wisping up and down rows, dodging in and out of view and leading my dog through every deep puddle. Here among all the mourning their surroundings represent, two little dogs are having the time of their lives.

Kath arrives carrying a posy of white dianthus. I had thought of bringing flowers, but decided against it. I felt it might be too familiar. There is a big pile of turf under the cypress by Jenny's grave, growing its own fine covering of bright green whiskers. I ask Kath when it will be put back over the grave site. She doesn't know. She clears away some of the dead flowers still remaining since the second funeral, mostly shrivelled up in their cellophane wrappings. When she moves the bunches, dead heads of flowers and brown petals fall out and tumble like potpourri all over the clay. I don't help. Again, I think it might be too familiar. I rescue a length of wet tartan ribbon from one of the bunches she's thrown on the nearby rubbish pile and wind it around my fingers, keeping it to tie in a bow on my dog's collar—a memento of our visit. I'm waiting until Kath has finished for a good opportunity to take some photos. I don't think she'll want to be in them.

'I haven't been here since the funeral,' she tells me, as she empties the dead flowers and water out of the vase at the top of Jenny's gravestone.

'May I take some photos of the headstone?'

'If you want, but I hate that inscription,' she says fiercely, as we walk back from the tap where she's filled the vase. This surprises me.

'What inscription?' I ask, puzzled.

'That one,' pointing to Jenny's headstone. The inscription reads: 'In loving memory of Jennifer Ruth Tanner. Died 14 November 1984, Aged 27 years. Loved wife of Laurence James. Dearly loved mother of Samuel James. Loved and remembered always.'

'He chose the words—we weren't asked about anything. See how it doesn't say Jenny loved anyone, only that *they* loved *her*. She was a loving mother to Sam—she loved him very much—it doesn't say that anywhere, does it? Anyway, if she was so loved, how come ... ?' Her lips tighten in the now-familiar line Kath adopts when she is holding her counsel.

I think it wise not to be drawn into this family conflict and say nothing. She moves quickly away to the side as I aim at the headstone and fire away with my camera.

There's not much else we can do here; it's all been done twice already. We walk out to our cars together, detouring around past the troopers' headstones, and Kath gives me a little rundown on the history of the cemetery. My dog doesn't want to leave his new-found best friend and I have to chase them up and down rows. Quite Kafkaesque! The dogs have a distinct advantage. Finally I catch mine and meet Kath back at the cars, dog and I both dripping muddy water.

Beside our cars I ask her if she and Les are happy with the way the investigation is proceeding. She seems to be. The police either phone or call in if they're in Mansfield and she doesn't seem worried about progress. She's more worried about an outcome, thinking anything definite will be unlikely, due to the elapsed time.

∞

After leaving Kath, I call in to the *Mansfield Courier* to deliver a letter to the editor for publication the following week. In this letter I have said I'm writing a book about the death of Jenny Tanner and am seeking any information anyone could offer—confidentially or otherwise.

While I'm there, I interview the reporter who covered most of the stories about Jenny and the Adele Baily discovery.

'It's really hard for me,' she says plaintively. 'I'm very good friends with some of the Tanner family and the Blakes are such nice people—everybody likes them a lot. The paper can't take sides, and I have to stay objective. The way we've tried to handle it is to only report the police activities and direct quotes from the police, so we don't get into any editorial discussion about the situation.'

Again, I'm confronted by the difficulties created by small-town loyalties and High Country traditions. Even the newspaper can't report without fear or favour.

I find the newspaper's attitude hard to understand. At the time, Jenny's death was potentially a sensational news story for a small town where reporters and editors mixed daily with the townsfolk and couldn't possibly have avoided hearing the whispers. The sudden violent death of a well liked and beautiful young woman; the young baby left without his mother and his elderly grandmother stepping into the breach; the finding of two bullets in the brain; the inquest held right in Mansfield, attended by the Assistant State Coroner … this is the stuff of a journalist's dreams!

And what was reported? Nothing. Jenny's obituary a week later was the only mention of her death until the case was reopened. A former editor of the *Courier* told me the family company that owns the paper doesn't like upsetting other local families. It's bad for friendships and even worse for advertising revenue.

∞

I take the long way home because I want to eyeball Ian Welch about a new piece of information I've been given. Dusk is falling fast and I again miss the farm entrance and have to retrace a few kilometres back to the gate. I can just see the hump of grass growing in the middle of the tyre tracks on the driveway and I use this to guide me as I drive carefully towards the house. The emus drum me to the front porch and Welch comes out before I have a chance to knock.

'Hope I didn't interrupt your dinner,' I say.

'Nope. Haven't started yet.'

We stand in front of my car in the light from the porch. 'I wanted to ask you something on my way home. Kath Blake told me that the CIB went over to Springfield after Laurie's dog was shot. I just wondered if it was you who went?'

If he had a goatee beard it would be receiving a long massage. He looks at his feet and then over my shoulder towards my car.

'I've never been to that house—ever.' He seems to be reassuring my car.

'What about when Laurie's dog was shot, didn't you go over then?'

'I've never been there. Not for any reason.'

There is nothing to be gained from hanging around, and I still have a long drive. My little dog has barked himself into a frenzy at the strange sound coming from the nearby paddock and I know it's time to call it a day.

'OK. I'm off, then. Thanks for your time.'

'No problem,' he says and disappears into the lighted hallway.

I negotiate the deeply rutted driveway once more and head the car for home. A vaguely unsatisfying trip this time—I'm starting to get to know people and yet still feel like an outsider. A voyeur, peering in through the partly lit windows of people's lives.

12

The Professionals, 1984–85

THROUGH A mounting level of anger and frustration, I decide it's time to take a really good look at Jenny's treatment at the hands of the professionals involved in her case in the year after she died. Researching the facts about what happened turns out to be like digging a hole in dry sand. The deeper I dig, the more falls in. Many of the people I am trying to interview see co-operation with me as risky, as they are still practising their professions and want to distance themselves physically as well as chronologically from even the slightest hint of involvement. Even after twelve years, sensitivities and caution are uppermost. All the professional people I approach have already been interviewed by the new Task Force team, and some seem wary about sharing information that might subsequently be produced by the police as evidence in an inquest, and maybe by the Director of Public Prosecutions in a trial. Others, however, amaze me with their willingness to make sure I get the 'full' story, perhaps to protect their own backs. One even says to me, 'That's what it's all about—always making sure your arse is covered.'

Some have an axe to grind—they perhaps want any blame that may arise to be pointed in a particular direction. Denis Tanner is not popular, in or out of the police force, and much of the testimony given to me is obviously coloured by a pervading dislike of the man himself. I am left in no doubt that a lot of people would be very happy to see Denis in trouble, the more the better. He doesn't seem to have read many of Dale Carnegie's books.

There is always the danger that someone in my position will be fed selected pieces of a puzzle while other parts are withheld, for whatever reason. For example, it is only after months of talking to Bill Kerr that I discover the real reason no photos could be taken on the night. Finally someone else tells me that Sergeant Neil Phipps, the senior police officer on duty that night and official police photographer for Mansfield, was 'working a phantom'—police vernacular for being absent while rostered on duty. Phipps apparently left the station around 8.30 p.m. to attend to personal business, leaving Bill Kerr in charge until the shift ended. Astounded, I phone Bill Kerr, and he verifies this news. He hadn't volunteered the story himself during our various interviews, even though he'd been out of the police force for years. Probably I didn't ask the right questions.

He also didn't tell me he phoned his CI not once but twice, asking him whether he wanted to come to Springfield. This piece of the puzzle is eventually filled in by Don Frazer's recollection of events. It's a very important detail, as it demonstrates—to me, anyway—that Bill needed help on the night.

When I ring Bill Kerr again to confirm this piece of information (which he says he forgot to mention) we chat a bit about progress on the case. He's in a very jovial mood and says Paul Newman came to see him a couple of days ago. When pressed for a reason, he tells me triumphantly 'I found my file!'

'What file?'

'My file on the Tanner case. The one I thought had been "lost",' his voice heavy on the last word.

'Where was it? Did it have all the memos and notes on it you told me about?'

'Let's just say it was my complete file.'

'Oh, come on, Bill! If it does have all those notes in your superiors' handwriting and so on, it really lets you off the hook, doesn't it?'

'Well, you might say that, yes. Put it this way, Inspector Newman seemed pretty pleased to get it. He sat at my kitchen table going through it and every now and then said "Oh, yes! This is what I needed" and other pleased sort of noises. He drove down and back in a day.'

I'm pleased for Bill. I think he got a raw deal in many ways. 'So all those people have been blaming you for being incompetent, and now you'll have the last word? How did you find it so conveniently after all this time?'

'We had a wedding at our place in December and I had to clean everything out of the garage to hold the dancing in there. I pulled out some boxes and there it was.'

'Was it the official file, the one from after the inquest?'

'It was my working file. All my diary notes about my investigation. You have to keep detailed notes when you're investigating a homicide, and I had my suspicions that's what it was. Official stuff, memos and letters too—the whole box and dice. I photocopied a lot of stuff from the official file as well and kept it in my file, along with who I'd phoned and when and so on.'

'So the notes from higher up, saying "No further investigation warranted" and other notes for you to pull your head in are all there?'

'Yup!'

I'm grinning on the other end of the line. The discovery of Bill's file and its contents could be a godsend. The police involved in the first investigation all believe the official records are gone, and I have no intention of disabusing them of this notion during any interviews I conduct. Memories are notoriously unreliable, especially at a twelve-year distance. But Paul Newman has the file. Oh, good!

∽∾

Now that I know about Bill's file, I set out to interview everyone I can find who had anything to do with the case in the months after Jenny's death. It's a slow business. Sometimes I spend days at a time on the phone, trying to track people down. Mr Cosgriff, who was the Coroner for Mansfield at the time of the first inquest, is a good example. I want to find out why the District Coroner deemed a local suicide case important enough to be handballed to the Assistant State Coroner, so ask Bill Kerr who the local Coroner was. He can't remember. I ring Ian Welch—neither can he. I then progress through all the other senior police who had been directly or indirectly involved at the time. Ex-Inspector Tom O'Keefe thinks it was Lance Gilmour. Ex-Chief Inspector Duncan MacLennan disagrees. 'Definitely Cossie,' he says. I ring Homicide. They can't tell me immediately, so I tell them not to bother looking it up. I am assuming Mr Cosgriff, if it was him, might have retired to Melbourne, as he isn't in my well-thumbed Mansfield phone directory, so I try Telstra directory assistance, who are their usual unhelpful selves. For all I know, he could have retired to Timbuktu. (I'm willing to bet I'd get more help from *their* telephone company.) Then I phone the Blakes' barrister, Mr Ryan, and ask him. 'Yes, it was Brian Cosgriff. Still lives in Shepparton and I think he's out of retirement in Wangaratta and Shep, helping out. Shall I give you the Shepparton Court number?' Bless your conservative grey socks, Mr Ryan! And all this chasing for only one paragraph in my story.

The hunt for some of the more important people is no less difficult. Some days I start out with good intentions of 'finishing this chapter today' and get no more than a few pages done, because one phone call leads to another. It becomes like one of those child's necklaces made from different coloured popping beads. Just when I think I have a run of red beads, someone drops a name into the interview and I say, 'Hang on—who's that?' Then I think I'll have to find him, and go chasing after a blue bead to add to the chain. A very scatty methodology, which depended on lots of help from various leads, some amateur detective work, great good luck, miles of tape-recordings and copious note-taking and cross-referencing.

As Jenny's story has progressed it has become increasingly apparent that many, many people have been affected by her death. A murder leaves a different legacy from a gentler death. One of the officers I interview expresses the view this new investigation could all be in vain, with no answers to many questions and the only possible outcome being the same as now, with the wounds a bit deeper than they were the first time round. He could be right.

Seven police over eighteen months have travelled far and wide to find and interview more than a hundred people to investigate actions taken by their colleagues and other professionals at the time. Dozens of technical and medical personnel have contributed to trying to solve the puzzle. If the first investigation had been managed properly under the rules and regulations of the time, the new investigation would almost certainly not have been necessary.

Another still serving officer who was working at Mansfield in 1984 says, 'I wasn't involved in that investigation, for which I am eternally grateful. It has blighted a lot of careers. It also taught me some very, very important lessons. Don't assume anything. Do it once and do it right and be thorough. If you don't provide the best investigation you can, you shouldn't be there. In this job, you're always remembered for your stuff-ups—doesn't matter how many good things you do, you're remembered for the one day you made a blue. It's part of the pressure of this job, really. If you don't do what you could've done this is what happens. It's caused a lot of polarity in a small country town and left a bad taste in everyone's mouth. How much do you think people in Mansfield trust their local coppers these days?'

'It was all a long time ago,' I reply. 'Only four original members of the station are still there.'

'Doesn't matter. They're still "the cops". It's easy for me to say now, but a lot of things just were not done.'

'Like what?'

'First rule of evidence—bag and tag, bag and tag—and I mean everything. The scene wasn't even secured on the night, the gun was handled and moved, relatives were wandering round touching everything, packing clothes and whatever, maybe even exhibits. No gunshot residue tests done on Laurie or Jenny—just doing those tests at the scene could've saved a lot of hassle for people later. I mean, here's the situation right in front of you—it's happened within the last hour—you keep it together! I would've insisted on the CI coming over—I wouldn't have moved till he got his bum over there. I'm not saying it was Billy's fault—he was an unassuming poor devil, probably didn't know how to stand his ground.

'Mind you, you can't absolutely rule out the "passing stranger". We had so many escapees head up our way from Pentridge and other prisons, we were really beginning to think maybe it wasn't a coincidence—perhaps there was a safe house in the area they all headed to. Perhaps someone picked the wrong house that night and Jenny got in the way. Maybe she knew something? It's all speculation now, anyway.'

'But the killer would've had to know where to find the rifle and the magazine—they were kept separately—in separate rooms.'

'Yeah, well that's what everybody tells you, because they want you to think they're right up there with their safety procedures. For all we know, it could've been sitting just inside the back door fully loaded, so he could frighten his dogs. Let me tell you, don't always believe what people tell you.'

Bearing in mind that many of the players in this drama are still around today, even if many have been relegated to the sidelines, I want to present some objective information about how the first investigation was handled, without conveying my own opinions. After a meeting with my strategist husband, I decide to research the rules and regulations of the time, present them to demonstrate what should have taken place and then outline what actually occurred, to allow independent conclusions to be drawn.

One of the key things to take into account in this assessment is the almost sacred chain of command in the police force. Any profession requiring obedience, discipline, dealing with people in difficult situations—and perhaps being required to put life at risk or protect your 'mates'—adopts a similar approach to inducting and training its members. The police, the armed services, fire officers, nurses and others all practise a tried and tested procedure when signing on recruits. Strip them of their civilian clothes; put on a uniform (to minimise individuality); give them a number and rank (the lowest possible); treat them with large helpings of discipline and contempt (to weld them into a team and unite them with each other against the authority figures); instil the importance of seniority and their obedience to whoever represents it; deprive them of liberty and freedom of choice and give them a solid structure from which they may not deviate and through which they must work to achieve their needs—'a chain of command'.

I did not obtain this information from anyone in the police force—I speak from experience as the daughter of an army brigadier, a trained nursing sister and the mother of two serving soldiers and another trained nurse. (Some families are gluttons for punishment.)

Because it is easy to be critical with 20/20 hindsight, I have presented the existing 1984 rules and then outlined what actually happened, based on written records and interviews.

The police—Mansfield

The police are the agents of the Coroner, so they hold the most important position in an investigation of this nature. Under the Coroner's Act of 1958, Jenny's death was clearly a case for an inquest. Therefore, there were a number of clearly defined roles and functions to be executed from day one in relation to the preparation of the inquest brief according to the Victoria Police Manual 1981–86 'Inquests—Reports of Death and Matters Preliminary to Inquest'.

In 1984 the State of Victoria was divided into a number of police districts. Bonnie Doon and Mansfield fell into 'F' District, which also encompassed Benalla (where the District Headquarters was located), Wangaratta and Shepparton. It is important to remember that promotion in those days was not only based on exams, but also on seniority, that is, the length of time a member had served. Later on in my research, one of the Mansfield police added his own list of qualifications for promotion at that time: 'How tall you were; how strong you were; and your ability to take orders from people who didn't know what they were doing.' Length of service sometimes bore little relationship to ability. In turn, the promotion of certain members regarded by their colleagues as being unfit or less well qualified for more senior positions often created dissatisfaction in the ranks. There was also friendly (and not so friendly) rivalry between Operations police (uniforms) and Criminal Investigation Branch police (plainclothes).

In the Mansfield/Bonnie Doon area the chain of command was as follows:

OPERATIONS

District Chief Superintendent Eric Brewer (now retired): Based in Benalla, responsible for the smooth administration of Operations police in District 'F', consisting of Benalla, Seymour, Alexandra, Wangaratta, Shepparton and Echuca.

Chief Inspector Duncan MacLennan (now retired): Based in Mansfield, managed Division 3 of 'F' District. One of three Operations Inspectors for the district, the other two being in Division 1 (Benalla) and Division 2 (Seymour). Although Mansfield was a smaller area than Seymour or Benalla, the Inspector's position there was created largely because of the huge influx of tourists to the area.

Senior Sergeant Neil Walker (now retired): Station Commander of Mansfield. Responsible for the day-to-day running and management of the station's business.

Sergeant Neil Phipps (now retired) and Sergeant Doug McPhie (now Acting Chief Superintendent at Wangaratta): Both reported directly to Neil Walker.

Senior Constable Bill Kerr (now retired): Operations Branch 'foot soldier'. Senior in years to all other Senior Constables in Mansfield.

Senior Constable Don Frazer (now Sergeant at Ballarat): Operations Branch 'foot soldier'. Both these constables reported directly to either Neil Phipps or Doug McPhie.

CRIMINAL INVESTIGATION BRANCH

Regional District Chief Inspector (RDCI) Tom O'Keefe (now retired): head of CIB for 'F' District, based in Benalla.

Detective Sergeant Ian Welch (now retired): In charge of the Criminal Investigation (the 'CI') Branch for Division 3, reporting to Tom O'Keefe and based in Alexandra, about 70 kilometres from Bonnie Doon.

Three other Mansfield police had small roles. They were Senior Constables Jeff and Steve Adams, who were related by marriage to Roz Smith, and Senior Constable Greg Holcombe, who is only of interest because he played a game of basketball on the night of 14 November.

The chain of command was nearly always from the top down—no questions asked. Sometimes it was sideways; for example, the CIB could be notified regarding any suspicious or serious events by the investigating officer, whether uniformed Senior Constable or Inspector. There was also a regulation at the time about official photography. Only members who had completed the photography qualification course set down by the police training school were permitted to take photos of suspicious scenes.

If we look at the roles of the police involved in Jenny's death in sequential order, this is what happened:

On the night Jenny died the station records show Sergeant Neil Phipps (who was also the station photographer), Senior Constable Bill Kerr and Senior Constable Don Frazer were assigned to the afternoon shift—3 p.m. until midnight—with Sergeant Phipps in charge.

Sergeant Neil Phipps has no present recollection of being on duty that night, and told me he doesn't know where he was. According to the two other officers, as it was a quiet night, he apparently left the police station around 8.30 p.m. for personal reasons. He did not return and was unavailable by phone or pager. The first time he heard about Jenny's death was on his arrival at work the following morning. When Detective Sergeant Ian Welch came over to the station that morning, he and Neil Phipps (neither of whom had seen the body or the scene), hypothesised about how Jenny could have pulled the trigger and jointly arrived at the conclusion that she had done it with her toe. They based this hypothesis that it was suicide on the opinions of the two members who did attend. They were at that time unaware that there were two bullets in Jenny's brain.

Senior Constable Don Frazer left work that night to play a game of basketball near the police station on the police side of the local team with Senior Constable Greg Holcombe, who was off duty. Bill Kerr was thus left on his own, which he regarded as 'only natural— Wednesdays were usually pretty quiet'. Police members of the basketball team had permission from Inspector MacLennan to play in competitive games when they were on duty, providing the station was always adequately manned. Don Frazer returned before the call from the ambulance despatcher came in.

Bill Kerr was the senior of the two attending officers. During this part of my research I've finally discovered *his* nickname—'The High Plains Drifter'. There was some ill feeling among other constables about his chronological seniority and irritation at more senior levels from time to time about his apparent lack of independent thinking. Yet all who have served with him have highly praised his honesty, reliability and hard work—he was 'just unusual'. He wasn't 'a man's man, didn't go to the pub, always went home to his family'. (Could this have been because his wife was unwell and he had two small children?) He told me he stayed away from the pub because he'd 'had ten years on breathalyser duty talking to drunks' and is 'not much of a drinker' himself.

At the scene, he was required to implement Section 4.7 of the Victoria Police Manual:

(1) Where a member attends at the scene of an offence of such serious nature that the attention of members of the CI Branch shall be required he shall:
(a) preserve the scene
(b) ensure that as far as possible nothing is touched or removed; and
(c) protect all evidence pending the arrival of members of the CI Branch.

(2) In cases where murder is suspected he shall request any doctor who attends not to move the body until an accurate note of its position has been made.

Section 10.5 says:

(a) In homicides or suspected homicides, a full photographic record will be required, including photographs of the deceased in position as found.
(b) In suicides, photographs are usually not necessary, but in exceptional cases they should be obtained … in which case the photographs should show the deceased in position as found.

Bill Kerr had a long history of being assigned to highway patrols and breathalyser details. He was untrained in crime scene investigation, but approached the scene at Springfield pretty much 'by the book'. Being unable to notify Phipps as the next most senior member on duty, Kerr turned to CIB Detective Sergeant Welch, who instructed, 'No need for photos if it looks like suicide.' Kerr obviously thought the incident was 'of a serious nature', or he would not have made two calls to Welch, but was prepared to accept suicide 'on the face of it'. This meant it was not technically an 'offence' under Section 4.7, though it appeared a bit suspicious. Anyway, he did not know how to get hold of Neil Phipps to get photos taken.

Section 4.5 (4) of the Police Manual clearly says, 'The DDCI (or RDCI in country areas) will decide whether the investigation will continue or whether it will cease.' This instruction is related to investigations under way, but it demonstrates the decision-making power of the local CI officer. Bill Kerr told me if Ian Welch had directed photos to be taken, he would have driven back to get the camera and taken them himself.

The manual also states in Section 10.32, 'Where the circumstances indicate homicide or are suspicious, the member concerned must seek the assistance of the CIB and a medical practitioner as soon as possible.'

After making the first phone call to Welch, Bill Kerr found the extra empty cartridge case 'up the spout'. He and Don Frazer questioned Laurie about it. Kerr says he rang his CI again and told him about this new development, saying there could have been two bullets fired, as there were also injuries to the hands.

Section 10.27 of the manual states:

> Immediately upon receipt of a report of *any death which should be the subject of an inquest* the member concerned must proceed to where the body is lying and take charge of the body.

Of course Welch knew that other officers were already in attendance and he did not feel it was necessary to attend.

After telling Don Frazer, 'He's not coming' and making his sketch of Jenny ('out of habit—you cover your back—put on the old flak jacket') Bill Kerr contacted a doctor and allowed removal of the body. He says the house was empty and locked when he left. In his opinion, the scene was secured until the following day. He took the rifle and two spent cartridge cases with him. He did not touch any other evidence—or protect it by means of bagging and tagging it.

Don Frazer did as he was told by Bill Kerr. Even though Frazer perhaps had more crime scene experience, Kerr was his senior and did most of the phoning and interviewing on the night. Don Frazer was about to be promoted to Sergeant and moved to another police station. So he kept his counsel. He stayed with Jenny's body and returned to the house some time later to draw a plan of the house to comply with Section 10.5 (2), which says:

> When necessary and possible, the member concerned should forward with Forms No. 83 (1) and 83 (2) a carefully drawn pen and ink sketch plan of the house or locality where the body was found and where death was caused.

At the end of the night, after being told so vehemently by Jenny's parents that she could not and would not use a gun, Bill Kerr did not fully complete his Form 83, leaving blank the space indicating 'No suspicious circumstances.'

Detective Sergeant Ian Welch, for whatever reason, decided the following day to visit the scene, even though the night before he had decided it was unnecessary. We don't know what changed his mind. We do know from all his colleagues he was usually 'very willing to come over for anything … Even if he had a gut full of beer, he'd still come.' The next day Welch, coming from Alexandra, apparently drove straight past the gate of Springfield at around 9 a.m. and proceeded into Mansfield. If he had stopped at Springfield, he might have come across members of the Tanner family cleaning up the house. After he and Neil Phipps left the police station around 10.30 a.m. to check the scene, he was told on the radio the house had been cleaned up. Far from raising his suspicions, it appears this news caused him to return to Mansfield. Later that morning, he went with Denis to see Laurie. Laurie was still too distressed to give a formal statement, but did provide new information about Jenny's state of mind. After this informal interview Welch was convinced the case was suicide. Other than Kerr and Frazer, no police officer ever went out to check the property.

On finding out about Jenny's death, Neil Phipps, who had previously been attached to the Homicide Squad, attempted to reconstruct the scene with Ian Welch and Bill Kerr. He was also required to explain his previous night's absence to the Station Commander, Senior Sergeant Neil Walker. There was little cordiality between the men, and Neil Walker could be very blunt indeed when he was upset. He accepted that Phipps was 'missing in action' the night before and more or less told him to keep his nose out of the case, as he was being transferred within a few days to Bentleigh in Melbourne. It wasn't seen to be any of his concern, as he was leaving so soon and he'd missed all the action the night before.

Nevertheless, Welch and Phipps conferred on the situation and reassured Neil Walker that Jenny's death was 'simple suicide'. Walker says now he had no reason to doubt the opinion of his local CI and an ex-Homicide member. He can't remember when he found out the scene had been cleaned up, in spite of the instructions in Section 10.29 of the Manual:

> Before removal of the body from the place where it is found, the body and its surroundings should be carefully searched for anything which might throw light on the cause of death. All such things should be preserved for production ('bag & tag') at the inquest. A careful note must be made of the condition, position and surroundings of the body and of all injuries, instruments, articles or marks &c on the body or in the vicinity which may have any bearing on the cause of death.

The clean-up of the scene was not sufficiently important, it seems, to relay to the Station Commander, although it was allegedly done without permission by a serving police officer or officers, in direct conflict with the orders in the manual and at a time when at least some Mansfield officers held suspicions about the death.

Phipps took the only photos of Jenny's injuries at the Mansfield Hospital that morning. He also took the phone calls from Dr Dyte on the Friday and described to Dyte how the police believed Jenny had shot herself. He was the officer who requested the post mortem be expedited so Jenny could be buried the next morning. In the company of Ian Welch he questioned Denis about why the Altona police were unable to rouse his household during the previous night. Phipps told me Denis's answers were 'evasive'. Denis didn't seem to know anything about what went on at the trots meeting he said he'd attended. Phipps told me he knew Denis only from the police pistol club and seeing him around Mansfield on his visits from Melbourne. Phipps transferred to his new posting within about ten days and said he had no more to do with the case.

Senior Sergeant Neil Walker and Chief Inspector Duncan MacLennan were the two most senior police in Mansfield. Neil Walker just made it into the police force when the minimum height was five foot ten. He was 'fairly ordinary looking' and at around forty-five years he had dark hair already greying and beginning to recede. He was well known for being a bloke who'd get the best out of his team without being overbearing, a straight talker and a fair boss—in fact, he was usually addressed as 'Boss' by all members. One of his superiors was to say of him later, 'Walker was the best at keeping his books in order I'd ever seen.' Although he was often caught up with paperwork, he still liked to get out on the street when he could.

He told me he phoned Ian Welch on a number of occasions—particularly about the finding of the second bullet in Jenny's brain and after Roz Smith called from Queensland. He did not receive her call himself, but was told about it by Constable Jeff Adams. When Neil Walker asked Bill Kerr to follow up the inferences in Roz's call, Bill immediately put a whole series of actions in place with the CIB in Queensland, without going through his chain of command. Neil Walker said he was severely embarrassed by this, but could not ignore the outcome. He referred Roz Smith's statement to Ian Welch, who also could not ignore it. Walker knew Denis Tanner from his days as a trainee mechanic at the local garage, but had never worked with him.

Many of the instructions in the Police Manual refer to cases where there are 'suspicious circumstances'. Although 'on the face of it' a suicide was accepted, a lot of people went to a lot of trouble if the circumstances were not suspicious. Bill Kerr insists he was suspicious even on the night, and several of his actions substantiate this claim. Others will argue now they were not suspicious then, but some of their actions suggest otherwise. Frazer, O'Donnell and Kerr discussed murder by a passing stranger as a possibility while waiting for the doctor at Springfield. Dr Dyte's two phone calls indicated he thought things were not all they seemed, but this was brushed aside in the haste to get Jenny buried. In Neil Walker's own words, afterwards 'Bill was like a fox terrier with a bone.' Walker also says now, 'I played golf with Les Blake many times and never told him I had those deeprooted suspicions.'

The Police Manual Section 10.49 (5) prescribes behaviour for dealing with suspicious deaths:

The officer in charge of the station is responsible for the proper compilation of inquest briefs prepared by members under his control and for the transmission of such briefs through the divisional officer.

Duncan MacLennan was the District Inspector, with a tough and gruff reputation. His steel-grey hair always smelt of smoke from his battered pipe. He was generally regarded as a 'good cop and a tough but fair boss'. His inaugural address to the Apex Club began with the long-remembered statement: 'I came here without any friends and I'll leave without any friends.' He was a consummate politician. Nearly half of his twenty-year career to that time had been spent in Ararat, where he was twice elected mayor. He also knew the importance of good media relations. During the Jika Jika escape the year before Jenny died, he headed up the search in and around Bonnie Doon. He was quoted in the *Age* as saying, 'The press are the nexus between the police and the community. I believe the police are the public and the public are the police.' He also said, 'The positive side of these jobs [hunting escapees] is that they create a remarkable opportunity for the police to establish good relations with a whole lot of people; country people, local businessmen, travellers, the press, and support services, such as the Red Cross and the State Emergency Services. When things like this happen, people in the country take a large amount of comfort from the large numbers of police around. The greatest majority of these men [over 100 were involved in the search] I've never seen before, but it took only five minutes or so to establish rapport—because we're all policemen.'

It is hard to imagine this man being unaware of the impact on police and community relations of the discovery that Jenny Tanner might have been murdered. Or that this possibility had seemingly gone uninvestigated by his police—in her own home town.

In a police district consisting of 6000 people, which swelled to up to quarter of a million during peak skiing seasons, Duncan MacLennan had a fierce reputation for catching traffic offenders. He pitted the full resources of the Mansfield police against them on a daily basis. His record of catching and fining offenders was impeccable.

When I speak to him, he says his 'diary would show he had more than a passing interest' in the investigation. Duncan MacLennan's regulation diary, stored with old records at Benalla and unearthed by the new Task Force, shows he had, in fact, very little involvement, certainly not enough to initiate any serious investigation at the time.

MacLennan did not know Denis Tanner at all before Jenny's death, and he tells me he opposed Tanner's application to move to a vacancy in Mansfield after Jenny died. You'd think as the senior officer in charge of Mansfield Police Station he'd have shown some curiosity about why an officer in the CIB was seeking to transfer to his station following the unexpected death of his sister-in-law.

MacLennan in turn reported to the Area Chief Superintendent, Eric Brewer. The Manual Section 10.49 (1) says:

> Every brief of evidence to be taken at an inquest must be prepared in duplicate as soon as the necessary inquiries are completed and before the date of the inquest is fixed. The brief must, without delay, be referred to the officer in charge of the division, who will satisfy himself that it has been properly prepared.

It was clearly Duncan MacLennan's responsibility to oversee Bill Kerr's preparation of the inquest brief and Eric Brewer's to make sure it was accurate for the Coroner.

There was plenty of information in Section 10.50 of the manual about requirements for the Coroner's brief:

> As a guide to members of the Force in the preparation of inquest briefs, the following information regarding the duties of a Coroner and the methods which he is obliged to employ in conducting an inquest should be borne in mind:
> 1. The Coroner differs from the presiding Judge or Magistrate in an ordinary Court in that he must hold a full investigation;

2. The Coroner is therefore interested in factors as distinct from facts. He requires evidence of factors having approximate or even remote bearing upon the death of a victim;

3. He is interested in all allegations of negligence and suggestions of imputed negligence;

4. He is interested in information which may enable him to suggest methods of preventing the recurrence of an accident;

He is the only person upon whom the scope and choice of the evidence rests.

When preparing a brief for the Coroner's Court the member should, therefore, seek to place himself in the position of the Coroner. He should not limit himself merely to facts, but go beyond and seek factors which may produce deductions and suggestions for preserving other lives as a result of lessons learnt during the hearing of a case. However, if the member is required to give evidence he should be careful to avoid expressing his views as to the cause of death in the court. Opinions of this nature are to be confined to the 'Report of Death' Form No. 83.

Neil Walker and Duncan MacLennan had these instructions to follow. Bill Kerr laboured long and tortuously over the brief for the local Coroner, Senior Magistrate Brian Cosgriff. This should have been done under the supervision of Neil Walker, who would have then passed the brief to Duncan MacLennan for dispatch to the Clerk of the Court.

Kerr says there were a number of reasons why it took nearly seven months to prepare the brief. The file went to Queensland and back; then to Melbourne and back; then to and fro to Ian Welch a number of times with Kerr's requests for further action. Much of the brief was prepared by Kerr at night, out of his rostered working hours, as he did not want 'others' to get wind of what he was recording.

When I ask him, 'Which others?' he says that, as a member was 'under suspicion', he did not want the details of the investigation leaked to that member before he had been officially questioned. Before sending the file across to Ian Welch, Kerr prepared a list of questions he wanted an officer from Homicide investigations to ask Denis Tanner. These were included in the file. Kerr recognised the lack of senior support and wanted to get the brief documented to the best of his ability before it was presented to the Coroner.

Kerr was also keen to interview old Mr Tanner, as he and Jenny were reportedly close. He wanted Fred's opinion about her state of mind. Every time he tried to see Fred the family said he was 'too sick' to be interviewed. All these attempts and others he made to obtain additional tests on the rifle were recorded in the file he maintained on the case. In the end, Kerr gave up on interviewing Fred Tanner.

Kerr says Jeff Adams put pressure on him to tell Jenny's parents about the two bullets and suggest they might wish to get representation. In fact, this was no favour—he was required to do so under Section 10.60:

> In every inquest, the member in charge of the inquiry must ensure:
> (a) a relative (if any) of the deceased is notified in proper time of the day, hour and place fixed for the inquest …
> (b) the relatives of the deceased may be legally represented at the inquest …

This information was only given to Kath and Les about one week before the inquest.

The role of Detective Sergeant Ian Welch is crucial at this early stage of the first investigation. While duty CIB officer he elected not to attend the scene despite two phone calls from a Senior Constable, who was perhaps a bit out of his depth. The only way Bill Kerr could have got Welch to attend was to go over his superior's head and phone either the Regional Detective Chief Inspector, Tom O'Keefe, or D24 in Melbourne to get them to contact Welch directly. Either would have been a drastic step—not at all good for Kerr's career path.

Welch told Bill Kerr not to bother with photos. He made no attempt to view the scene before or even *after* it was cleaned up, although it is possible forensic material was still available even then. Neil Walker has told me Welch assured him and all others that he was, and still is, satisfied Jenny met her death at her own hands.

Welch did not verify Denis Tanner's statement regarding his whereabouts on the night of Jenny's death. He did not request that Tanner be interviewed until May 1985, although Roz Smith's statement was provided to Bill Kerr in February. When Tanner was interviewed, a Record of Interview was not conducted by an officer; a sergeant merely took a statement and provided a written opinion that Kerr's suspicions were based on rumour and innuendo, without even checking Denis Tanner's alibi. Welch and Walker failed to inform Jenny's parents about the second bullet for nearly ten months. They appeared to thwart all attempts by Bill Kerr to have ballistics examine the rifle and conduct other tests. Welch, MacLennan and others returned the working file to Bill Kerr on several occasions with (further investigation) 'Not warranted' written across it.

At the time of Jenny's death, Inspector Tom O'Keefe was the relieving Regional Detective Chief Inspector. His predecessor, Inspector Dallas McDonald, had been ill for some time and Tom O'Keefe had been in this relieving position for nearly twelve months. Because of McDonald's illness, the region had got badly behind in its paperwork—accounts, writing up diaries, briefs for court and so on. O'Keefe told me discipline had slipped and CIB members were conducting their affairs pretty much as they wished. O'Keefe brought in some new rules designed to keep track of what was going on in his region. One of these was an order that any member going outside their own district was to report this movement to O'Keefe.

A call came in from Ian Welch on 29 April 1985 to say he was going over to Shepparton the following day to see Dr Peter Dyte, a pathologist involved in a suicide case in his district. O'Keefe asked Welch to stop in on his way through Benalla. He told me this was the first time he had heard of Jenny Tanner's death and was not at all alarmed, as Welch was an experienced detective who was convinced it was a suicide and was visiting the doctor to confirm it. This occurred six months after the pathologist's first autopsy report was received. Welch persuaded Dr Dyte to change his report in a tape recording to include 'suicide' as a cause of death, to fit the police theory, in spite of Dyte's misgivings that 'she could have put her hands up in defence and been shot by someone'.

According to City Morgue staff I interviewed in 1997, this was a highly unusual course of action for both doctor and police officer— almost unheard of for a member to make such a request and a doctor to accede to it, especially on tape (which, incidentally, Ian Welch kept safe in his own possession until contacted by Homicide during the new investigation). The tape recording was not produced at the first inquest, and its existence was only revealed by Welch's evidence under cross-examination.

In his evidence to the second inquest O'Keefe says Ian Welch was an excellent officer and very thorough and can only explain the lack of CIB investigation of Jenny's death as a 'hiccup' in an otherwise exemplary career. Welch did call in on his trip and they had a cup of tea. O'Keefe says he had no further involvement in the case that he can recall.

The current investigation, however, has revealed that Ian Welch's diary records at least three conferences and a number of other con-versations with Inspector Tom O'Keefe to discuss Jenny's case.

Ian Welch was a popular police officer with a good reputation in his district. He has remained there after his retirement and is well known and well liked by townsfolk. He was 'one of the boys'— definitely a 'man's man'. He did not meet Denis Tanner until Tanner came to Mansfield Police Station the day after Jenny's death. Bill Kerr told me, 'I always thought Welchy was a good bloke. It hurts a bit these days to find out he has such a low opinion of me. He never expressed it to my face then. He was the kind of bloke that you'd model yourself on. I would've liked to have been like him.'

Welch somehow knew the file had 'gone missing' after the inquest—he says it did not come back to his office. He confirmed this during my first interview with him. This was one of the reasons he gave me for taking no further action after the open finding was handed down. He also mentioned approaching Christmas commitments and his lack of officers to assist him.

Section 10.62 of the Manual states:

> When an inquest is concluded all the papers and documents connected therewith (signed where necessary by the Coroner) shall be sent without delay by the member in charge of the case through official channels to the Office of the Registrar General except where a Clerk of the Court [in this case, Senior Sergeant Peter Fleming] has attended, in which case he shall attend to this duty.

So at least one copy of the results of the inquest would have been available to Ian Welch and Eric Brewer if they'd wanted to obtain it. It was still there on file in 1996, when the *Sunday Age* obtained it without any difficulty.

Section 10.63 says:

> The results of every inquest, in the exact words of the Coroner's finding, must be reported to the officer in charge of the district concerned. If an inquest brief has been prepared the finding will be recorded thereon, but if no brief has been submitted the finding will be entered on Form No. 83(2). In all cases an entry must also be made on Form No. 83(2) showing how the property found with the deceased has now been disposed of.

The officer with overall responsibility, District Chief Superintendent Eric Brewer, has no recollection of receiving the results of the inquest. When I interviewed him, he said he was off sick following a spinal operation around that time. All his diaries were lost in the floods of 1993. Neil Walker told me that if Eric Brewer had received the file, in view of the Coroner's scathing remarks about the way the brief had been prepared and presented, he would have expected to hear roars from Benalla. 'Once it was over, I can't believe those comments I read in the *Sunday Age* were put on the file. They didn't come back to me at Mansfield.' Walker claimed this was the first time he'd seen the finding. 'I can't believe Eric Brewer didn't raise merry hell. It should have gone through the CI (Ian Welch). I don't think the file ever came back.'

It's very easy with hindsight to blame Bill Kerr, as the man on the spot and lowest in the chain of command, for not securing the scene properly and not insisting his CI attend the scene. But once he had completed the required paperwork about Jenny's death, Bill Kerr had no official support and nowhere to go with his unease about the case. All he had were hunches. Doubts. A feeling a blind eye had been turned towards justice. Building a solid case requires facts, witnesses, physical evidence, confessions—a logical, methodical process, layer upon layer. Bill Kerr didn't have any of those, hadn't been trained to pursue them, and no-one seemed inclined to help him get any further.

The police—Melbourne

Detective Senior Constable Denis Tanner was at Footscray CIB when Jenny died. His colleagues from Altona allegedly were unable to obtain any answer when they called at his home twice, or three times, or 'every half hour' (recollections differ) between midnight and 5.30 a.m. on the night of Jenny's death. If he was home, neither he nor his wife answered the door. Their bedroom was the first room off the hallway inside the front door. From the police duty rosters of that night, the Task Force detectives conducting the present investigation located one of the police officers who tried to raise the Tanner house-hold. In his company they have revisited the location of the Tanners' old house to make certain it was the right house and ascertain the methods employed to try to wake the household. The garage is a closed building, so it was impossible to say whether Denis's car was there or not.

We do not know why Denis changed his alibi from the trots to the bingo. In any case, the statement to the police regarding his whereabouts on the night of 14 November 1984 appears to be unsupported by reliable independent evidence. His evidence in court about his visit to Springfield shortly before Jenny died also conflicts with evidence given under oath by Roz Smith.

Denis certainly participated in the thorough clean-up of the scene the following morning and made it a priority. He has never denied this to me on the several occasions I have spoken with him during my research. He was seen leaving his home at around 6.30 a.m. with his wife and baby. According to his later statement, he and Lynne, with their baby, went straight to Springfield, before he went on into Mansfield to comfort his grieving brother and offer his assistance to the family. The drive to Bonnie Doon usually took about two-and-a-half or three hours (although as a police officer racing to comfort his family in bereavement, he could have risked driving much faster). He apparently met one of his brothers and they had everything tidied away by 10 a.m. or earlier. His wife has said that after the fanbelt was repaired the family continued on into Mansfield.

In the Tanner family, Denis, Frank and Lynne all had some crime-scene experience. No-one sought permission from Bill Kerr, the investigating officer, or thought to advise him of the clean-up, but no secret was made of it when Denis arrived at Mansfield Police station some time after 10 a.m. Several officers recall him telling everyone at the police station that the house had been cleaned. Denis was a CIB detective who had only just completed his Sergeant's course, and would have been aware of the Victoria Police Manual entries about scene preservation.

On the face of things, Denis Tanner does not seem to have had a motive for killing Jenny, but he is the present investigation's prime suspect. The police Task Force also appears to be investigating any link between Denis Tanner and Adele Baily. He was the last officer to annotate her file, in his own handwriting, 'Failed to Appear' when she did not show up for her court appearance after being bailed on a prostitution charge in 1978. He made this notation in spite of the fact that someone else was the police complainant and in the normal course of events he would have had nothing to do with the file on that day.

This record was still available to the current investigating team by mere chance, as the old part-leatherbound notebooks holding the St Kilda Police Station records from that time were in good condition and were kept for the police museum as an example of the way things were before computers. Most books from that period have been destroyed.

Denis is in his early forties and seems to have few admirers, in or out of the force. There is a danger that perhaps a desire to manoeuvre him out of the force for other reasons could be a motivation for putting pressure on him in a number of ways. Using the crime suspect formula of 'motive, means and opportunity' in relation to Jenny's death, Denis may have had an opportunity, he could have had the means—he may have still been in possession of Laurie's rifle and certainly knew how to find it and use it—but what was his motive?

Denis's wife, formerly Senior Constable Lynne McKenzie, had been in the force for twelve years and was very popular. She is mentioned here for only two reasons. The first is the question about why she did not answer the door (or the phone?) between midnight and around 5.30 a.m. on the morning of 15 November 1984. The second is that in the same old St Kilda records, a diligent search has unearthed the fact that Lynne Tanner was the last person to sign out Adele Baily's file. The records do not show why she examined it. The new investigation team has not been permitted to ask her. She has made no comments to the police, which is her right.

Senior Sergeant Peter Fleming is now a Superintendent at the Ethical Standards Branch. It may give him some degree of personal satisfaction that this case has now been reopened, but it is probably a Pyrrhic victory. As the police officer assisting the Coroner in 1985, he discovered a number of 'major black holes' in the brief prepared for Jenny's inquest. Despite his best efforts, he was unable to elicit a response from the entrenched chain of command. His own Acting Chief Superintendent, although senior in rank to the Homicide Squad members—Ritchie, Merrigan and Fry—who refused to take the case further at Fleming's request, appeared to have no jurisdiction to encourage these officers to participate in a more thorough examination. If an Acting Chief Superintendent couldn't get any action from Homicide, what hope had a police sergeant? In a different way, Fleming was stymied by the same police culture as Bill Kerr. Even though he had more rank and more influence, he still couldn't penetrate the protective barrier surrounding this case.

Several of the statements presented at the inquest—nearly one-third of the total—were obtained by Fleming within days of the inquest. The inquest seemed to be flawed from the start, because witnesses could only be examined on their original statements and they all made those statements having been told Jenny had committed suicide. Several now say, with the clarity of hindsight, they would have thought of other things to include if murder had been mentioned. Sergeant Fleming also finally arranged for the forensic examination of the rifle, ten months after the event.

Senior Constable Adrian Barry was a senior officer at the Firearms Identification and Toolmarks Section of the Victoria Police. This section was established in 1928 as part of the Forensic Science investigation team. Their job was to record what they saw and treat every case as open. Barry (now retired) has a scientist's approach to being interviewed, both on the witness stand and for this book.

He is rather heavy going at first. 'I never volunteer information. I record what I see in a report. If people don't ask the right questions I don't volunteer. The Coroner can ask questions as well—he has very wide, sweeping powers. In 1985, I answered direct to the Coroner. Sometimes I'd attend four inquests and three homicides in a day in court. To give you an idea of our status at the time, I was called to the scene at Hoddle Street after the mass killing there in August 1987 and was there for many hours. The Chief Superintendent of Police could have come and told me to move something or change something and I wouldn't until I was satisfied.'

Section 10.20 of the Manual states:

> In the event of a death by shooting the State Forensic Science Laboratory, Criminal Investigation Branch, will assist in making an

examination of the weapon and any cartridge or bullet suspected to have any connection with such death; and a member of the Laboratory staff will attend the inquest if necessary, to give expert evidence.

In 1985 Barry was 'disappointed rather than surprised' when asked to examine a rifle that had killed someone ten months earlier, particularly in view of the fact that the inquest had already started and was technically still in progress, having been adjourned to enable him to conduct his examination.

He was disappointed about getting the rifle so much later because since 1981 it had been standard practice for members of his section to be called to participate in investigating the crime scene itself or at least attend the autopsy. 'If the police had been present,' he told me, 'the course of the autopsy could have been different.'

I asked him if it was standard practice for his section to be called to the country. 'We were the *Victorian* Firearms Identification and Toolmarks Section, not just Melbourne. I've driven from Sale to Warrnambool in a day'—a trip of 455 kilometres—'We all had beepers and cars—any member or doctor could ring D24 and they could page us. We'd go anywhere, that was our job. Before 1980, in the early days, we didn't attend scenes. The other members brought us exhibit items. But they got contaminated or lost and we started to push for attendance by our own people at a scene. That was introduced in 1981 and has been standard practice since.'

Barry had no opinion about how or why the rifle had been fired. 'The nut behind the butt is of no interest to us.'

When he examined the rifle in 1985 he photographed some smears that showed something was wiped on the weapon—or the weapon was wiped on something. These photos and others of the rifle were not produced at the inquest and he therefore answered no questions about them. They now seem to have disappeared altogether. Barry's evidence that the rifle was 'last fired at fifteen degrees from the vertical' was not explored in detail by any of the legal counsel present.

My question to him about whether that could mean vertically

down as well as vertically up was initially met with 'wait for the next inquest', but he did not argue with me later on that up or down is still on a vertical plane. Was the evidence there all the time and over- looked, because everyone wanted to wrap up this case as a suicide as quickly as possible and distance themselves from it? Mr Barry would not comment.

At Homicide headquarters in Russell Street in May 1985, Detective Senior Sergeant Jim Fry obtained a sworn statement from Denis Tanner—the statement later produced at the first inquest. Fry did not conduct a formal interview. As Executive Senior Sergeant he had the job of assessing files as they came in, and was given the Tanner file for review by his boss, Inspector Brian Ritchie. The file contained requests from the investigating officer (Kerr), the Detective Sergeant in the local CIB (Welch) and covering letters from Inspector MacLennan and the Regional Chief Inspector of the District (O'Keefe) asking Homicide to conduct various investigations.

Fry did not check Tanner's statement of his whereabouts on the night. He wrote a detailed report to his country counterparts telling them that, in his view as an experienced Homicide detective, Jenny Tanner's death was clearly suicide and Kerr's suspicions were based on rumour and innuendo. He discussed the matter with Inspector Ritchie and also gave him a written report. Fry's opinion was reiter- ated by Ritchie in a written report back to his country colleagues, in spite of the fact that Ritchie now says he never read the file but 'was told enough by Fry to be satisfied the investigation had been brought to a satisfactory conclusion'. Ritchie also says in sworn evidence in 1998 that he did not know there were two bullets in Jenny's head until he read about them in the paper in June 1996; yet in the file there is a memo to him from Jim Fry, dated 22 May 1985, *telling* him there were two shots in Jenny's head.

In the lead-up to the first inquest, Fry spent more than an hour with Peter Fleming while Fleming was attempting to obtain more information. Apparently with the backing of his senior officers, Fry refused to conduct even a cursory investigation into some of the mys- teries surrounding Jenny's death.

Jim Fry is now retired and growing chestnuts in the country. He tells me he was quite satisfied with Denis's statement at the time. Denis showed no hesitation when asked to make a statement and was 'very confident' in what he said. Fry says he didn't know Denis then and has never seen or spoken to him since. The file came to Fry from the Coroner's Office with a query because 'some of the allegations being made by Bill Kerr were pretty serious—there were a lot of suppositions by Kerr in his original typed statement attached to the brief. His report and statement contained a lot of possibilities.' It also contained the list of questions from Bill Kerr—none of which Fry asked.

Fry tells me he thinks a lot of fuss is being made now with little possibility of an outcome. 'You should never chase gold. If you don't solve a case in three days you have less and less chance of it. If Tanner wasn't at the bingo—so what?' he challenges.

I don't know if an answer to this question is expected, so say nothing. He goes on to tell me a story about a shotgun death at Omeo, in country Victoria. 'The young guy was shot twice in the head inside the house and had only half his brain left. He walked to the outside door, used the handle to open it and started down the outside steps. It wasn't until the last two steps he fell over and actually died. It was a famous case in the area—James Henry Macnamara. They say you can do it on memory, like a reflex. Your body functions on automatic for a few seconds. With this Tanner case—hindsight is a marvellous thing. They should have done residue tests, would have saved a lot of hassle.'

I wondered if he thought Jenny was so familiar with firearms she'd be able to shoot herself 'on memory, like a reflex'.

Senior Sergeant John Rankin (now Chief Inspector at Horsham) was on duty at D24 the night Jenny died. He is reluctant to speak to me about his recollections of calls received from Bill Kerr or Altona police on that night, as he is now a very senior member and the case is still under investigation. He does say he has made a statement to Homicide.

The doctors

The first medically trained person at the scene of Jenny's death was not a doctor but Gerry O'Donnell, the ambulance officer. After months of fruitless searching, I finally discover he works five minutes' walk from my house and lives not much further away.

Gerry has left the ambulance service. He tells me Jenny Tanner's death brought his career as a country ambulance officer to an end— it was 'the final straw. It's too difficult in a small town—we lived right next door to her in-laws. I'd see them every day and it was just too hard to live with.' He declines to be interviewed in detail for fear of breaching patient confidentiality, but he speaks to me briefly and confirms the evidence he gave at the inquest. He says the 'passing stranger' theory was short-lived, mainly due to the lack of any obvious disturbance. He did accept it was suicide on the night, although the absence of a note puzzled everyone. Gerry O'Donnell did everything by the book, and no doubt fulfilled his role professionally and compassionately.

The significance of my brief discussion with Gerry was that he was the first person to tell me murder was suspected, for a short time at least, on the night. If it was so obviously suicide, why was such a possibility even canvassed? Bill Kerr says the absence of a note was a major factor. But as murder *was* discussed, why were more precautions not taken to keep the scene intact for the CIB?

Dr Gilham argued at the inquest, and still says today, that all he was asked to do was issue a death certificate. In his own evidence he says he 'made a presumption and didn't examine the body closely'. He was told Jenny had committed suicide and had no reason to question this at the time.

The Police Manual Section 10.15 (2) says:

> The death of a person must be certified by a doctor before the body is conveyed to a mortuary, except where the death occurs in a hospital.

The main purpose of Dr Gilham's presence was to pronounce life extinct so Gerry O'Donnell could take Jenny to the morgue at Mansfield Hospital. The procedure for custody and delivery of her body and the death certificate, which Gerry O'Donnell followed to the letter, was also outlined in the Police Manual.

Ross Gilham, however, had knowledge the police didn't have and he did not share it on that night. Jenny was not his patient, but Laurie Tanner was. A number of visits from Laurie had developed into listening and counselling sessions about his troubled marriage. Gilham could have kept silent for several reasons—patient confidentiality, feeling it was irrelevant, not thinking of it at all. Whatever the reason, he said nothing then or later. He did no detailed examination of Jenny's body and did not even look in her mouth to see if his 'presumption' had any substance.

He seems to have made no attempt to follow up Laurie's state of mind or counsel him after Jenny's death, other than visiting the Tanners' house that night to sedate Laurie and sit with June and Fred for a while. He says Laurie made a 'good recovery after the incident and his behaviour was quite appropriate at the time'. If Gilham had followed up the investigation, he might have been able to contribute more. If he'd known about the second bullet on the night he says he would have conducted his examination differently and taken more notice of the surroundings. As one of the bullet holes was hidden by Jenny's blood-soaked hair, a slightly more thorough examination of her injuries on the night, after Don Frazer had given him permission to touch her body, would have revealed the fact she had been shot twice in the head. This might have encouraged Dr Gilham to insist that Ian Welch attend, and the course of the investigation could have been completely different.

Dr Peter Dyte died soon after the first inquest. His family is unhappy about the way he was treated in the *Sunday Age* article, which indicated he went along with the police theory because he was 'obliging' and 'easily influenced'. Respect for the feelings of the survivors, however, should not allow the facts to be buried with those who haven't survived. I have written to Mrs Dyte and offered her the opportunity to provide more information, but through a family friend she has indicated her wishes are to put this tragic episode behind her, which is her right entirely.

Dr Dyte was a highly respected member of his profession. At the time of the autopsy on Jenny his illness, which was very rapid, severe and painful, either had not been diagnosed or was in its very early stages, so it should not have interfered with his professional approach to his duties as a government pathologist.

Dr Dyte was described for me by Dr Terry Schultz, one of his colleagues at the time, as follows: 'Peter was a very likeable, intelligent, and knowledgeable man. You mention that he was described as obliging, and indeed he was, but you also said that he was easily influenced, which any of his friends will tell you is a false statement. The implication of the latter comment is that the police were easily able to convince Peter that this was "just a suicide". In assessing this assertion, you should bear in mind the whole context of the situation. [A senior forensic professor] has indicated to me that he has a great deal of sympathy for the position in which Dr Dyte was placed. He had an exceptionally good relationship with the police and the Coroners, as one would expect, and no reason to doubt their word. Nevertheless, he was still clearly not happy with the situation, hence the telephone calls to the local station, where he was reassured of the supposed presentation of the "facts".'

The fact of Jenny's autopsy are:

Jenny was escorted to Shepparton Hospital by the Mansfield police and presented to Dr Dyte as a self-inflicted gunshot wound. He commenced his autopsy on the basis that Jenny had shot herself and that his report would be produced as evidence at a later inquest. No member of the police force stayed with the body during the post mortem.

Before he discovered the second bullet, he did not take any photos or X-rays, although he did order X-rays after he had discovered the two shots. These X-rays were never produced and have been lost. He did not conduct any gunshot residue tests on Jenny's hands or feet. Early in the autopsy he found two holes in Jenny's forehead. Towards the end of the autopsy he found the two bullets and a fragment in her brain. According to my discussions with staff at the Melbourne City Morgue, at this point he should have stopped the autopsy and called the CIB or Homicide. The autopsy should not have continued until they were present. They said, 'When a doctor believes a reportable death is suspicious he does not continue with the autopsy.' This is supported by what Adrian Barry told me.

He did stop the autopsy and, because of his good relationship with the police, he rang the station responsible for the investigation and reported his misgivings—twice! Although the pathologist is in complete charge of the body and the direction the autopsy should take until he has completed his report to his own satisfaction, Peter Dyte allowed a police sergeant to persuade him his misgivings were unfounded and that he should continue and complete the autopsy as quickly as possible. This was despite the fact the police only have an investigative role, not a medical role, in an unexplained death and the police officer he was speaking to was not medically trained and had not even attended the scene of the death. In view of the fact that Jenny's body had been brought to Dyte by the police, it was automatically a death 'under investigation' and what is known as a 'Coroner's body'—that is, it 'belongs' to the Coroner, who has total jurisdiction over it. Dyte's report was vital to the direction the investigation would take. It determined whether Jenny would be buried as a suicide or the police would look further for someone else who might have inflicted the wounds.

Following the conversations with Neil Phipps, Dr Dyte was obviously still unconvinced himself, as he then walked across the car-park to another building and sought the opinion of a pathologist much junior to him in years and experience. From their own experience and with the help of a textbook, together they tried to develop an explanation for the two bullets in Jenny's brain in terms that would be compatible with the police suicide theory.

According to all the accepted practices and guidelines laid down in 1984, Peter Dyte had a number of other options at this point. One of them was to err on the safe side, in view of the fact that two bullets fired from the front of the head directly into the brain was such an extreme outside possibility. He could have phoned the local Coroner for direction, or the City Morgue in Melbourne. He could have phoned the local RDCI in Benalla or even the CIB officer in Shepparton, five minutes' drive away. He could have phoned Mansfield police station again and gone above Neil Phipps to speak to Neil Walker or Duncan MacLennan. He could have phoned D24 and asked for someone from Adrian Barry's department to drive up to Shepparton, only a couple of hours from Melbourne.

At the time of his discussion with Neil Phipps he was informed that Jenny was related to a police officer, who was awaiting the return of the body for burial. In view of this new information, he could have been more careful about detail. He could have taken photos. He could have done gunshot residue tests. He could have refused to release Jenny's body until someone had examined her forensically. But *because* he had such a good relationship with the local police he made the gross assumption that the hand wounds were consistent with the head wounds, which were consistent with suicide. He and Sonenberg, trying to 'assist' the police, arrived at a vague agreement that it was 'possible' she could have fired two shots herself. He completed the autopsy as quickly as possible and released the body that afternoon. He did not offer a written opinion about how death could have been effected on his autopsy report, as this was not the usual practice, but the release of the body so quickly at the request of the police, without causing any further investigations to be done, implicitly indicates that he accepted the word of the police regarding the suicide theory.

Five months later, when he was unwell, he allowed Ian Welch to persuade him to add crucial information to his original single-page report. He provided a taped opinion suggesting the hitherto undocumented presence of powder burns around the wounds on Jenny's hands. In spite of the fact he had mentioned 'defence' wounds, he still went along with suicide as the cause of death. This was highly unusual. Welch's request must have sounded some alarm bells for Dyte in view of his problems with the two bullets at the time of autopsy. Unfortunately, Dr Dyte was too ill to present his own opinions and his reasons for them at Jenny's inquest and he died soon after. Any conclusions drawn from his professional opinions regarding her case can only be speculative, as he is not here to discuss them in person.

Dr Terry Schultz was, as indicated earlier, a colleague and friend of Peter Dyte. He worked with him at Shepparton before moving to a more senior position at Wangaratta, where he still lives today. It was only a few days before the inquest when he was asked to give evidence—his opinion about Dr Dyte's autopsy report. He reviewed the report and had some questions about it, which he decided to raise with Dr Dyte. However, when he travelled to see him, Peter Dyte was already very ill and Terry Schultz felt it was inappropriate to question him in detail about something that was of no great importance to a dying man, although of extreme significance to others. He did, however, obtain an assurance from Peter Dyte that his opinion about suicide had not altered.

Dr Schultz was now in a difficult position. He disagreed with his colleague and maybe would have conducted the autopsy differently, but he could only offer an opinion, not evidence, on a senior colleague's professional findings at an autopsy in which he did not participate. He told the court, 'I think it unlikely that the deceased would not have lost consciousness after the first wound to the head, whichever of the two it may have been. In addition, it is noted that the rifle was a bolt-action type requiring manual operation.'

His opinion was too late to change the course of the investigation into the cause of Jenny's death. He was fascinated by the case for years afterwards and researched multiple gunshot suicides, keeping records on file at home. Some time later he was entertaining Professor Stephen Cordner, Head of the Forensic Institute, and mentioned Jenny's case as an 'interesting' one that Professor Cordner might wish to follow up. Professor Cordner was used to having his attention drawn to 'interesting' deaths, and did not pursue the matter. Neither doctor dreamed Professor Cordner would spend about six months investigating this very puzzle in 1996.

Dr Norman Sonenberg was the junior pathologist at Shepparton who conferred with Peter Dyte on Jenny's injuries during the autopsy. He had been at Shepparton for approximately two years, filling his first position as a specialist. He is now a pathologist in Gippsland. He had already left Shepparton Hospital at the time of

Jenny's inquest and was tracked down by Peter Fleming from the Coroner's office to provide testimony about Dyte's autopsy report.

Sonenberg supported Peter Dyte. He said he had no doubts then that suicide was the cause of death. His evidence at the first inquest gave professional credence to the suicide theory, even though he did not participate in the full autopsy and only had the opportunity to examine Jenny's brain *after* Peter Dyte had uncovered the two bullets.

When I interview Dr Sonenberg he cannot remember this critical piece of evidence he gave at the inquest. He tells me he only provided a written opinion for the Coroner's Court. When I read him back some of his testimony, he recalls the event, but says he gives evidence at so many inquests they all run into each other.

Doctor Geoffrey Patience is a well-respected general practitioner in Benalla. When asked why Jenny made the 160-kilometre round trip from Bonnie Doon to see him ten times while she was pregnant, he says it was because Ross Gilham did not have 'delivery rights' in Mansfield and thus could not see the pregnancy through to its conclusion. Kath Blake says Jenny did not like Dr Gilham and that most of the young women in the Mansfield area had their babies delivered at Benalla Hospital. (Dr Gilham also told me that he thought Jenny did not like him, but had no idea why.)

Dr Patience saw Jenny throughout her pregnancy and afterwards. He noticed she was withdrawn and 'taciturn'. When I ask if her demeanour could have been the result of anger just as easily as depression, he agrees that any deep-seated emotion could have been the cause. He said in evidence that Laurie, who was also a patient from time to time and still is occasionally, had consulted him about Jenny's 'moods'. I ask him if he can recall how soon before Jenny's death these consultations took place and without the benefit of his notes he says it was between two and four months before. This would have been around the same time as Jenny consulted Dr Patience about having a second baby. Dr Patience says he was aware from Laurie there were problems in the marriage, but he cannot discuss the case any further with me due to patient confidentiality.

He treated Jenny professionally while she was alive and gave evidence at the inquest that he had no reason to believe she would take her own life.

The legal practitioners

The first legal practitioner involved in this case was Senior Magistrate Brian Cosgriff, who received the brief from Mansfield police in about June 1985. The length of time taken to prepare it was not unusual, but perhaps a little longer than normal for a 'simple suicide'. Under the old Coroner's Act there was no requirement for local or regional coroners to report any death to the Melbourne office, as officially the State Coroner's office did not exist. There was a Senior Coroner and Assistant Coroner, but the establishment of the State Coroner's Office arose from the new Act.

Mr Cosgriff tells me he excused himself from the case and sent the file to the Assistant Coroner in Melbourne because there were 'a number of aspects about it he didn't like'. He thought it should be heard 'by a magistrate who had better access to the main Coroner's Court', although it was a great pity it arrived there almost ten months after Jenny's death, when any possible evidence against a suicide was cold. Some people have told me Mr Cosgriff thought the case was 'too hot to handle' and wanted someone more senior from outside the area to take it on 'just in case'. When the brief arrived at the Melbourne Coroner's Court it was given to Mr Hugh Adams, SM.

Mr Adams' neat grey suit and clipped greying hair predict his orderly and economical approach to questions. He indicated he was unable to answer many of my questions as the case was still in progress. He was the Assistant Coroner for Victoria at the time, but agreed to travel to Mansfield to hear the case, so that a number of local witnesses did not have to travel to Melbourne. In view of his scathing comments at the time I find it difficult to understand why his office did not ensure that there was some sort of follow-up to the inquest, rather than letting the file 'disappear'. I also find it difficult to understand why the brief was accepted in the form it was and the inquest was not adjourned until a full investigation had been conducted, especially in view of the representations from the Blake family. Interestingly, the Tanner family never pressed for further investigations to be conducted. On the contrary, they said they thought it was 'a very thorough and complete investigation at the time'. It should be remembered that Mr Adams specifically cleared Laurie and Denis Tanner of any involvement in Jenny's death.

Mr Joe Gullaci is now a senior barrister with his own chambers in Melbourne. He is constrained by lawyer/client privilege from making any comment to me about the case. I comment that I feel some opportunities were missed in the cross-examinations at the hearing. He says from his point of view it was 'an interesting case forensically'. In those days he often acted for police members who required representation and it was quite in order for any interested party to have representation at an inquest. He has never seen a transcript of the case. 'Would you represent the same clients if asked again?' I ask. He refuses to comment. I ask him if he was pleased with the finding in 1985. Again he won't comment. 'Well, did you leave the courtroom smiling or frowning?' I persist. He laughs. 'I can't tell you that, either!'

Later, when I call him to check some details in a nearly completed draft, he asks me who is 'legalling' my manuscript. He say he has a lawyer friend who does 'that sort of thing', whose wife is involved in the movie business. If I'd like to send my MS to him he'll pass it on. I thank him, but decide when I hang up that would not be a very clever idea. What if he's just got back an old client?

Mr Rodney Ryan sees me in his office in Mansfield after I make an appointment with his secretary. I haven't explained why I wanted to see him. As I sit down I tell him the reason for my visit and offer to pay for the time I am spending with him, as I am preventing him from seeing other real clients. He generously refuses payment, but he also refuses to discuss the case in any detail. He is quite firm about one issue—Kath and Les Blake had told him they wanted an open finding and that is what was handed down. He says he thinks they were pleased with this outcome and he fulfilled his brief, so he felt quite satisfied at the time.

I ask him why he was not more aggressive in some of his cross-examinations and he gives me the same reply about getting the open finding. When I point out a number of discrepancies in the evidence about time and place and details he didn't appear to follow up at the inquest, he replies the same way again. I decide I'm being treated to the old 'broken record technique', though in the nicest possible way. I ask him whether he now thinks that he was too gentle in his conduct of his clients' case at the inquest. He denies this and points out that Mal. Ryan, Jackson & Glen have been in business in Mansfield for nearly one hundred years. I say they must be doing something right in that case. He sees me out and I thank him for his time. He is very gracious. 'Not at all. It was much more interesting than a divorce, which is what most unaccompanied women I've never heard of come to see me about!'

Kath and Les Blake are satisfied that Mr Ryan did a good job for them. He got them the finding they wanted.

∞

The more I investigate the 'processing' of Jenny after her death, the more I feel she was caught up in a chain of events, each one perhaps significant enough in itself to be of major concern, but put together, looking very like a series of actions to avoid the consequences of mistakes.

It appears the police made genuine mistakes early on and then willingly or unwittingly became enmeshed in a cover-up, part of the police culture of the day to protect the brotherhood and avoid criticism for the early mistakes.

The doctors did not follow accepted procedures. By his own admission Ross Gilham did not do a full examination of Jenny. Peter Dyte and Norm Sonenberg were willing to accept the police suicide theory over the evidence of their own eyes, and Dyte's autopsy report was silent on some key issues. Various excuses were subsequently put forward for these shortcomings—'police on the night only wanted life pronounced extinct'; 'police said it was suicide'; 'a senior colleague needed confirmation of his findings' and so on. Viewing merely this medical chain of events, as a mother and former nurse, I say it was not good enough! Jenny deserved better medical attention to detail, even if she was dead.

Because of his rigid adherence to his clients' brief, Mr Ryan seemed reluctant to query professional opinions when opportunities presented themselves at the first inquest. Even then, new evidence solicited by cross-examination would not have been too late to reactivate the investigation. Mr Ryan had the power to ask questions that would give the Coroner additional 'factors as distinct from facts ... having approximate or even remote bearing upon the death of the victim', as the Police Manual puts it. Mr Ryan had power but, for whatever reason, did not use it.

Mr Gullaci, on the other hand, properly used this same power quite often to deflect lines of questioning away from any slight imputation on either of his clients' movements or actions.

Mr Hugh Adams cleared both Tanner brothers in his open finding and shut the door on any further investigation in either direction. The police seem to have used the open finding as an excuse to lose the file altogether and take no further action.

Even the media of the day were silent. For fear of alienating the living, the issues were buried with Jenny. If some of the questions being asked over gateways and fences were asked by the *Mansfield Courier*, perhaps the police would have put more energy into quelling media stories with some measurable investigative processes. While the town quietly simmered with disapproval below the surface without a legitimate release valve, the police had nothing to fear.

13

Motives

AT LAST my husband and I are ready to head north. We pack our computer gear in the station wagon and set out, aiming for North Queensland. As we drive we speak often of Jenny. We have plenty of time to speculate on motives. For 3500 kilometres we go over the possible scenarios, coming up with some wild theories and some not so wild. Why did Jenny die? Who benefited? Was her murder covered up? Who benefited from a cover-up? Why was so much energy being expended now on a case with a trail colder than yesterday's mashed potatoes?

On the way we visit Jenny's friend Roz Smith near Brisbane, and test out a couple of our new theories. She is still deeply affected by Jenny's death. It is 42 degrees the day we are there, and nothing is moving except the thermometer. Wrapped in the heat as we walk to the car, she says in parting, 'I really hope they get enough evidence to have another inquest. Maybe the truth will come out this time.'

Certainly Paul Newman's words are reassuring: 'A case is never closed until I get my man.' Whatever the police hierarchy's motives for ensuring the reopened case is kept active—to see justice done or to head off media criticism—there is no doubt the new investigation team is making every effort to get to the bottom of Jenny's murder and Adele's disappearance and death.

The investigators are convinced of their quarry and have pursued him relentlessly. His own training would tell him exactly what they're looking for—and they don't appear to have found it.

During discussions with the Task Force, I have expressed the hope their motives were not so blurred by their wish to 'get their man' that they overlooked some other man (or woman) in the process. This case has become a mission for some of the investigating team. By the time the second inquest begins, at least seven Task Force members and dozens of outside experts will have lived and breathed it for nearly two years. They think it, speak it, live it, reconstruct it, imagine it, discuss it, analyse it, even dream about it. Just when they think they have the brief wrapped up, another piece of the jigsaw surfaces and its position has to be identified and recorded. New pieces of the puzzle often dislodge other pieces already in place. The cost of the investigation leading up to the second inquest is about a million dollars. It's hard to believe the Victorian Force Command would authorise this level of expenditure for public relations alone—or merely to serve the interests of a long-dead woman and her family.

Perhaps another, deeper motive drives this difficult investigation. It would be safe to assume that no-one at Force Command wants a police scandal. The new investigation of Jenny's death has shown the first investigation was at best incompetent and at worst a conspiracy of silence up to pretty high levels in the police force. So now their best, most squeaky-clean Inspector is on the job—to make sure there is no evidence out there that could implicate a member.

Inspector Paul Newman has become single-minded about pursuing his prime suspect. He personally believes beyond doubt that Denis has more than a few curly questions to answer. If Force Command has a hidden agenda, Paul Newman seems totally unaware of it.

Whoever was responsible for the deaths of Adele Baily and Jenny Tanner—and it may have been two different people—what really rankles is the way they have got away with it all these years. Three families devastated, two women dead, dozens of people affected in so many ways, and the murderer/s going around free, perhaps even laughing about how thoroughly everyone was fooled.

How could anyone living with a cold-blooded killer not know? Jenny's killer would have been covered in blood if he or she attempted to sit Jenny up on the couch, wipe the rifle and place it between her legs, wrap her bleeding hand around the butt and prop her up. It was someone strong; a dead woman Jenny's size is no

Left to right: Denis Tanner, Joe Gullaci, Tony Hargreaves, Laurie Tanner at the Coroner's Court, March 1998. Photo by the author.

Artist's sketch of how Jenny was found, an exhibit in the second inquest. Photo by the author.

June and Denis Tanner, December 1997. Photo by Ray Kennedy, the *Age*. Reproduced by permission.

Inspector Jeff Calderbank (left), Inspector Paul Newman (sitting on desk) and Senior Constable Graham Miller (at desk) in the police room at the Coroner's court, with some of the inquest evidence. Photo by the author.

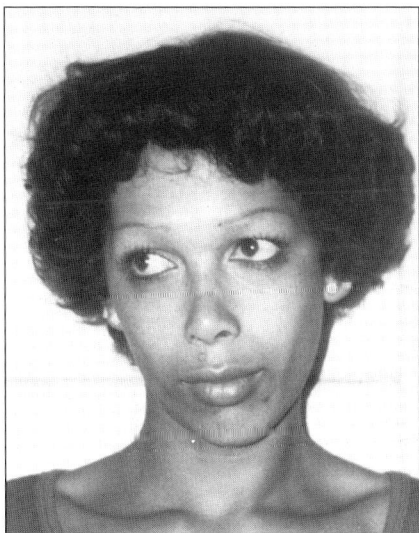

Adele Baily,
Courtesy
Victoria Police.

A knife sent to Helen Golding.
Photo by the author.

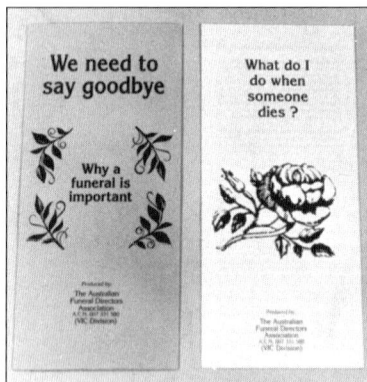

Sympathy cards sent to Helen Golding.
Photo by the author.

lightweight, especially if she had to be lifted from the floor. What happened to the killer's clothes? Were they packed and removed that night? Did the killer wear them home and dispose of them at leisure?

If we accept that Jenny's killer was known to her (which is likely given the coffee, the biscuits, the cigarette butts and the lack of any obvious signs of a break-in) it is likely other family members would know that person too. Any uncharacteristic behaviour or unexplained movements on that night would stand out like a beacon, highlighting their suspicion.

The most fascinating question, apart from who killed Jenny Tanner, is why was she killed? What was the motive for this seemingly execution-style killing? I think the killer went there to have something out with her, knowing Laurie would be late home. Mind you, whoever it was took a big risk in not killing Jenny until so late in the evening, as Laurie could have come home at any time after his cleaning job.

Jenny's uncharacteristically long conversation with Angie McCormack may have been a ploy to buy time. Maybe the killer had the rifle at her head the whole time, but allowed her to answer the phone. Perhaps the call sliced into a heated argument and Jenny stayed on the phone longer than usual to allow tempers to cool. If her visitor was already there when the phone rang, it's interesting that Jenny didn't mention it. This indicates to me that whoever was visiting was either someone Jenny did not want known, or someone of whom she was not at the time afraid; otherwise, surely she would have seized the opportunity to tell Angie she was not alone? The real threat must have come after she hung up, between 9.30 p.m. and around 10 p.m., allowing for the killer to be gone before Laurie arrived home.

The killer fired at her from close range. Perhaps a couple of shots were fired through the white towel (or was it a nappy?) that was left on the couch, and she instinctively put her hands up to protect herself. Maybe more than three or four shots were fired—the magazine held ten bullets and only two remained. Other shots could have gone into the couch, the floor or the walls. Jenny would probably have fought like a wild cat, knowing that anyone who would shoot at her like this could not allow her to tell the tale. She knew her baby son was asleep in the next room, and she would have been frightened for his safety. If her killer was an uninvited visitor she would have been expecting Laurie home any minute. Perhaps she fought for time, arguing or abusing. Perhaps she tried to run for it.

It took more than one bullet to kill her, even though the killer aimed at her head at close range. Why did the shot miss, especially if the killer was familiar with the use of firearms? Jenny knew she was fighting for her survival, although she may not have believed her attacker would really go through with it. Perhaps she moved at the last second, but not quickly enough. Stubborn in life, Jenny refused to die quietly. Was she still conscious after the first shot to her head? Several doctors think she could have been. Did she continue to fight and curse her killer, or did she lie still and bleed into the couch cushions, her moaning the only sign that she still wouldn't die? By this time the killer must have been pretty angry and frantic. A nice simple execution turned very messy and difficult to explain away as 'simple suicide'. This killer, however, was pretty damn sure of what the police might be looking for. In spite of the hand wounds and the two obvious bullets, a suicide scenario might still be possible. Hastily, the scene was rearranged. Did the killer push Jenny's blood-soaked hair over the second bullet hole, hoping a cursory examination would overlook this incriminating injury?

How did the killer escape from the house? It's unlikely a car was parked in the driveway for anyone passing to notice and for Laurie to block in when he arrived home; it's more likely to have been hidden at a discreet distance from the house in the lane between Springfield and Stanleys, or inside the gate behind the fence at the rough entrance to the paddocks on the western side of Springfield. This is a country area, where every unusual car is noticed. If it was parked visibly at Springfield and it was a car not usually parked there, during daylight saving when it didn't get dark until nearly 9 p.m., why didn't anyone see it? Country neighbours notice visitors as they drive by.

All things considered, the killing was a pretty risky exercise. It might not have been premeditated, even if the visit was planned. Yet the stakes must have been high and the motive strong for the killer to take those risks. There was a certain cold-bloodedness—or foolhardiness—in expecting police to overlook other indicators and accept a suicide theory in the absence of a note or any obvious reasons for Jenny to take her own life.

My patient husband and I thrash out so many scenarios we even outdo the police investigators at times. From time to time I call Paul Newman and say 'Hey, what about this idea?' Mostly the police are months ahead of us, but a couple of times we highlight a new possibility or provide some food for thought. In any event, I've always viewed this case as Homicide's to solve and mine to write about. As Paul Newman once said, dismissing some theory of mine: 'As a writer you make a lousy cop.'

∞

My endless speculations always centre around motive. I don't believe anyone would risk murdering another human being, especially in such circumstances, without very strong motivation. Something was driving the killer to abandon caution and 'take care of business' almost regardless of the potential consequences.

Why do people kill? Passion. Jealousy. Financial gain. Anger. Accidentally. Psychopathically. Randomly.

So how about passion? Several people have intimated Jenny was having an affair, possibly with a police member, at the time of her death. June Tanner certainly thought Jenny was being unfaithful to Laurie and allegedly said so to a number of people after Jenny died. If she was involved outside her marriage, passion may have caused her death.

Maybe her lover visited that night and Jenny told him she was staying with Laurie and tempers flared irretrievably. In creating one hypothetical scenario, my husband and I link Neil Phipps' absence from work that night to Jenny having an affair with a policeman and make five. On my next trip down from Queensland, I set off looking for 'Phippsy', to ask him face to face if he killed Jenny Tanner.

∞

After driving a long way from the main road through some of the prettiest countryside in Victoria, I finally find his Nirvana. I'd planned to say I was just passing, but I don't think I'll get away with that ten kilometres off the highway. So I broach the front door rather nervously, and when he answers I tell him I have two important questions to ask him. We've spoken on the phone but not met face to face before. Sitting in his kitchen over a welcome cup of tea, I pop the first question.

'Were you having an affair with Jenny Tanner? Is that where you were that night?'

He laughs. 'I didn't even know her! The only time I saw her was when I took a few photos the following day at the morgue. For years I thought she was Jenny Black. It was only recently, when the Task Force came to see me, I learnt it was Blake. Years later, I even worked with Les Blake for a while and never knew she was his daughter—the suicide, I mean.' I think this is a little odd, given the size of the town, his involvement at the time (which could have been much greater, but which was still small and crucial) and the notoriety of the case among police officers, but I let it through to the keeper and bowl him the next one.

'So you didn't nip out of the police station at 8.30 that night and drive out to Springfield and shoot her?' I challenge him, watching his face all the time.

This time he really laughs. 'No way! I didn't even know her. Fair dinkum.'

'So I can cross you off my list, then?'

'You can cross me off both lists.'

'Both lists?'

'Yeah. I wasn't having an affair with her and I didn't kill her.'

I flatten my left palm and with my right finger I draw a big cross on it.

'OK. Consider yourself off.'

Neil Phipps comes across as my idea of a country cop. I'm not 100 per cent convinced he's been completely frank with me, but I believe his answers to my two crucial questions.

While we finish our tea I tell him how I've driven all over the countryside looking for him, stopping to ask directions a couple of times (not a bad idea to have a few locals knowing whom you're visiting) and at one stage helping myself to a handful of ripe figs off a tree in an empty front garden for a very late lunch.

'You have to admit, it's a bit weird in a way—your driving around all over the place doing interviews for a book about a dead girl you didn't even know.'

'I'll tell you what's even funnier, Neil,' I confide. 'I turn up unannounced at your front door and you invite me in for tea and I ask you the most intimate and impertinent questions and you answer them! Now that's what I find really amazing!'

He agrees it is a bit odd, and I tell him all my friends think I'm insane for embarking on this project. I ask him what he's doing in retirement.

'I run a small farm and make pens.'

'Pens! You mean writing implements or sheep containers?'

'No. Pens to write with. I've just done an advanced course in making the resin barrels and I'm making a few to sell to boutiques in Melbourne.'

'Can I see?'

From a battered old backpack he produces a travelling salesman's polished wooden display case glittering with beautiful colours and patterns in resin—crushed opal, tortoiseshell, polished bone and ivory, swirling crimsons and turquoises—all neatly lined up in black velvet trays. They are quite amazing, especially in this setting. Out of idle interest I discuss prices with him and then decide to buy a couple. I ask him if he'll take a cheque.

I select a slim tortoiseshell and a thicker polished bone number and we walk to the car, where I write the cheque leaning on the bonnet.

As I make my way back to the highway I have a little chuckle to myself. I can hear my husband's voice in my head saying 'Only you could turn a murder interview in the middle of the bush into a shopping opportunity.'

∞

Try as I might, I can't track down anyone in or around Mansfield with whom Jenny could have possibly been having an affair. I ask her friends and enemies, her mother, her doctor, the local gossips, everyone I can think of except June Tanner, who still won't talk to me, but I can't get the remotest clue. The only possibility would be a well-hidden paramour in Melbourne whom she visited during her shopping excursions.

So … how about jealousy as a motive? If Jenny was involved with someone else, there would be a number of people who could be jealous. First, Laurie—if he knew, or suspected, he would have been very jealous. But Laurie says he was in Mansfield and so do Curly and Angie. His temperament and reputation do not seem to equip him to be a calculating killer. And if Laurie had killed Jenny, his actions would have had to be planned and timed to precision.

On the other hand, several people have indicated Laurie was quite insecure in both his marriages to young attractive women. He has a shy nature and is sensitive about his looks. In both relationships he displayed a degree of possessiveness that was noticed by others. Once, when Jenny was on an outing with girls from the bank in Melbourne, he allegedly phoned her grandmother, with whom Jenny was still living at the time, and checked that Jenny was where she said she was. 'I couldn't trust the first one,' he explained. This was a long time before Laurie and Jenny were married.

∞

Next day in Mansfield, I call again at the Tanners' house. It's early afternoon and old Fred is sitting on the front veranda, soaking up the last of the season's sun before the chill winds come slicing down from the High Country.

'Hullo! Who have we here?' Fred asks. I remind him of who I am and ask if Laurie is out at the farm today. He tells me he thinks he's working at Doon, so I tell him I'll be back for a chat later, jump in the car and head straight for Springfield. Although Laurie has sold the house and surrounding land, he is still using the adjoining paddocks and some shearing sheds.

I drive slowly past Springfield, looking for a driveway or road on the western side of the farm to test my theory that a car could have been hidden there on the night. Bingo! There it is! An access drive and gate to the paddock, and enough stuff growing over the fence to conceal a small car in the dusk. (I realise twelve years ago there could have been less growth—or even more—but this drive is close to the house and it's on the side away from where Laurie and the police would approach.) I take a quick photo and drive on to Prowds Road to do a U-turn. I'm not sure how I'm going to find Laurie and I don't want him to be cranky with me for trespassing. Not a good way to start what might be my only chance to talk to him.

As I drive the three or four hundred metres, I glimpse a small figure outlined against the sky on top of a high grass verge bordering the highway. A glance in the opposite direction and I would have missed him. He's wearing some sort of cap, not the usual farmer's broadbrimmed hat, and it makes him look almost childlike. He's mending a fence. As I pass he stops and watches me. I think of Bill Kerr watching every strange car that slows down outside his house. But this is the busy Maroondah Highway—why would my beat-up white Corolla hire car attract this man's attention?

I turn and drive back as if I am going somewhere, but look up at the man on the hill. He's gone back to his fence, twisting wire around something. From here he doesn't look as if he has a beard. The outline of his face looks too small. His 4WD with two kelpies in the back is parked in the paddock a few feet behind him.

I wonder if it's Laurie. Only one way to find out. Out of his line of sight I do another U-turn in Springfield's driveway and slowly return along the highway. This time the man straightens up and shades his eyes as he looks towards me. He starts rolling up his wire like a nervous deer.

I pull onto the gravel and clamber up the steep bank. The man at the top stares down at me. He looks small and thin, dressed in daggy old work clothes with a weather-beaten, life-worn face. No beard. Pain and sorrow seem to be deeply etched—or could those lines be the remnants of a chainsaw injury?

'Hi! Are you Laurie Tanner?'

'Who wants to know?'

It's him! 'Laurie, I'm Robin Bowles—I'm sure you've heard of me—I'm writing a book.'

Laurie is instantly defensive—a cornered terrier. 'I'm not contributing to your book. I don't want to talk to you. There have been too many lies told already and when all this is over, heads are going to roll!' He throws his bundle of fence wire into the back of the 4WD for emphasis. Fortunately, a good tradesman never leaves his tools out in the weather and while he gathers his pliers and hammer I have enough time to reach the top of the bank. Here we are, separated only by a few wire strands on a beautiful autumn afternoon. I pull at some long dried grass stalks to give me something to do with my hands. If only Laurie knew it, I'm as nervous as he is.

'Look, Laurie, I don't want to upset you. I just want to introduce myself. I'm writing a book about a very important event in your life, and how can I make sure it's accurate without talking to you?'

Laurie moves towards his car. He tells me he doesn't want to be quoted and that Jenny's death was the beginning of a lifelong nightmare for him. I assure him I won't quote him unless he says I can. He turns his back and makes towards his car. I call out to him that when I read the *Sunday Age* article I thought he'd killed Jenny himself. This provokes an unexpected reaction—Laurie bursts into tears. He climbs into his car and slams the door and I think I've lost him. But suddenly he winds down the window and blows his nose. He sits looking partly ahead through the windscreen and a quarter on to me, resting his right arm along the window sill. We talk for more than half an hour, with Laurie in tears most of the time, blowing his nose and wiping his eyes as we talk. I begin to feel awful about upsetting him so much. His hurt and sorrow seem palpable. His anger at Jenny's family tumbles out in a no-holds-barred torrent. Laurie seems convinced the Blakes have told some terrible lies about him, although he doesn't expand on what they might be and I can't think of any.

He reaffirms his inquest evidence that he was in Mansfield when Jenny died and that she had been throwing around statements like 'Life is not worth living like this' for some time. I tell him one of my reasons for thinking he might have been involved was that his statement to the police in 1984 said he didn't go to Jenny when he came in—'I believed from the way she looked she was dead.'

He is stung. 'I did go to her! Of course I went to her—I loved her! You would check if you loved someone!'

I point out his statement doesn't say that, and ask him if he still thinks Jenny killed herself.

He says he does. 'You weren't there that day. You didn't know her. She was very, very determined.'

I ask him if I can quote him on these two things at least. He agrees.

'You can. Of course I think she did it. I checked her first and then went to check the baby, in case she'd done something to him as well.'

This is the first time it has occurred to me that this was why he went so quickly to the baby and didn't bother much with Jenny once he saw he could do nothing for her. His actions on the night seem a bit more realistic with this slant on them, and I say so.

We discuss the devastating impact of Jenny's death on him and his family. He expresses deep love and concern for his son. We get into a discussion about raising boys and their ways of dealing with problems and I start giving him some advice about getting through the teenage years, since I've survived four episodes with my own sons. I imagine a little bird sitting on the fence listening to this discussion and saying to itself, 'This is the most surreal conversation I've eavesdropped on for years.'

I am moved to tell him I feel very guilty about stuffing up his afternoon, but that I really had to talk to him. This prompts a fresh lot of tears. Laurie is a very sad and lonely man. I think he is only going through life's motions, and if it were not for his son he mightn't bother. We talk a bit about that too.

Finally, I feel I've intruded enough. We're both pretty wrung out.

I say, 'I'm not close enough to shake hands with you, Laurie,' but reach out my hand over the wire anyway. Laurie blows his nose and gets out of the car. His rough farmer's hand is firm as he shakes my soft one. I'm impressed he's had the good manners to climb out of his car to shake my hand, and I feel even more to blame for his apparent distress. I bid him goodbye with 'I guess I'll see you at the inquest.' He doesn't answer.

I slither down the bank and Laurie wheels his 4WD around, leaving a solitary dust trail across the top paddock. I do a U-turn too and for a little while we are running parallel but far apart, as I follow the highway below. I feel very unsettled by this meeting and start thinking: what if the police and forensic people are wrong? What if Jenny really did manage somehow to do it herself? Wouldn't that be something?

I'm opposite Hughie Almond's place and I think I'll try once more to see him. I feel unsettled by my interview with Laurie and need some confirmation from Hughie about events on the night. I pull into his driveway and drive almost to the back step. No dogs, no cars—the place looks deserted. Do farmers have holidays? The small house dam reflects the sky like an unblinking eye, waiting for the boat on the trailer next to it to get its keel wet. The back porch looks like one of those run-down Historical Society museums you find in little towns—rusty wire hanging baskets supporting plant skeletons draped in cobwebs; coils of rope and an assortment of dusty harnesses which all look as if they'd ease apart at the slightest strain; a boot collection past its best-by date and an old round-shouldered fridge covered in Harley-Davidson stickers. It presents a picture of neglect. Hughie, however, is not in it.

I shrug off my doubts as I drive into the main street of Mansfield. I still have the feeling a suicide would have been physically impossible and emotionally improbable, but Laurie's demeanour has shaken me a bit. After all this time and all these interviews, here I am thinking Jenny might have done it after all.

∞

Before returning to my Queensland hideaway, I have lunch with Paul Newman in Melbourne to check some procedural details in my manuscript. Afterwards, while I'm walking around the city, someone takes the long shoulder strap off my small wallet, which I'm carrying around inside an open woven straw shoulder bag. This freaks me right out. I just can't imagine how anyone could do this without my noticing. The strap can only be detached from the wallet by unclipping two tiny clips like the ones on the end of dog leads. Because they're small they're tricky. Someone must have taken the whole wallet and strap out, removed the strap and then replaced the wallet. Nothing has been stolen from the wallet. Why take the strap and not the wallet?

I phone my husband that night in tears. He makes 'there, there' noises, and I'm cross he doesn't seem to understand just how baffling it is. When I get home and show him similar clips on another bag, he agrees it is odd.

Two weeks after I get back to Queensland, an envelope arrives addressed to 'R. Bowles—Book Writer'. Inside the envelope is my strap.

∞

Still thinking about jealousy as a motive, my husband and I thrash out a few other scenarios. It could be the phantom lover, jealous and angry about Jenny's apparent decision to stay put. Or it could be the phantom lover's lover.

All this time we have been thinking about a man, but perhaps a woman visited Jenny that night. A woman anxious about an actual or imagined relationship Jenny was having with someone close to her. Maybe a woman who heard Jenny was planning to leave Laurie and thought that might have consequences for herself.

Whoever visited stayed for some time. Five cigarettes, even if

Jenny smoked a couple, indicate at least half an hour to an hour, depending on the smokers. A cup and saucer could indicate a female visitor—in the country it's likely a man would be given a mug.

What if a woman visited Jenny and brought her baby, whom she changed on the floor by the heater? A young baby in the room would explain why the heater was on so high and why Jenny had left the nappy on the floor instead of putting it away, which she would have done automatically if it was Sam's. In any case Sam, once in bed, would most likely be changed in his bedroom if he'd woken. Jenny preferred him to stay in his bed during the night and it's unlikely she would have brought him out to join visitors, especially if an argument was in progress.

It is very likely Jenny's visitor was there when the McCormacks rang, as within about forty minutes of this call Jenny was dead. Not long enough to be sociable with cigarettes and cups of coffee as well as stage a suicide. What if the change in her demeanour detected by Angie McCormack was tension from being interrupted in a fierce argument? It is likely Jenny did not view this visitor as a threat, and so didn't mention any one else was there. It is also possible this visitor may have come and gone before Jenny died.

What if a vital clue was left behind? A disposable nappy on the floor near the heater? It's another possibility, anyway, but the police don't think so.

∞

One of my concerns all the way through this investigation has been that Denis had no motive. Every time I have asked the investigating team why they have Denis so firmly in their sights when I can't think of a motive, they say: 'Money'. When I point out Denis had no financial interest in the property at that time, they say: 'Family money'. But that doesn't stack up.

I decide to find out just what the financial situation was at Springfield at the time of Jenny's death. It's very difficult to keep any of your own business to yourself in a democracy. Ownership of and transactions relating to land and property are a matter of public record at the Land Titles Office.

I conducted a detailed search on the property known to locals as Springfield and to the Land Titles Office as Crown Allotments 32, 33, 34, 34A and 35B in the Parish of Brankeet. It showed that until the beginning of 1977 the property was owned by June and Fred Tanner.

On 8 February 1977 Fred and June moved into the house in town and transferred their ownership of Springfield to Laurie and his first wife, Sally. Little or no money changed hands during this transfer, as previous mortgages on Springfield had already been discharged, but it looks as if the elder Tanners left some money in or borrowed from the Bank of New South Wales, as there are subsequently a couple of mortgages to the bank, and June and Fred were also registered mortgagees on the property. In essence, though, the families did a swap and Sally and Laurie moved to Springfield so that Laurie could work the farm more easily, Fred could semi-retire (although someone forgot to tell him at the time) and June could improve her golf.

The registered ownership of the property was shown as a two-thirds share to Laurie and a one-third share to Sally, as tenants in common. When a property is owned by tenants in common rather than joint tenants, one part-owner can sell, give or bequeath their share independently from the other owner or owners. After Sally left Laurie, Denis came to his brother's aid. A Land Transfer form dated 27 July 1978 shows that Denis, who was about twenty-four at the time, paid $43 100 to purchase Sally's one-third share. Although this form is signed and initialled by Sally, she is adamant she only received $20 000 and an agreed share of the household contents.

On 4 March 1981, a couple of days before Laurie and Jenny were married, Laurie became the sole owner of Springfield, buying back Denis's share for $46 050. This transfer also discharged Denis's mortgage commitments, which had been incurred on 17 August 1978 and 4 April 1979, to the Bank of New South Wales and his parents respectively. As he said in his statement to the first inquest, 'I relinquished any ownership rights in so far as Springfield was concerned … leaving Laurie the sole owner of Springfield, with finance commitments.' It appears most of Laurie's commitments were to his parents, who held three separate mortgages over the property by 1986.

Jenny had no registered ownership of Springfield. If she had left Laurie and wanted money, she would have had to wait twelve months and then take Laurie through the Family Court, unless a prior settlement was made. But, as there was no real risk of his parents foreclosing on Laurie's mortgage, it is unlikely that he would have 'lost the farm'.

In fact, in 1986 Laurie subdivided the farm into ten separate titles and sold most of them, including the lot containing the homestead of Springfield, for a good enough price to enable him to discharge all his mortgages and purchase a larger historic property in nearby Preston. His financial gain would have been substantial. The subdivision was commenced on 19 September 1985, and the Council sealed the new boundaries on 21 August 1986. It was completed and mostly sold by 27 October 1986. If Laurie had the means to subdivide the property within two years of Jenny's death, realising a tidy profit, it seems he could have paid Jenny half of the value of an unsubdivided Springfield (which is all she would have been entitled to if she'd left before the subdivision commenced) and still made a profit. But if he had been planning to subdivide for some time and Jenny knew of these plans, the money motive may hold more water.

Keeping Denis up front for a little longer, I can't think of any supportable motive for him to have killed Jenny Tanner, and it seems, neither can the Task Force. The Task Force's theory requires them to believe that Denis's motive was financial. I find it difficult to believe money was the sole motive for her death and the Land Titles search seems to demonstrate a fatal flaw in their theory.

Maybe Denis and Jenny were attracted to each other, although all Jenny's friends say not, as does Denis himself.

I've also puzzled a lot about the way in which Jenny's death was investigated in 1984–85, and listened carefully to the evidence given to the second inquest by the first investigators. Try as I might, I can't believe Denis Tanner, as a newly promoted Sergeant, could really exert enough influence over the complicated chain of command—uniforms and plain-clothes, many of whom he didn't know, in four separate locations—to manipulate or influence any sort of cover-up, about anything, after her death.

However, a cover-up did occur. Not a cover-up of murder, or even any kind of conspiracy to protect a fellow police officer, but a systematic cover-up of incompetence. This, and the further cover-up to protect reputations, was clearly recognised by all who attended the second inquest and was commented upon often by the Coroner. The sad outcome of this cover-up to protect reputations was that it prevented a diligent investigation into the way in which Jenny Tanner died and so became, ipso facto, a cover-up of a murder.

Perhaps Jim Fry thought he was doing Denis Tanner a favour by turning a blind eye to some obvious inconsistencies, but Denis could have been done a disservice in one way. If the list of matters Bill Kerr had wanted raised with Denis by an officer had been followed up and Denis's alibi checked properly at the time, he might not still be trying to maintain his reputation all these years later.

And I still have one last question about motives which I cannot answer. Why did the police re-open the investigation into the death of Jenny Tanner after the discovery of Adele Baily? What, in their minds, is the actual connection?

∞

We could speculate that an accident was the cause of Jenny's death. Perhaps whoever visited her picked the rifle up from near the back door, where Laurie had left it on Sunday after firing at the dogs, and waved it around to threaten her, without any intention to kill. Jenny, thinking the rifle was not loaded because of her repeated instructions to Laurie to keep the ammunition separate from the rifle, refused to be intimidated. Maybe the killer pulled the trigger accidentally, or did it to frighten her, not realising the rifle was loaded. Perhaps Jenny, thinking the rifle was not loaded, grabbed the barrel and pushed it away, causing it to discharge through her hand. Enraged and in pain, she might have made threats of retribution, escalating the conflict to its deadly conclusion. The other player in this scene could have been anyone Jenny knew—or even a passing stranger who wandered in from the highway. But if it was an accident, why attempt to make it look like suicide? If more than two bullets were fired, a cool person picked up the other cartridge cases, leaving only two to be discovered. The passing stranger would certainly be the most palatable solution for everyone, including the police. Perhaps one day he or she will come forward. It has happened before.

14

Where Angels Fear to Tread

I DECIDE I have to talk to Denis Tanner. It is ridiculous trying to write a story about real people if you've never set eyes on them. So many people have told me about Denis, and few of the descriptions are heart-warming, but I've yet to form my own impression. It's time to see for myself. My husband agrees, but says, 'Be careful.' I'd like a dollar for every time someone has said that to me since last June.

I fly to Melbourne from my tropical hideaway and rent another cheap car. I spend the night before my trip speculating with friends about whether Denis will talk to me at all, or if he'll chase me off his property with a shotgun. He's assumed bogeyman status. I've informed Paul Newman I intend to visit Denis, but I haven't sought his permission. He can't really stop me anyway. To avoid compromising his ethics, I don't ask him for Denis's address—there are plenty of ways to find someone in a small town, especially someone with a high profile. I've heard Denis is on sick leave with a broken collar bone after falling from his pushbike on a weekend ride, so I hope to catch him at home.

I stay up so late talking with my friends that I sleep in, and I don't get on the road until 7.45 a.m. I'm cross, as I had visions of trying to catch Lynne alone after she took the kids to school before talking to Denis himself. Now I'll arrive too late to put this plan into operation.

The two-and-a-half-hour trip up the Hume Highway to Benalla in my Rent-a-Wreck is boring—not the most scenic route in Australia. I have plenty of time to reflect on what I want to ask Denis and whether he'll answer. I want to ask him if he had an affair with Jenny. I want to know where he was on the night. If he was home, as he said he was in his inquest evidence, why didn't he answer the door? I also want to know if he thinks anyone who cared for baby Sam would depart from the house after killing Jenny, leaving the iron and the gas heater on. It doesn't seem the act of someone who cared about the baby's welfare, unless the killer just panicked. They are my key questions, and I want to eyeball him and ask them. I keep reminding myself this is a real murder and Denis is a real Detective Sergeant in the CIB. This is no game for amateurs and that's just what I am. For the first time, I wonder if I'm not being a bit silly and self-important.

I have a diversion just before reaching the Euroa exit. Looking down to check the map on the passenger seat I notice a seven-centimetre split in the outer seam of my blue drill pants. Oh damn and blast! How can I go and see Denis with a blob of leg poking out? Today I need all the self-confidence I can muster. I wheel into the detour road and pray St Vincent de Paul made it to Euroa. God is looking after me, and I find a three-dollar pair of quite passable grey jeans with a designer label. They're actually better than the ones I've been wearing. Not so tight, either.

Arriving in Benalla, I easily find Denis's street and drive slowly past the house. It's about 10.30 a.m. Big elms shade the footpaths, and most of the houses are elderly but cared for. Denis's double-fronted weatherboard and front garden are undergoing some renovations. Two little squares of newly planted grass flank gardens bordering a pathway to the front door. There's a man in overalls with his back to me standing on a scaffolding beam, doing repairs to the eaves of the house. I wonder if it is Denis. He doesn't turn round, so I can't see his face. Would he be doing repairs with a broken collar bone? Probably not. From behind he looks thinner than I imagined. I double back at the next intersection and cruise by again. My mouth is dry. I think I'll go into town and get a cup of coffee first.

I'm halfway up the main street looking for a coffee lounge when I sternly give myself a lecture. 'You've flown over 3000 kilometres to see this man. What if it *is* him on the scaffold and he goes inside before you get a chance to confront him and he slams the door on you when you knock? Now's the time to see him. At least he'll have to climb down and go inside before he stops listening. Get back there at once!' I obey myself and give away the idea of coffee until after the interview. It may be soon anyway. Two minutes later I park under the elm tree in front of his house, let myself in through the wire front gate and walk halfway up the path. I inadvertently put one foot over the garden bed onto the lawn while looking up at the man on the scaffold to see if it is him. He looks over his shoulder.

'Hullo. Is this Lynne and Denis Tanner's house?'

Denis fixes me with a cop's analytic stare, guarded and distrustful. 'Yes, it is.'

'Are you Denis? I'm Robin Bowles. I'm writing a book, as I'm sure you know, and I really wanted the opportunity to meet you. Would you be prepared to talk to me for a few minutes?'

'Not if you don't get your foot off my new lawn.' From the tone of his voice, he is used to being obeyed. He looks at the spot where my foot has trespassed onto his tender grass shoots.

I look down too. My sneaker has flattened a saucer-sized area. Damn! What a way to start off, getting Denis cranky about his grass. I apologise and nervously lean down to fluff up the little patch with both hands so the squashed blades line up with their neighbours again.

'I'm really sorry. I'm a gardener myself. I don't know what I was thinking of.'

Denis climbs down off his scaffold. We have a bit of a heated exchange about how I got his address. He's convinced I got it from Paul Newman, but he's wrong. I gain the impression he won't talk to me at all unless I answer him. I explain that it didn't require any great detective skills to get his address, as his profile in Benalla is so high. We walk out onto the nature strip to talk in the shade of the elms. He asks me if I'm taping the conversation. I've deliberately decided against doing so and am glad. I lift up my jumper and give him permission to frisk me if he wishes. He shakes his head and seems satisfied and more relaxed. I suppose frisking me would look a bit funny to the neighbours. Even my spontaneous gesture of lifting my jumper over my head and turning in a full circle in front of him could cause gossip in a country town. Just as well I'm wearing a clean skivvy. He tells me he is talking to me against legal advice and he doesn't want to be quoted. I agree I won't quote him unless he gives me permission.

We size each other up. Denis is around 180 centimetres tall (six feet for those who still have difficulty visualising centimetres) and looks fit. I expected him to be fatter and look older. He's forty-three. He has dark hair, well cut in a regulation service style, which suits him. He is quite nice-looking in a brooding sort of way. He is tanned, and under his overalls he's wearing an old short-sleeved blue police shirt, which still shows the outline of his Sergeant's stripes from where they've been ripped off and promoted to a newer uniform. From time to time my eyes stray to these faint outlines, reminding me I'm talking to a real live policeman whom Homicide say is a murder suspect.

We stand out there on the nature strip for about two hours. During that time many cars pass by, which seems curious in a quiet residential side street. All of them slow down and the drivers wave to Denis. He waves back. It's almost as if word has got round that Denis has a strange visitor and he needs a show of town solidarity. I remark that he may not be very popular in some circles but he sure seems to have a lot of friends in Benalla. He is aware of his reputation and lack of popularity, but quite unconcerned about it. He doesn't feel the need to be popular, but acknowledges he has a lot of friends in Benalla. He's proud of his business connections and his reputation in town of being tough but fair.

I tell him a lot of people think I'm crazy for coming to see him and that many people I've interviewed said they are scared of him. He finds this pretty amusing and tells me he can't see any reason for anyone to be scared of him—I'm obviously not, or I wouldn't be there. (Appearances aren't everything, though I must admit I'm no longer nervous.) I occupy my hands with my rental car key, and Denis picks up a long stick and proceeds to break little pieces off it as if measuring his responses. He throws them in the gutter while we talk.

We talk a lot about Jenny. He tells me Lynne and Jenny were close friends. He was usually out working when she visited. His statement to the inquest tells of Jenny's numerous trips to Melbourne and long stays with Denis and Lynne, before and after Sam was born. Neither of them knew what Jenny did when she was out. Lynne looked after Sam for her—even during the night Lynne would care for Sam if he woke, to let Jenny rest, as Lynne had no children of her own. On Denis's visits to Bonnie Doon he was rarely around at the house socialising. He helped his family with the farming, as he'd told the police in his statement.

Denis is still convinced it was suicide. He talks about other dual shot cases he has come across during his police career. He quotes the evidence he and others gave at the inquest. Jenny was depressed. She was determined. Laurie was in Mansfield. Denis was at home.

'Were you at home?' He confirms the statement he gave in 1985, that he was home by 10 p.m.

I tell him I've been told that Homicide have tracked down one of the police officers who was sent to give him the news on the night. He's been to the house and tried to reconstruct his visits for Homicide.

'If you were at home, why didn't you or Lynne answer the door when the police came to see you during the night?'

He looks knowingly at me and tells me I don't have the full story. He has also found an officer on duty that night who remembers being asked to go around, but went to a divisional barbecue first and didn't come by until 5.30 a.m. (Seems unlikely to me; if there's a death in a member's family other members wouldn't go out socialising for hours before going to inform him.) I ask him if he has told Homicide about this and he basically indicates he's not obliged to help them.

I'm thrown a bit by this information. I don't accept it at face value, but it indicates Denis has been preparing his own case, in case. He intends to attend the new inquest. He thinks he'll be subpoenaed anyway. I ask him whether he's obliged to answer questions if he's a known suspect and am told he can answer some and not others if he wishes. He seems keen to get on the stand and give Paul Newman heaps.

Our discussion turns to Paul Newman and the way Denis has become the prime suspect. Anger emanates into the space between us. He thinks he's been unfairly singled out for investigation. He says,

'Your mind is like a parachute—it has to be open to function.' I tell him I haven't heard that before and ask if I can use it. He doesn't mind. He tells me he believes he was tricked into going into Ethical Standards to be questioned by the Task Force. He tells me how it happened and I ask him if I can use this information in my book. He says I can, so I get my note-pad from the car to take it all down. This is how he tells it.

'On a Friday last October [1996] I was phoned by Chief Inspector Peter Keogh from Ethical Standards who was investigating something I had approached him about. I had made a statement about this incident, and Chief Inspector Keogh had made some alterations to this statement. He wanted me to come down to sign them off. I said I'd check baby-sitting arrangements with my wife and call back, as the trip may involve an overnight stay. Later that afternoon Keogh called back and suggested fairly insistently I come to Melbourne the following Wednesday, 30th October.

'When I arrived I waited a long time in the foyer for Keogh. The girl at reception wouldn't look me in the eye, and I had a feeling something was up. Keogh eventually appeared with some very minor changes—I felt he'd been marking time. He told me to read these and he'd get me a cup of tea. When he came back he said, "I saw Inspector Newman upstairs. He'd like a word with you, since you're here." I said, "Well engineered, Peter." He reckoned it was just an accident Newman was in the building. [Paul Newman was at that time working on the opposite side of the city.] I said to Keogh, "I didn't come down in the last shower. I don't believe you." When I got into the interview I said to Inspector Newman, "What did you do this for? I would have come in." He said, "It's nothing like that," or some such thing. Jeff Calderbank and Newman interviewed me.'

I ask what they talked about. He won't say. It is the only question I ask him in two hours he refuses to answer. I understand why. It's pretty cheeky to ask anyway. I ask why he seems to dislike Paul Newman so much.

He says I can put this in my book too. 'One day, part way through the Task Force investigation, I was on duty at Benalla Police Station.

Newman arrived unannounced with Inspector Ross Smith from Seymour. I'm not one of his favourite people either, but he saw this whole thing happen and you can ask him if you like. They were rummaging around in the storeroom and I went to offer them a hand. Inspector Smith introduced me to Newman—I hadn't ever met him before. I offered him my hand, while we were standing on the top landing outside the store, and he stared me down and wouldn't offer me his hand back. I virtually pushed it under his nose and he took it— he had to. Then he turned away. He didn't say anything. I said, "If you tell me what you're looking for I might be able to help you find it," but he didn't reply. Before that, he and Calderbank had been all over the place in Mansfield and elsewhere asking questions and they made no effort to get in touch with me until the end of October, by stealth.'

Refusing to shake someone's hand obviously means a lot to Denis, I think. Better remember that.

I wonder aloud why he didn't contact them during the investigation, since he knew they were asking all these questions. He says had no need to. He was satisfied with the investigation and the outcome of the first inquest, which absolved him and Laurie of any involvement in Jenny's death. Why wouldn't he be satisfied?

He goes on, 'The first time I knew Jennifer Blake's inquest was involved in that article was when that reporter rang me on the Friday before it came out. He taped my conversation. He wasn't supposed to quote some of the things I said—it was off the record.' He obviously thinks book writers are a bit more understanding, or we wouldn't be having this conversation.

I ask about the impact the hunt for Jenny's killer has had on his family. Of course it has been tough. Fortunately his kids have escaped all but a couple of little incidents—he puts this down to his acceptance in Benalla.

Suddenly from the street behind me Lynne arrives home at the wheel of the family station wagon. She drives straight in and doesn't acknowledge Denis or me. I can't get a good look at her, as she's approached from the wrong direction, but I can see she has a toddler in the car.

Soon, Denis's little son comes out to play on the nature strip and gives us both a distracting focus when we need a break to collect our thoughts. His shoelace is undone and I automatically call him over to tie it. He has masses of golden curls—must take after Lynne, as Denis is so dark. He's the youngest of four. We talk kids for a while. I tell Denis I have no intention of approaching Sam. His hard cop face comes back. He indicates I'd better not!

The postie arrives on his pushbike and stops for a brief chat. Another friendly face. I smile too. I want him to remember I'm here in case Denis later says I've never been to see him. Denis gives the little boy the mail to take in to his mum. A few minutes later Lynne comes to the gate, looking for her son, who has obviously been distracted somewhere on the way in. Lynne doesn't come past the gate. She's about 170 centimetres (5 feet 6 inches) tall and well covered without being fat. She has straight strawberry-blonde hair cut in a short bob. She wears glasses, and looks strong, plain and capable. Brian Cosgriff, the former local Coroner, told me, 'The older Tanner boy and girl are terrific cyclists. She's a great mum, she drives those kids all over the place so they can compete in races.' She looks the part. She doesn't come out, just asks after the baby. Denis tells her he's sent the boy in with the mail, and she disappears to look for him.

Denis and I are winding up. He's ready for lunch, and after a couple of hours I can't think of any more questions he'll answer. I offer my hand. He takes it immediately. His hand feels big and strong and a bit callused. I half-expected him to have one of those 'see-how-strong-I-am-you-wimp' grips that crush my rings into my fingers, but no—it's firm and dry. I wish him good luck. One way or another, I think he'll need it. I thank him for spending so much time with me when I've arrived unannounced. I say I'll probably see him at the inquest. He says he might talk to me some more once it is 'all over'.

I drive off feeling a mixture of triumph and perplexity. I've seen Denis and survived! He wasn't nearly as bad as I expected. I think he cultivates the mean, tough image, or at least does nothing to dispel it—perhaps it suits him to do so. In person he hardly lives up to it— not today, anyway. There were a couple of times though … like when he spoke of Laurie and Sam and particularly Paul Newman. I certainly wouldn't want to be in his bad books. I'm still no wiser about Denis's role, if any, in Jenny's death. I use my mobile to phone my husband and my friends in Melbourne as promised, to say I'm leaving Benalla in one piece.

∽

As a going-away-to-Queensland gift a friend gave us a food storage jar with 'Food for Thought' written on its label. Inside are 365 separate sayings and inspiring quotes, a year's supply, all folded up like Chinese fortune cookie messages on different coloured paper. It's become a ritual for my husband and me to take turns to select one each morning and read it out. A week after my visit to Denis, back at home, it was my turn to choose. I reached in and came out with this: 'Your mind is like a parachute—it has to be open to function.'

15

The Professionals, 1995–98

ONE OF the police I spoke to told me the process of investigating a suspected homicide has changed little since last century. Certainly there are more effective scientific tests now, 'but the good old-fashioned police work—secure the scene, protect the evidence, the hard slog, the endless questions, following up hundreds of dead ends, spending much of the time writing reports and more of it mixing with the scum of the earth—hasn't changed at all. It's rare someone in a murder investigation will open their front door, invite you in for a cup of coffee and sit there and spill their guts to you while you drink it.'

Homicide detectives come to know their victims and their killers intimately. They don't know which information will prove to be important, so they collect minor scraps and personal secrets about people they haven't heard of the day before. They'll never know the victim except through others' opinions and memories, but they begin to understand the killer better than they understand their own partners.

In most cases, homicide is an irrational act, and it's the rule rather than the exception that those who commit homicide act irrationally afterwards as well. Profilers have made a career out of telling the police and potential informants what to look for to spot the murder suspect. This irrational behaviour is why so many are caught.

The investigation of Jenny Tanner's death is virtually an exercise in futility, so long after the event. No-one at the Coroner's Court can remember another instance in the State's history where such energy has been expended on such an old case. Pathologists and forensic technicians working for the Coroner can only remember two or three exhumations in the past five or six years. The reason is that all the necessary investigations have usually taken place before a victim's body is buried. Samples are taken and stored, pathology tests are conducted, photographs and reports are recorded. Even if the case is not solved at or soon after the time of death, the information is stored to assist at any time.

In addition to the lack of physical evidence available to Jenny's investigators, the time elapsed is well beyond the capacity of most people's memories. Investigators are sifting through chronologically warped recollections. Many of the locals who were around at the time are friends with one or other family—or both. Some of them have not told all they know. Others are likely to concoct impressions unconsciously to please or impress. In reality, Jenny's sudden death, apart from creating a ripple of sympathy and gossip, was not important to most of the locals at the time. It's only now that the event has assumed such importance, has split the town, has caused people to whisper or speak obliquely of having to 'be careful', or suggest the topic is 'too dangerous' to discuss—with me or the police. Many have clammed up altogether. People I interviewed in and around the district told me the police would never be told the full story, and that I probably wouldn't either. The town has closed ranks to protect the victims, but, in doing so, has protected the murderer as well. This realisation has now come too late. Police cannot ascertain if petrol-station attendants served any strange people on the night of 14 November 1984. They can't obtain accurate reports of strange cars or unexplained absences. They can't be certain where people were and what they were doing. Where were *you* on the night of 14 November last year? Almost no-one would remember. So why have the Victoria Police initiated such an expensive and thorough, but probably futile, murder investigation?

∞

Inspector Paul Newman has been allocated an unenviable task in heading up the investigation Task Force. He's a quiet, determined man who looms high in the estimation of all the police I interview. Even those who don't know him personally have opinions. A former Inspector says: 'I haven't worked with him, but I've heard nothing but good about him and his abilities as an investigator.' A retired Deputy Commissioner concurs: 'Newman's as straight as they come. You couldn't have a better investigator on that case.' I'm beginning to think Newman's primary role is to be the beyond-reproach crusader after an impossible Holy Grail, to ensure there is no potential for the force to be embarrassed. (He probably views this task differently, but Inspector Newman is nobody's fool).

No-one could accuse him of not trying as hard as he can. The difficulties encountered in the search for Jenny's killer have been like no others in his career. New ground has been broken, legally and historically. The application to overturn or quash the findings of the first inquest has created a legal precedent in Victoria.

Hundreds of vague leads have been followed up. Many people have been afraid to make formal statements, because of a perceived threat of retribution. At times this reluctance has proved exceptionally frustrating for the police, as people gave them information and then refused to formalise it in a statement that could be used at the inquest. Some other informants have offered to provide leads in return for 'deals'—a reduction of sentence or withdrawal of police pressure about some other matter. Newman has done no deals.

Everyone wants immediate answers—but investigating is a painstaking process, especially many years on. To give one example of the tedious nature of this type of investigation, an extraordinary amount of police time was spent looking for a motor vehicle said to have been lent to a suspect at around the time of one of the murders. It's quite likely this vehicle 'is now a sardine can anyway'. Paul Newman has traced the car through a series of owners and uses. At one stage he thought it had been found in a paddock, being used as a chook-shed. Even if he'd found the vehicle he was seeking, there was an infinitesimal chance that forensic technicians would be able to find any physical links to victim or suspect. But you have to try. What if there had been something there and he hadn't looked? Criticisms are sometimes levelled at homicide investigators for taking too much time or spending too much money. While Newman had to account for expenditure, he had virtually an open budget for this investigation.

The Task Force team was made up of five experienced Homicide investigators. The initial leader of the group was Detective Senior Sergeant Jeff Calderbank, who had ten years in Homicide (I later discover he was actually attached to Homicide at the time of Jenny's death, but that he was not involved with the brief 'investigation' undertaken by Sergeant Fry). His career spans 22 years in the police force. He has a family who don't see as much of him as they'd like. He's missed birthdays and anniversaries and Speech Days while away from home tracking down another tiny piece of whatever jigsaw he's currently collating. He looks tough because he's big. I think he has quite a wide gentle streak, which he lets out for a run when his colleagues are looking the other way.

Jeff Calderbank moved onto the Jenny Tanner investigation as a follow-on from his involvement with Adele Baily's case, where he was the most visible investigator in Mansfield and did most of the liaison with the local media. He travelled to New Zealand to interview Adele's family and attend her funeral. He was a big hit with Adele's mother, bringing her some duty-free cigarettes. He followed the funeral cortege past all Adele's old haunts and attended the service. I was very impressed when I heard this, but I think a lot of homicide police are closet romantics. They care for and nurture the families left behind. They spend so much time with the survivors of tragedy they become expert counsellors. Jeff Calderbank also had an unenviable task, trying to find the killer of a long-dead transsexual prostitute— the type of person who had many detractors and few mourners, with a family outside Australia. If the case had not been so closely linked to Jenny's death it's unlikely it would have proceeded as far as it has. While Adele and Jenny had little in common in life, in death their fates are inseparably linked through the police investigation. It is possible that there were two different murderers, although the police generally discount this theory of mine.

A new Task Force was put together to support Jeff in his search for information about Jenny. They were Detective Sergeant Marty

Allison, Detective Senior Constable Jacqueline Curran, Detective Senior Constable Paul Solomon and the police analyst, Senior Constable Graham Miller.

Marty Allison spent a lot of time in and around the Mansfield area with Jeff Calderbank and later Paul Newman. Residents of Mansfield and Bonnie Doon say the police virtually moved in for weeks at a time. The Bonnie Doon pub, which locals use as their own private club, became a daily rumour exchange. Police used the pub as a base while they were interviewing everyone they could find in the area who could tell them anything about Jenny, her life and her death. They heard gossip and malicious hearsay, facts and fairy stories, accurate information and tips not worth mentioning. The people they really wanted to talk to, Jenny's husband's family, didn't want to talk to them. The only way they could get Laurie to speak to them was to lie in wait near the Preston shearing sheds to surprise him and obtain a new statement—or, on another occasion, wait until he left his house to go to work in the morning, follow him down the road a way, then pull him over and ask him to accompany them to the police station to assist them with their inquiries. Although police may ask people to accompany them to a police station, there is no power to compel any person to do so, short of arresting him or her. And, except in special circumstances, such as a driver of a car being asked their name and address, no person is obliged to answer any question put to them by a member of the police. Laurie did speak to them at that time and has on a couple of occasions since, but he is still convinced Jenny committed suicide and will not answer most questions.

Jacqueline Curran and Paul Solomon did a lot of travelling. They did interviews in South Australia, Queensland and New South Wales. The entire team shared the travel around Victoria; back and forth to Mansfield, Ballarat, Bendigo, Western Victoria, Gippsland, the Mornington Peninsula, and many places in between.

Every police officer who had been involved with Jenny's case at the time was found and interviewed. Many had retired, but some are still in quite senior positions in the force. They were asked for their recollections and impressions and why more was not done at the time. I know Homicide interviewed them all, because I tracked them all down myself, usually asking many of the same questions. The Task Force searched old records at the Melbourne Coroner's Court, and at police stations in Benalla, Mansfield, St Kilda, Altona and Russell Street Headquarters. Police radio transmissions, diaries, rosters and reports were unearthed and scrutinised for the smallest detail. This was not a process of trying to allocate blame—more one of trying to discover answers to some pretty baffling questions. Dark mutterings from the investigating team indicated deep dissatisfaction with some of the processes undertaken and the lack of investigation following Dr Dyte's phone calls.

At every turn Bill Kerr copped a bucketing from his former colleagues and superiors, and until he rediscovered his file it looked as if he would continue to be the scapegoat of the 'A Team'—my nickname for the 1984 investigators. But his file on the entire investigation, painstakingly maintained in sequential order, provided ample indication that the course of the investigation ran pretty much as he said and that he, as a senior constable, was blocked at much higher levels than he'd ever had the rank or the audacity to challenge. At first he recorded general daily entries during his shift, but later he began writing down minute details late at night, as he seemed to realise he might get shafted on this case. Perusal of his working file confirmed much hearsay and innuendo. Bill Kerr was now certain his stance was vindicated, and felt much more relaxed about the forthcoming inquest with his old file firmly in Paul Newman's hands.

Tapes he'd made of conversations were sent by the Task Force to a laboratory in Queensland for micro-enhancement and transcription. Copies of correspondence from his file were pieced together to form a sequential picture of inaction. Don Frazer was interviewed again to clarify some of the issues raised in Kerr's file.

The police analyst, Senior Constable Graham Miller, had the laborious task of transcribing and recording every detail of the past and present investigations onto his computer. This formed a central record, allowed data to be cross-matched, and finally helped Paul Newman to prepare the brief for the Coroner. Miller can cross-reference names or dates or localities over thousands of pages of transcribed information. He can access the files for information at any time to prepare flow charts, balance of probability charts, date lines and almost any other diagram you'd need to present evidence and information in a simple format in court.

Country police have been involved in Jenny's investigation with smaller roles to play—people like Ian Coutts, who attended her exhumation, Senior Constable Charles Fleming, the Mansfield officer who accompanied her to Melbourne, and others.

The others who have not featured in this story by name so far are the senior police—those telling Paul Newman what to do. An Inspector sounds like a pretty high rank to devotees of Inspector Wexford and Inspector Morse, but in the Victoria Police there are several ranks above Inspector, and in a hierarchical organisational culture every rank counts. The higher the rank the greater the clout, and several interested parties now have a lot of clout in the police force. I've also been told by several people the Chief Commissioner is taking a personal interest in this investigation, which can only conclude in one of two ways—a suspect can be charged, or the file can be returned to limbo as an unsolved case. I've wondered why a police officer who was supposed to be the primary suspect was left on full-time duties. Was it because the police didn't have enough evidence to embarrass him into standing down? (Denis Tanner was on sick leave for the latter part of this investigation with a collar bone he told me was broken in two places.) Tanner himself has told me he believes the Director of Public Prosecutions had the new inquest brief for around three months, combing through it for enough admissible evidence to charge him. As he pointed out, speaking to me from his office in Benalla, the file had gone to the Coroner's Court—an indication to him at least that his colleagues had collected no evidence—other than circumstantial—they could produce in a court.

Officers senior (and junior) to Paul Newman have questioned his wisdom in assisting me to the extent he has in my own investigations. Denis's comments during my first meeting with him certainly suggested he thought I'd had much more 'help from an officer—an

Inspector' than I actually have, so someone has told him Newman has been 'helping' me. I have been at least as aware as Paul Newman of the constraints on our exchanges of information. I realised from our first meeting that part of his job was to feed me the Task Force party line and hope I wouldn't tear off at an embarrassing tangent. He joked with me once that if I solved this murder his job wouldn't be worth having, and I joked back that if I did solve it I'd give him the answer so he would get the glory. He looked embarrassed and told me he wasn't looking for glory. I believe him. I wonder if anyone is meant to get to the bottom of this investigation.

∞

When I meet Paul Newman for lunch in March 1997, he indicates this might be our last encounter before the inquest, for a number of reasons. He confides to me (as if I don't already know) that I have been a 'tool of his investigation', as I've been places and interviewed people he hasn't and this alone makes it permissible for us to meet. But I haven't told him everything, just as he hasn't told me much I couldn't find out anyway. I may have come late to this investigation business, but I've worked hard at making up in enthusiasm and cheek what I've lacked in training and experience.

I tell him then I've prepared a sealed package containing my manuscript to date on disk and left it that morning with my solicitor, along with all my transcribed notes and tapes. I want a record of my story as it was before our conversation, so no-one can say he's broken any rules. He doesn't seem to think this is necessary, but I've already done it. Across the medium rare buffalo and grilled barramundi I repeat the first lesson I was given in police investigation—'Watch your back!'

I read him some passages from this story, including some that are not very complimentary to his colleagues. He is not very happy with some of them, saying the police do a lot of good work too, which often gets overlooked. I agree and always have, but I'm convinced in 1984 they stuffed up!

I also read out a quote from the trial barrister summing up for Ted Bundy, the infamous serial killer in the United States. I tell Newman that when I saw it I wrote it down, as it struck me as perhaps being relevant to the current investigation.

> There are basically two ways for the police to investigate a crime. They can go to the crime scene, they can look for the clues, and they can follow the clues to their logical conclusions and find a suspect. Or they can find the suspect, decide on the suspect, and decide to make the evidence fit the suspect and work to make the evidence fit only him.

'Any danger of that happening in this case?' I ask.

He returns my stare with a fixed one of his own. 'None whatsoever.'

I phone Paul Newman from Queensland days later. From a few pieces of gossip I'd heard while in Melbourne I tell him I have a feeling his career might be compromised if we meet again before the inquest. I thank him for his co-operation and say I'll see him in court.

∞

It's now time for me to play 'Hunt the Experts'. The only measurable difference in police investigations since 1984 is the degree of scientific accuracy that can be obtained in regard to certain evidence. Many of the tests we take for granted today after watching so many courtroom dramas and detective movies on TV—fluorescent tests for old bloodstains, DNA identification, electron microscopes and other now commonplace tools of trade for the forensic team—did not exist or were very primitive in 1984, only thirteen years ago.

Professor Stephen M. Cordner is the Director (Forensic Pathology) of the Victorian Institute of Forensic Pathology and Professor of Forensic Medicine at Monash University. He is responsible for the provision of forensic pathology services to the State of Victoria. He also supervises the research activities of the Institute, and has written a number of books dealing with forensic science, including one in collaboration with Professor Plueckhahn, whose opinion on multiple gunshot injuries carried so much weight with Dr Peter Dyte.

In February 1997 I phone Professor Cordner, who, after checking with Paul Newman, agrees to speak to me, but not to say much. He is hampered by the confidentiality of the evidence he has gathered. He says the case has occupied him for a huge amount of time over the past six months. When he began, he had no idea it would become so all-consuming. His method was to start from the premise that it was suicide and try to demonstrate, through forensic testing, whether it was possible or not.

He says to me, 'If you start from the position that someone with a bit of lead in their head can walk around, then you can't automatically assume murder because of two bullets. You must have other evidence.'

He does not tell me, but others have, that a re-enactment, as far as possible, was performed and videoed for the inquest. Although they could not find the same model couch, they did find a chair from a lounge suite identical to the one Jenny had in her house. Using this and a policewoman about Jenny's size, they tested various hypotheses in regard to the loading, positioning and firing of the rifle. They measured angles and potential bullet pathways and matched these to the actual injuries. Professor Cordner tells me, 'You ask what are the possible permutations and ways the rifle could have been held to produce the pathways of the bullets—to recreate with any certainty the paths of the bullets. You start with a suicide—take a favourable position to start with and think about it long enough to hope you've covered all the possibilities.'

He cautions me against too hastily rejecting the possibility of suicide by multiple gunshot injuries and quotes an article from the *American Journal of Forensics* 'Hudson 1981—Multi Shot Firearm Suicide—Greater awareness of the entity of multi shot firearm suicides may reduce the number of misdirected homicide investigations and diminish unwanted public arousal.' But it doesn't say anything about shots directly into the brain, does it?

On Tuesday 9 July 1996, Dr Matthew Lynch (who supervised

Adele's return to the daylight and performed her autopsy) deputised for Professor Cordner at the Mansfield cemetery, supervising Jenny's exhumation. A pathologist from the Coroner's Court must attend an exhumation. The exhumed remains of Jenny Tanner were delivered to the City Morgue in Melbourne for a new autopsy to be conducted by Professor Cordner.

At the Coroner's Court in March 1997, I retrace the path Jenny's remains would have taken. I phoned earlier to arrange this visit, and on my arrival I am told 'the Prof' has been contacted and he has no objection. I'm escorted around by Jodie, who leads the way into the first area by pushing through a pair of overlapping plastic hospital doors. She pauses halfway through and looks over her shoulder. 'You've seen dead bodies before, haven't you?' I respond quickly 'Oh, dozens!' She disappears and I follow, to be immediately confronted by a naked male corpse a metre away, yellowish and supine on a stainless-steel table. For a moment I'm stopped in my tracks; I calculate the last time I've seen a dead person was about fifteen years ago. Gulp! Oh, well, seen one, seen 'em all. I casually ask a few questions so Jodie won't notice my discomfort and the tour continues.

Jenny's remains arrived in the delivery area and were taken straight into this reception bay, where they were weighed, X-rayed and videoed—standard procedure for all new arrivals. The video of newly arrived corpses was introduced for identification purposes, but also serves as a complete record of all items delivered with the body. From there she was placed in a locked refrigerated unit until her autopsy the following day.

Professor Cordner carried out the procedure in the theatre, which is overlooked by a viewing booth, sealed from the theatre by thick glass. Observers and the medical team communicate by micro-phone. Observers are usually members of the Homicide investigation team and sometimes other doctors, forensic technicians and students. The investigators can ask questions during the procedure and request the pathologist to look for particular clues or injuries. Judging by the pile of reading material in the booth—*Who Weekly*, *TV Week* and a golfing monthly—many observers suspend emotion in these rooms, or seek other distractions. Jodie jokes that some observers go to sleep.

All Jenny's remains were examined, but special attention was paid to her hands and skull. Jenny's hands were given to Dr Chris Briggs, a forensic anthropologist, who is a Senior Lecturer in the Department of Anatomy and Cell Biology at the University of Melbourne and is on 24-hour call to Professor Cordner's Forensic Pathology team as a consultant in physical anthropology. He assists the Institute by providing expert examination and analysis of skeletal material. Forensic anthropology is concerned primarily, although not entirely, with the analysis of skeletonised or partly skeletonised remains known to be, or suspected of being, human, with a view to identifying the deceased and offering opinions about the circumstances surrounding the death.

Since the establishment of the on-call service there have been 35 cases in which a formal opinion has been expressed. Cases have fallen into three general categories: distinguishing animal from human remains; confirmation of identity where visual examination and forensic odontology have been unable to assist; and confirmation of identity in the case of suspicious death. Jenny Tanner and Adele Baily were in the last category.

When Dr Briggs received Jenny's hands there was some tissue still attached to the bones, but it was too decomposed to show anything of significance. I express surprise that it is there at all, and he tells me it largely depends on how quickly the body is buried before decomposition really takes hold. If the burial is in summer the coffin goes into dry ground where there is not much seepage at the bottom of the grave. Once the grave is closed in, the temperature remains pretty constant, slowing the decaying process.

We discuss the details of his findings over the phone. He tells me it was difficult for him to draw any definite conclusions, because some of the bones were not recovered. In particular, a small bone from the right wrist and a couple of thumb bones were missing. These bones were crucial to his investigation and his subsequent findings. My heart beats faster as he speaks. I have visions of grave robbery or tampering with evidence.

As casually as I can, I ask, 'How do you think those bones in particular could have been lost? Dr Lynch and Ian Coutts told me Jenny's remains were lifted in total from one coffin to another with extreme care, just so nothing would be lost.'

'I doubt they were removed,' he replies, maybe discerning my thoughts from the tone of the question. 'They could have been so badly fractured they disintegrated and decomposed, or they may have just been lost. There was a lot of dirt and other matter recovered with the body. I agree the loss is more unusual in this situation because of the means of transfer, but it's not impossible.'

He did find some damage on the left metacarpal (thumb bone)— some slight markings on the back of the bone—and on the right hand two areas of roughening on the bones which still remain.

His report concludes that there is 'no other significant finding'.

Because of his specialised skills, Chris Briggs was also involved in trying to obtain some answers from Adele Baily's remains. During the autopsy conducted by Dr Matthew Lynch, it was Dr Briggs who identified the bones as those of a male Caucasian with a mixture of another racial group, and estimated her height and age. He was right on all counts. Considering the huge number of fractures and bone fragments present, it was a neat piece of anthropological detection.

∞

Professor Cordner's task of trying to piece together the physiological possibilities associated with Jenny's death has provoked some questions about the exact angles at which the bullets entered her skull. Using all the other measurements he has obtained from the rifle, the height of the couch, the length of Jenny's arms and so on, he is asking the same questions I asked myself that Sunday morning so long ago. Not *did* she do it, but *could* she do it?

To provide the Firearms and Toolmarks experts with more detailed information he called in Ron Taylor, Forensic Sculptor. Ron works with Associate Professor John Clement, who is the Head Odontologist at Melbourne University School of Dental Science. Professor Clement joined this facility from England, where forensic odontology was further advanced at that time. Soon after his arrival a body was washed up in a reservoir, too decomposed to identify, and his assistance was sought to identify the body from dental work. During this process colleagues mentioned Ron Taylor, who was at that time the maxillo-facial dental technician at the Peter MacCallum Clinic, making new eyes, noses and ears for cancer patients who'd had radical surgery. Professor Clement responded with 'Oh, good! He can join them up!' and Ron Taylor's new career was launched.

Ron and another dental technician are the only experts in Australia recreating skulls using dental acrylics. The use of this material gives them accuracy to less than a millimetre.

Jenny's skull was brought to Ron on Thursday 11 July 1996. His job was to construct an exact replica to be produced in court to demonstrate the angle of entry and damage inflicted by the bullet wounds.

The holes in Jenny's skull—one well above the hairline, according to Ron Taylor—were different sizes. This could have been because the end of the rifle was a different distance from her head when each shot was fired, or because the hollow-nosed bullet had begun to fragment after it passed through her hand on its way to her head. It is impossible to say accurately. The locations of the bullet holes as described by Professor Cordner's autopsy and by Ron Taylor differ from those detailed in Dr Dyte's report. Dyte's report has them one centimetre apart, but Ron Taylor says more like 3.6 centimetres. Even this close proximity is unusual in self-inflicted wounds, especially with a bolt-action rifle, which has to be moved away, reloaded and fired. 'It doesn't go Bang! Bang! in quick succession like an automatic, so the entry points would have to be more distant from each other,' he said. The lower shot was between the eyes, the other directly above the first.

The reconstruction of Jenny's skull was unusual for a number of reasons. Since it was the second autopsy, her skull was in two pieces—the large lower part and a smaller 'skull cap' to allow for her brain to be removed. Secondly, this is only the third exhumed case Ron has completed in the past five or six years. He says exhumation is very expensive—over $7000—and is not undertaken lightly. The work

Ron does for the Forensic Institute is honorary, although the Institute pays for materials—in this case around $800. Finally, the replica was required urgently, so tests could be conducted while allowing the remains to be returned to Laurie for reburial. The pressure was on, and this job is not easily done under pressure.

The process is tedious and exacting, and very time-consuming. Every tiny aperture must be filled with molten wax. Then a split mould (one layer inside and one layer outside) is made by painting layer upon layer of silicone until a thickness of around three milli-metres is reached. This process took Ron about 80 hours of actual work time, from Thursday morning to the following Tuesday night. He worked until two and three in the morning and all weekend. Finally, on Tuesday night they very gently peeled the mould off for the pour. The unmoulding is just as delicate. 'You have to be gentle while rushing to meet their deadlines. The sweat pours off you. It's very tense.'

When they removed the mould from around the newly created model of Jenny's skull, the silicone peeled perfectly in one piece—and tore!

'We couldn't believe our eyes! Usually we can get fifty or sixty copies off a good mould—we can sell them for study—but this time we had one shot.'

Maybe Jenny has had enough of people poking and prodding her for the truth.

The skull made by Ray and his colleagues sits in a box on Professor Cordner's desk. He may have been looking at it the whole time we were talking on the phone. Jenny Tanner is going to have her day in court after all.

∞

My last stop on the expert trail is Firearm Examiner Senior Sergeant Ray Vincent. Ray Vincent is very reticent when I ask him to tell me about his tests on the rifle, which has been brought out of storage after all these years. He makes this profound pronouncement—'When

I saw the rifle it had the appearance of being having been stored.' Uh oh! This has all the promise of a stone wall. He also tells me he is 'not at odds with anything Mr Barry said' in 1984. I ask him about Mr Barry's evidence that the rifle was fifteen degrees to either side of vertical when it was last fired. He repeats that he can't confirm or deny anything new I'm probing for until the inquest. I suggest he checks me out with Professor Cordner and I'll call back. That approach has worked well so far. He agrees and I call again a few days later.

Still no joy. This makes me suspicious. Everyone else has been pretty open with me—at least thrown me a few crumbs—but this is different. He was very guarded. Have they found something new or incriminating, or is Ray Vincent one of the 'old school'—watching his back?

He agrees to talk in generalities about firearm identification and not specifics about that BRNO .22 rifle. Ray tells me no two weapons will ever leave the same marks on a bullet—'it's better than a fingerprint … to the exclusion of all others'. I ask if the cartridge cases found in Jenny's lounge room that night were fired from the rifle he had examined for Professor Cordner. A barely perceptible break in our conversation follows.

Then—'I can't answer that question, I'm afraid.'

'Can't or won't?' I push.

'Can't, I'm sorry. The cartridge cases seem to have been lost somewhere over the years.'

I wonder aloud how that could happen, but receive no reply. I remark that the bullets have never been produced either. Dr Dyte must have disposed of them at the autopsy. This means it is impossible to be absolutely certain, beyond the shadow of doubt, that this weapon was actually the one that caused Jenny's death, as the bullets from Jenny's brain were never forensically linked to Laurie's BRNO rifle.

We go on to discuss the phenomenon of the .22 rifle and how he can say with absolute certainty it was last fired fifteen degrees to either side of vertical. 'Because you have a closed breech, which affects the pressure in the barrel, this affects the distribution of powder in the barrel. It leaves a characteristic pattern. Usually residue is left as an even deposition in the bore of the weapon, but if this particular type of rifle is fired within fifteen degrees of either side of vertical a partly burnt section can dispose itself around the bottom of the barrel. The only weapons in which this very specific phenomenon occurs are the .22 bolt actions and some centre fires.'

'Vertical can mean up or down along the vertical plane in this case?'

'That's correct.'

'So Jenny could have been lying on her back on the couch, or crouched on the floor, and someone could have pointed the rifle right between her eyes and shot her at a downward angle?'

'That's pure speculation and I cannot comment at this stage.' He withdraws from this discussion, telling me it will all be explained in great detail at the inquest and if I want to know more I should be there.

'Oh, I'll be there,' I agree. 'It's the most important date on my calendar this year.'

∞

A couple of months later, while researching in the Office of Corrections Library, I come across an article in the *Police Bulletin*— 'Deaths Caused by the Discharge of Firearms'. It was written by Senior Sergeant Henry Glaser, who was attached to the same Firearms and Toolmarks Section as Ray Vincent. This article refers to Force Circular Memo (FCM) 6/90 (meaning it went out in June 1990) regarding a new policy for dealing with all deaths by firearms— including suicides.

On the off-chance of reaching Sergeant Glaser to ask him what had prompted the memo, I phone the Firearms and Toolmarks Section again. Glaser is on leave but I luck onto Senior Constable Alan Pringle, who is in his seventeenth year with Firearms and Toolmarks.

He tells me how very difficult it is to investigate such an old case. The evidence can appear inconsistent, and you are missing some of the players. He says this is an unusual case for a number of reasons, not the least being the direct involvement of members as relatives of the deceased.

I liken this investigation to one into the Mafia—the code of silence to outsiders and networks and favours being used internally to protect and prevent discoveries. He doesn't disagree.

He says the memo on death by firearms was issued following two apparent suicides by firearms in Melbourne in quick succession. One was a well-known building magnate, who left a note, and the other was a police member, who didn't. On closer examination of the member's firearm, it became apparent that for some reason he had failed to take adequate precautions when cleaning his gun. He removed a key piece of the mechanism when there was a cartridge still in the magazine, the gun fired accidentally and killed him. (I was hoping the memo had been prompted by the circumstances surrounding Jenny's death, but in a true story you can't always get what you want.)

The memo says any member attending the scene where a death has occurred by firearms must notify the Firearms and Toolmarks Section—around the clock. Nothing must be touched until the Firearms Examiner, these days Ray Vincent, decides if he needs to attend or not.

I ask Alan if this differs much from the procedure in 1984. 'Not really, but back then you didn't have to go if you were satisfied it was suicide.'

'Can I put a hypothetical scenario to you? Suppose a country police officer—uniformed and untrained in crime scene investigation—found someone who looked like a suicide in 1984. He was unable to contact his local CI so he phoned D24 to reach you. He described the scene. What would you say?'

'Describe the condition of the firearm. If it was a bolt-action firearm, for instance, you wouldn't expect to find an ejected cartridge case—that would indicate straight away more than one bullet had been fired, because the case from a single bullet would still be in the breech. I'd ask him to give me a detailed description of the condition of the wound—like if there were black residues around the wound and so on. If he was satisfied I would probably say, "It seems OK to me if you think so".'

So I continue. 'He hangs up. Soon he rings back. He's found another cartridge case in the gun and a hole in each of her hands. What do you say then?'

'Oops! We would have to attend the scene. We'd check the number of shots. We'd attend the post mortem. At that time we'd possibly get on to Homicide.'

'But we're talking 1984 now. Would you have attended then, especially out in the country, two or three hours away?'

'Of course,' Alan says. 'We're always eager to go bush. It's a great break away, and it's usually interesting.'

'Did you have pagers in 1984? Someone told me you may not have had them that early?'

'Yep. No doubt about it. We were always on call.'

'Another police officer told me that if Bill Kerr had any suspicions about it not being suicide it would have been impossible for him to carry out gunshot residue tests on Laurie Tanner at Springfield, as he wouldn't have had the capacity to do them. Even the CI didn't have the technology. They would have had to say to Laurie, "Put your hands on the table and don't move for three hours until the ballistics guys get here from Melbourne." Is that true?'

'Yeah, that would be right,' Alan concedes. 'And it's not something a mere constable would do, given he was faced with a dead girl, a grieving husband, a crying baby and a worried grandmother in a country town. What would you do? Anyway, gunshot residue tests in those days were very volatile. It was before the scanning electron microscope and the chemicals used were not very reliable. The results were not admissible in court because they were either done with sodium nitrite or gas chromatographs. These tests could be destructive of the tissue, so you only had one go. You couldn't check them or replicate them, so I think that's why they had little evidentiary value. Even if they'd found residue on her feet or hands, it wouldn't have been conclusive anyway.'

This surprises me. 'Why not? Surely that would have indicated whether or not she fired the rifle?'

'Not at all.' When a gun fires, Alan goes on to explain, three residue elements appear together—lead, antimony and barium. Two clouds of residue are formed, one from the breech and one from the muzzle. The size, distribution and composition of each cloud is different. Antimony is the primer used in the cartridge of a bullet. When a gun is fired, the nitrocellulose that creates the accompanying gases also releases a component of the primer; 90 to 100 per cent of the antimony exits the muzzle. Anyone familiar with firearms in 1984 would've known this. If a murder had been committed, but the killer wanted it to be thought a suicide, he or she could have shaken the breech over the victim's hands (or feet) to leave enough particles of residue from the breech on the skin to create doubt.

'Of course now, with *Phoenix* and all the other police shows on TV, lots of people know about this,' he concludes. 'All the crims know it—we wish they didn't, but it's pretty common knowledge.'

Well, it's news to me.

∞

Once the media became involved in Jenny's investigation, the gossip in and around Mansfield and Bonnie Doon intensified. For example, I was told by a local that after the TV segment featuring Angie McCormack, 'hundreds of calls were received by Crime Stoppers. They could hardly cope.'

In order to test this out (and try to find out what sort of information was phoned through) I contact Crime Stoppers. Senior Sergeant Val Smith is in charge of Crime Stoppers and he takes my initial enquiry. Again I am struck by the sensitivity of Jenny's case. He tells me he will have to obtain clearance to give me any information and call me back, which he subsequently does. His reticence is not only related to Jenny, but also to the confidential nature of calls received by Crime Stoppers. Many people don't want to be identified as having supplied information that leads to someone's arrest, so a large proportion of the potential rewards for this type of information go unclaimed. All calls to Crime Stoppers result in an Information Report. This is then checked to see if it has any value. For instance, a caller could say he saw someone accelerating away from outside a robbed bank in a green Ford van with licence number '123'. Crime Stoppers checks if there is a green van with that number plate. Sometimes that number belongs to, say, a red sports car, and the information supplied by the caller is then deemed of no real value. If it does match and if such a vehicle is considered to be of interest, the report is passed on to the appropriate police for further investigation. Intelligence analysts follow up this first report, and if it 'has legs' it will be investigated by the relevant police on the case. If not, the original Information Report is returned to Crime Stoppers as 'no value', for filing.

The more specific the crime, the fewer the calls of any value. A traffic accident on a busy street corner may produce a lot of calls because there could be many potential witnesses. A child abduction (or a murder) may produce very few, as information relevant to such a specific incident would only be known to a very few people. The publicity about Jenny's investigation stimulated two calls. Both the Information Reports were returned as 'no value'.

The investigating Task Force used their best efforts to enlist support from local media during their visits to Mansfield and Bonnie Doon. They were probably unaware of the editorial reticence that precluded broader stories about the locals involved. Most of the local media coverage during the period following the discovery of Adele Baily and the reopening of Jenny's investigation consisted either of direct quotes from the police or excerpts from their media releases. Police employ a number of their own little tricks when dealing with the media, one of which is to withhold small but vital pieces of information that could be known only to the real culprit. This was done in both cases, but so far no-one seems to have fallen into the trap. Maybe it's because the suspects know the rules too. The *Courier* ran short passages about the directions the investigation was taking, but surprisingly, nothing from or about the Tanners or the Blakes.

My own letter to the editor produced no response.

In the *Mansfield Courier* on 12 June 1996—only three days after a sensational news article rocked the district and resulted in a sell-out of the *Sunday Age* from Seymour to Benalla—a two-and-a-half-column photo of the blessing of the Mt Buller snowfields dwarfed a narrow half-column par headed 'Police to investigate Doon deaths'. The last paragraph in this story was a single blunt sentence—'Homicide squad members are in Mansfield this week.' In a later issue 'Vandals at St Mary's Hall' who caused $600 worth of damage were given a bigger headline than 'Police seek to re-open Tanner inquest'. Neither of these stories was on the front page.

Compare this with the *Sunday Age* article, where the editor of the paper backed his journalist's hunch that this was a story worth nearly three pages—a story that had the potential to severely embarrass senior police and expose a possible cover-up involving dozens of police, from a low-ranking constable in Mansfield to the head of Homicide in Melbourne, to protect a member of the police brother-hood. The crime journalist, Andrew Rule, and his colleague, John Silvester, have been dogging police for years on all manner of issues. Silvester has written several other stories about the Task Force's prime suspect, Denis Tanner, before and since the story about Jenny was published in 1996. Some of their stories are based on information released by the police, but more often they are uncovered through investigative journalism, using the network of contacts established by these journalists over the years. Both have written books about police corruption and criminals. In this case, Andrew Rule won a journalism award for the newspaper story, but decided not to write the book.

I wonder what would have happened if the suppression order had extended for months. Would the story have been shelved? Would other issues have taken priority?

At least in one other area the media were working as a positive force. The article in *Outrage*, which was seen by Adele's mother's friend in New Zealand, was a critical breakthrough in the Adele Baily investigation, enabling her to be identified as a St Kilda prostitute. This identification later established in the Task Force's collective minds circumstantial links with Denis Tanner. Without that article Adele might have remained unidentified, and Jenny Tanner might still be resting in her undisturbed grave.

But is this a 'whodunnit' without a culprit behind bars? As the details of the first investigation have emerged, it has become more like a 'who didn't do it'. After two years of solid investigation, it seems we've all come full circle, though at least Jenny's family will now have the satisfaction of everyone knowing Jenny loved them and did not take her own life.

Perhaps my friends at Homicide have been keeping a few cards close to their chests. Will the second inquest provide any answers?

Part Four

The Outcome

Though justice be thy plea, consider this,
That in the course of justice none of us
Should see salvation

SHAKESPEARE,

THE MERCHANT OF VENICE

16

The Second Inquest I

The relocated Melbourne Coroner's Court is at the posh end of town, with one of Melbourne's best business addresses—Kavanagh Street, South Melbourne. The building itself is imposing and contemporary, a solid white concrete edifice with smart blue trim and a bright yellow feature wall. Landscaped greenery contrasts sharply with the still-new white walls and softens the asphalt expanse of car-park at one side. Flanking the main entrance, the Victorian and Australian flags signify a building of status. It looks more like a corporate headquarters than a court. Back in the depths of the building are the Institute of Forensic Science, the City Morgue and an education facility for doctors, police, lawyers and others connected with the industry generated by death.

Above the entrance is a full-colour replica of the Victorian coat of arms. Beneath this, etched in concrete as deeply as time itself, is the motto 'Veritas omnia vincit.' I remember that motto from one of the endless succession of schools I attended—'Truth conquers all.' We wish!

Students are huddled around the front entrance having a last gasp on a cigarette and gossiping about their weekend before turning to the sober business of Monday's first forensic lecture. I move past them into the imposing lobby.

Solid blue carpet cushions the nervous pacing of witnesses. Upholstered seating lines the walls. The entire space is dominated by a soaring feature wall of amorphous modern sculpture—a part of the building, yet separate.

The doors leading to the two courtrooms are off to the right. I make my way to Court One—the larger of the two, selected for Jenny's inquest because of the large numbers of spectators expected. 'TANNER' is printed on a slip of paper in a slot on the door. It's early and there's hardly anyone here yet. I wanted to be certain of a seat. After all this time, it would be dreadful not to get in. My mouth is dry and my heart is beating fast. Who would have thought, twelve months ago, I'd be standing here today, a fringe participant in an inquest to truthfully establish the cause of death of Jennifer Ruth Tanner?

I am the first person to enter Court One, apart from the Court sound-recording technician, who is arranging microphones. I try out three different seats before choosing one that gives me a clear view of the witness stand, the various counsel and the coroner. I leave my bag and coat on the chair and buy breakfast from a takeaway across the road—the only place within cooee to get drinks and food. I eat quickly and return to Court One.

Witnesses dribble in. I have a sense of disembodiment, sitting on the sidelines, trying to put names to various faces known only to me by their voices on the phone. Familiar faces arrive too: Kath and Les Blake, supported by a phalanx of friends and relatives; Jenny's three sisters, all so different but all with a familial resemblance—Kris, immaculately dressed with fashionably streaked silver-blonde hair, Miriam tense, dressed in a miniskirted black suit, with tousled shoulder-length dark red hair, looking as if she's had little sleep the night before, and Clare, with a brown bob and simple black dress, looking far younger than her thirty-two years.

At first Jenny's family members sit in my row and the row behind me. Then Denis and Laurie Tanner come in and sit in the row in front of us, and the Blakes move en masse to the opposite side of the court, leaving Denis and Laurie isolated together on one side of the room, with me and a smattering of journalists occupying a few seats behind them. Journalists are everywhere—maybe twenty of them—almost outnumbering the family and witnesses.

Denis is imposing and pretty cool in a navy suit, Laurie awkward in light grey pinstripes, anxiously chewing gum. Denis's face is like a mask most of the time, but he does acknowledge me with a nod and 'Hello.' And surprise! His counsel is Mr Joe Gullaci—not tall, smooth and elegant as his telephone voice had indicated, but power-dressed, short, swarthy and balding. I feel pleased I didn't take up his offer to get one of his mates to 'legal' my manuscript. I wander across to him to introduce myself and chaff him about trying to get 'the inside story' to assist his client. He grins sheepishly and replies, 'Well, you can't blame me for trying!' Laurie's lawyer, Mr Tony Hargreaves, is younger and less imposing. His brown tweed suit is a bit tight from the rear view, and his boyish face, steel-rimmed glasses and curly hair remind me of a woodwork teacher I'd had at one of the co-ed stages of my education.

Everyone is tense—including me. Some people have waited a long time for today and others no doubt hoped the day would never come. The police arrive—Jeff Calderbank looking bigger than I remember in a tailored double-breasted suit and flash tie; Paul Newman, dressed down in sports jacket and elastic-sided boots; Marty Allison, suave and tall, looking more like a model than a Homicide cop, his conservative suit offset by lairy socks that only peep out when he crosses his legs; and Paul Solomon, thickset in a navy bomber jacket and jeans—someone says he's working undercover on another job. Graeme Miller, the police analyst whose pleasant English voice at the end of the Homicide phone number always made me think of a holiday resort reservation clerk, now materialises in a dark navy suit topped by very English shiny scrubbed cheeks and a luxuriant black moustache. No sign of Jacqueline Curran, though. All the police carry lots of luggage—the Coroner's brief and their supporting material. The statements folder alone is eight centimetres thick. Paul Newman hasn't been kidding me.

Mr Jeremy Rapke is appearing for the Director of Public Prosecutions and the police. I ask Kath Blake if Jenny's family is represented and she says, 'We have Mr Rapke—he's appearing for all of us.' Mr Rapke wears one of those beards that look like the skin on a kiwi fruit. (I always wonder how this look is achieved—it must be more trouble than shaving properly.) His mild-mannered demeanour could easily lull witnesses into a relaxed state. He'll not be a man to underestimate.

The witness list shows 45 names. Denis and Laurie Tanner are not among them. Denis has had to take recreation leave to attend, as his superiors would not allow him to use police time and he was not sub-poenaed. (Another police strategy to exert pressure on him?) Frank Tanner is helping with the farm to allow Laurie to attend. I count six people on the witness list I haven't interviewed and haven't heard of. Good. There might be some surprises.

It all seems very disorganised. People wander in and out of the court, chatting as if at a social gathering. Paul Newman and Denis Tanner both look tense, but don't look at each other. Everyone else is greeting, catching up or, in the case of myself and the media, sussing out who is there. The police have called ten witnesses per day and five standbys, so the first fifteen on the list are in attendance. These are mostly the first police investigators (the 'A Team') and a couple of names unfamiliar to me. The old guard huddle together in a little clutch, still unaware of the existence of Bill Kerr's file. When I talk to them it's obvious they're going to tough it out, support each other and paint Bill Kerr as an incompetent who couldn't hack the heavy demands of police work and retired early due to stress. Jenny Tanner shot herself twice in the head and through both hands by using her toe to pull the trigger. Simple suicide. The Party Line. Former Inspector Duncan MacLennan, looking exactly as I had imagined— red-faced, loud-voiced and overbearing—tells me, 'We were a pretty good team, you know. I don't care what anyone says—we did a great job, didn't we, boys?' hitching his suit pants for emphasis every so often.

The 'boys' are former Sergeant Neil Phipps, not as good-looking in a suit—farm gear looks better; former Station Commander Neil Walker, small and dapper in a navy blazer, still sporting his regulation haircut, and former Detective Sergeant Ian Welch, even smaller than I remembered, wearing the light tan suit favoured by people who don't wear suits very often.

On the outer of this circle is Sergeant Don Frazer, in uniform. He looks so much like an old friend of mine they could be twins. I feel as if I've known him for years. This makes it easy to chat, and he seems much more relaxed face-to-face than on the phone. Perhaps he too thought his phones were bugged?

The Coroner arrives and suddenly we all become solemn and businesslike. Mr Rapke stands and informs us we are here to ascertain the cause of death of Jennifer Ruth Tanner at Springfield, Bonnie Doon on 14 November 1984.

His soft monotone address summarises the story and outlines the type of evidence some witnesses will be giving to the court. He makes reference to Denis's controversial visit to Jenny on either 22 or 29 October (still unresolved) and the fact that Laurie told Paul McCormack, one of Curly's brothers, that Denis had 'cleaned the mess at the farm' early the following day. Drifting along with his speech, I wonder if I will learn anything new—maybe this last chapter of Jenny's story will be an anticlimax.

Then the first bombshell drops. 'There will be evidence from a Sergeant of Police, Helen Golding, a close personal friend of Denis Tanner's wife and an acquaintance of both Denis Tanner and the late Jennifer Tanner. She will tell Your Worship that a couple of weeks before Jennifer died she was at the home of Denis and Lynne Tanner for dinner and Jennifer was being discussed. Denis Tanner mentioned he had been up to see Jennifer and told her to treat his brother, Laurie, properly. Denis Tanner told Golding he had driven up and back to Bonnie Doon in one evening, just to tell her that she had to start looking after Sam, being the baby, and to start treating Laurie properly. Golding has a recollection that Denis Tanner claimed to have told Jennifer that it wasn't fair for Laurie not to be getting any sex. Golding gained the impression that Denis seemed quite pleased he had been up and spoken to Jennifer and rectified the situation. Golding got the clear impression, based on what she was told by Denis Tanner, the visit had taken place at night-time.

'Sergeant Golding will also tell Your Worship that she had the clear impression that Denis Tanner disliked Jennifer intensely. She observed him display a distinct lack of respect for the deceased and, on occasions, display anger at what he perceived to be the poor treatment his brother Laurie was receiving from Jennifer.

'On other occasions, Golding observed Denis Tanner to display anger over his perception that Jennifer was not looking after the baby. He commented that Laurie had to come in every four hours off the land to change the baby's nappy and to feed him. On other occasions she witnessed Denis Tanner expressing strong views on other matters concerning the way in which Jennifer was handling the baby and running the household.

'In early September last year, Sergeant Golding informed her old friend, Lynne Tanner, that she had made a statement to the police about Jennifer Tanner. She outlined the contents of her statement. A few days after that meeting, Lynne Tanner advised Sergeant Golding she had told her husband, Denis Tanner, about the contents of Golding's statement. A few days later, Golding received threatening telephone calls at her office at the Geelong Community Policing Squad. The male who made the calls told her she should be ashamed for what she had done and that she would not make it to court. She was also called a "bitch".

'On 25 September last year, Denis Tanner rang Sergeant Golding's private residence and, in a conversation with Golding's husband, Tanner made references to "the pricks in the job that try and fix up other members, but their turn will come".

'Sergeant Golding has also received threatening letters, one of which reads:

> Are you ignoring the warnings you have received. Do you think they are idle—not so. Your movements are known—as you can see by the attached roster—and you have a new car. How nice. Do not follow through with this—life is not worth it and won't be worth it. You should have the message by now and if not you soon will. That prick in Melbourne, fucking cunt that he is, will get his soon too. If this goes ahead 'YOU'RE DEAD' but not without pain or alone. You won't get another warning, the moment you make a move to Melbourne start watching your back. J.F.T.'

Denis's face is expressionless throughout this reading—about the only face in court that is. I watch him closely all the time, and there isn't even a twitching of that little muscle near the temple men twitch when they get angry. He's tough and he's cool. Laurie chews his gum so fast his jaw nearly goes into spasm. The rest of us are dumbfounded. Many exchange amazed glances. Journalists scrawl pages of notes. Mr Rapke continues as if he's just read out the stock exchange report, but the atmosphere in court has changed. We are all sitting up, listening carefully.

We are soon further rewarded for our attention. After making much of the various explanations Denis has offered for his whereabouts on the night Jenny died, Mr Rapke tells us about a motel deal Denis, Lynne and Laurie were investigating in 1989. During discussions with the person commissioned by Denis to find a suitable property, Denis was asked if Laurie definitely wanted to be included in the deal, as Denis and Lynne did not have sufficient capital without him. Denis's alleged reply was, 'Laurie will do as he's fuckin' well told, because if it wasn't for me the second slut would have got the lot.' After summing up the outcome of the first (now quashed) inquest, Mr Rapke sits down, a stunned audience at his back.

Joe Gullaci rises to his feet. At first I think he's going to object to the inflammatory nature of the opening address, but instead he requests that all witnesses be excluded from the court until after they give evidence, because the long time lapse could perhaps leave memory gaps that might inadvertently be filled by other witnesses' testimony. Although the request is unusual, and Mr Rapke argues, the Coroner, Mr Johnstone, agrees. All witnesses except family file out disgruntledly. Thank goodness I haven't been subpoenaed—I wouldn't have seen a thing!

Hughie Almond, nuggety and weather-beaten, takes the stand. He goes over his role in the finding of Jennifer and steps down. Nothing new there.

Next up is Bill Kerr, cocky and playing to the media for all he is worth. He tells me during the lunch break, 'Now I know how Princess Diana must have felt.' His suit is the regulation light tan and his shirt too small. His tie valiantly struggles to keep the unbuttoned edges of his collar in place.

Bill's evidence is well known to me, but the journalists lap it up. He says his superiors totally ignored his requests to obtain forensic tests on the rifle and they whitewashed the interview of Denis Tanner when he was asked to account for his whereabouts on the night. Towards the end of the day, while ten or so disgruntled witnesses are milling about outside, Bill is still enjoying the limelight. He produces his old file and flourishes the list of questions he sent to Homicide attached to his request that Denis Tanner be interviewed by an officer.

MATTERS I BELIEVE SHOULD BE CLARIFIED PRIOR TO PRESENTATION OF THIS MATTER TO THE CORONER.

1. Is there any proprietary interest in the property Springfield held by Dennis Tanner or his wife Lyn? [sic]
2. Is there any possible future interest in the property held by Dennis Tanner or Lyn Tanner?
3. Is the allegation that Dennis attended the Bonnie Doon home on the night of 22 October 1984, unannounced, true?
4. If true, is this a normal pattern for Tanner to follow?
5. Is the allegation that he told his wife Lyn that he was going to the races true?
6. If so, could the statement by Tanner that on the night of the deceased's death that he went to the races be true or false?
7. What were Dennis Tanner's movements on the night of the deceased's death? Can they be substanciated? [sic]
8. What was the topic of conversation with Laurie on the phone at about 5.30 p.m. that night?
9. Could a possible financial interest in the property Springfield present or future and the possible threat of further financial burdens on Laurie and the family property be sufficient motive for Dennis to contemplate the commission of a serious crime?
10. Was the fear of a possible marriage breakup so strong as to require drastic action?
11. It has been alleged there was no love loss [sic] between the deceased and Dennis. Is this true?

12. Did Dennis Tanner in fact attend at Bonnie Doon on the night of 14 November 1984, and point the rifle at the deceased when it went off?

Although the above questions are based on rumour and conjecture I believe that they must be answered prior to the Coronial Inquest into the death of the deceased Jennifer Tanner.

Clearly few of them *were* answered, but they clearly indicate the extent of his concern at the time.

The rest of this memo reads:

The fact that there are two gunshot wounds to the forehead of the deceased has not been made common knowledge. Although the doctor performing the post mortem considers that what he believes to be the first would not have killed the deceased it would have had a telling impact. Could the deceased in fact have fired the two shots when

The entry holes are so close?

The weapon is of bolt action type and has to be operated manually?

Could the second shot have been fired by the deceased after receiving a wound of the magnitude of the first?

OR Could the second shot have been fired by some other person in an attempt to have the same entry point as the first in the hope that the matter would be written off as suicide?

This memo is dated 19 April 1985. Bill's concerns about the infliction of the wounds exactly reflected the ones I had when I read the article in the *Sunday Age*. Why didn't anyone take him seriously in 1985?

Mr Rapke reads out a memo from Tom O'Keefe, former RDCI at Benalla, dated 6 June 1985, which dismissed Bill's concerns as rumour and innuendo and instructed 'no further investigations are required in this matter'. He then quotes from another memo by Detective Senior Sergeant Jim Fry at Homicide in Melbourne, dated 30 May 1985, stating that 'the points raised by Mr Kerr were based on rumour and conjecture and our examination of the documents vindicate [sic] our previous feelings that innuendo made by relatives and friends are [sic] not supported by any factual evidence and no further investigation is warranted'. This was accompanied by another memo from Inspector Brian Ritchie, head of Homicide, which said, in part, 'This matter has been investigated by a member of Homicide and confirms our opinion that innuendo from well-meaning friends and relatives has no basis. The matter should now be concluded and prepared for the Coroner.'

The file was returned to Alexandra CIB, where Detective Sergeant Ian Welch couldn't help adding his opinion 'It appears relevant matters have been clarified—return file to Coroner.' It looks as if Bill was really up against it.

With the hammy air of a magician, Bill then produces a statement he claims was attached to his original compilation of the Coroner's brief. This statement is a couple of pages longer than the one read into evidence at the first inquest, which Bill agreed at the time was his full statement. In the missing section, we are told that Denis Tanner allegedly told Bill he feared the family property would be lost in a property settlement. Bill says he gained a strong impression Denis would do almost anything to prevent another divorce.

This statement causes a minor sensation. All eyes are on Denis. Not a good first day for him. When Mr Rapke asks Bill why he took the file home and kept it after his retirement, Bill replies, 'I probably didn't trust them to investigate it properly.' (Nothing about covering his back, as he told me last year.)

Laurie's and Denis's lawyers are understandably peeved at the production of this new file, to which they have not had access, along with several enhanced copies of Bill's secret tape recordings. Mr Johnstone directs that the additional material be made available and we all stand up while the court is adjourned. I whisper to Denis that it might be a good idea to phone his mother to protect Sam a bit from the news. All four TV channels are outside, waiting for the Tanners to leave. The day has flown.

∽

Day Two: much more of Bill Kerr. Too much, in fact. He's tripping over himself and changing his evidence from hour to hour. He tells us he was 'just a dumb country copper', and he seemed to be trying hard to prove it. Dr Patience, who is in the waiting crowd of disgruntled and edgy witnesses outside, announces that he must be heard on his appointed day as he has a full patient list tomorrow. Perhaps sensing we all need a bit of a break from Bill, His Worship consents to hearing Dr Patience interspersed between Bill's increasingly ragged testimony.

Geoffrey Patience presents like a retired naval officer, crisp, upright and sparse. He speaks precisely in clipped tones. He gives his evidence concisely. While he repeats his early statement about Jennifer's taciturn and shy nature and her lack of joy in raising her young child, he emphasises that he had never thought she was suicidal or depressed. (Presumably he means clinically depressed, as he does say she had early problems with young Sam, who was twice referred to a paediatrician.) He is also asked about Laurie's visits to consult him, and discussions they might have had about Laurie's relationship with Jenny. He gives the court a full rundown of the dates and reasons for Laurie's visits. Patience is on and off the stand in twenty minutes. This is more like it. Bill is becoming very boring!

The rest of the day is spent investigating a hypothesis that some scoundrel might have assisted Denis in some way to avoid further investigation by doctoring the second half of Bill's statement and 'disappearing' it. Bill goes along quite happily with this line of questioning, saying senior police—he does not know who—cut back his statement. 'I felt it was wrong, but that's the way the system is. I was fighting the system … I eventually gave up … the whole thing seemed to be a whitewash.' Among the comments excluded from his original statement were claims that Jenny was not considered suicidal; that Denis appeared to have conflicting alibis for 14 November; that Denis was said to dislike Jenny intensely, and Bill's list of 'Matters'.

In all, four different files regarding the first inquest have now been produced, including the original inquest brief, which had apparently been at the Coroner's Court since December 1985. So much for the

'A Team' not being able to access a file! Bill's somewhat vague answers under cross-examination by Mr Gullaci at the first inquest begin to make more sense to me. He obviously didn't agree then with some of the hypotheses being put to him, but didn't feel brave enough to say so. If his statement had been tampered with, that in itself would be a clear indication to Bill that justice could be manipulated to suit a desired outcome. Who was he to buck the system?

Bill goes on to say he subsequently came under intense pressure from two senior police officers, which eventually forced him to resign from the force. One of the officers he mentions is Chief Inspector John Rankin, who I remember was in charge as a Senior Sergeant at D24 on the night Jenny died. He was reluctant to give me any information when I phoned this year to interview him about that night.

I feel for Jenny's family, sitting stoically through all this. While Mr Johnstone is looking increasingly displeased by the inference that a coronial brief might have been tampered with, the rest of us are letting our minds wander.

Then we are snapped back to the present by a question from Mr Hargreaves. 'During your investigations, did you interview a Dawn Kipping who, rather than Mrs McCormack, appears to be the last person to have spoken to Jennifer on the phone between 9.30 p.m. and 10 p.m. on the night she died?'

Bill's apparent confusion reflects my own. Who is Dawn Kipping, and how has this conversation been kept secret for so long? And why? She's one of the unknown people I've marked on my witness list. This rather narrows the time frame in which Jenny had been killed. As soon as I return home that night I track down Dawn Kipping through my well-thumbed Mansfield phone book, but can't raise her. She's probably already in Melbourne. So I resign myself to waiting to hear her evidence—if they ever get Bill off the stand!

∞

Next day we are treated to a demonstration of just how extensive the powers of the Coroner are. A surprise first witness, before Bill resumes his evidence, is Detective Superintendent Peter Fleming, now in charge of Ethical Standards. He's been moved up the list of witnesses to appear before His Worship. He tells me he just 'dropped everything' to attend. The Coroner takes precedence over all, it seems. Peter Fleming's dark grey suit and iron grey hair project seniority. He's short—calmly confident, with a quiet voice that commands attention. He tells us he has never seen the longer version of Bill's statement. Security with files had been lax at the Coroner's Court at the time he was assisting Mr Adams. Files were kept in a small office just inside the front door in an open cabinet filed under the hearing date, or in metal boxes in the foyer. In fact, one of his tasks was to tighten up procedures and security while he assisted in introducing the new Coroner's Act in 1986. He says he thinks the first investigation was incompetent, and said so to Mr Adams and internal investigators at the time. He believes senior Homicide detectives, including Sergeant Jim Fry, prevented him from making further inquiries into Denis Tanner's whereabouts on the night, even though Denis's alibi had not been checked.

Fleming is followed by another surprise witness—David Stevens, who assisted me so extensively on the phone about Coronial Court procedures and the Coroner's Acts. He bounces into court with a big smile and a mass of unruly curls, looking much too cheerful to be the manager of an undertaker's firm (a recent job change) whence he has been summoned to be examined on security procedures in 1985. He looks extremely happy to be back in his old environment and exchanges a few quick pleasantries with Mr Johnstone before settling down in the witness box. David, who was Mr Adams' clerk during Jenny's first inquest, tells us he was certain he kept the brief file in a safe at the court, but might have sent the original across to Homicide. The Coroner is taking the intimation that Bill's statement might have been tampered with extremely seriously.

Bill's evidence concludes at last—almost four days on the stand— with his assertion that Jenny might have been killed in another room and moved to a staged position on the couch, given the way her left finger and thumb made a circle around the rifle barrel with her other fingers splayed out. He now agrees he did not search the house so couldn't say whether entry had been forced, if there was blood in any other room or whether there was, in fact, a suicide note. Poor Bill!

Mr Gullaci makes him look even worse, but Bill doesn't seem to notice. He departs the stand triumphantly for his media interviews and negotiations for a starring role in a TV current-affairs show. It's becoming obvious that this inquest isn't going to finish in the eight days allocated. Will we get an extension, after waiting so long for a conclusion, or are we going to be put on hold once more?

Roz Smith, tiny and shrinking into herself after a four-day wait outside in the foyer, gives the same evidence she gave at the first inquest. Her voice quavers, but Mr Gullaci can't shake her story about Jenny's phone call recounting Denis's allegedly threatening visit. She says when she heard of Jenny's death she felt the telephone call 'had become a reality'.

She leaves the stand limp with relief to race to the airport. She confides to me that she only brought one white shirt with her and has worn it back to front on alternate days for variety, washing it every night in her motel hand-basin. Inquests can be pretty tough on witnesses, in more ways than one.

The Task Force has been to Surfers Paradise to find the Browns, whose farewell at the bingo Denis said he attended on the night of 14 November 1984. Mrs Brown can't remember seeing Denis at the bingo on 14 November because she wasn't there that night. Her recollection was that a small and informal presentation was made to her and her husband and that she had to be called over from her nearby home to receive her gift, as there was no specific notification that a ceremony of any sort would occur. She could not, however, recall if that happened on a Wednesday night. When challenged by Mr Gullaci about the accuracy of her recollection after so long, she replies confidently that she remembers it very well, as she'd thought what a miserable lot the bingo organisers were, only giving her and her husband a box of chocolates and a bottle of whisky after all the years of voluntary work they'd put in. She also tells us Denis was not the only off-duty police officer who used to 'moonlight' there, and that they were all paid in cash—$25 per night. Mr Johnstone's eyebrows meet in the middle.

Don Frazer follows Mrs Brown. Don looks embarrassed and awkward in his Sergeant's uniform, preferring to stand up while giving his evidence. He keeps his hands tightly clasped around the edge of the witness box and leans forward attentively. He tells us that the way Jenny's hand was 'gripping' the rifle caused him concern on the night. His face reddens when he agrees photos should have been taken on the night and the scene should have been examined by crime scene investigators. He also reveals it was he, not Bill, who discussed the empty cartridge case in the rifle with Laurie. Don now says he can't remember how many times Bill had phoned the CI, as he was in the lounge room and couldn't hear Bill in the kitchen. This differs quite a bit from what he said when I interviewed him.

The Coroner asks Don a number of questions about his apparent lack of follow-up during the subsequent investigation. His Worship seems at a loss as to why Bill had been left so much to his own devices to investigate Jenny's death.

Don responds that it was all 'a delicate situation from start to finish. On the night, you couldn't lock Laurie out of his own house while we treated the scene as a crime scene—it wouldn't have been right. As a country copper you know all these people and he was so upset, his wife was dead. I was trying to treat it one way until we knew the CI wasn't coming and then we treated it just as suicide.' Don shakes his head and looks pleadingly at the Bench for understanding, but is fixed by a stony stare. He sighs. 'I've been very troubled by this event since then. I've thought of it often. You have to understand, we were just two country constables trying to do our best. We had no detective training. If the CI wouldn't come over, we had no choice but to treat it the way we did. I did not stick my nose in later in the investigation, or voice my concerns in my statement, because it was not my place. I did try to get the file from Bill to read it. Like everyone else, I was curious, but he kept it pretty close to his chest. In fact, I never saw the file at all.'

Don comes across as honest, but shy and a bit hesitant—who knows how much more so he would have been twelve years ago? He looks so miserable I have an urge to hug him, but I'm cross with him too. He should have stood up more for Jenny. Police culture and the hierarchical chain of command have had a very strong influence on Don Frazer. He believes his involvement in this case has somewhat blighted his career.

I corner him outside the court before he escapes in his police car back to Ballarat.

'Don—are you absolutely sure the nappy on the floor was disposable?' I ask.

'I'm certain. I had plenty of time to observe it—I was in there with Jenny for over an hour and I've got kids myself. I've seen hundreds of them. It was curled upwards, as if it had just been taken off. The weight of the wetness probably held it in that cup-shaped position. There's absolutely no doubt in my mind it was disposable.'

In his cross-examination of various witnesses who saw the nappy, Mr Gullaci suggests it could have been there since the playgroup meeting that morning, but I don't believe that for a minute.

∞

Another new development confronts us on arrival at court the following day. Three uniformed police officers are stopping and searching everyone going into Court One. We are also scanned with the electronic metal detectors used at airport security points.

I ask what is going on.

'Coroner's orders. Witnesses have been threatened and this additional security is to ensure their safety.'

'Additional' security is stretching it a bit, in my view. Generally people seem to come and go as they wish.

The buzz around the court is that Helen Golding, godmother of Denis's four children, Lynne Tanner's former best friend and Sergeant of Police, will be in court today, and indeed she is. Led into court shaking and extremely anxious, Helen Golding looks as if she would rather be anywhere else in the world.

She seems very frightened, alone up there in the witness stand. She says in her evidence she has received a number of death threats after making a statement to the police in August 1996. In that statement she made some of the damning allegations read to the court during Mr Rapke's introduction to the inquest and provided further information regarding her knowledge of Denis Tanner's 'intense dislike' of his sister-in-law and his scathing comments about Jenny as the 'town bike'. She further recalls that Lynne Tanner phoned her early on the morning of 15 November 1984 to say she was unable to make a cake for Helen's grandmother's funeral that day, as Lynne and Denis were leaving immediately for Bonnie Doon, where Jenny Tanner had 'died as a result of a gunshot wound'. In her statement Helen said that Lynne also told her the police had brought this news 'soon after 5 a.m.' and that 'Denis had been out all night and had arrived home only shortly before the police had attended'. She said she was glad Denis had arrived home before the police got there, as it would have been hard to get the news when she was by herself.

The Coroner asks Sergeant Golding why she did not come forward to assist the first inquest into Jenny's death.

She replies that she read the transcript soon after the first inquest and the Coroner had brought down an open finding and specifically said he could not implicate Laurie or Denis Tanner in Jenny's death. 'At the time I thought: if that is the decision of the Coroner, then who am I to question his decision?'

Sergeant Golding goes on to tell us that on 5 September she told Lynne Tanner she had made a statement to the police. To her surprise, Lynne subsequently told her she'd passed this news on to Denis.

On 10 September she received two threatening calls at work from a male she did not recognise. On 25 September Denis Tanner phoned her at home, which was very unusual, ostensibly to speak to her husband (also a police officer). As her husband was unavailable, Helen spoke to Denis for some time. During this conversation he allegedly told her the bosses in the job 'always think they have something on you, but they will get what's coming to them'. This was the call referred to by Mr Rapke, in which Denis spoke of 'the pricks in the job that try and fix up other members, but their turn will come'.

Helen Golding says that most of this latter conversation concerned problems her husband was having at work, but she, 'in my paranoia', decided there was a double meaning, as Denis was very forceful in what he said and repeated himself several times.

On 7 October she received an unsigned 'With sympathy' card with the words 'YOU'RE DEAD' written inside. On 5 December a knife with red nail polish all over the blade was delivered in a box with a motif saying 'Merry Christmas'. In March 1997 she found a wreath addressed to her in her maiden name at her home front door, accompanied by a card saying 'Time runs out.' In April she received three unsolicited letters at work from various funeral directors thanking her for her enquiries about pre-paid funerals (which she said she had not made). In June a .22 calibre bullet was posted to her at work. On 8 July she received another envelope containing her work roster, a card and a two-page letter—the one read out by Mr Rapke in his opening address.

She says she believes the threats were an attempt to keep her from testifying, and they nearly succeeded. 'To be totally honest, I'm terrified. I have stopped seeing people. I haven't walked the dog or ridden my horse. My health has degenerated.'

The silence in Court One is suffocating. Most people can hardly believe their ears. Denis is implacable, as always, but reacts occasionally with a grimace or by writing furiously and passing the resulting pages to his counsel. The journalists can't scribble fast enough. I'm pretty surprised myself. I knew about the knife, but this was a campaign, not an isolated incident.

Helen Golding goes on to present the most difficult part of her evidence about one of the toughest decisions of her life. She tells us about the circumstances in which she informed Lynne Tanner about the contents of her statement to the police. As both women lived in regional towns some distance apart, she arranged to meet Lynne for an overnight shopping visit to Melbourne and booked a hotel room for them to share. At the urging of the Task Force, and knowing she might be charged with an offence if she refused, she agreed to allow the conversation between herself and Lynne Tanner during their overnight stay to be secretly tape-recorded. She told the police the name of the hotel and left it to them, but believes they installed a listening device in the room before she and Lynne arrived around 6 p.m.

Mr Gullaci is outraged. He springs to his feet, objecting and blustering and pouting because he's been kept in the dark yet again. 'We know we're at the mushroom end of the table, Your Worship, but this is too much!' He demands copies of the tapes and transcripts and refuses to cross-examine Helen Golding on anything to do with this incident until he and his learned friend Mr Hargreaves have perused the transcripts. Considering there would be around twelve to fourteen hours of tapes, I think it will take more than overnight to meet his requirements. Poor Helen! She will probably have to be recalled. The Coroner adjourns the hearing, saying, 'I want to think about something for a few minutes.' What next? Tension in the court is oppressive, but no-one leaves, not knowing how long His Worship will be away and not wanting to miss anything.

I reflect on the high price Helen Golding has paid for co-operating with her police colleagues. Her friendship of many years with Lynne Tanner is in shreds; she's unlikely to see her four godchildren again; she's certainly on Denis Tanner's list of least favoured persons; she's suffered public exposure, private anxiety, loss of freedom to do as she pleases, ridicule and censure at work, and so the list goes on. Is it worth it? I'm not allowed to ask her, as she might be recalled and I have to wait to speak to witnesses until their evidence is completed. That's the price I pay for being permitted to remain throughout the proceedings.

His Worship returns and pronounces: 'I've sat in a large number of inquests. At no stage has any witness appeared before me with a number of threats against them and I find it very troubling. The serious nature of those threats prompts me to say this. The system of justice means you can give evidence freely in any court. Commanders at Force Command Level ought to ensure Helen Golding receives the highest level of support, security and assistance.'

Either insensitive or oblivious to the Coroner's mood, Mr Gullaci presses His Worship further about obtaining the transcript of the motel tapes. His Worship looks down fiercely from his exalted position. 'Mr Gullaci, the tapes will be supplied when I am ready and not before. This is my investigation and I will retain control. I am not about to prejudice this investigation, which is still in progress.'

We are then treated to one of those artificially polite court exchanges full of suppressed heat, where counsel are calling each other 'learned friends' when they really would like to wring each other's necks. While Helen looks on from the stand, the Coroner is drawn in to adjudicate about whether her cross-examination should be suspended until the production of the tapes. The Coroner will not budge and Gullaci is directed to cross-examine on other aspects of Helen's evidence pending the Coroner's decision about the tapes.

Mr Gullaci stalls for time by asking for Helen's police diary to be produced to substantiate her harassment claims. It's a three-hour return trip to her desk in Geelong, so she's excused to collect it, escorted by another police officer.

There is a short recess and I wander over to Denis. 'Your wife must be pretty upset by all this, Denis. Did you know about the secret tape?'

'No, we didn't. All we know is there's a lot they're keeping from us.' He seems quite happy to chat, and Laurie looks more relaxed with the heat off him for a while. I am pleased they both seem comfortable enough to exchange pleasantries with me. I've tried very hard to be neutral in my dealings with everyone.

The clerk calls former Detective Sergeant Ian Welch to the stand. He's been outside 'on ice' for more than a week, wondering what is going on inside, and must be relieved his turn has finally come. His tan suit is becoming rumpled.

Ian Welch's evidence is a mixture of material I already know and a revised version of some events and recollections. At one stage I write in my notes: 'Columbo's memory is VERY BAD! He now can't remember anything!'

He tells us he kept his own file after his retirement 'in case, due to the open finding' and handed it over to Homicide when they interviewed him last year. He explains that his visit to Dr Dyte was to clarify the 'powder burns on both hands'.

'What else did you do in relation to the investigation?' asks Mr Rapke.

'Probably not much,' comes the reply. 'I had a liaison role, I was not in charge of the case.'

Mr Rapke reminds him of his sworn evidence to the first inquest that he had 'overall responsibility for the case until he was satisfied'.

'Were you satisfied it was suicide?'

'Yes.'

'Why then did you endorse Kerr's request to interview Denis Tanner?'

'Kerr raised these doubts, I still had no doubts, but the query had to be answered, we had to do the interview.'

'What use could this interview be other than to protect you?' Mr Rapke fires off. 'You were a detective in the CIB for nine years—how could someone shoot themselves twice in this fashion?'

Welch mumbles the now-familiar 'A Team' Party Line.

Mr Rapke asks if Welch, as a trained investigator in the CIB, wasn't concerned when Bill Kerr rang him back to tell him there were two cartridge cases found at the scene.

'He only phoned once, said it looked like a suicide to him. The first time I heard there were two cartridge cases was from Phipps the next day. I'd never investigated a homicide—still haven't, as a matter of fact. I didn't go out on the night as I was too ill. I had undiagnosed cancer at the time.'

'Were you drinking on the night Jennifer Tanner died, Mr Welch?'

'I have no idea.'

'Are you sure you did not go to Springfield that night, either at the time you were called or later?'

'I did not attend on the night. Kerr phoned when I was asleep in bed. He told me he was satisfied it was suicide. Photos were not discussed. I assumed they would have been taken, even for a suicide. There was no need for crime scene investigation or fingerprints or other tests for gunshot residue. If the officers were satisfied it was suicide there was no need for CIB involvement.'

'Why then did you travel to Mansfield the following day?'

'I heard from Neil Phipps about the two cartridge cases.'

Through a series of questions about the contents of Welch's own file, which is now evidence, Mr Rapke seems to be trying to get Welch to admit he was in charge of the investigation. This is when Welch's memory fails him completely. 'I can't recall' rolls out repeatedly.

His Worship stares at Welch intently through all this, but Welch does not look his way. His replies are aimed directly at an air space between Mr Rapke and the Bench.

He virtually denies all of Bill's evidence. Denies he knew anything about Bill's concerns about Denis Tanner and his alibi. Denies knowing about the 'rumours and innuendos' about Jenny leaving Laurie and so on. He says he doesn't think he spoke to Sergeant Fry at Homicide and goes pale when his police diary is produced for his identification. (I smile to myself. I know this exhibit is the result of Paul Newman's visit to the Benalla storeroom the day he met Denis on the stairs.)

Mr Rapke reads him a diary entry dated 15 May 1985 about a conversation with Fry. He asks Welch to find, in his own file, a copy of Bill Kerr's statement, sent to him with the request that Denis Tanner be interviewed. (I write in my notes—'I bet it's the longer statement, with all the concerns about Denis. Yes! It was the long statement!')

Welch stares at the four pages and mumbles, 'It must have slipped.'

Mr Rapke reads aloud the material containing Bill's concerns and asks Welch if he can think of any reason why this might have been removed from the file. He can't. He didn't remove it. He doesn't remember ever hearing about any of this material. He doesn't know we have already heard his memo agreeing with Sergeant Fry's assessment—'Return file to Coroner.' I don't think he realises Bill kept his file too!

The Coroner leans down towards the witness box. 'Your first inquest statement says there was blackening around each wound indicating the shots were fired at close range. How did you know that?'

'I was told by the pathologist powder burns were evident on both hands.'

'How could that be? Explain it to me.' His Worship directs.

'I don't understand.'

'How could there be blackening around all four wounds if only two shots were fired?'

Welch finally saw the trap. 'I can't explain. I'm not a firearms expert.'

'But you were an experienced investigator?'

'I must have overlooked it.'

His Worship looks far from satisfied. 'Mmm.'

Mr Rapke resumes his attack. 'Did you approach the whole matter with a fixed mind about suicide and didn't allow any conflicting evidence to compute? Prior to the first inquest you knew about the two shots, the two alibis from Denis Tanner, Kerr's statements and concerns, et cetera. How did you arrive at suicide?'

'I don't know how Kerr arrived at a suicide outcome. I wouldn't be confident now it was suicide. I did believe it was a suicide I should have gone to the scene that night, but unfortunately I can't turn the clock back.'

Moving in for a final admission, Mr Rapke asks Welch, 'Was the investigation bungled?'

'Yes, it was.'

'How should it have been handled?'

'The scene should have been visited and preserved and a full and proper homicide investigation conducted.'

Jenny's father sits slumped, looking sad.

Surprisingly, Gullaci and Hargreaves have no questions. Ian Welch leaves the stand red-faced and heads straight back to the safety of his non-judgemental emus.

Former Detective Senior Sergeant Jim Fry is tall, greying and fashionably dressed in navy. He's as smooth as a used-car salesman and
outside waiting in the foyer, telling the same bad jokes. He strides
confidently to the witness stand, unaware that his predecessor in that
hot seat has just undergone such a harrowing experience. (It wasn't a
bad idea of Mr Gullaci's to separate the witnesses.)

Mr Rapke gives Fry Kerr's long statement to read and reminds
him about his discussion with Welch on 15 May 1985. He's asked why
he wrote the memo saying the allegations regarding Denis were based
only on conjecture and rumour. He replies with The Party Line.

Mr Rapke leaps straight in. 'I put it to you, you had not seen the
scene or any evidence, so you were singularly ill-equipped to decide
whether it was suicide or murder.'

For some unknown reason Fry replies 'Exactly', sinking himself
like a stone.

Perhaps trying to recover ground, he begins to relate another
unusual case in his Homicide portfolio. I think it is going to be the
one he told me about James Henry Macnamara of Omeo, but no. This
one is about a young man who poisoned himself and then put a rope
around his neck, stood on a chair and then hit himself over the head
several times with an axe in his determination to commit suicide.
'People do funny things,' says Fry. No-one laughs.

Mr Rapke asks Fry many questions about why he took a simple
statement from Denis Tanner instead of conducting a record of interview and checking Denis's alibi for the night. Fry's memory is worse
than Welch's. To alleviate the boredom, I start counting the number of
times he replies 'I can't recall'.

He finally agrees, 'With hindsight I should not have written that
report. I've now seen evidence—what I've read in the papers, caused
me to change my mind.' Evidence?

Mr Rapke asks Fry if he knows Denis Tanner.

'I've only seen Tanner three times in my life.'

'Did you make contact with Denis Tanner by phone in June 1996,
following the publication of an article in the *Sunday Age*, and advise

him to obtain legal advice and offer him your assistance to fight it if necessary?'

Fry is too taken aback to say 'I can't recall.'

('Must have been taped!' I write in my notes.)

Fry is not an impressive witness. I would not buy a used car from this man.

∝∝

A long procession of former and serving police officers follows on.

Superintendent Peter Fleming returns to the stand and tells us he thinks the first investigation was grossly unsatisfactory. He had concerns about the presumptions regarding the cause of death. Anyone with homicide experience should have been suspicious of the circumstances; the rumours surrounding a member should have been properly checked and laid to rest with factual evidence. He regrets that he was unable to persuade the Homicide Squad to renew their interest. He felt there was a reluctance to investigate further with an open mind and he was disappointed his own superiors did not allow him to take the matter further up the ladder as it was not his jurisdiction.

After the first inquest he didn't think it would be taken further due to the lack of interest at Homicide. Today, he favours the theory of incompetence over a cover-up. Things were just not done correctly soon enough.

Former Assistant Commissioner Werner, Peter Fleming's old boss, says he shared Fleming's concerns, and was 'quite perturbed. The circumstances were highly unusual, to say the least. They did not have the ring of truth about them at all.'

(I write in my notes—'Where was the ring of confidence to do something about it??')

He concludes, 'I felt I'd done all I could. I couldn't help wondering if it was laziness, incompetence or some other reason.'

Les and Kath Blake at last have their day in court. Both give evidence, adding little to the chats we've had across tables in Mansfield. Kath tells us Sam used to go to bed at 7.30 p.m. and rarely woke till the next day. She also says that Laurie received $24 000 from Jenny's life insurance.

She registers her strong objection to her daughter's being discussed as the 'town bike' and says Jenny had only three or four boyfriends before getting married.

Mr Johnstone adjourns the case to December. What a nuisance! It seems we'll never get to the end.

∞

On a balmy late October day Detective Senior Constable Jacqueline Curran and Detective Senior Sergeant Marty Allison sat in their unmarked police car in the main street of Benalla. They were waiting for Lynne Tanner to make her daily visit to pick up milk and bread. They approached her as she emerged from the shop and requested a few words.

Lynne says she was told that if she'd agree to tell all she knew about Jenny Tanner's death she would receive police protection, a change of identity and money to support herself and her children and help to obtain an intervention order against her husband. The offer was similar to being placed in the Witness Protection Program. The two detectives said they believed Lynne was in fear of her life from Denis Tanner. She rejected their offer and told her husband about it. Around the same time, Denis Tanner was transferred from active CIB duties at Benalla to the police pool at Wangaratta, effectively removing him from face-to-face contact with the public and giving him little to do with his days.

∞

For my own part, I now have six weeks to fly back to Queensland, pack up the house, drive back to Melbourne, unpack and do the Christmas shopping, as the inquest is expected to run until 19

December. It has been extended by two weeks because of the long periods already spent analysing the first investigation. In fact, my suspicions are being proved correct. We seem to be spending an awful lot of time trying to allocate blame for the first 'bungled' investigation, rather than on how Jenny Tanner met her death. Maybe Part Two, with the roll-call of expert witnesses still to come, will shed some light on that matter.

17

The Second Inquest II

The return to Court One is almost like coming back to school after the term break. All the players are there, greeting each other and catching up with events since our last gathering. Little groups gather in the foyer, drinking coffee from polystyrene cups and exchanging news and information. I make my way through the security check (still in place) and secure my old seat. Denis and Laurie are in court already, huddled with their counsel. They turn to greet me. We are becoming quite friendly, in a careful sort of fashion. Laurie and I have a chat about the sale of his fat lambs; he seems quite pleased with the price he's obtained. Shearing is nearly done, but there's always something pressing to do on a farm. Denis has taken more leave to return to court. His briefcase is open on his chair, very orderly. He fiddles with his row of pens, lining them up exactly, while he listens to me and Laurie chatting.

'It must be costing you a fortune, Denis,' I say, out of Mr Gullaci's hearing. 'Why do you feel you need to have two lawyers here representing you, day after day?'

'You've seen what the media is doing to us. We're being crucified. I'm just protecting my interests, that's all.'

Indeed the media have been pretty direct with their reporting of each day's events, often lining Denis up as 'the prime suspect'. I feel this is jumping the gun a bit, as the Coroner has not formally found anyone to be responsible for Jenny's death. Although we all have our own views by now, suspicions are not evidence.

Privately I ponder: if money was a motive for Jenny's death and Denis was involved in any way, it would have been cheaper in the long run for her to be 'paid off and pissed off' than spending all this money later. She's extracting her pound of flesh from the grave.

When the Coroner emerges he makes special mention of a current-affairs programme featuring Bill Kerr and a graphic 're-enactment' of the events on the night Jenny was killed. He says he finds it 'very inappropriate' that witnesses in this case had spoken to this programme.

Mr Hargreaves then asks His Worship if he's planning to call Laurie Tanner as a witness, as he's not on the witness list.

He's told Laurie will be called at the end of the proceedings, by the Coroner himself. A little jolt runs around the court. I am waiting for Mr Gullaci to ask about Denis, but he doesn't. Maybe they're hoping he won't be called.

The Coroner has relaxed his witness exclusion ruling in regard to expert witnesses, so several of them are scattered around the court. The procession commences with Professor Kay, an eminent neuro-surgeon, who has been commissioned by the Coroner to attempt to ascertain whether the deceased could have inflicted the injuries on herself. Professor Kay differs with Dr Dyte's findings in some areas, although he agrees the top shot to her head was the second shot and definitely fatal. (If the top shot was the first shot, she could not have fired any other shots herself.)

The police bring in a square cardboard box and pass it to Professor Kay. Before he opens it, the Coroner, who has shown remarkable sensitivity towards Jenny's parents on a number of occasions during these proceedings, warns them a model of Jenny's skull is about to be pro duced and points out that, while it is only a model, it's very realistic. He offers them the opportunity to leave if they wish. Tension in the court is palpable while the Blakes lean into a little whispering group. They stay. Professor Kay continues, using the skull to illustrate his points. He disagrees emphatically with the opinions of both Dr Dyte and Dr Sonenberg in most areas. He tells us 'it was stretching the bounds of credibility and extremely improbable' Jenny had the required motor skills to fire the shots. He is in agreement with

Professor Cordner's report, sent to him for evaluation, that 'it would be hard to conceive of a reasonable ability for the deceased to have committed suicide'.

Aha! At last we have two experts saying she couldn't have killed herself. The media keep scribbling. Dr Sonenberg looks miserable. The Coroner is totally absorbed.

Dr Norm Sonenberg has the misfortune to follow Dr Kay's expert and very professional presentation. He looks like a middle-management public servant with terrible taste in ties, nervously blinking at us through wire-rimmed glasses as he swears on the Bible to tell the truth.

He has already sat through all of Professor Kay's evidence, so he's in no doubt it severely conflicts with the 'expert' opinion he offered the first inquest. When a new statement he made in September 1996 is read out, he asks for it to be amended from 'probable' to 'possible' that Jenny could have shot herself. Shortly afterwards he agrees when asked by Mr Rapke if it is 'highly improbable the deceased was able to hold the rifle in a way she could inflict the injuries on herself'.

He tells Mr Rapke 'It's difficult to remember twelve years ago. There was no suspicion by the police ... we were trying to make the wounds fit with suicide ... was it possible? ... Both Peter [Dyte] and I were channelled towards the finding of suicide ... we spent a lot of time trying to make the wounds fit.'

Mr Rapke asks, 'Have you ever seen a woman suicide with a gun?'

'No.'

'Have you ever seen anyone suicide with a central wound to the skull?'

'No.'

'Have you ever seen anyone suicide with two bullets in the brain?'

'No.'

'Can you remember any X-rays being done?'

'No.'

'Do you still hold the opinion that the hand wounds could be consistent with the rifle being held against her head?'

'No.'

Mr Rapke obviously feels Dr Sonenberg has suffered enough, but Mr Gullaci steps in. 'So you don't disagree with Professor Kay?'

'No. We were trying to make a round peg fit a square hole. We weren't happy. Nobody wanted to help. Dr Dyte rang a number of people.'

'What's that got to do with your function, to obtain findings and present them to the Coroner?'

'We had suspicions, but more information was not forthcoming. It wasn't my case—Dr Dyte did most of the dissection.'

'Did you say deception?' asks Gullaci, quick as a whip. 'Oh, dissection, sorry.'

'Having been confronted with the new expert opinions, I was wrong when I gave my 1985 evidence.'

That must have cost him, I think. Hard to admit so publicly you were so wrong. Les Blake leaves the court, almost in tears.

'For what reasons did you change that view?'

'Professor Kay's opinion, Professor Cordner's opinion and the viewing of a video reconstruction of the various possible rifle angles.'

Pretty impressive line-up. Why wouldn't he change his mind?

This seems to be the first time Mr Gullaci has heard of the re-enactment video. I'm glad I've kept my mouth shut about a few things. It's much more fun seeing the impact they have when they come out in court. Mr Gullaci calls for the video to be produced, and the Coroner assures him it will be, in due course.

Ross Gilham is next. His face is pale and pasty and his shoes look as if he'd walked the 96 kilometres to Melbourne from his home in Torquay. He adds nothing new to his first inquest evidence.

Gerry O'Donnell follows, confirming a few things he was unwilling to discuss in brief interviews with me.

He tells the court that Laurie told him on the night 'I knew it was bad, but I didn't think it was this bad.' Laurie also said he'd been out at an Apex meeting. When Gerry arrived, he got the impression Laurie had not yet checked the baby. He noticed what appeared to be blood and brain tissue behind Jenny and sprayed up to the left on the wall. Gerry asked the police to move the rifle for his own safety while he recorded his examination of her body, so it could not have been in position very long. He remembers a disposable nappy on the floor.

He also recalls some discussion about the police going back to Mansfield to get the Polaroid, but can't remember how many times the CIB was phoned.

Next, Liz Thomas takes the stand. Like many witnesses, she's been waiting a long time, but is no more than ten minutes giving her evidence. The main reason she's there is to confirm that Jenny had never discussed suicide or marital problems with her, and to reinforce the testimony about Jenny's dislike of guns. She also explains that the poster with the baby and gun was a warning to Laurie to be careful of firearms.

Shirley Pike is a smiley, mumsy lady, who was secretary/book-keeper to the bingo game at the Carmelite Hall in 1984. She's also a hoarder, and has located her diaries for 1984. A couple of entries read:

31 October—Joy and Keith, Bingo—their last night

11 November—Joy and Keith, send off.

She also informs us Jack O'Hanlon phoned her quite some time afterwards, saying, 'I need to know now when Joy and Keith left', but he couldn't hold on while she found her diary.

∞

The media outside are becoming a bit of a joke. Even nobodies like me are filmed and photographed coming and going, in case we feature later on. Witnesses from each day who've never experienced anything like this are followed to their cars with cameras and microphones stuck in front of their faces. The Tanners run the gauntlet morning and evening and rarely go out at lunch-time, but have sandwiches brought into the witness room.

I strike up a conversation with a tall greying man in the foyer one day. When I ask him who he is, he tells me he's Denis's friend, delivering lunch. I say I'm a writer, finalising a book on the case.

'Oh, I know who you are. You're Robin and you live in Parkville, don't you?'

Even this far into the story I get a little chill hearing one of 'Denis's friends' saying he knows where I live. Silly, of course. It's no secret. I'm in the phone book.

'But how did you know about me?' I ask.

'You live next door to a couple of friends of mine and they told me all about you without knowing I know Denis. I've known him for years, went to his wedding.'

Just then Denis comes out of court. I tease him, 'Hey, you're having me watched, eh?' He laughs too and says he has been for months. I say, 'That would have been a good job for someone, following me round the Whitsundays,' and we all laugh again. Still spooky, though. Melbourne is a village.

∞

Day 10—still not much closer to an answer. Former Senior Sergeant Neil Walker strides in, looking more confident than he feels, no doubt, after reading all about his former colleagues in the papers. He says he had several meetings with his boss, Inspector MacLennan, to discuss Bill Kerr's suitability for the job. He keeps telling us he thought Kerr didn't have enough experience, even though he'd been a police officer for fifteen years and had completed the sergeant's course. Walker said he wanted to transfer the case to someone else, but took no action to achieve this in his capacity as Station Commander. 'The scene had been botched up by Frazer and Kerr and nobody else wanted to handle it.'

He can't recall making any enquiries about who cleaned up the scene. He can't recall chastising Bill Kerr for criticising his colleagues for allowing the clean-up. He agrees when Mr Rapke puts it to him that 'Any competent police officer of any rank would know the scene should not be interfered with until further investigated.' He can't recall reprimanding Neil Phipps for 'doing a phantom' the night before. He says he thought Bill Kerr was an authorised photographer and didn't know why he didn't take photos himself. (He was the only person who thought Bill was qualified.) He does remember telling Phipps to go and take photos in the morgue. He agrees the proper preparation of the Coroner's brief was ultimately his responsibility.

He tells us 'alarm bells rang' on many occasions. (My notes say: 'Lucky he wasn't the fire chief!') Jeff Adams' information about the call from Roz Smith he viewed as extremely serious, because if her account was correct, it indicated Denis could have threatened to kill Jenny only two weeks before she died. He passed on her phone number to Sergeant Welch, who never rang her.

Mr Gullaci strenuously objects to this 'mischievous and potentially sensational' material, as the contents of the phone call and the events during Denis's visit to Jenny are unproven. The Coroner instructs the press to 'be careful' with the way this material is used, but will not place a restriction order on it. He tells us this is an open court and he's reluctant to restrict anything.

Walker says that Property Room procedures required property to be checked every month, so 'Bill Kerr could definitely not have kept the BRNO rifle in his locker. I wouldn't allow it. There was no attempt to preserve the rifle for fingerprinting—too many people had handled it. Phipps, Kerr and others had manhandled the rifle while trying to demonstrate how Jenny may have used it. I knew it was never going to be used for fingerprinting.'

When cross-examination begins I detect a new tactic. It seems as though both Mr Hargreaves and Mr Gullaci are virtually taking over where Mr Rapke leaves off and are also trying hard to demonstrate the first investigation was totally incompetent. Perhaps this will be used later in summations to show that no definitive conclusions can be drawn such a long time later, because the groundwork is so unreliable. In any event, from about this point on they proceed to peel the police witnesses apart, layer by layer.

Mr Gullaci puts to Walker: 'It would be fairly difficult to clean up bullet holes in a short time. You wouldn't need to be Inspector

Clouseau to work out there may have been some remaining evidence, even after the clean-up. The couch was presumably still there.'

'There was no point in going back to see the situation once it was cleaned up. The groundwork for the investigation had been botched up.'

'But any police officer in his right mind would know an examination of the couch would yield more information?'

'Yes.'

Walker is excused after a series of questions from Mr Gullaci showing him in a fairly poor light. Even though he's in the witness box for over an hour, I think he gets off pretty lightly. The boss should always carry the can.

My estimation of Neil Phipps plummets when he gives his evidence. Soon after taking the stand he tells us, 'I thought it was always one wound. I thought both bullets went through the same hole. I thought that until I read the *Herald-Sun* this morning.'

This evidence is given to us by an experienced police officer who retired as a Chief Inspector and who was homicide trained.

He tells us he has 'blanked out' details about the incident because he transferred a few days later. He says he was unaware that Denis Tanner applied to replace him in Mansfield.

Phipps cannot recall discussion about two bullet holes in Jenny's forehead at any time, then or since. This seems strange, as I discussed it with him myself over a cup of tea in March this year.

Mr Rapke asks him about a discussion he had on the phone with Dr Dyte regarding Jenny's injuries. He reminds Phipps that his statement—read to the court and acknowledged by him as correct—said in part: 'I have read a transcript of a micro cassette recording and agree it depicts in general the conversation between myself and Dyte.' Mr Rapke produces the transcript from Bill's 16 November 1984 tape recording of Phipps' conversation with Dr Dyte. On 15 August 1996 Phipps read and signed four pages of this transcript, which were shown to him by the Task Force. On the first page was Dr Dyte's statement that there were 'two wounds in the forehead of this lady'.

Mr Rapke asks Phipps if he read this statement before signing the bottom of page one.

Phipps says he must have.

The Coroner is curious about how Jenny could have managed to shoot herself twice through the same hole. He leans towards Phipps and asks, 'How could that occur?'

'I'm sorry, Your Worship. What occur?'

'The two bullets entering the same hole. How could it be that you thought there was only one head wound when you had discussed two wounds to the head?'

'The hypothesis was that the gun was somehow left in the same position when the second shot was fired.'

A small titter ripples through the court. (I write in my notes: 'Jenny gets more proficient every day!')

Mr Rapke asks 'Who put that hypothesis?'

'I think it was Bill Kerr.'

Phipps is then asked if he can recall being told about other injuries, the blood, the number of wounds, the number of cartridge cases found, the coffee, heater and so on.

He can't recall any of that, nor can he remember discussing the case at all the following day with Sergeant Walker.

Mr Rapke looks resigned. 'If you have no recollections of being told of any of the circumstances, I put it to you that you were singularly ill equipped to pass a hypothesis on the morning following her death about how this woman was killed.'

'Had you been a member of the Homicide Squad before this event?' asks the Coroner.

Phipps says he had been at Homicide but further says he relied on Dyte's expertise to reassure him about Jenny's ability to fire the rifle herself. 'He was the pathologist.'

'Did you go 'up the mountain, doing a phantom' as has been suggested?'

'It's probable that as I was due to be transferred I had gone to collect some personal gear from the police depot at Mt Buller.'

'Possible or probable?'

'I think it's probable.'

'Mmm' from the Coroner.

Phipps *does* remember, though, that the day after Jenny's death he asked Denis Tanner about his whereabouts on the night and he said he'd been at the trots. 'From my recollection Denis was non-specific in his answers, which left me feeling uneasy with his answers on the basis he was a policeman. I suppose, in reality, because of the tragic circumstances, I didn't take the matter any further.'

Under cross-examination from Mr Gullaci, Phipps tells us much of his memory is so bad because he has 'tended to switch off' all the information about the case as he was told to by Inspector MacLennan because he was due for a transfer. It was not his responsibility. 'I've had nothing to do with the case since 16 November 1984.'

He can't remember what shift he was supposed to be working that night, or what time he signed off, or what he did after that—nothing in fact, until he arrived at work the following day. A complete blank.

'Were any other members there when you signed off?'

'No.'

'So you can't recall signing off, but you can recall the other members weren't there.'

In the next break, Denis moves over to speak to me.

'What did you think of that?' he asks. 'He's got an immaculate memory about how uneasy I was, but he can't remember a thing he was doing.'

'True,' I have to admit.

The mystery witness Dawn Kipping appears next. She has little to say other than that on the night of Jenny's death her husband wanted her to leave a message for Laurie and she was trying to get through for some time before 9.30 p.m., but the phone was engaged. She did get through eventually, but couldn't say at what time. All she can be certain of was that Jenny told her Laurie would be home after 10 p.m. and he'd call her. She could have phoned any time between 9.35 p.m. and 9.55 p.m. Even though we are no closer to a time of death, her evidence does seem to indicate that Jenny knew Laurie would be home at a specific time and that at the time of this call Jenny sounded 'quite normal'.

I wonder why Kipping hasn't come forward before. It seems strange to me. I phone her later and ask her. She tells me she didn't want to get involved in 1985. She was scared of repercussions on her family and didn't think her story could add much anyway. She says the police really leaned hard on her this time to get her to testify.

The next day Mr Gullaci raises the issue of the previous night's headlines on the TV news, where the words 'Threats to Kill' were screened behind the newsreader reporting Denis's visit to Jenny before she died. Gullaci more or less tells His Worship 'I told you so.' Again I am struck by the Coroner's powers. He hasn't seen the news, so orders copies of the offending footage and a VCR and suggests that the TV station in question might wish to be legally represented while we all view the tape in court, first thing after lunch.

After this by-play, Laurie's first wife Sally gives some pretty straightforward evidence about her time with Laurie. The only significant item for me is her statement that when she lived with Laurie 'He never kept the gun loaded', which is at odds with Laurie's claim that he usually left an empty cartridge case up the spout for safety reasons.

Max Harvey, current owner of Springfield, dressed as a gentleman farmer, looks very uncomfortable in court. He says he might have left a key on the fence post for the carpenter, but he can't remember because he was in New Zealand at the time. He says the insurance loss assessor decided the 1995 fire was caused by an electrical fault from the timer on the kitchen light. He's not excused when he leaves the witness stand, which seems to cause him further discomfort. The coroner says he might want him back.

Former Chief Inspector Peter Mangles is one of the names on the witness list I haven't interviewed, although I did have his name in my research notes. After hearing him give his long, convoluted evidence I'm not sorry I missed him out. He does have something important to add, though. On 22 May 1990, Denis Tanner made an official request to him, as a senior officer in Benalla, for the return of Laurie's rifle. Denis said he bought the rifle for his brother, who was wondering if the police had finished with it. After producing his police diary for that period, which he'd kept because he knew 'one day between now and the day I die I'll need it', Mangles takes us through Property Book procedures and his diary entries about checking for Laurie's rifle at Mansfield police station. He found 'Returned to L. Tanner' in the book, when it clearly hadn't been. He reported this to his superior, Inspector Stevenson, and was told to go no further; others would investigate.

Much later he was told that a Constable Winters had seen him check the Property Book and had realised it was he (Winters) who had written 'Returned to L. Tanner'. Worried that he might be in trouble, as the rifle was actually still in the station, Winters gave it to a colleague, Sergeant Steve Adams. Adams became anxious when Inspector Stevenson started investigating and said he threw the rifle in Lake Eildon.

It also transpired that Mangles was relieving at Mansfield when the Coroner's brief prepared by Bill Kerr was first presented.

He said, 'There was nothing in it. I was shocked that a brief could be submitted in such a poor fashion. I sent it to Homicide to see if they could patch it up', but he was back in his old job when it came back.

Later he said he did not follow up the open finding as 'it was not my area. I had a lot of faith in Dr Dyte. He said it was a suicide. Two holes in the head is unusual, but not impossible.'

He earnestly assured us he had supported Denis and Lynne through their latest ordeal by giving them eggs and vegies and his friendship and 'if I thought Denis had anything to do with it I wouldn't have supported him'.

After lunch the 'mushroom end of the table' introduces a further surprise. Mr Hargreaves tells us Laurie has seen a doctor and is too ill to attend until further notice. The nasty rough media outside are partly to blame. Mr Hargreaves tells His Worship, 'I cannot comment on whether this indisposition will extend until my client will be required to give evidence.'

The Coroner dryly replies, 'I don't expect it to extend long enough to prevent him being called.'

The next witnesses are Bryan Shannon (the fire chief), followed by Angie and Curly McCormack. Nothing new emerges except a couple of comments from Curly, who was not called to give evidence at the first inquest. 'I saw Laurie on the Friday. He told me his brothers helped clean up the mess. He's told me he thinks the police are hounding people through this new investigation.'

Retired Sergeant John Winters agrees he made the entry in the Property Book about Laurie's rifle. He remembers Don Frazer signing it out on 15 November 1984 to take it for forensic tests ordered by the first Coroner. After this it was returned to the Property Room at Mansfield. Subsequently Laurie was asked to collect the rifle from the police station. He came to pick it up, but didn't want it. He said he never wanted to see it again and asked Winters to dispose of it, signing away his ownership in the Property Book at Winters' request. Winters gave the rifle to his Mansfield colleague, Sergeant Steve Adams. He is aware that Adams told the inspector investigating Denis's query about the rifle's whereabouts that he'd thrown it in the lake.

The case is beginning to take on the aspect of a French farce. What is being investigated here? Jenny Tanner's death or police culture? People in court are trying not to laugh, it is so unbelievable. And all the time the rifle has been lying over there near Mr Rapke for a string of witnesses to identify. I've never heard anything about them dragging the lake.

Mansfield officer Sergeant Adams, arriving in court in police uniform, is the same officer I interviewed on my first trip to Mansfield—it seems a lifetime ago. He corroborates Winters' story. He said Winters brought the gun to his house. He used it for a while, then registered it in his name so he could sell it to a country dealer later on. At a disciplinary interview resulting from the investigation into the rifle's whereabouts, he said he'd thrown it in the weir, as it had a history and he didn't want it. After reading the story in the paper about the new investigation into Jenny's death, he realised the rifle would be needed and confessed the whole story to the Task Force in

June 1996. They were able to track the rifle down and bring it back into the picture. Neither officer was charged, as they both said they were sorry and wouldn't do it again.

What a can of worms Denis opened when he wrote that memo! I go home that night feeling frustrated and furious. My poor husband cops the brunt.

'These are the Boys in Blue! They're supposed to look after us, not sneak off duty, pinch rifles, tell lies and cover things up. Where was everybody when Jenny needed them? Too busy feathering their own nests or not getting involved because it wasn't their area, or blaming other people—or they can't remember!'

I throw things around the kitchen as I prepare dinner. Although today wasn't the worst day in court, the cumulative impact of every-thing being said day after day slams into me. I nearly don't want to hear any more, but I am addicted by now and determined to see it through to the end.

∞

The arson experts open the next day's testimony, basically telling us they can't tell us anything. The house was so badly burnt that only powder ash remained. Absolutely nothing left to investigate.

Retired Chief Inspector Duncan MacLennan arrives to share with us his version of events. His opinion of Bill Kerr is that he was 'hon-est, reliable and trustworthy, industrious but different. He had an idio-syncratic approach to policing—he was the odd man out. In the four years he worked for me I never found him in error or not doing a task correctly.'

He goes on to say he'd never seen the coroner's brief, had never been asked by Bill Kerr to get the rifle tested, had never discussed Bill's suitability for the investigation with Walker or Phipps, had never been asked by Bill Kerr to request an interview with Denis Tanner, and had never seen Bill's list of 'Matters', even though he was the one who wrote 'No Further Action' on the brief when it returned from Homicide.

Mr Rapke commences to refresh MacLennan's memory with documents either addressed to him or signed by him, including his signature on the coroner's brief. He agrees it must have crossed his desk, but says he had only a supervisory administrative role; Walker was actually the hands-on 'manager'.

'If His Worship came to the view that this thing was thoroughly incompetently handled, would that not be your responsibility?' Mr Rapke asks.

'Yes.'

'You're the one ultimately responsible in the police station, aren't you?'

'Yes, yes. But Walker did not come to me to ask for assistance. Never having been a detective, I can't really comment on the investigation.'

Later on he confides that 'people widely believed at the time Jenny's death wasn't suicide'.

The Coroner asks exasperatedly, 'If people widely believed she didn't commit suicide, why didn't someone *do* something about it?'

MacLennan gives us the A Team Party Line hypothesis again.

The Coroner persists, 'Why wasn't it followed up?'

'I've no idea. I had no knowledge of the Coroner's finding then, only after I read it recently in the *Sunday Age*. Steve Adams sent it to me in New South Wales.'

Putting equal emphasis on each word, the Coroner asks again slowly: 'Why wasn't it properly investigated? Can you explain to me precisely why the death of Mrs Tanner in 1984 wasn't properly investigated?'

'I can't answer that, Your Worship.'

'What are the alternative reasons?'

'With the benefit of hindsight, specialised people were not involved.'

'Mr Fry was involved. He'd had a number of years in Homicide, specialised knowledge. How do you explain that? If it wasn't the subject of a cover-up, what was it?'

'Obviously a case of inept police work.'

'Are you suggesting that ineptitude ran right through to the Homicide Squad?' the Coroner asks.

'I have no knowledge of that, Your Worship.'

Mr Gullaci takes over. MacLennan is far from off the hook.

'Can I suggest to you as an alternative scenario that it was badly handled by every policeman who came in contact with the case at Mansfield?'

'Yes, you can suggest it, but I don't have to agree. There were only Frazer, Kerr, a Senior Sergeant and myself, and I have no knowledge of anyone else with particular input to the inquest brief.'

'Well, the ones you've named are all tarred with the same brush and now, with the benefit of hindsight, you're all trying to cover your own backs and protect your reputations.'

While MacLennan is collecting his thoughts, the Coroner breaks in and asks if he could explain the editing of Mr Kerr's statement in the brief.

'It would appear most irregular, Your Worship, but I have no knowledge of it. It implies a possible cover-up.'

Mr Gullaci picks up the baton. 'Every senior officer of Kerr's has given evidence it wasn't him who told Kerr to delete his evidence. People handled this in an incompetent, unprofessional way and are now trying to cover their own position, and that includes you.'

'Well, I categorically deny that, of course. My involvement was limited.'

The Coroner breaks in: 'As the senior officer at the station, wouldn't you be the least curious when an officer was seeking to transfer to your station following the violent death of his sister-in-law?'

'Perhaps with hindsight ...'

The Coroner is pretty testy by now. He must be feeling the same way I do. 'It doesn't require much hindsight. It requires very little hindsight.'

Mr Gullaci resumes. 'Did Bill Kerr bring his concerns to your notice? The rifle, the phone call, the two alibis et cetera?'

'I never heard anything from Bill Kerr about his concerns.'

'But he's told us he did bring those concerns to your notice. And you've just described him as honest, trustworthy and reliable.'

The Coroner interrupts. 'Do you think it wasn't properly investigated because a police officer was involved?'

'No.'

'As far as you were concerned the investigation was done properly?' asks Mr Gullaci.

'I was an administrator, not an investigator! I haven't changed my mind on anything. Apparently a lot of other people have.'

He leaves the stand red-faced. My notes say 'Poor Duncan. Let down a bit by "the Boys", eh? Gullaci shredded him.' I am feeling very warmly disposed towards His Worship and Mr Gullaci for asking some tough questions.

The rest of the morning is taken up with minor witnesses: the truck driver who reported the fire and may or may not have seen a shadowy figure, and a couple of others. Mr Rapke is saving today's lead act until after lunch. There is a certain amount of showmanship involved in court procedure.

Kevin Russell is the motel broker quoted in Mr Rapke's opening address, which now seems so long ago. He's currently a car salesman, but you'd never guess from his mild manner and quiet voice. He tells us that he was introduced to Denis Tanner through another policeman, and outlines his subsequent business dealings with Denis and Lynne.

Mr Rapke puts to him, 'On the face of it he makes some fairly extraordinary statements to you in some of those meetings. Would you agree with that? I don't suppose it's every day of the week that someone refers to his brother in the terms in which he did refer to him?'

'No, no, that's—that's right.'

'Or goes on to say,' continues Mr Rapke, 'that "his brother will do as he's fucking well told because if it wasn't for him", that's Denis Tanner, "the second slut would have got the lot"?'

'That's fair to say that, yes.'

'Did those sorts of comments, those remarks, stick in your memory?'

'Yes, they did.'

'Now, I take it that you weren't at the time either recording these conversations or making notes of them?'

'No.'

'What was it about the conversations that you've included in the statement that enabled you to record them eight or nine years later?'

'Well, at the time—when—when it was said I thought it was fairly extraordinary—not a normal thing that someone would say to you anyway ... Denis Tanner's the sort of fellow that once you meet him he's a very difficult person to forget. He's a very—very predominant character.'

Russell's statement to the inquest also contains this evidence. 'I recall him [Denis] once telling me about a fuel distributor in Benalla. An employee of this man had been caught stealing some money and Denis investigated the matter. There was some agreement that the employee would pay the money back and Denis told me that employer didn't give him the normal thank-you of 10 per cent. I asked him what he meant and he said, "Normally, in the city if we saved someone some money, we'd get 10 per cent." I didn't know whether to believe him or not.'

Russell recalls a meeting at the Farmers Arms Hotel where there was some discussion about Laurie's son and his divorce and the second wife's suicide. Denis allegedly told him something like 'Laurie's first wife stuck it right into him, she wanted this and wanted that and Laurie wouldn't listen to me and do it my way, he wanted to do it his way. So Laurie had to pay out his missus, which meant that me and the family had to tip in and pay her out. Laurie's a ripper bloke, but he's not that worldly and I've had to help him and guide him, otherwise plenty of pricks would have ripped him off. I've made sure that's never going to happen again.'

Mr Gullaci gives Kevin Russell a very hard time, trying to shake him on his memory for dates, meetings, times and recollections of conversations, but although he's rattled and obviously uncomfortable, he won't budge from his original story.

At one point Russell appeals to His Worship for guidance. 'Do I have to keep going over and over these details when I've already answered?'

His Worship says Mr Gullaci is only doing his job. I guess that's why Mr Rapke doesn't intervene with any objections.

I watch Mr Gullaci doing his job (very well, I should say) and muse that it's no wonder more citizens don't come forward to assist the police if they get this sort of treatment. I have a coffee with Kevin Russell later on and he says it was a very hard decision to tell the police what he knew—he has a wife and kids and he was afraid of the possible consequences, but he has 'a conscience like most people'.

'Not like most people,' I reply. I'd certainly buy a used car from him.

∞

The next day the sensations continue.

Several members of the Tanner family have been subpoenaed the night before—Lynne along with June, Bruce and Frank—leaving them little time to prepare for a reluctant family reunion in Court One. Denis is tight-lipped and furious, coiled inside, but externally a model of self-control. He tells me his wife's parents have both died this year, very close together and not long ago. Lynne is finding it difficult to cope at the moment—with everything.

Lynne is brought in first, white-faced and red-eyed. She seems to have lost weight. She appears to be dazed, not knowing where to go or what to do, in spite of her twelve years in the police force. Her passage through the courtroom is hesitant, as though she expects to collide with an obstacle on the way.

Once in the witness box she appears extremely nervous, sighing and rolling her eyes upwards. Is this an act, or is she so distraught she isn't in any kind of control?

'Where was your husband on the night Jenny Tanner died, Mrs Tanner?' Mr Rapke's first question indicates he isn't mucking about.

'At the bingo.'

'How do you know?'

'He told me that's where he was going.'

'What time did he return?'

'I got up to feed the baby at 1 a.m. and he was there. I had a baby that didn't sleep too well.'

Lots of questions follow about conversations or discussions Lynne and Denis might have had. Lynne tells us they 'never discussed' Jenny, the way she died, when Lynne first learnt about the two bullets, the first investigation process, Denis's reaction to the open finding, the relationship between Jenny and Laurie, Denis's complaints (if any) about the way Jenny looked after Laurie, the likelihood or otherwise of Jenny being suicidal, Jenny's temperament or post-natal depression, what Denis did at the bingo and how much he was paid, Denis's trips to and from Bonnie Doon, Denis's interest in guns, motel dealings, Denis seeking to get Laurie's rifle back, or virtually anything at all to do with this family tragedy.

At one point Mr Rapke asks with a straight face, 'Mrs Tanner, do you still live with your husband?'

More sobs from Lynne.

'Mrs Tanner, do you think your husband, as a police officer, knew the importance of telling the truth about his whereabouts on the night?'

'Yes.'

'After the open finding did you ever say to anyone, "Well, that's a bit peculiar, we've always thought this was suicide"?'

'The whole thing was peculiar.'

'Why?'

'Well, the mere fact that someone would want to do that. I couldn't understand it.'

'And you still can't?'

'No.'

Between bouts of tears, holding a tissue over her mouth, Lynne tries to explain that she and Denis didn't discuss many things at home in an effort to provide some sort of normality for their four children. The Coroner asks how long Lynne had been a police officer, as if he can't believe she would have shown no interest whatsoever in this event.

'Did you attend the first inquest?'

'No.'

'Did you read the transcript?'

'No.'

Mr Rapke asks, 'After your husband gave evidence at the first inquest, did you ask him how it went?'

'I guess I did.'

'What do you guess he said?'

'Okay, I suppose. I don't remember. It's a long time ago.'

Lynne breaks down and the Coroner calls a recess, even though she clearly wants to continue and get it all over with. Mr Rapke doesn't look too thrilled about having his line of questioning interrupted either. Lynne races to the seclusion of the Witness Room. Denis stays in court, impassive. I move along my row of seats and whisper, 'Denis, why don't you go and comfort her? You look pretty hard-hearted sitting here.'

He replies with a stony face, 'I can't. I don't want to be seen to be influencing anything she says.'

On her return, Lynne is taken through the events of the morning after Jenny's death. She was up feeding the baby when the police arrived around 5 a.m. Denis was in bed, but answered the door, as the bedroom was next to the front door. They left for Mansfield after a few phone calls, but broke down on the way, several kilometres before Springfield. She waited in the car with the baby. It was hot. Denis hitched a ride to get some tools from Springfield to fix the car. They continued to Mansfield. They did not go to Springfield. They arrived around lunch-time. She doesn't know if any of the other Tanner brothers went to Springfield that day.

'I knew Denis had not gone there because we went straight past. As far as I know he did not go down there.'

Mr Rapke presses on, asking Lynne if Jenny's suicide surprised her. She replies, 'When Jenny made up her mind to do something, she did it.'

Lynne denies she told Helen Golding that Denis hadn't arrived home until 5 a.m. on the morning after Jenny died. She explains he often worked shifts and she'd told her friend she was glad he had been there when the news arrived. She wouldn't have liked to get the news alone, as she would have if Denis had been working.

'Where was your husband on the night of the Springfield fire?'

'I don't remember.'

'Did you discuss the fire?'

'I don't remember.'

'So your husband's family home of several generations burns down and you didn't discuss it at all?'

'I don't remember.'

Mr Hargreaves objects. 'I've sat here patiently, but if the witness says she can't remember something it's improper for my learned friend to continue to base his questions on the alternative proposition. He shouldn't do it. If she can't remember, she can't remember.'

Mr Rapke starts to ask her about her visit to the motel with Helen Golding. Mr Gullaci objects. He still doesn't have the transcripts. He has no questions. Mrs Tanner is excused.

This is a new version of the events of that morning and the trip to Springfield and Mansfield. It conflicts in several places with what I know from Denis's statement, the time he was first seen at the Mansfield police station and discussions I've had with Denis.

My recollection is that during an earlier phone conversation with Denis he said the fan belt on his car had broken and he hitch-hiked to the property to get some tools, fixed the car and then went to clean the house. I asked if Lynne had helped clean up, and he said, 'No, she continued on to Mansfield with the baby.'

When I asked, 'How did you get into town?' he replied, 'I got a ride with the person helping me.' I asked, 'Was that Frank?' to which he replied, 'I think you're mixing up my brothers, but I don't want to say any more because Mr Newman would like to know all this and for all I know he's listening in.' This conversation took place on the Benalla CIB line, so for all I know he was!

I wonder why Lynne wasn't asked more about this critical clean-up, but she wasn't. She scored nearly as many on 'I don't remember' as Neil Phipps and Jim Fry with 'I can't recall'. It's interesting that Mr Hargreaves and Mr Gullaci objected vigorously several times when Mr Rapke tried to stretch Lynne Tanner's recollection of crucial points, but when Mr Gullaci gave Kevin Russell at least as hard a time, it was 'just doing his job'. Maybe Russell should have cried. (I did think he was close to it a couple of times!)

Bruce Tanner is elegantly dressed in an expensive suit. He gives his profession as company director and looks it every inch. When Jenny died he was school principal at Girgarre, near Kyabram, about 180 kilometres across country from Mansfield. He's obviously extremely annoyed about being required in court and gives his answers reluctantly and belligerently.

His evidence is that his mother phoned him around 6 a.m. on 15 November and told him the news. She also informed him the police had told her she was expected to clean up the house. He told her there was no way she was going to do that, and said he'd call in on his way through and fix whatever needed fixing. After arranging for a fill-in teacher he went to Springfield, found the back door open, observed the scene, saw a lot of congealed blood at head height on the sofa and a line of blood running down a cushion of the couch on his left-hand side. He cleaned up one lot of congealed blood from a cushion, locked the door and left. He went overseas about three weeks later for thirteen months. 'Thirteen years later I have my own life I need to live. A lot of water passed under the bridge while I was away.'

'What did you do when you got to Springfield?'

'I was there long enough to take one piece of congealed blood off the sofa and I got out and locked the door with keys which are kept on a nail beside the door and that was it. I didn't want to stay.'

'How did you clean up the blood?' asks Mr Rapke.

'How do you normally clean blood?' Bruce spits back.

'I don't know, Mr Tanner. Do you want to tell us, or is it a secret?'

'With a bucket of cold water and a cloth—you usually use cold water for blood', Bruce explains with exaggerated courtesy.

'Was any other cleaning up done that day or the following day?'

'We went back the following day to feed the animals. No further cleaning had been done. The house was locked.'

'Did you know Jenny Tanner?'

'Yes. She and Laurie appeared to be very happy. She was very moody.'

'Why do you think she was moody?'

'She was a woman, wasn't she?'

Mr Rapke responds wryly, 'That should please half the people in this court.'

'I'm not about to try and please anybody,' Bruce frowns.

'Did your brother Denis Tanner go to Springfield that day?'

'At some stage I met Denis on his way through to Mansfield. I had to change a fan belt when I went to Mansfield.'

'So you met him on the road, did you?'

'No. He hitch-hiked up to ... towards Mansfield and I was leaving and I saw him on the road.'

'Right. Nowhere near Springfield.' Mr Rapke seems to be concentrating on the exact location of this meeting.

'He was coming past Springfield.'

'But do you know if he went up to the property?'

'No. He didn't.'

'He told you that, did he?'

'I was there. I helped him fix the car and we went on together to Mansfield.'

'Do you know what Denis did that day?'

'I was his brother, not his keeper.'

No questions from Mr Gullaci.

Bruce's evidence concludes Day Thirteen of the inquest. Another version of the clean-up and the breakdown. For Bruce to have encountered Denis on the road on his way to Mansfield, Denis's car would have had to break down after passing Springfield, not 'a few kilometres before' as Lynne said. It is all becoming very messy.

After court that day Denis's control finally snaps. The media crush around the Tanner family as they try to get into their cars. Incensed by this insensitivity, Denis uses his heavy briefcase to hit a photographer directly in the groin. Bruce's temper also gets the better of him, and he whacks the same photographer on the back with his car door. A winded and sore photographer is examined by a forensic medical officer while the Tanners drive off. It's a Pyrrhic victory. Denis is bound to be charged with assault.

∝∞

Frank Tanner is quite a contrast with his rather brooding brothers. More open-faced and with a less hawk-like nose, he sits as if freshly scrubbed, with his shirt-sleeves rolled up and shirt neck open, looking eager to get the whole thing over with and go back to the farm.

Frank says he was still a police officer on night duty at Hamilton when his wife took a 6 a.m. call from his mother about Jenny's death. His wife phoned him at work. He worked the following night and set out on Friday 16 November in the morning to go to Mansfield. It was his father's birthday, so he had some time off. He'd always been close to Laurie, helped out around the farm when he could. He didn't go to Springfield on 16 November. 'I felt it's nothing to do with me, I'm not a gory sort of person.' He did call in with his wife and kids a few days later on his way home and saw the couch covered up on the front veranda. He always thought it was suicide. He says he was not that close to Denis, and he didn't follow the investigation or the first inquest.

Mr Rapke says, 'You could not believe that any member of your family would stoop to murder?'

'I still believe she committed suicide, but obviously I'd be a fool if I didn't think about it, wouldn't I?'

'As an ex-police officer thinking about it, have you considered how Jenny could have got the number and type of injuries she sustained?'

'Well, I've thought about it.'

'And what did you come up with?'

'I haven't come up with anything.'

'Do you find it hard to believe any of your brothers would be involved in the murder of a young woman?'

'There's no reason for anyone in my family to have harmed Jenny. Anyone that takes a mother away from their little baby is pretty ordinary.'

He feels the bone is being pointed at Denis and that the media have treated his brother unfairly.

Frank says Laurie only found out about the reopening of the investigation when Andrew Rule phoned him for comment while he and Frank were out fencing one day in June 1996. 'Laurie was a bit surprised when he heard.'

I have a brief talk to Frank in the foyer afterwards. He says he wants to catch up with me, but Mr Gullaci appears and whisks him away just as we are warming up.

On the stand, June Tanner is in control. She looks straight ahead and answers in a strong voice. You can tell immediately where her sons' aquiline noses come from. She's quite adamant that Denis never had any financial interest in Springfield (didn't the boys tell her about Denis helping Laurie out with Sally's pay-out?). Even when Mr Rapke refers to the Land Titles documents in front of him, she's convinced they are incorrect.

She says she normally got home from bingo around 10.45 p.m. or 11 p.m. She recalls Hughie Almond phoning her, not getting a message from her husband as a result of Laurie's 10.15 p.m. call. She didn't phone Denis or Frank to ask, 'What will we do?' She was more interested in going straight out to help Laurie.

She did not subsequently speak to Gerry O'Donnell and tell him the boys had cleaned the mess, 'and what's more Denis wasn't there'.

She 'certainly didn't tell Bruce to clean up the house. Didn't tell any-one to clean up the house.' She can't remember any policeman telling her to clean up the house. She doesn't know when Bruce cleaned up the house. She says Denis and Bruce turned up at her place after she had notified them both and Bruce and Denis went back down the road with the tools to get the car going. She knows nothing about the number of wounds Jenny had or how she was shot. She doesn't read the papers, and can't recall any recent discussion at home about how Jenny died or any other family interest in the event.

'I had no interest in how she died. I still haven't. I'm just interested in my own life and bringing up my grandson. It doesn't really concern me. I was very upset that she died like that, but you have to get on with your own life. I wouldn't like to think it was murder because that would be shocking.'

Mr Rapke asks, 'Bruce did the cleaning up?'

'Yes.'

'What did Denis do?'

'Denis wasn't there. His car broke down as far as I know, down the road, and they had to get help to get the car going. When Denis did turn up later on, they went back down the road to help him. Took tools and things to try and get the car going.'

'Who did?'

'Bruce, I think.'

No questions from Mr Gullaci.

Picking her way through what is obviously the venomous vicinity of Paul Newman, Jeff Calderbank and Mr Rapke, June Tanner walks out with her head high. She smiles at Denis as she passes. I look across at the Blakes. Kris, impassive for so many days, is crying openly.

Jenny's uncle, Mr Thomas, briefly gives evidence about a letter he'd written to Bill Kerr early in 1985, detailing Jenny's family's con-cerns about the way Jenny met her death. The letter is in Bill's file. The main purpose of Mr Thomas's appearing in court seems to be to demonstrate that a) you didn't need to be police-trained to pick up some startling inconsistencies about Jenny's death and b) people in her husband's family, although police-trained, had seemed quite satisfied with the direction of the investigation, asking no questions.

Mr Adrian Barry, retired firearms expert, gives similar evidence to that which he gave at the first inquest. The Coroner asks him about whether he thinks the bullets are consistent with causing Jenny's injuries. He tells His Worship the same thing he told me months ago. The cartridge cases were available to him at the time and had been fired by that rifle. They have since been lost. He has never seen the bullets. No-one has since Dyte and Sonenberg.

'In that case, Mr Barry, can you be sure the rifle was actually the firearm which killed Mrs Tanner?'

'No, Your Worship.'

What a way to end the day! Maybe Jenny was shot by a different gun. That would make it premeditated murder, not an escalation of an argument or an accident. Can anything else new be introduced to this case?

∞

The next morning Mr Harold Wrobel, a forensic firearms expert, gives lots of technical evidence about lead wipe, lead particles and so on. The most relevant piece of information, following on from Mr Barry yesterday, is that it is impossible to determine the calibre of the bullets that entered Jenny's head.

Senior Constable Ray Vincent from Firearms and Toolmarks looks exactly as I imagined, earnest, spare and serious. He takes us through all the experiments his people have conducted regarding gunshot residue and says that even firing through a sheet of paper would prevent any residue from collecting around a wound. To make his point, he shows us several pieces of paper with holes surrounded by black marks. 'The bottom shot was direct, nothing between the rifle and the head. It's the classic contact wound. Both shots are uninterrupted.'

The Coroner asks, 'Is there a possibility this wasn't the weapon that was used?'

'I'd have to say that is a possibility. The accepted scenario presents difficulties. We don't have the bullets—that's the bottom line.'

Former Chief Superintendent Brian Ritchie is called next. In 1985 he was an Inspector and head of Homicide. At the time Jenny's file was sent down for review, he was the person who passed it over to Detective Senior Sergeant Jim Fry, whom he considered the most experienced homicide investigator in the State at that time.

He assures us he has never read the file. He 'was told enough to feel satisfied the investigation had been brought to a conclusion and properly conducted by my discussion with Fry. In my experience the actions of death can be very, very peculiar.'

Mr Rapke produces a memo addressed to Ritchie from District Chief Inspector Tom O'Keefe in Benalla, attached to requests from Kerr, Welch and MacLennan for further investigation of Denis Tanner's alleged two alibis and his visit to Jenny Tanner in October the previous year.

'How could it have been that a proper record of interview was not conducted?'

'Tanner wasn't a suspect.'

A memo dated 22 May 1985 from Fry to Ritchie detailed the injuries to Jenny Tanner.

The Coroner leans forward. 'Surely that would raise serious questions in your mind—immediate concerns as a homicide investigator?'

'Not at all, when I am relying on an experienced homicide investigator and the pathologist.'

'If you knew about the conflict in the alibi, what would you have done?'

'My options would have been to get Fry to revisit the file or put another team on it.'

This brings us to his memo back to O'Keefe. 'The evidence has been reviewed, Denis Tanner has been interviewed and his statement taken.' This memo led to the string of notations on the file as it made its way back to Bill Kerr—all adding up to No Further Action.

Mr Ritchie tells us he knew Denis Tanner at St Kilda when

Ritchie was a patrol officer in the district. He says, 'I didn't like his reputation.' But he didn't elaborate.

Mr Rapke is looking genuinely puzzled. 'How can you explain how every level and branch handled the investigation so incompetently?'

'It's a system where circumstances of the investigation depend on the facts. In this instance, by the time the file reached us there was an absence of hard evidence. Blame the coronial direction at the time that suicides not be treated as more serious deaths for investigation. For example, taking photos and so on.

'At any inquest, all the information available to the Homicide Squad is not necessarily available to the Coroner. You could review any Homicide file and find all matters have not been finalised. I doubt very much whether a police suspect would have influenced the course of the investigation.'

Mr Rapke asks Ritchie's opinion of the calibre of the investigators working on the case.

'Ian Welch was a very, very high-level investigator. Jim Fry was seconded by a Supreme Court judge to assist him in an investigation because of his excellent reputation, but they are part of the system. People make mistakes. There was no ploy at all to protect Tanner, in fact it would probably be the opposite in my case. I can't explain why nothing was done after the first finding. I don't know when it was brought down.'

Mr Rapke turns a couple of pages of his notes and pauses. We wait. He's such a performer, subtle but deadly.

'The problem with all these highly experienced police officers being involved in this investigation is that they are all incompetent. How can that be?'

'I don't think they are. It was the system.'

What can anyone say to that? I feel very flat. No-one, from the bottom to the top, is accepting any responsibility for anything.

During the lunch break Denis tells me he thinks the Coroner is biased against him, because of the questions he's asking, and because in Denis's opinion he's blocking a lot of Gullaci's and Hargreaves's objections and requests for material held by the Crown Prosecutor's office. I think His Worship is asking a lot of questions that should have been asked in 1985, and I say so. 'He has to be seen to be doing the most searching investigation, Denis, but I must say it has looked bad for you on a few occasions.'

Denis doesn't agree it has looked bad at all, but says he can take it, he has nothing to hide. He tells me today is his birthday. I don't wish him Many Happy Returns—it doesn't seem appropriate, somehow.

Professor Stephen Cordner looks just like his photo on the Internet, eminent, commanding and reliable. His evidence has been largely pre-empted by Professor Kay and the firearms forensics experts. He produces the long-awaited 'video re-enactment' with the caution it is not definitive in its accuracy, merely an attempt to confirm or rule out Jenny's physical ability to shoot herself according to the long-held hypothesis. A policewoman of similar size and build to Jenny, using the Moran seat from the same lounge suite, attempted numerous contortions followed by falling back on the chair into the pose in which Jenny was found. It is almost embarrassing to watch it for about an hour—no matter how hard she tried, the substitute 'Jenny' couldn't get it right.

The TV reporters are dying to obtain copies of this footage, as the video is tendered in evidence. Normally, if an item is tendered it's fair game—or, more correctly, on the public record—and is permitted to be reproduced. Unfortunately for the anxious reporters, His Worship places an indefinite restriction order on this material, as well as on photos of Jenny's exhumed skull and its model.

Professor Cordner indicates his research and tests show at least three, maybe four or even more shots were fired, which meant, as my husband and I have worked out months before, that someone removed the extra cartridge cases at some time, either before the police arrived on the night or some time later.

Dozens of statistics related to suicide by firearms are produced, in essence saying that Professor Cordner could not find a single instance in published literature of anyone committing suicide with more than three shots. In the Hudson report he had quoted to me on the phone, 3500 suicides were studied, 38 involving multiple shots and 7 involving two shots to the head, but in all cases the first shot did not enter the cranium or, if it did, it either missed the brain or involved only the less vital frontal lobes.

Professor Cordner tries to explain the curious circle made by Jenny's left forefinger and thumb as they were found around the rifle barrel. There is an outside chance of cadaveric spasm, a rare phenomenon in which the body spasms as it dies, the 'clutching at a straw' concept occasionally found when someone has drowned and clutched onto flotsam in a river at the last second. But he doesn't seem very convinced that this was possible in Jenny's case.

He feels that a suicide scenario in any form is 'stretching the limits of my imagination'. From Professor Kay's evidence we already know Professor Cordner's final conclusion: 'It is hard to conceive of a reasonable suicidal explanation of this death, bearing in mind the other forensic evidence.'

18

The Accusers

DAY 16—only two more scheduled days to go. Considering most inquests last between one and five days, Jenny has set another precedent. Today we are to hear from Paul Newman and Jeff Calderbank. I have a few goosebumps of anticipation. Will Inspector Newman really stand in the witness box and point his finger at fellow police officer Denis Tanner?

Paul Newman is in his suit today, looking grim and determined, jaw set and eyebrows knitted. He stands straight and takes the oath in a strong voice. He tells us his opinion of the first investigation—'It was appalling.'

The Coroner asks him to put himself back and say what should have been done. Newman lists all the obvious things outlined in the Police Manual. He also says, 'The body should have been taken to Melbourne for examination by a forensic pathologist. The premises still should have been forensically examined. Blood may still have been evident and bullets and other material.'

Mr Rapke tells His Worship he wants to play us the tape of Denis's interview with Newman and Calderbank on 30 October 1996—the one Denis said he was 'tricked into' last year.

Silence prevails in the courtroom as the tape begins to roll. The videotape reveals a small interview room with a table and three chairs, each occupied by one of the key players. Denis is squashed into a corner and we see Newman's hands on the table. There's no sign of Calderbank till he goes to make Denis a coffee, but we hear his voice.

Denis is initially co-operative. He asks Newman why he resorted to tricking him into the interview. He wants to know what further information Newman requires that is not contained in his 1985 state-ment. He agrees tentatively to a formal interview. He looks a lot less confident than the Denis we've seen in court every day. Of course he knows he's being filmed, so he can't let too much emotion show, even if he's cornered—in a manner of speaking. He's cautioned and offered an opportunity to speak to his legal adviser. He accepts. They all go away and come back.

Denis crosses his arms over his chest (my notes say 'defensive or aggressive?') and tells Paul Newman he's going to reply 'No com-ment' to any question related to Jenny Tanner's death.

Denis is within his rights to do this. The police regulations provide for a commissioned officer to question members if they are suspected of any unethical behaviour. With minor breaches of discipline or ethics, a member who refuses to answer questions put by a senior offi-cer can be charged with refusing to answer the questions being put—itself a disciplinary charge—in the absence of any mitigating information. With a murder inquiry, however, police have exactly the same rights as other citizens. They can refuse to speak to the police at all, insist on the presence of a lawyer, or agree to attend an interview and then refuse to answer any questions that may incriminate them.

Undeterred, Newman starts the questions, 229 in all, covering everything we've heard in three weeks of evidence in this court. Where, what, when, who and why are fully canvassed and all answered with the same 'No Comment'.

Newman arrives at question number 229: 'I put it to you that on or about 14 November 1984, you drove to Springfield, entered that property, had a conversation with Jennifer Tanner and then shot her to death.'

'I have got no comment.'

The tape ends. No-one moves except Mr Rapke, who stands and asks Paul Newman why he asked that damning question. 'Did that question or the allegation contained in that question accurately reflect your state of mind at that time?'

'It certainly did. On the date of the interview Detective Sergeant Denis Tanner was a prime suspect in what we believed was the murder of Jennifer Tanner. During our detailed investigation, all roads tended to lead towards Denis Tanner.'

'Can you see any justification for not interviewing Denis Tanner in 1985?'

Newman replies, 'I can't see much justification for anything done at the Homicide Squad in relation to this particular inquiry, especially as they were approached twice, by Kerr and Fleming. I can only suggest that initially the job was botched—the rot started at the scene. I believe Welch received two phone calls. Alarm bells should have rung. Frazer and Kerr couldn't get help from Welch—then there was Phipps. Phipps was the ...'

Mr Gullaci leaps to his feet. 'Your Worship—I object to this witness summarising the evidence in this manner. With respect, it's the Coroner's function to pass judgement, not Mr Newman's.'

Mr Rapke explains to us, 'The witness has put to a suspect in a formal record of interview he's a murderer. I am trying to determine why.' He apologises for the open-endedness of his earlier question and asks, 'What had you turned up in your investigation that led to that question being put to him?'

Paul Newman counts the points off on his fingers:

Tanner tried several times to get the boundaries changed to put Mansfield under his CIB control.

The evidence from Helen Golding.

Corroboration of Roz Smith's evidence.

On 15 November Lynne Tanner allegedly told Helen Golding Denis had not returned home until 5 a.m.

Concern about the two alibis.

The send-off for the Browns was not on 14 November.

The fire at Springfield—'for eighty or ninety years it was OK, then just when we might have examined it, it burned down'.

The truck driver saw an open gate and car in the drive, but the gate was locked when the fire truck arrived.

The finding of Adele Baily would have occurred in the area under Tanner's control, if he'd been successful in getting the boundaries changed.

Tanner was always interested in any little crime in the Mansfield area, but completely lost interest following the finding of Adele Baily.

Tanner claimed ignorance of details of wounds, but since he was present at the first inquest he must have been aware of them.

A lot of people, including police, had said they had suspicions about Tanner's involvement at the time.

Mr Gullaci leaps up again, interrupting our strained attention. 'Your Worship, I can't sit through this! Allegations are not evidence! This witness is summarising and commenting on the credibility of the information before the court. That is not his role.'

The Coroner supports Mr Gullaci. 'Try to list the concerns you had without commenting on their credibility, if you can.'

Newman nods and continues:

Denis and his family never showed any interest in the way Jenny met her death.

The desire to retrieve the firearm.

The threats to Helen Golding.

His absence during the police attendance at his Spotswood home.

No violence or forced entry at the scene.

The firearm's locality must have been known to the killer.

'Did you have any material available to you from Mr Russell at the time of your interview?' asks Mr Rapke.

'No, I don't believe so,' Newman replies.

In cross-examination Mr Gullaci makes a valiant attempt to elicit from Newman whether there are any more undisclosed tape recordings of conversations. Newman refuses to go along with this line of questioning, claiming the case is not closed, is still under active investigation and he will not be put in the position of jeopardising the outcome.

The Coroner looks almost inclined to support Mr Gullaci in his quest, but is then told firmly by Newman that if he's directed to answer these questions he will have to seek advice from the Crown Solicitor to protect his ongoing investigation. He looks determined. Mr Gullaci loses with bad grace.

'Your Worship, there's been a witch-hunt in this court, orchestrated I would submit by my learned friend Mr Rapke, aided and abetted by him and various members of the police department—materials have been leaked to people.'

I look at my knees. I hope I'm not one of the people he's referring to. I've done my own research.

The Coroner says placatingly, 'It's late in the day, Mr Gullaci.'

'It's very late in the day, Your Worship. There's got to be some balance. My client just sits there and has to wear it, and, whether it's late or early, the way that it's been portrayed is not to give my client any sort of natural justice. The innuendo and prejudice and trial of my client through the media just continues every day, unhalted, unabated and without any great deal of substantiation, in my respectful submission.'

Mr Rapke is waiting for his turn. 'I resent the suggestion I've been orchestrating a witch-hunt. I'm doing my job as Counsel Assisting.

This witness [Newman] has been prepared to put in a formal record of interview to a witness in these proceedings that he's a murderer, and I should probe the basis on which he put that allegation. Now, my learned friend might get terribly twitchy about this, but the fact is that I'm asking with a view to see how substantial the basis was for the allegation.'

We wait for the Coroner to adjudicate. He looks at the clock. Nearly lunch-time.

'Well perhaps now is a good time to adjourn.'

We all stand.

When we return Jeff Calderbank is sworn in. His large frame contrasts with his soft voice.

The bulk of his evidence centres round a long tape-recorded interview he did with Laurie in the company of Marty Allison at the Preston shearing sheds. Jeff and Marty 'sat off' the sheds from 6.30 a.m. on an icy August morning, waiting for Laurie to arrive. He finally fronted at around 9 a.m. The interview was a surprise and was taped for an hour and a half without his knowledge with a recorder attached to Marty Allison. Most of the interview occurred inside the shed and was interrupted often by a disobedient dog called Tammy, which had obviously taken a liking to Calderbank, who did not return the affection. 'Why do I attract them?' he asked plaintively. (I write in my notes: 'Must have been his tie.')

What strikes me about this interview is that Laurie responded with either evasiveness or apparent naivety but didn't actually answer any questions of substance. For the most part he claimed his memory after twelve years was poor or that he was zonked out for most of the crucial period being investigated. Of course one could be sceptical about someone not remembering a significant and traumatic event that changed his life, but it's also possible it was so bad he's just blotted it out altogether.

He comes across as weak and indecisive, yet that fits awkwardly with our knowledge of Laurie 'the champion bloke', president of the Agricultural and Pastoral Society, married to two attractive young women, clever enough to subdivide his property and make a living off the land when a lot of others have failed. He can't be stupid.

Calderbank asked him about his life with Jenny. Was Sam planned?—'Yes'; Jenny's care of Sam—'She'd leave him in his bassinette for hours on end'; her health and moods—'She had PMT and a split personality and she'd lie in bed till lunch-time sometimes'; and his movements on the night of her death.

'The shithouses were playing up. If I hadn't been called in there that night and Angie hadn't just been talkin' to Jenny, what would've happened? I'd be lookin' pretty bloody ordinary now, wouldn't I?'

'I don't follow what you mean.'

'Angie said she'd just got off the phone from Jenny. If I hadn't called in and I'd just gone home, I couldn't have proved where I was.'

I reflect that there was still half an hour between the earliest time Laurie could have arrived home (about 10.05 p.m.) and Hughie Almond's arrival (about 10.35 p.m.). Even if he hadn't gone to the McCormacks', so what?

Calderbank asked about his relationship with Jenny. 'I thought we had a very close relationship. We had good times together. I'd say she was a fun-lovin' type of girl. Liked nothin' better to go out to the pub and have a meal and a couple of drinks. But of course you get tied down a bit after you have a kid, don't you? You can't get out as much. We visited people, had tea at someone's place and a drink. You don't do the same things as before. That's when her mood swings started.'

He was asked who phoned his parents the night Jenny died. He thought it was either Hughie or the police. He can't recall making the 10.15 p.m. call Fred told me about, although he does say later in the interview that if he was in trouble or needed someone to confide in it would be 'prob'ly my mum, I s'pose.'

'Who notified your other brothers?'

'Don't ask me. I got home and got a stab in the bum and that's the last I remember of it.'

He did remember discussing the future subdivision of the property with Jenny, which would have given her a much bigger financial claim on him if those plans were known to her and she decided to divorce him. But he could recollect no marital problems or talk of her leaving.

Calderbank asked about Sam.

'Well, he's gone very quiet and deep, won't discuss anything. I told him about the exhumation and the tests and he closed up. Kath thought he might want to go to the funeral [which was scheduled for the day after this interview] and I asked him if he wanted to but he said, "No thank you, I don't want to go." I'm not gonna force him.'

Jeff Calderbank is cross-examined by an indignant Mr Hargreaves, who takes him to task for lying in wait for his client and secretly taping his open and honest answers. He also castigates Calderbank for giving Laurie a caution, but then not giving him the prescribed time or opportunity to contact legal counsel if he wanted to. A big slip for an experienced detective. I think Jeff is blushing.

After he steps down the Coroner gives us another surprise. He adjourns until February, because he wants 'some further inquiries' conducted.

Mr Johnstone also makes the following comment.

'There have been some serious issues raised regarding serving police and retired police. I may, and I'm only saying may'—with a stern look at the press corps—'be critical of some of these police. Counsel assisting will make contact with these people to allow them the opportunity to make written submissions on their own behalf. Court will resume on 23 February.'

'All stand.'

His Worship leaves and we mill about a bit before dribbling away to our families and Christmas preparations. What will the new year bring? Who could believe the wheels of justice could creak along at such a slow pace?

∞

MONDAY, 23 FEBRUARY 1998
We reconvene on Day 17. The atmosphere is different—everyone says so. There are lawyers everywhere, their dark suits emphasising the

contrast between the court proceedings and the fine summer day outside. I've been told every police officer involved with the first investigation, except for Peter Fleming, has received the equivalent of a 'please explain' letter from the Coroner. Maybe that's why there are so many lawyers here today?

People are looking weary. Kath wants an outcome. Les is fed up. Paul Newman is power-dressed in a navy double-breasted suit with padded shoulders, making me think of a gladiator about to go into battle. He'll be on first, to resolve the outstanding point of law about whether he has to answer questions about his continuing investigations.

There are no security checks in place, and word filters out that the Coroner is most displeased. He refuses to commence the hearing until Security arrives, so we hang around, frustrated at another hour's delay.

The lawyers use this time to negotiate on today's programme. Mr Gullaci is again complaining that he never knows who's on till they're on. He and Mr Hargreaves, along with another lawyer they've brought along, make theatrical tutting noises and heave big sighs as they canvass Mr Rapke's proposed order of proceedings. All part of the performance. I suss out the new lawyer—a Mr Holdenson. He's blond and sparse and looks as if he rarely smiles. I ask Denis who he is. Denis is cagey. 'He has a role to play,' is all he'll say.

There are two more lawyers at the bar table. Mr Brian Dennis, appearing for the Chief Commissioner's Office (and therefore Paul Newman) and a Mr Geoffrey Steward, who, once we finally get under way, tells His Worship he's appearing for Lynne Tanner.

Mr Steward advises His Worship that Lynne Tanner's doctor, who is also in court in case he's required, says Lynne is unwell and will not be able to return to court 'for the foreseeable future'. Since we hope we'll be finished this week, that means she won't be back unless we have another adjournment—oh no!

Mr Rapke fingers a small pile of cassette tapes and looks as if he's weighing up the pros and cons of insisting on Lynne's return. He probably thinks that, if she's so unwell, any evidence she might give may not be totally reliable anyway. He says, 'I won't press for her

attendance at this time. But that decision should not at any stage pre-clude Mrs Tanner from returning to give evidence if she wishes to.'
Lynne's lawyer leaves with the doctor in tow.

A legal argument on the matters of relevance and public interest in regard to Paul Newman's methods of investigation takes us through until lunch-time. The Coroner wants to know all the players and asks Mr Holdenson for his first name.

'O. P.' comes the reply.

'Your *name*, Mr Holdenson?'

'Paul, Your Worship.'

Everyone in court then spends the boring parts of the argument speculating on what the 'O' stands for—so embarrassing he can't tell us?

The essence of the argument is first about the relevance of the information Mr Gullaci wants. Mr Holdenson presents the argument that the police are in possession of material they refuse to share that may assist the Coroner. ('And them,' I write in my notes. 'The info may also assist his clients.')

Mr Rapke argues, 'To press the police to reveal the methods by which they gathered information is irrelevant, as the police have already said they've given the Coroner everything relevant.' He says that to force their hand would be to doubt their credibility.

Mr Dennis adds considerable support to Mr Rapke. Eventually the Coroner rules the police methodology is relevant. Round One to Mr Holdenson, who then argues it is therefore in the public interest to disclose it.

Mr Dennis offers to give His Worship a confidential affidavit from an undisclosed author. Mr Holdenson wants a copy. Mr Dennis tells the Coroner this affidavit is for his eyes only and he must be 'irre-trievably be bound by its confidentiality' if he reads it. If he feels he must share it with anyone, the Commissioner's office will take the matter to the Supreme Court.

Mr Gullaci protests, 'That is waving a big stick over Your Worship!'

The Coroner replies wryly that he is just as susceptible as anyone else in court to being threatened with a higher authority. He takes the affidavit and retires to read it. He returns and says, 'It is not in the public interest to disclose the contents of this affidavit.'

Mr Rapke is on his feet immediately. 'Please call Deputy Commissioner Graham Sinclair.' Who? He's not on the witness list.

Mr Gullaci leans in to Holdenson and Hargreaves and mutters, 'Are we just going to swallow that?' Mr Holdenson leaps up and seeks leave to argue the ruling. Deputy Commissioner Sinclair goes outside again and another legal tap-dance follows. The Coroner upholds his earlier ruling and moves on. Denis's team is cranky. Paul Newman relaxes. I wonder who wrote the affidavit. Deputy Commissioner Sinclair takes the stand.

He outlines his role in the series of meetings held between police and Mr Russell, the motel broker. It seems he is present solely to rule out any suggestion of impropriety on the part of the police in obtaining Mr Russell's statement, as it seems Mr Russell himself had a little bit of unfinished business with the police, which has since been dealt with through the normal channels. As he told me months ago, Paul Newman has done no deals. Another little stone turned over to make sure no spiders lurk underneath.

Then we have Assistant Commissioner Graeme McDonald, who comes to tell us about a conversation held in his office at a mates' reunion attended by Fry, himself and another ex-Homicide detective. McDonald says that in this conversation Fry indicated that it was common practice to edit statements on inquest briefs and added that it was not only likely Bill Kerr's statement was edited, but also likely Mr Adams and David Stevens knew about it. He told us Fry said he'd had a discussion with David Stevens about editing of inquest statements in the foyer of the Coroner's Court before he gave evidence.

This conversation took place last October, and I wonder why it's being related in March. By an Assistant Commissioner.

Ray Vincent from Firearms and Toolmarks is recalled. He tells us he now cannot guarantee 'the very specific phenomenon which occurs in .22 bolt actions and some centre fires', that is, the tell-tale residue deposit indicating a shot was fired at 15 degrees from vertical. He'd accidentally banged the rifle on a table during further laboratory testing and dislodged the residue. 'Taking into account the rifle was moved on the night, maybe thrown in a car boot, stored in a locker, handled and so on, we can't now attach any significance to the residue found when the rifle was first tested.'

Does this revelation have any real significance to the outcome? Probably not.

Chief Superintendent Peter Hester takes the stand. Last October he'd been appointed by His Worship to investigate the possibility that Bill Kerr's long statement had been shortened after reaching the Coroner's court. He's conducted a number of interviews and reports his conclusions: 'The longer statement was never available to the original inquest.'

I hope this is the last we hear of Bill's statement. It's had nearly as much examination as Jenny's death. What are we trying to prove here?

∞

Day 18—no anticipation or excitement; we're all a bit jaded. Maybe Denis and Laurie will be called today—that will make us all sit up. Jeff Lockhart gives evidence about his role in the Springfield fire and why he cut the chain holding the gate instead of using his key to the padlock. (Quicker in the dark.) Questions are slanted towards trying to demonstrate that Laurie has a key to the gate. So what? we all think.

They call retired District Chief Inspector Tom O'Keefe. He's a tall, grandfatherly man with a ruddy complexion setting off bright white hair. He's supposed to have been unwell and experiencing memory difficulties. I hope it isn't contagious—there seems to be a lot of it around.

Mr Rapke takes him through what he can remember. He remembers Sergeant Welch having a cup of tea with him on his way to see Dr Dyte in April 1985—the 'first he'd heard of Jenny's death'. Mr Rapke asks him why he thinks, as chief of the entire district, he did not hear about Jenny's death, or any details about her injuries, or that a fellow officer might have been involved until six months after the event. He doesn't know.

He's asked about referring the file to Homicide for Denis to be interviewed. He never saw it on its way to Homicide, only on the way back, never knew about two bullet holes, never saw any information from Welch or MacLennan, never wrote a covering letter to Homicide requesting an interview of Denis Tanner.

Mr Rapke shows him the memo addressed to him from Welch— 'In view of the allegation from Mrs Smith I believe Sergeant Tanner should be interviewed'—never seen it before.

He is then shown the memo from MacLennan—'the closest confidentiality must be observed in this matter'—never saw this either.

Mr Rapke hands him a memo dated 8 May 1985 addressed to Mr Ritchie, containing comments such as 'this case is alleged to involve a member of the police force' and signed by Tom O'Keefe RDCI. He's never seen it before.

The Coroner is fascinated. He leans over, eyebrows arching and asks, 'Who would have written it?'

'I don't know.'

'Why would someone else write it?'

'The signature looks like mine. My recollection is I told Ian Welch to look into it.'

The Coroner is insistent. 'But you wouldn't get Ian Welch to write this letter? Can you explain why you don't remember writing this letter?'

'I can't offer any explanation for it, Your Worship.'

The Coroner leans back and remarks vexedly, 'That seems to be a common facet of this inquest.'

'I can't help that. If I'd written that I'd remember it.'

More questions from Mr Rapke about O'Keefe's knowledge at the time about the details of the case. More denials from O'Keefe.

The Coroner interrupts again. He now sounds cross.

'The truth is, you *knew* about this incident and you *were* briefed on it.'

'Er—I was not briefed in full.'

I thought the Coroner was going to say 'Bullshit!' but he actually said, 'But you had sufficient information to know what was going on, didn't you?'

'I don't accept that, Sir.'

Mr Rapke intervenes, summarising all the briefings O'Keefe would have received from his subordinate officers. O'Keefe says he was 'rather surprised that a number of subordinate officers did not brief me on this matter'.

Mr Rapke asks, 'Were you not in possession of *any material at all* that even hinted that Detective Sergeant Tanner was a suspect?'

'I first became aware that Sergeant Tanner was a suspect when it was printed in the newspaper.'

After more grilling from Mr Rapke, Tom O'Keefe breaks down in tears. In spite of his obvious desire to get to the truth, the Coroner is pretty considerate. We adjourn to allow Mr O'Keefe to collect himself.

Outside the Court, O'Keefe wants to talk to Kath and Les Blake. He apologises to them for the lack of proper investigation into Jenny's death. At the same time, I am talking to Jenny's aunt. 'Poor old thing,' she says. 'It must be hard for him after all this time.'

'I'm not sorry for him at all,' I respond. 'He was in charge of the district.'

We resume and Mr Gullaci hoes in, emphasising the lack of proper investigation at the time. He seems to be building a case for dismissing the first investigation and, with it, all aspersions cast on his client. 'Did you ever make any enquiries about Jenny's death rather than waiting for people to come to you?'

'No forensic enquiries. All those would have had to come through me.'

'So you had final say. You'd make a judgement on the details to justify calling them out. So you *knew* when Welch saw you in 1985 that no forensics had been done.'

'I would inasmuch as I hadn't authorised it. A policeman being involved is a seven-day wonder, like a bank manager or anyone else. But I would have remembered if Tanner had been involved, because I had investigated him for something else fairly recently before that.'

Mr Gullaci quickly dismisses this interesting little detail and reminds O'Keefe that this previous investigation is of no interest to this court. Of course, we're all agog, but his point is taken and no details of Denis's alleged misdemeanour are revealed.

Tom O'Keefe leaves the stand redder faced and more stooped than when he arrived.

∞

David Stevens is recalled. He is asked about his conversation with Fry—'Yes, it did take place'—and if he had any role in editing Bill Kerr's long statement.

'No. In all my time as a Coroner's clerk I've never edited any statement, although I have sometimes been asked by the Coroner not to read aloud hurtful material from statements.'

The Coroner then proposes a very unusual course—to call Mr Hugh Adams to the stand. I am quite pleased about this plan. Maybe Mr Gullaci will ask why the open finding was never followed up, to demonstrate conclusively his client had no involvement in Jenny's death.

Mr Adams sends in his place a very senior barrister, Crown Counsel Professor Colin Howard, to argue that under Section 62 (1) of the Coroner's Act:

> A Coroner … must not be called to give evidence in any court or judicial proceedings about anything coming to their knowledge in carrying out their powers, duties or functions under this Act.

In view of this, the professor asks the Coroner to set aside the subpoena summoning Mr Adams to attend.

The Coroner seems a bit put out. He discusses points of law with Mr Rapke and Professor Howard and deliberates whether Section 62 (1) also applies to the previous Act, but then reminds himself Mr Adams was a Coroner under both Acts. There's also talk about whether this is even a court of law—or is it an inquisition? No-one seems too sure. His Worship decides we'll hear what Jim Fry has to say and then we'll see about Mr Adams.

Jim Fry has been waiting outside for a day and a half. The papers gave him a hard time yesterday, saying he knew about the 'doctoring' of Bill Kerr's statement. He's pretty cross and not looking anywhere near as cocky as he was in October. 'The Boys' have all gone safely home and he's on his own, although his wife is with him to provide moral support.

The Coroner is still intent on getting every bit of information about Bill Kerr's long and short statements.

Jim Fry answers tersely. He says he disagrees with Deputy Commissioner McDonald's assertions that he [Fry] commented on Bill Kerr's statement during the meeting at his old mate's office. Fry was alleged to have implied that Bill Kerr had gone too far in including unsubstantiated hearsay and opinion, and said that 'in keeping with established practice, some of the controversial evidence was deleted before the original inquest'.

McDonald said Fry had 'left him with the impression that Kerr's original statement had been reduced in content prior to the first inquest with the knowledge of Mr Fry, Mr Stevens and Mr Adams, the presiding Coroner'. Fry disagrees with this allegation.

'We weren't concentrating on Kerr's statement, we were talking generally. I have also formed a very strong opinion that Mr Peter Fleming knew the contents of Kerr's long statement.' Fry is still insistent the file came to him from the Coroner's office, though this seems unlikely, in view of all we have heard to the contrary.

Fry tells us he thought the long statement was edited by someone because 'the Coroner would have had pups when he saw that statement'.

This sparks our Coroner's interest. 'Why would the Coroner "have pups", as you put it?'

'The hearsay and innuendo. Junior members sometimes got carried away.'

The Coroner asks him about his meeting with Peter Fleming and why he refused to make further inquiries into the circumstances of Jenny's death.

'I've said it and will keep on saying it—there was *no evidence* that involved Denis Tanner.'

'Why didn't you investigate the two alibis?'

'I considered he'd made a mistake. I committed him to the bingo.'

In between giving these rather astonishing replies, Fry suffers greatly from memory loss. He answers 'I can't recall' fourteen times.

The Coroner tells Mr Fry he's free to go 'at this stage'. What does that mean?

Then he tells us—so are we! I can't believe it. Adjourned again—for another five weeks. Andrew Rule makes the comment that the Blakes are getting justice on a time-instalment plan.

∞

TUESDAY 3 MARCH 1998
NEWS FLASH! POLICE SEARCH SERVING POLICE OFFICER'S HOME IN DAYLIGHT RAID.

On Tuesday 3 March, Denis Tanner was one and a half hours' drive from home, attending a crime conference on a river-boat—out of touch and out of reach—when five members of the Ethical Standards Department, accompanied by a police officer attached to the Coroner's Court, arrived at his house. They waited outside until Lynne Tanner returned from her morning chores.

On Tuesday 24 February 1998—the day after the Coroner's Court had been supplied with a detailed opinion regarding Lynne Tanner's fragile mental health, which led to her being excused from providing further evidence to the inquest—Mr Johnstone ordered a search of Denis Tanner's house under the little-used Section 26 of the Coroner's Act. The search was to be conducted within one month of his direction.

The search party assembled at her front door and passed the coronial authority around the wire screen. Lynne says she asked for a minute to read it, but the police pushed straight in, knocking her down. The police say she collapsed. Either way, she ended up on the floor as the search party walked in. They were very thorough: they searched in the roof, under the house, and among boxes of mementoes from her recently deceased parents. The authority specifically listed two items of interest—any photos or registration papers relating to a vehicle owned by the Tanners in 1984 and a pair of binoculars—although Section 26 says the Coroner can 'take possession of anything which (he) reasonably believes is relevant to the investigation and keep it until the investigation is finished'.

Lynne Tanner says she gave the police photos of the car. (Had the Coroner forgotten that very early in the inquest Mr Gullaci had tendered a photo of the Tanners' house in which the car was clearly visible, parked outside?) A set of binoculars was also seized in the search. These items will be examined by police before we reconvene. When I contact the police officer attached to the Coroner's Court, he will not comment on anything to do with the raid.

Anything seized under Section 26 cannot be produced in a court as evidence, so even if they did find something incriminating (and I bet they didn't—Denis isn't that silly) it's unlikely it will be produced if there's ever a trial.

While the police searched, Lynne was eventually able to contact Denis, who returned home as quickly as he could. He was very angry. He says his colleagues didn't follow police guidelines during the search and were still looking through Lynne's jewellery when he arrived home. He says Lynne 'took the invasion real hard and is now suffering from a speech impediment'. He is trying to make an official complaint for assault on Lynne's behalf—the police deny it.

He tells me his family is now under siege. 'When you're put in this position, you start thinking like a crim. But it doesn't matter what they do to me,' he goes on with bravado, 'they can't make strawberry jam outta shit—no matter how much sugar they put in.'

∞

CORONER'S COURT, MELBOURNE
2 APRIL 1998

We reconvene. The crowd is much smaller. The Blake family is still represented in force. Far fewer journalists, though. Have they lost interest?

Denis is wearing his favourite tie, with rows of romping koalas—

an incongruous choice for a big, tough cop. 'My kids gave it to me,' he says proudly.

'This might be your big day,' I say. 'Are you ready?'

He says, 'I'd rather be out the front of this court than on a slab out the back.'

For once, we start more or less on time. Mr Rapke calls his first witness, Doug McPhie, now Acting Chief Superintendent in charge of 'P' District, based at Wangaratta—and Denis's boss. He looks full of authority in his uniform badged with rank, but he seems nervous, and stumbles several times over the wording of the oath. He tells us he was 'the other sergeant' at Mansfield when Jenny died, but had nothing to do with the investigation.

He remembers sitting in the muster room one or two days after Jenny's death when Dr Dyte rang to tell Neil Phipps about the second bullet. He tells us he said, 'There goes your suicide theory', or words to that effect. Phipps replied, 'It could still be suicide.' McPhie then walked out.

He seems vague about the entire case. He thinks Peter Fleming was involved, and that Bill Kerr had a Queensland witness, but is 'not entirely sure'. He says it was 'all sort of periphery, there was just a dis-cussion around the station, but I know Jimmy Fry was involved in it, and that was pretty much it'. He was unaware of the wounds to Jenny's hands 'until this inquest'.

I feel surprised that his knowledge is so sketchy, considering he was Bill Kerr's only immediate superior for quite some time after Neil Phipps left Mansfield. Besides, he's now working in the same station as Denis, and the details have been in all the newspapers.

'I wasn't that keen on the thought she'd committed suicide,' McPhie says. 'I thought it was strange that someone could shoot themselves twice with a single shot rifle to the head.'

('*Another* one who said nothing!' I write in my notes.)

Mr Gullaci takes over and, after a few questions about the rifle, he presses McPhie on his role in the investigation. 'Having formed the view you say you formed at the time, that suicide was questionable, did you keep an eye on the investigation?'

'There was discussion with Sergeant Phipps, who was assisting Mr Kerr, and Homicide were involved—they were the experts.'

Mr Gullaci asks nine more questions in an attempt to clarify what kind of assistance McPhie 'believed' Bill Kerr was receiving from Neil Phipps, but no new information is forthcoming. Eventually McPhie is excused, and former sergeant Terrence Cahill takes his place on the stand.

Cahill tells us that he transferred to Mansfield police station as a sergeant in February 1985, filling the vacancy created when Neil Phipps left the previous November, ten days after Jenny died. After Cahill was appointed, but before he had actually moved, Denis Tanner phoned asking him to withdraw in his favour. Denis said there had been a tragedy in the family and he wanted to be near by. Cahill refused to withdraw.

Cahill says he had no knowledge of Jenny's death before he went to Mansfield and 'played no part at all in the investigation' of her death, although he was aware that Bill Kerr was conducting an investigation and preparing a brief. Cahill did not even set eyes on the brief; in fact, if he ever knew anything about the episode, he seems to have forgotten it.

What happened to the chain of command, I wonder, if Bill Kerr had no sergeant to report to right through that crucial time? Is this a 'missing link'?

After Mr Cahill steps down, Mr Rapke says, 'Call please Denis Tanner.' A murmur travels around the onlookers.

Denis walks across the front of the courtroom, buttoning his navy suit jacket. He looks cool and confident. At 10.31 a.m. he holds the Bible high and says the oath.

Mr Rapke asks, 'Mr Tanner, can you tell me please where you were on the night that your sister-in-law died?'

The Coroner leans down and cautions Denis about his right to remain silent.

It seems a long time before Denis replies. We wait. Finally he says, 'Sir, I decline to answer that question. I've sought legal advice from Mr Gullaci. Mr Gullaci's instructions are that I decline to answer questions on the grounds that any answers I made—may give—the questions *may* tend to incriminate myself.'

At 10.33 a.m. Denis leaves the witness box. Nineteen days in court and two minutes on the stand! Unconscious of having held our breath for so long, we all breathe out.

'Mr Rapke?' says the Coroner.

'Your Worship,' says Mr Rapke, 'I don't think I can ask any questions of Sergeant Tanner that would not have that tendency to which he's referred.' He announces that he will not press for Denis to be required to answer, and calls Laurie Tanner.

Laurie doesn't look too nervous. He unfolds a sheet of paper and lays it in front of him. I think he's going to read a statement.

Mr Rapke asks Laurie what he and Denis discussed over the phone on the afternoon of Jenny's death. The coroner cautions Laurie, who then reads from his sheet of paper: 'I've had legal advice from my lawyers. I object to answering any further questions because the answers may tend to incriminate me.'

'Take a seat behind counsel, thank you.' Laurie's stint on the stand is even shorter than Denis's—only one minute. What a let-down! I thought Laurie would answer some questions—why would he refuse?

As soon as he is seated Mr Gullaci stands up. 'Your Worship, there is a matter I want to raise now, as it may affect further proceedings.'

He launches into an eighteen-minute speech, most of which is read from prepared notes. He criticises the conduct of the inquest, complaining that he and Mr Hargreaves were not given statements and other evidence, and were not told the details of further inquiries being made by the Coroner, only that they would be informed of the outcomes 'in due course'.

Mr Gullaci seems particularly annoyed that he was not present when the Coroner inspected Springfield and the Jack o' Clubs mine. He and Mr Hargreaves were aware the Coroner was going to Springfield, and Mr Rapke had given them the option of coming along, but they had decided not to attend. They would have come along, however, if they had known that the Coroner intended to view the mine as well.

'It would be clear, we would say, that the view which occurred relates to the Baily matter and not this matter, and it is of grave concern to us that Your Worship … has had a view in the presence of investigators, where things may have been said to you in our absence.' He objects to the linking of the Baily case with the current inquest, and complains that his team's request for access to the Baily brief has been denied.

He is scathing about the raid conducted on Denis's house on 3 March. Was it a ploy to put pressure on Mrs Tanner? Why has no evidence from the raid been presented? Why has no explanation been given, and why have the seized items not been returned? Why did it take six police to carry out a raid on a house where a sick woman was home alone? Was the exercise deliberately planned to take place while Denis was away? And was the search lawful? After all, the Coroner had given Jeff Calderbank the authority to search, but he was not present.

For the first time during the inquest proceedings, I see Paul Newman smile. I smile too. Mr Gullaci is certainly getting a lot of mileage out of his speech.

He continues by attacking the media coverage of the case, and in particular Andrew Rule's story about the raid on Denis's house. He claims that his team only found out about the raid when the *Age* report appeared. (I'm surprised; I thought Denis would have been on the phone to Gullaci as soon as he discovered it had happened.) He suggests that Andrew Rule has a 'deep throat' connection 'either within the Task Force or within the confines of Your Worship's office', and points out that 'The article included great detail, and also included the address, the street, and of course it's a small town—it wouldn't take people too long to find out exactly where our client lives.'

Mr Gullaci's voice gets louder. 'We've never sought any favours on behalf of Denis Tanner,' he says. 'We've been prepared to listen to the evidence. We've been prepared to listen to the innuendo, and we've been prepared to put up with the media witch hunt, but surely somebody must consider the effect of these things on our client's family— his wife is sick, his four children who attend school in that area.'

Then his speech takes an unexpected turn. 'I tell Your Worship that my client, in view of the matters that have occurred, has lost confidence in the way this inquest has been conducted, and, accordingly, my instructions are to take no further part in it. I do not propose to take any further part. I propose to withdraw from these proceedings and, indeed, as a matter of courtesy, I seek your permission to leave the Bar Table.'

While he is packing up, Mr Hargreaves stands up and says he is also instructed not to participate any further.

We all sit with our mouths open as Gullaci, Hargreaves and the third lawyer, Holdenson, file out of the courtroom.

Mr Rapke fill the void. 'I'm staying, Your Worship. I've got a job to do.' He suggests a short adjournment so that they can consider where the proceedings should go from here. The Coroner agrees eagerly, and out we go. The media besiege Denis and company, but they're definitely leaving.

What a finale! I ask around. The Coroner's Court staff can't recall this ever happening before. I sit and write a short list in my notebook:

Reasons for walkout?

Costs escalating—doesn't want to spend the $10–20K on fees for submission. To express contempt for the way they've been treated. Denis upset about police invading his house—wanted to have a swipe at the Coroner and put it on the record before they walked out.

∞

A subdued group files back into court. We're all wondering what this means for the conclusion of the inquest.

The Coroner begins by answering some of Mr Gullaci's allegations about the conduct of the inquiry. He says, 'The very nature of an inquest is that it is an investigation … It has required us to look into matters that have not been previously looked at; to look for evidentiary material, both forensic and otherwise, that might have been missed. It is not appropriate to telegraph that information to others.'

He goes on to say that the material would have been made available to the Tanners' counsel when and if it became relevant.

He tells us that Mr Rapke will still make his written submission available to the Tanner team, and they will be invited to comment. Without their comments, he adds, some of the balance of the process would be lost. 'I hope they will reconsider their position.'

He is about to adjourn when Mr Dennis, who is appearing on behalf of the police, stands up.

The Coroner says, 'Oh, Mr Dennis. *You're* still here.'

Mr Dennis asks for a moment to get instructions from his clients. After a quick consultation, he again addresses the Coroner, trying to draw him on his foreshadowed criticisms of members of the police. Who is he likely to criticise? Should Mr Dennis's submission be concerned with anyone who wasn't involved in the initial investigation, or hasn't given evidence?

His Worship is not very forthcoming. He puts the ball back into Mr Dennis's court: 'It's a matter for you to look at the evidence and decide whether or not, if those police officers are still serving police officers, you choose to make comment on their evidence.'

Mr Dennis then refutes some of Mr Gullaci's criticisms of the present Task Force. He says the suggestion there was a leak to the media is 'absolutely untrue'. He rejects Mr Gullaci's claim that the raid on the Tanner house was unlawful because of Jeff Calderbank's absence. He denies the allegation that the search was deliberately engineered to take place when Denis was absent. Finally, he says it is 'a little surprising that these matters were raised by Mr Gullaci in this manner … this melodramatic assertion from the Bar table this morning about all of these matters without any warning'.

I'm surprised Mr Dennis is surprised that he wasn't forewarned. That would have destroyed the impact of Gullaci's performance. But his comment is now in the record

Mr Rapke stands up and registers his surprise for the record too. He says he had no advance notice, even though he and Mr Gullaci had spoken on the phone this morning, and goes on to refute the criticisms of the conduct of the inquiry. 'Nothing that I or those assisting me have done in this inquest has been designed or intended to cause unfairness to any interested party. Further, I am confident that no unfairness or prejudice has in fact occurred to any person. I reject any suggestion of impropriety or unfairness that has been levelled at me or my assistants during this inquest.'

Mr Rapke says he will deal with the criticisms in his written submission, which will be sent to Mr Gullaci and Mr Hargreaves. Now, though, there's another matter that he wants to comment on. 'It is to be observed that Mr Gullaci's carefully crafted speech … was made after Mr Denis Tanner and Mr Laurie Tanner declined to give evidence at this inquest, on the grounds that their answers may tend to incriminate them. When I come to prepare my final submissions, Your Worship, I shall deal with the significance of the refusal of those two men to give evidence.'

The Coroner asks that submissions be put in writing, and again expresses his hope that the Tanners' counsel will reconsider. He adjourns the inquest to a date to be fixed.

So that's that. Five weeks for Mr Rapke to write his submission, and who knows how long for the Coroner to present his finding?

Everyone disperses so quickly I don't even have time to seek out the Blakes to ask their reaction. At the tram stop on my way home I write another list:

Coroner has heard all the evidence. Prosecution says they have no further witnesses. If they find anything to inculpate anyone, Denis and Laurie will have to be given another opportunity to speak. Gullaci and Hargreaves have withdrawn from the case and don't intend to put submissions. Murder is a foregone conclusion. It's unlikely Denis and Laurie will be charged.

∞

Denis and I speak the next day. I say some people may draw adverse conclusions from the fact he and Laurie had refused to give evidence.

He says they've already given evidence and been cross-examined at the first inquest. They have nothing to add. They've already been tried and convicted by the media, so what's the point? Their legal advice was to make no comment.

I reply that Mr Rapke will still make a meal of their failure to give evidence at this inquest.

Denis says, 'As far as I'm concerned, he can sit on my finger and spin.'

Epilogue

So—THERE you have it. The best investigators and legal minds in Australia haven't been able to prove who killed Jenny Tanner. I don't know who killed her, but I do have an opinion. It might be different from yours.

The number of surprises we experienced at the second inquest and the sheer volume of statements and evidence collected by the Task Force showed me they have really left no stone unturned in this new investigation, as they promised. They have clearly demonstrated their dedication and single-minded purpose. On the other hand, I have still have vague concerns about whether their investigation has been completely open-minded. If Denis Tanner did not exist, I wonder, might the Task Force's concerns have found a different target?

Unlimited resources have been devoted to the investigation, and no evidence has been uncovered which could convince the Director of Public Prosecutions to charge him or anyone else. Explicitly cleared of any suspicion by the first coroner and then exhaustively investigated by the police, it now seems clear that there is nothing to suggest that Denis Tanner has committed any offence.

After the inquest I was speaking to a very high-ranking police officer who told me: 'If the Coroner sends the file back to Victoria Police for further investigation I don't know what we'll do. I don't think there is one single avenue left unexplored.' And I believe him. I don't think the killer of Jenny Tanner will ever be brought to justice. The investigation has not been 'too little', but it has certainly been 'too late'. The reality is, some people *do* get away with murder.

At least the new investigators set the record straight. I think the responses of the professionals at the time amounted to a scheme extending to the highest level to protect members of the police force—to cover up the incompetence of the early investigation in their own interests, not in the first instance to cover up the murder. The police culture of brotherhood and protecting their mates is compellingly demonstrated by the calculated avoidance of pursuing facts in this investigation.

The early stuff-up was probably just great good luck for the killer. The police probably were not certain it was murder until two bullets were discovered, and by then it was already too late for some. Jenny's interests, and those of her bereaved family, became secondary to police status and career paths. After all, Jenny Tanner was just a country housewife—what did she count for in the greater scheme of promotions and reputations? Why shine the light on your mates when the victim can't complain?

I should say that this cover-up met with little opposition. Whether people knew about it or not, few of them asked any probing questions. The Blake family and the children who will never know their aunt—Stephanie, Ashlee and Joshua—may never be fully satisfied.

Most of those responsible for the first investigation have long been superannuated out of the police force with, until now, their reputations intact. Unfortunately, although the Coroner may be critical of the handling of this case by some of Victoria's 'finest investigators', no sanctions can now be applied.

And has justice been arrived at through this hugely expensive and protracted exercise? Who paid the greatest price apart from Jenny? Sam Tanner, who for twelve years thought his mother had abandoned him in a lonely farmhouse because she was unhappy after his birth, and who now has to come to terms with the police investigating a trusted member of his family on suspicion of involvement in his mother's death. Good luck, Sam Tanner. You deserve it.

My own interests? Was my involvement in this story merely opportunistic—the chance to write the book I've wanted to write for so long—or was I motivated by my need to uncover the injustice done by the system to a young woman and her family? Maybe it started out in one way and finished in another. Jenny Tanner's story has taken over my life for nearly two years. I feel I know all the cast intimately. Dates, times, locations, conversations, details—test me and I'll pass. In the Coroner's Court, the Blakes, Tanners, police, media, counsel, witnesses all approached me and shared conversations with me when I approached them 'because you're sort of neutral in all this', said Kath Blake.

Neutral, I hope, but not disengaged. I'll never forget Jenny Tanner, or the lessons her story has taught me. I've now seen at close quarters how justice suffers when those who administer the law place their own reputations ahead of the interests of those who have been wronged. I've gained some alarming insights into a police culture where the recipe for success is to 'keep your arse covered'. And I've come to realise how conspiracies of silence thrive when ordinary citizens—and sections of the media—are reluctant to speak out against injustice. When silence prevails, justice will remain blind.

∞

One day recently, feeling rather flat after the inquest, I was at my desk packing away the piles of notes, tapes, drafts and photos I'd assembled during my own search for the truth. A friend of more than thirty years sat chatting to me while I sorted and filed. Among the photos I found the one of Laurie and Jenny at the airport and put it separately on the desk to return to Kath, as promised.

My friend reached over and picked it up. 'How did this get in there?' he asked.

'It's been there since the beginning,' I replied.

'But why include an old photo of you in all this?' he asked. 'Who's the chap you're with, anyway? I don't know him, do I?'

'No, Ralph, you don't.'

Silently I retrieved the photo from Ralph, slipped it into an envelope and put it in a drawer, which I firmly shut.

That's how Jenny's story ended for me.

Cast of Characters

* Names marked with an asterisk have been changed for reasons of privacy.

The Blake family

Kath Blake	Jenny Tanner's mother
Les Blake	Jenny Tanner's father
Kristine Blake	
Miriam Blake	Jenny's sisters
Clare Blake	

Jenny's friends

Liz Thomas★
Rosslyn (Roz) Smith
Debbie Collins★
Senior Sergeant Jed Moffit★ Jenny's former boyfriend

The Tanner family

Laurie Tanner	Jenny's husband
Jenny Tanner	née Blake, Laurie's wife
Sam Tanner	son of Laurie and Jenny
June Tanner	Laurie's mother
Fred Tanner	Laurie's father
Bruce Tanner	
Frank Tanner	Laurie's brothers
Denis Tanner	
Carol Tanner	Laurie's sister
Lynne Tanner	Denis's wife

Laurie's friends

Curly McCormack	farmer
Angie McCormack	his wife
Mick McCormack	Curly's brother
Anne McCormack	Mick's wife
Hugh Almond	farmer and neighbour
Sally James★	Laurie's first wife

Others who have asked to remain anonymous

Police, 1984–85

District 3: Mansfield, Alexandra, Benalla, Bonnie Doon

OPERATIONS (UNIFORMED)

Chief Inspector Duncan MacLennan	(retired)
Inspector Peter Mangles	(retired)
Senior Sergeant Neil Walker	(retired)
Sergeant Neil Phipps	(retired)
Sergeant Doug McPhie	(now Acting Chief Superintendent at Wangaratta)
Senior Constable Steve Adams	(still at Mansfield as a Senior Sergeant)
Senior Constable Jeff Adams	(retired)
Senior Constable John Winters	(retired)
Senior Constable Bill Kerr	(retired)
Senior Constable Don Frazer	(now a Sergeant at Ballarat)

CIB (PLAIN-CLOTHES)

Regional Detective Chief Inspector (RDCI) Tom O'Keefe	(retired)
Chief Inspector Eric Brewer	(retired)
Detective Sergeant Ian Welch	(retired)
Sergeant Jim Sullivan	(retired)

Melbourne

OPERATIONS

Senior Constable Lynne Tanner	(resigned 1989)
Senior Sergeant Peter Fleming	(now Superintendent, Ethical Standards Branch)
Senior Constable Adrian Barry	(retired)
Senior Sergeant John Rankin	(now Chief Inspector, Horsham District)

CIB

Detective Sergeant Denis Tanner

| Inspector Brian Ritchie | Head of Homicide in 1985 (retired) |
| Detective Sergeant Jim Fry | Executive Sergeant at Homicide in 1985 (retired) |

Others who played small but significant roles are mentioned in the text.

Medical officers, 1984–85

Gerry O'Donnell	ambulance officer
Dr Ross Gilham	general practitioner, Mansfield
Dr Geoffrey Patience	general practitioner, Benalla
Dr Peter Dyte	pathologist, Shepparton
Dr Norman Sonenberg	pathologist, Shepparton
Dr Terry Schultz	pathologist, Wangaratta

Legal practitioners, 1984–85

Mr Brian Cosgriff SM	Coroner, Shepparton
Mr Hugh Adams SM	Assistant State Coroner, Melbourne
Mr Joe Gullaci	counsel for the Tanner family
Mr Rodney Ryan	counsel for the Blake family

The Adele Baily connection

| Adele Baily | transsexual prostitute |
| Karen Baily★ | Adele's sister |

Dave Worsley★   mine shaft explorer
Mick Bladen★   mine shaft explorer

Police, 1994–98
Country
Sergeant Ian Coutts   Wangaratta
Constable Charles (Bob) Fleming   Mansfield

Melbourne
Inspector Paul Newman   Ethical Standards Branch
                                   (ex Homicide)
Detective Senior Sergeant Jeff Calderbank (now inspector)
                                   Homicide Squad
Detective Sergeant Marty Allison   Homicide Squad
Detective Senior Constable Paul Solomon Homicide Squad
Detective Senior Constable Jacqueline Curran
                                   Homicide Squad
Senior Constable Graham Miller   Homicide Squad
Senior Constable Ray Vincent   Firearms and Toolmarks
                                   Section
Senior Sergeant Val Smith   Crimestoppers
Others who have assisted with information but not been directly
involved

Medical and forensic professionals, 1995–98
Professor Stephen Cordner   Head, Institute of Forensic Science
Dr Matthew Lynch   Pathologist, Coronial Services
Dr Chris Briggs   forensic anthropologist
Professor John Clement   Head Odontologist—School of
                             Dental Science
Ron Taylor   forensic sculptor

Legal practitioners, 1995–98
Mr Graeme Johnstone   State Coroner
Mr Jeremy Rapke   counsel assisting the Coroner

Mr Joe Gullaci   ·   counsel for Denis Tanner

Mr Tony Hargreaves   counsel for Laurie Tanner

Mr O. P. (Paul) Holdenson   counsel for Denis and Laurie Tanner

Mr Brian Dennis   counsel for the Chief Commisioner's Office

Crown Counsel

Professor Colin Howard   appearing for Mr Hugh Adams

Other lawyers appeared briefly for Lynne Tanner and Channels 9 and 7.